LAW'S COSMOS

Recent literary-critical work in legal studies reads law as a genre of literature, noting that Western law originated as a branch of rhetoric in classical Greece and lamenting the fact that the law has lost its connection to poetic language, narrative, and imagination. But modern legal scholarship has paid little attention to the actual juridical discourse of ancient Greece. This book rectifies that neglect through an analysis of the courtroom speeches from classical Athens, texts situated precisely at the intersection between law and literature. Reading these texts for their subtle literary qualities and their sophisticated legal philosophy, it proposes that in Athens' juridical discourse literary form and legal matter are inseparable. Through its distinctive focus on the literary form of Athenian forensic oratory, *Law's Cosmos* aims to shed new light on its juridical thought, and thus to change the way classicists read forensic oratory and legal historians view Athenian law.

VICTORIA WOHL is Professor of Classics at the University of Toronto. Her previously published work includes *Love Among the Ruins: The Erotics of Democracy in Classical Athens* (2002) and *Intimate Commerce: Exchange, Gender, and Subjectivity in Greek Tragedy* (1998).

LAW'S COSMOS

Juridical Discourse in Athenian Forensic Oratory

VICTORIA WOHL

CAMBRIDGE
UNIVERSITY PRESS

CAMBRIDGE UNIVERSITY PRESS
Cambridge, New York, Melbourne, Madrid, Cape Town, Singapore,
São Paulo, Delhi, Dubai, Tokyo

Cambridge University Press
The Edinburgh Building, Cambridge CB2 8RU, UK

Published in the United States of America by Cambridge University Press, New York

www.cambridge.org
Information on this title: www.cambridge.org/9780521110747

First published 2010

Printed in the United Kingdom at the University Press, Cambridge

A catalogue record for this publication is available from the British Library

Library of Congress Cataloguing in Publication data
Wohl, Victoria, 1966–
Law's cosmos : juridical discourse in Athenian forensic oratory / Victoria Wohl.
p. cm.
Includes bibliographical references and index.
ISBN 978-0-521-11074-7 (hardback)
1. Forensic oratory – Greece – Athens – History – To 1500. 2. Rhetoric, Ancient.
3. Law, Greek. I. Title.
KL4115.A75.W65 2009
340.5′38 – dc22 2009043211

ISBN 978-0-521-11074-7 Hardback

For E.

Contents

PART III TIME, MEMORY, REPRODUCTION: LAW'S PAST AND FUTURE

Preface: before the law

> "I don't know this Law," said K. "All the worse for you," replied the warder.
>
> Kafka *The Trial*

Athenian law is a notorious historical dead end. Unsystematic, with no formal legal theory, no unified lawcode, no written verdicts or system of precedent, it falls off the map of Western jurisprudential history, whether common law or civil. Both as forensic practice and as jurisprudential philosophy it is "before the law" as we know it, an evolutionary oddity. The subject of this book is neither the practice nor the philosophy of Athenian law, but something between the two, the juridical discourse generated by and embedded in the courtroom speeches of the fifth and fourth centuries BCE. These texts, as I hope to show, offer complex (though not necessarily coherent) meditations on law and justice. They create and sustain a juridical world-view and a juridical world, a world not completely segregated from its surrounding cultural environment, of course, but recognizably distinct in its rules, logic, and structure. While Athens' legal practice may be deemed an irrelevant detour on the path of jurisprudential history, Athenian legal discourse, I suggest, is an important part of that history, offering an early example of a developed, if unsystematic and largely latent, body of jurisprudential thought and a self-consciously juridical relation to life.

This book is not a quest for origins although, as Derrida has remarked, that is one temptation created by the law's apparent resistance to history.[1] Instead it is the archaeology of a neglected site of legal knowledge. It aims

[1] Derrida 1992b: "To enter into relations with the law . . . is to act as if it had no history or at any rate as if it no longer depended on its historical presentation. At the same time, it is to let oneself be enticed, provoked, and hailed by the history of this non-history. It is to let oneself be tempted by the impossible: a theory of the origin of law, and therefore of its non-origin . . . " (192). I use "law" or "the law" throughout as umbrella terms that encompass juridical discourse, forensic practice, legal institutions, and the principle of legality. As context dictates I will also refer to more specific aspects of the law such as litigation, forensic procedure, the lawcode, statutory regulations, or the idea of justice.

to trace the dimensions of Athenian legal discourse in all its complexity. That complexity, it argues, lies in the specific rhetoric of the speeches in which it is embedded; thus it seeks to understand Athens' juridical discourse through close reading of selected forensic speeches. We have approximately 100 of these speeches, a tiny fraction of the total, written between roughly 420 and 320 BCE by expert speech-writers (logographers) for litigants to deliver in court. We don't know why these texts were preserved – they may have been circulated as pamphlets to humiliate a defeated opponent, vindicate an acquitted defendant, or drum up further business for the logographer – nor how much the written versions we have differ from the version delivered orally in the courtroom. We almost never have opposing speeches from the same case and seldom know the verdict. Situating a given speech within a determinate historical context is often impossible; sometimes it is impossible even to identify the author.

These uncertainties become less pressing when we approach forensic oratory not as individual texts but as a genre. In the pages that follow, I offer detailed close readings of individual speeches and interpret their specific language and thought. But in most cases, the language and thought are themselves typical. Indeed, forensic oratory is a genre made up of typicalities, as Aristotle's exhaustive list of rhetorical strategies in the *Rhetoric* illustrates. Every trope I analyze could be extensively cross-referenced (and some works on the genre are little more than such cross-references); virtually every idea could be found elsewhere. So although I will argue that the meaning of any given text emerges only when its strategies are examined in their specific rhetorical context, its very "genericness" justifies treating the canon as a genre. For this reason, I do not enter into debates over authorship; no individual author, whether we call him Demosthenes or [Demosthenes], has a full monopoly over his own language.[2] Furthermore, although there were real and significant changes in legal practice over the course of the century, the jurisprudential issues that preoccupy Athenian forensic orators and the language in which they express them remain generally consistent, so my study is synchronic not diachronic.[3] Finally, the question of how closely the published speeches reflect those given in the

[2] Where a speech is of disputed authorship, I will refer to it by its traditional attribution without weighing in on the validity of that attribution. For a theoretical justification, see Foucault 1977a. On the problem of authenticity in forensic oratory, see Dover 1968; Usher 1976; T. Cole 1991a: 115–38; Trevett 1992; Todd 2007: 26–32.

[3] See Ober 1989a: 36–37, Christ 1998a: 6 for justification of a synchronic approach to the corpus. Diachronic surveys of Greek law are offered by Ostwald 1969 and 1986; de Romilly 1971. See also Gernet's study of "prelaw" (Gernet 1917, 1981a and b, followed by Foucault 1994: 16–32), and Farenga's analysis of the cognitive developments leading to the jury trial (Farenga 2006, esp. 262–345).

courtroom is irrelevant to my purposes: as long as those speeches are the product of a classical Athenian imagination, they fall within the purview of Athenian juridical discourse.[4]

This book examines that discourse within the genre of forensic oratory. Sometimes it will speak as if the two – juridical discourse and forensic oratory – are interchangeable, but they are not. Forensic oratory is a seminal part of Athenian juridical discourse but isn't coterminous with it. A full study of the discourse of Athenian law would include discussion of those legal statutes that can be reconstructed from inscriptions and other sources. I engage with such statutes in the same way the orators do – obliquely and with my own argumentative goals in view – but in doing so I rely heavily on the work of others and do not pretend to offer original solutions to any of the complex technical problems surrounding Athenian law as an institution.[5] Likewise, discourse should properly encompass practice – procedural options and alternate modes of dispute settlement, para-legal action like arbitration, the physical experience and performance of the trial – but I treat such topics only when they become issues within a specific forensic speech.[6] In focusing on the forensic *logos*, I necessarily overlook much about the forensic *ergon*, but it is part of my argument that the *logos* is the essence of the *ergon* in Athenian law.

On the other end of the spectrum, I engage only infrequently with Athenian legal philosophy such as Plato's *Laws* and Aristotle's *Rhetoric*, *Politics*, or *Nicomachean Ethics*. These texts have much to teach us about ancient law and constitute an important part of Athenian discourse on law, but they offer a very different jurisprudential philosophy than the indigenous theories that emerge out of legal practice. For one thing, these philosophers attempt to systematize and totalize a legal discourse that is

4 On preservation and publication of the texts see Dover 1968: 148–74; Humphreys 1985b: 318–21; Todd 1990a: 165–67; Worthington 1991, 1994: 115–18, 1996; Trevett 1992: 50–76; Johnstone 1999: 142 n. 63; Edwards 2000; Lavency 2007. Worthington goes the furthest in arguing for the extensive revision of the speeches for publication. I don't find his stylistic arguments persuasive, but the issue is probably not resolvable.

5 Of the scholarship on technical aspects of Athenian law I have found most helpful Harrison 1968, 1971; MacDowell 1978; Gagarin 1981; Osborne 1985; Hansen 1974, 1975, 1976; Carey 1996 and 1998; Carawan 1998; and especially Todd 1993, which reconstructs the logic of Athenian law from the institutional structure of its practice. Superb discussions of the law can also be found in the commentaries on specific orations, especially Wyse 1904; Carey and Reid 1985; Edwards and Usher 1985; Carey 1989; MacDowell 1962, 1990; Gagarin 1997. For a survey of earlier work see Todd and Millett 1990.

6 Humphreys 1985a: 251–57 stresses the interrelation in legal discourse between theory and practice, speech and action; see also Humphreys 1988; Ober 2005, esp. 408–11; and more generally Goodrich 1987: 125–212; Kahn 1999: 86–90. On procedure, see especially Hansen 1974, 1975, 1976; Osborne 1985; Boegehold 1991; Scafuro 1997.

essentially dynamic and asystematic, and in the process they translate it into a foreign language. Aristotle's *Rhetoric*, for instance, offers an abstract taxonomy of legal arguments that is interesting in itself but utterly fails to convey the subtle and creative ways in which such arguments function within a real forensic speech.[7] My focus is instead on legal oratory's own theorizations of its practice, philosophies that are both implicit within and complicit with a particular forensic argument and cannot be translated from the courtroom to the academy without significant loss of meaning. That said, however, there is no absolute line between the philosophers of law and the forensic speakers, and the two should better be imagined as part of a continuum between theory and practice in which forensic oratory (written if not in fact rewritten) would already stand at some distance from pure practice. Chapter 3 examines a text that falls somewhere in the middle of that continuum, Antiphon's *Tetralogies*. Abstract legal arguments staged (rather unconvincingly) as model trials, these cases offer a mimetic theorization of Athenian forensic practice within its own terms, a philosophy in the courtroom.

Finally, my book is not a survey of Athenian attitudes toward the law. The Athenians thought and talked often about law outside the *dikastēria* (courtrooms) and a number of scholars have productively explored the lines of convergence between the courts and, for example, the comic and tragic stage.[8] Plays like Sophocles' *Antigone*, Aristophanes' *Wasps*, and the comedies of Menander are a vital part of Athenian juridical thought and an important counterpoint to the discussions within the courts. The boundaries between law and literature are permeable, of course, and like all discursive boundaries are products of the discourse itself as it negotiates its relation to and autonomy from other modes of cultural expression. I examine forensic oratory in isolation not because I believe it existed in isolation – obviously it did not – but because I wish to define and describe this one genre of Athenian legal thought in its own discursive specificity. To this end, though with a keen sense of the road not taken, I have set deliberately circumscribed parameters on my study: tempting as it is to follow all the paths that lead from the *dikastēria* to the dramatic stage, the philosophers' academy, or the streets and houses where juridical thought

[7] The discontinuities between philosophy and forensic oratory are well discussed by Mossé 1987; Humphreys 1988: 477–78; Carey 1994a, 1996; D. Cohen 1995a: 34–57, 1995b; Nightingale 1999; Allen 2000a: 183–90, 245–91.

[8] Dover 1974: 23–33; Ober and Strauss 1990; Bers 1994; Porter 1997; Scafuro 1997; Christ 1998a; Allen 2000a; Hesk 2000; Omitowoju 2002: 137–233; Lape 2004; Wohl 2009, Wohl (in press). See also de Romilly 1971 and Havelock 1978, who trace the evolution of notions of law and justice in a broad array of Greek philosophical and literary texts.

was enacted in everyday life, I have decided to stay within the confines of the courts. In part this decision was practical – one book cannot do everything and those that try risk doing it all superficially – but largely it was methodological, as I hoped to bring into sharp relief a genre of writing and thought that can too easily fade into the background of Athens' broader cultural and political landscape, and to examine that genre not primarily in its emerging distinction from other modes of thought (though that, too, is a tempting project) but in its internal processes of self-structuring. Forensic oratory was "a node within a network," to be sure, but my focus here is the node, and I leave it to others to trace the network.[9]

Even inside these parameters, with a corpus and a topic as large as this one is especially aware of one's limitations. There are many texts I would have liked to include but couldn't; there are others I wish I could have treated more fully. Readers who make it to the end may be relieved to hear that two chapters were cut along the way. I suppose to this extent I know how Kafka's "man from the country" felt, sitting abjectly before the law, and I'm glad not to be sitting there until I die. But in a more positive form, that sense of incompleteness is part of what I hope to convey with this book: there are more forensic speeches than you realized, and more to say about them than you thought.

*

Writing this book has often felt like a trial, and I am indebted to all those who have provided advocacy, counsel, and aid during the process. Ryan Balot, Karen Bassi, Matt Christ, and Erik Gunderson offered me insightful comments on all or part of the manuscript: I very much appreciate their encouragement and their generosity with their time. The detailed comments of Michael Gagarin and Simon Goldhill, the two referees for Cambridge University Press, improved the manuscript in myriad ways, large and small: I could not have asked for more expert or more open-minded readers. Marie-Pierre Krück and Ariel Vernon provided indispensable research assistance in the final stages and saved me from many embarrassing errors. I am also thankful to the audiences who heard parts of the project in oral form and gave me helpful feedback and to the students in my ancient law seminars at the Ohio State University and University of Toronto, whose interest (and, occasionally, skepticism) pushed me to

[9] Foucault 1972: 23. Cf. Humphreys 1985a: 251. These same methodological considerations have also led me to include very little comparative material. While I engage throughout with legal theories based on modern law, and to that extent am always weighing Athenian law against the contemporary assumptions behind these theories, I do not undertake sustained comparison between Athenian legal thought and modern jurisprudence.

refine my arguments. Earlier versions of parts of Chapters 4 and 5 were published in article form as, respectively, "Time on Trial," *parallax* 9.4 (2003, 98–106) and "Rhetoric of the Athenian Citizen," in E. Gunderson, ed. *The Cambridge Companion to Ancient Rhetoric* (2009, 162–77). Generous material support was provided by the Elizabeth and J. Richardson Dilworth Fellowship (which sponsored a productive and enjoyable year at the Institute for Advanced Study), the Virginia Hull Award for Research in the Humanities and a Faculty Professional Leave from the Ohio State University, the Connaught Start-up Fund at the University of Toronto, and the Social Sciences and Humanities Research Council of Canada. Generous moral support was given by my parents and sister; by my friends Sandra Macpherson and Luke Wilson, who first got me interested in legal studies; and especially by Erik Gunderson, who like Kafka's K has, through no fault of his own, lived for many years under the shadow of the law. I am grateful to him not only for his patience and encouragement, for countless discussions and rereadings, but also for the exemplary paradigm of his own work on Roman rhetoric, which has taught me how to appreciate and read Greek oratory. Finally, I would like to acknowledge my intellectual debt to two scholars who died just as I was beginning this project, Nicole Loraux and Jacques Derrida. I was not fortunate enough to know either personally, but their influence will, I hope, be felt in the pages that follow.

Introduction: the rhetoric of law

> What if the law, without being itself transfixed by literature, shared the conditions of its possibility with the literary object?
>
> Derrida 1992b: 191

> The study of law is a very specialized form of literary pursuit.
>
> Goodrich 1986: 91

This book charts a legal cosmogony. It studies the creation of a juridical cosmos in the courtroom speeches of classical Athens. This cosmos, as its Greek etymology implies, is both orderly and ornamented. On the one hand, it is a legal order: not just an arrangement of laws or an organization of behavior into categories of legality and illegality, but a discursive order that is shaped by, even as it gives shape to, the concept of "law." It describes a legal world and a legal world-view: a specifically juridical way of thinking, speaking, and being. On the other hand, this cosmos is an aesthetic order, the product of the creative arrangements and expressive strategies of forensic rhetoric. In Athens' juridical cosmos, legal and aesthetic order are inseparable. What the texts say about the law is a function of how they say it. The tropes of forensic oratory themselves constitute a mode of jurisprudential thought.

This book traces the outlines of this juridical cosmos in the texts of the Attic orators. It examines the strategies by which forensic oratory authorizes this world; the metaphysics of causality and probability that govern it; where it draws the boundaries of legality and how it secures them. It looks at the subjects who inhabit this world and how the law permeates their desires, decisions, and relations to one another. Exploring its memory of the past and imagination of the future, it asks how this juridical discourse reproduces itself over time. And even as it delineates a project of discursive world-building, it is attentive to the exclusions that project seems to demand – the individuals banned from legal personhood, the thoughts that cannot be parsed within the grammar of the law, and the events that cannot be comprehended by its logic – and to the legitimate and legitimating violence that enforces them. Above all, this book stresses the inseparability of order and ornament, thought and expression. It does not, however, assume that they are homonymous. Athenian juridical discourse emerges in and through legal rhetoric, but sometimes also in spite of it, the product of an uneasy stand-off between the legal and the rhetorical.

In its insistence on the simultaneity of the two senses of *kosmos*, this book intersects with the concerns and questions of the modern law and literature movement.[1] One leitmotif of this critical school has been the call for law to return to its rhetorical origins. Law began its life (the story goes) in classical Greece and Rome as a branch of rhetoric. Over the centuries, in the course of increasing professionalization and in an attempt to declare its disciplinary autonomy, the law has suppressed its rhetorical nature, but in defining itself as a cosmos of order not of adornment it has lost its connection with language, narrative, imagination. The law and literature movement has sought to reunite these long-lost cousins and promised that the reunion would enrich them both, forcing the two disciplines to acknowledge their similarities and differences, and in this way allowing each one both to supplement and to critique the other.[2] But despite its rhetoric of return, the law and literature movement has been curiously uninterested in the historical details of that origin to which it appeals. There are good reasons to be wary of this nostalgic narrative and suspicious of its gestures toward a lost plenitude. Nonetheless, it does seem that classical Athens might provide an exemplary (though by no means uncomplicated) case-study for what it means for law and rhetoric to be united.

That Athenian law was rhetorical is a truism. "Rhetorical" is a literal description of the Athenian legal system, the core of which was the courtroom speeches: typically two for the prosecution and two for the defense in alternation, written by expert logographers but delivered by the litigants

[1] By way of example, see J. B. White 1985, 1990; B. Thomas 1991; Cornell, Rosenfeld, and Carlson 1992; Cover 1993; West 1993; Ward 1995; Brooks and Gewirtz 1996; Minda 1997; Goodrich 1998; Freeman and Lewis 1999; Brooks 2000; Felman 2002, esp. 54–105 and the extensive bibliography at 192 n.1. Derrida 1992b: 191 and Goodrich 1986: 91 (which serve as epigrams to this chapter) articulate succinctly some guiding methodological principles of the movement.

[2] Goodrich 1994b, 1996: 112–37, 1998; Peters 2005 (expressing skepticism); Brooks 2005. Sarat and Kearns 1994: 4–7 figure the "rhetorical turn" in modern legal criticism as a reunion of terms (rhetoric and justice) that Plato first set asunder. Peter Goodrich's work examines in detail the historical foundations of the rhetoric of law (predominantly English common law) but he locates those foundations in medieval not classical jurisprudence: see especially Goodrich 1990a.

themselves and heard and judged on the spot by a jury of citizens.[3] In the absence of a fixed code of law, a binding system of precedent, professional lawyers, or even a judge, these speeches construct the legal world; in them, the speakers shape the legal event, define themselves and their opponents as legal subjects, build a legal framework for understanding social interaction and for resolving conflict. They also construct "the law" both in the narrow sense, as they produce and interpret the specific statutes relevant to their case, and in the broad sense, as their speeches implement a latent theory of jurisprudence. Thus many scholars would agree with the claim of one recent study that "Athenian law was essentially rhetorical."[4]

What does it mean, though, to say that Athenian law was rhetorical? The statement is not merely descriptive. It is also prescriptive for the way we read these speeches and interpret the legal discourse they generate. When scholars say that Athenian law is rhetorical, they usually mean rhetorical in Aristotle's sense of the word: "the ability to see the possibilities of persuasion in every case" (*Rhet.* 1355b25–26). The equation of law with persuasion is not altogether felicitous for those (both critics and speakers alike) who wish to see law as a discourse of truth, grounded by an authority more secure than a speaker's self-interested manipulation. But in another respect, this definition is quite reassuring, as it situates the law within a familiar ontology, the linguistic product of a man who knows his own mind and controls his own words. Those words may bend or distort the truth, but their deeper meaning can be decoded within this general hermeneutics of persuasive intent. The language of law, on this view, becomes purely instrumental: even when it is lying it speaks the truth about the purposeful will of its speaker.

This view of legal rhetoric strikes me as inadequate both as a theory of language and as a description of the linguistic practices of Athenian forensic oratory. In these speeches, as I hope to show, language constantly exceeds or eludes the persuasive intent of its speaker. The rhetorical elaboration of legal arguments produces figural meanings that clash with the speaker's

3 There was some variation within this general rule: in many cases litigants gave only one speech; litigants who could not afford to buy a speech presumably wrote their own; in some instances (like Demosthenes 21 and Lysias 12, discussed in Chapters 4 and 5) the logographer was the litigant and he delivered his own speech.

4 Johnstone 1999: 1; the quotation is the first sentence of the book. He expands: "In Athenian litigation, the law was not opposed to, or even separable from, rhetoric. In the absence of authoritative legal specialists, the only historical sense in which the law existed in Athens was in and through the rhetoric of litigation" (1). Yunis 2005 takes a similar approach. This rhetorical focus characterizes much Anglo-American scholarship on ancient law, but is less prevalent in continental scholarship.

literal meaning. The tropes and images in which he expresses his intent work against it, leaving it unreadable within a hermeneutics of truth (and its distortion) or persuasion (and its failure). Rhetorical ordering skews legal ordering: one *kosmos* destabilizes the other. Athenian law is rhetorical, then, not in Aristotle's sense but in Paul de Man's: it operates within the figural dimension of language that makes a text's meaning undecidable in the terms of its own grammar, logic, or putative intent.[5] If we wish to call this dimension of language "literary," then in Athenian forensic oratory law is literature.

*

Forensic oratory is often treated as the bastard child of Athenian literature.[6] Falling into the gap between historical and literary studies, it is often condemned by both for being wholly or merely "rhetorical." For literary scholars this has been a problem of originality: dismissed as a monotonous collection of empty rhetorical clichés, the genre is often viewed as an embarrassment to the unique and innovative imagination of the Athenians.[7] For historians, on the other hand, the problem of oratory's rhetorical nature has been one of truth: because they are speaking to persuade a jury, orators freely embellish, conceal, or distort the truth, and thus their words are precarious sources for ancient history.[8] Ironically, texts that were preserved for 2,000 years precisely as models of rhetoric have come to be scorned for their rhetoricity.

In recent years, however, these problematic texts have again become central to discussions of classical Athenian history. Scholars approaching forensic oratory from an anthropological or sociological perspective

[5] De Man 1979, esp. 3–19, 103–31: "The grammatical model . . . becomes rhetorical not when we have, on the one hand, a literal meaning and on the other hand a figural meaning, but when it is impossible to decide by grammatical or other linguistic devices which of the two meanings (that can be entirely incompatible) prevails. Rhetoric radically suspends logic and opens up vertiginous possibilities of referential aberration" (10). Norris 1988 analyzes de Man's contribution to a reading of the law.

[6] Todd 1990a: 159–63 concisely summarizes the history of the reception of Athenian forensic oratory. See also Yunis' (2000–01) discussion of the reception of Demosthenes' *On the Crown*.

[7] George Kennedy's important study of Greek rhetoric begins: "One of the principal interests of the Greeks was rhetoric. Classicists admit the fact, deplore it, and forget it. After all, the Greeks condoned animal sacrifice, homosexuality, watered wine, and cock fights. But we will never understand the Greeks unless we understand what is peculiar about them" (Kennedy 1963: 3). Compare Loraux 1986: 221–62 on the supposedly monotonous genre of the funeral oration and on the meaning of originality in such a genre.

[8] Todd 1990a offers a thoughtful analysis of the problems. See also Harding 1987; Worthington 1994 (who argues that the more rhetorically sophisticated a passage, the less likely it is to be true, 119–27); Harris 1995; Golden 2000, and the interesting general comments of Crook 1996 on legal history and general history.

have attempted to resituate it within its cultural context, as a site for the expression and negotiation of Athenian ideology and social relations. In studies informed by comparative anthropology, Sally Humphreys and David Cohen examine the role of the courts in structuring, respectively, kinship systems and the zero-sum enmities of an agonistic honor culture.[9] Josiah Ober has analyzed oratory as a site of negotiation between Athens' democratic masses and its political elite, an ideological mediation that, he argues, contributed significantly to the stability of the democracy over its nearly 200 year history.[10] Other scholars have taken a similar approach in order to explicate the Athenians' views on their own judicial practices: Danielle Allen has looked at the way the orators represent pity and anger, law and desert, as part of a broader phenomenology of punishment in Athens; Matthew Christ has studied representations of legal excess and abuse within forensic oratory and explored their implications for the Athenians' attitudes toward litigation and their own notorious litigiousness.[11]

This scholarship has cast exciting new light both on Athenian legal oratory and, through it, on Athenian thought and society. It has neatly solved the historiographical problem of the genre's rhetoricity by embracing it and locating the speeches' value as historical sources precisely in their redundancy and unoriginality. Instead of seeking the truth of the text in its surface statements (which, being self-interested, are always potentially false or distorting) they seek it in the text's unspoken assumptions. Gabriel Herman lays out the methodological principle:

> [Forensic orators] are lying through their teeth. The connection between what they are saying and what really happened is at best minimal, at worst non-existent. However, they are lying in a manner which is extremely valuable for our [i.e. modern historians'] purposes: rather than revealing what really happened, they are revealing what the dikasts wished to hear. By tailoring their accounts to the dikasts' expectations, they provide us with the best clue a historian could possibly dream of to their society's ideal norms. The passages I paraphrase or cite are therefore not just ordinary passages. They are unique and truthful reflections of the Athenian value system – of what the collective Athenian mind perceived as desirable patterns of behaviour.[12]

[9] Humphreys 1985a, 1985b, 1986; D. Cohen 1995a. [10] Ober 1989a, esp. 3–52, 293–339.

[11] Allen 2000a, esp. 147–242; Christ 1998a. Other social-historical uses of the Attic orators include Cartledge, Millett and Todd 1990; Herman 1993, 1994, 1995, 2006; Hunter 1994; Foxhall and Lewis 1996; Hesk 2000: 202–91; Wolpert 2002a; Roisman 2005.

[12] Herman 1994: 106, and cf. Herman 2006: 136–54 for an extended defense of forensic oratory as evidence for Athenian moral norms (with critiques by Christ 2007 and Balot 2008). See also Dover 1974: 5–6, 8–14; Todd 1990c: 164–69; Christ 1998a: 6; Sternberg 2006: 17.

Because speakers aimed to persuade their mass audience, they shaped their arguments as much as possible to cohere to communal norms. Forensic orations become historical sources almost in spite of themselves, less for what they say than for what in them goes without saying.

In a sense, then, the texts become most revealing where they are most generic, where they are presumably telling jurors what they already believe. Ober proposes that the frequently recycled rhetorical topoi so often ignored as empty clichés were in fact full of symbolic meaning for the mass audience of jurors and were repeated so frequently for that very reason. Instead of ignoring these tropes as stylistic embarrassments, he takes them as symbols pointing to "the political ideology of the citizen masses."[13] By reading the speeches' generic rhetoric as a vehicle for symbolic communication between speaker and jurors, Ober and others are able to use these texts as windows onto the ideology and structure of Athenian democracy.

In order to use forensic oratory as a window, however, the historian must render it transparent. He or she salvages the texts' truth by conceding – indeed, accentuating – their rhetoricity, but that rhetoric is denied any density or interest in itself. Instead, it is reduced to an empty instrumentality. It is imagined as a tool manipulated by skilled speakers or as a vehicle of communication between speaker and jury.[14] The text's rhetoric is rendered meaningful, but its meaning lies beyond it, in the wider ideological or cultural structures to which it points. One does not so much read the texts as one reads through them. Excerpting selectively (on the grounds that a cliché is inherently mobile), one creates out of these rhetorical tesserae a mosaic of historical meaning that goes far beyond that contained in any given speech. This mode of reconstruction relies on a functionalist hermeneutics in which all of the speech's linguistic qualities are subsumed within and judged by its ostensible mission to persuade its audience. Only what is normative is persuasive in this context (the implicit reasoning goes), and only what is persuasive is culturally significant. In their instrumentalization of rhetoric, recent historical studies cross paths with the earlier generation of literary readings which, taking their cue from Aristotle's *Rhetoric*, analyzed

[13] Ober 1989a: 44.

[14] See, e.g., D. Cohen 1995a: "a topos . . . to be manipulated according to the exigencies of the particular case" (72), "a powerful vehicle for the articulation and expression of shared moral, social, and political judgments" (192); and Ober 1989a: "a primary means by which mass-elite relations could be discussed publicly" (45), "instrumental in the regulation of mass-elite relations" (45), "a primary vehicle for resolving tension" (308), "a natural medium of social mediation" (312).

every trope, argument, or metaphor in terms of its persuasive force.[15] In both cases, the language of the speech is just a means to an end, for the original speaker no less than for the modern historian. To note this is not to invalidate the historiographical use of forensic oratory: looking through the lens of forensic rhetoric, it has exposed to view many fascinating and important new vistas. But in focusing its gaze on those other vistas it frequently renders the texts' rhetorical substance insubstantial and all but invisible.

My study aims to restore rhetorical opacity to the texts of Athenian forensic oratory and pursues juridical discourse not *through* the rhetoric of the legal speeches but rather *within* it. It proceeds through close readings of the specific language and rhetorical structure of selected speeches. These texts are, admittedly, not densely textured or complexly allusive literary works. They are light on metaphor and imagery; their characters tend to be one dimensional; their plots are often technical and overly complicated; and much of their language is, as readers since Aristotle have stressed, formulaic. They are designed to be understood on the surface and they present as smooth and lucid a surface as they can. In this sense, they ask to be read as they usually are read, as straightforward, unambiguous, transparent. But that smooth surface is illusory and on closer reading cracks appear. Points are raised and not developed. Arguments are made that contradict other arguments. Details intended to prove a case sometimes subtly undermine it, while suppressed details insinuate themselves within a speaker's language and quietly disrupt a case that requires their exclusion. The rhetorical strategies by which speakers attempt to efface their rhetoric instead often cast it in relief. On this rough surface of the forensic speech lies a depth of jurisprudential meaning and it is here, in the form of the speeches, that I seek the content of their juridical thought.

While I take it for granted that the speeches were designed to persuade, my interest is in the rhetorical features of the speech that fall outside this interpretive framework, elements that do not fail to persuade so much as they fail to be fully explained by the sole criterion of persuasion. Even if we accept the cognitive and discursive assumptions behind the notion of speakers who hone or manipulate their rhetoric to convince a large democratic jury (assumptions that include an intentional and masterful subject of language and the felicitous efficacy of speech acts), and even if

[15] For instance, George Kennedy, whose seminal history of Greek rhetoric is entitled *The Art of Persuasion in Greece*, uses persuasion (or its perceived failure) as his primary criterion for assessing the forensic orators (1963: 125–51).

we were able to overcome the epistemological limitation of not knowing whether a given speech was in fact persuasive or why, this functionalist model seems to me to provide an inaccurate description of the rhetorical texture of forensic discourse. We know, to start with the most obvious point, that litigants often go to court with a different goal from the one they present in their speech. Sometimes their real target is not the defendant but a friend or ally of his; sometimes they are pursuing a different goal altogether, bringing a murder case, say, in order to secure an inheritance claim, or an inheritance claim in order to strengthen their hand in a property dispute. Such cases do not undermine the notion that the speaker's rhetoric aims to persuade, but they do alert us to the fact that persuasion may not be as straightforward as it appears and that the persuasive purpose of the speech may itself be a complex rhetorical strategy instead of a simple organizing telos for all rhetorical strategies.

Moreover, although these texts present themselves to us in the form of monologues, of course they were actually extended dialogues between prosecution and defense, and the opponent's argument is always speaking within the argument designed to silence it. We no longer have direct access to half of that dialogue, but we do catch echoes of it. Litigants sometimes acknowledge opposing arguments explicitly, referring back to a point already made, or anticipating a point they have learned in the course of pre-trial arbitration or through the grapevine will be made, or imagining (usually in order to misrepresent) a point they think might be made. Even when not explicitly mentioned, each litigant's case shapes the other's, determining the way each narrates the dispute and represents himself.[16] This means that every speech also contains its own counter-argument and that in making the case for its own position it also imagines – if only in an attempt to preempt, discredit, or otherwise negate – the case against it. The arguments that would undermine its persuasiveness are not external to the text but contained within it, and never as wholly contained as the speaker would like, for once they are admitted – even under negation – they have a presence within his speech and can exercise a differential force that divides the speech's unitary persuasive purpose.

Each speech is in dialogue not only with its counter-speech, but also with itself. Athenian forensic speeches tend to be structured by what Freud termed "kettle logic," after the old joke: "A. borrowed a copper kettle from B. and after he had returned it was sued by B. because the kettle now had a big hole in it which made it unusable. His defense was: 'First, I

[16] Johnstone 1999: 46–69.

never borrowed a kettle from B. at all; secondly, the kettle had a hole in it already when I got it from him; and thirdly, I gave him back the kettle undamaged.'" In this mode of faulty reasoning, which also characterizes dreams, "each one of these defences is valid in itself, but taken together they exclude one another."[17] If for Freud this "mutual cancelling-out" is a dynamic of the unconscious, it is also a feature of legal argument: the same joke is attributed to Chief Justice Theophilus Parsons.[18]

Athenian legal rhetoric operated according to a similar narrative overdetermination. In Lysias 16, for instance, a speaker who is being barred from appointment to the Council on the grounds that he served in the cavalry under the oligarchic regime of the Thirty argues, virtually in a single breath, that he was not in the cavalry nor was his name on the registry, but even if he was on the registry, you can't trust that because the lists can be forged; if he had been in the cavalry he would admit it and be proud of his service (which he would prove was spotless); anyway, many other people who were in the cavalry now serve on the Council, and he wouldn't even bother to defend himself on this score if his opponents weren't telling barefaced lies about him (16.6–8). Moreover, he continues, even if they aren't lying about this they are lying about everything else, and he should be exonerated for his blameless life and patriotic bravery. In his eagerness to produce every possible argument for his case, this speaker even produces conflicting arguments. Hypothetical statements ("even if I were in the cavalry . . . ") compete with declaratives ("I wasn't in the cavalry . . . "). Evidence is simultaneously presented ("I'm not on the registry") and withdrawn ("the registry isn't reliable"). His speech does not proceed in the straight path of persuasiveness but instead zig-zags and doubles back, cedes ground and stumbles over itself.

The kettle logic of Athenian forensic oratory is just one manifestation of a discursive hyper-productivity that is always generating more narratives and more meanings than can readily be accommodated by a model of rhetoric premised on the intending subject and his persuasive ends.[19] In their zeal to persuade, these speeches aim for an argumentative exhaustiveness that includes even what they wish to exclude: arguments, images, and objects that not only have no functional role in the speech's manifest trajectory but in fact derail it. This book follows many such rhetorical

[17] Freud 1960 [1905]: 62, 205. The joke is also told in reference to the dream of Irma's injection in Freud 1953 [1900]: 120.

[18] Parsons 1861: 218–19, cited by Ferguson 1996: 85–86 and 249 n. 5, but without making the connection to Freud.

[19] On this "jurisgenesis," or proliferation of legal meaning, see Cover 1993.

detours. An argument about *nomos*, the rule of law, produces *phusis*, nature, as an unruly by-product that undermines the speech's entire jurisprudential framework (Demosthenes 25). A speaker's dramatic story about the murder of his old nurse at the hands of his vicious opponent reveals his own complicity in this violence, as well as the institutional cruelty of the legal system (Demosthenes 47). Inheritance cases based on one genealogical narrative inadvertently produce counter-genealogies that disrupt the natural reproduction of the family and of family law (Isaeus 6).

To reconstruct the profusion of counter-narratives and superfluous meanings is merely to take seriously the force and fertility of rhetoric, which always exceeds the control of any given speaker. Language slides, legal language no less than any other. It means more than it is intended to, and sometimes one meaning runs athwart another. It speaks in various registers at once, slipping between the literal and the figurative: thus, for example, the contract becomes the guiding metaphor in a case concerning a contract dispute, and metaphors of contractualism displace the real contract, which may or may not actually still be legally valid (Demosthenes 48). Form and content are inseparable but not necessarily moving in the same direction, and one seemingly random word can open rifts in an argument the speaker hoped was sealed tight.[20]

The chapters that follow will analyze many such slips and ruptures within Athenian legal speech. Here I offer only one brief but particularly vivid example, from one of the best-known speeches in the corpus. Lysias 1 is the defense speech of Euphiletus, who has confessed to homicide but argues that it was justifiable because he caught the victim, Eratosthenes, in bed with his wife and the law on adultery condoned killing in such circumstances. Eratosthenes' relatives have apparently claimed that Euphiletus entrapped Eratosthenes, luring him into the house as a pretext for killing him. Euphiletus works to dispel that imputation in a colorful narrative that depicts him as a guileless and devoted husband, laughably slow to recognize his wife's adultery. The narrative culminates in the confrontation between the two men. Euphiletus, discovering Eratosthenes in his house, gathered witnesses (who will testify in the trial to the truth of his account) and

[20] This slippage and friction constitutes what Derrida calls the "structural unconscious" of the text, the non-saturation of the text by the conscious intent that animates it (1988: 18, 73–77). This notion of a structural unconscious of the legal text has been developed in a specifically psychoanalytic idiom by Peter Goodrich. See especially Goodrich 1995: 181–222 (cf. 1994a), which posits analysis of forensic rhetoric as a psychoanalysis of the legal unconscious. On the "juridical unconscious" see further Goodrich 1995: 29–30, 1996: 112–14; Felman 2002. My own study is elaborated in terms more deconstructive than psychoanalytic; the dynamic I trace, however, might well be termed a juridical unconscious.

took his lawful revenge: "It is not I who will kill you," he reports saying as he struck him, "but the law of the city, which you have transgressed and subordinated to your own pleasure" (26). The death, he asserts, was unpremeditated, the righteous act of an insulted husband and one not only allowed but in fact demanded by the law (34). Euphiletus ends his speech with the declaration that far from being a crime, his revenge was actually a service to the state, upholding the laws against adultery and discouraging future philanderers. If you are not going to acquit me, he tells the jurors, then you should erase the laws and write new ones protecting adulterers, "for that would be far more just than allowing citizens to be ambushed (*enedreuesthai*) by the laws that bid a man to act as he wishes if he catches an adulterer" (49).

His point in this closing section is clear, but the expression is striking. In a genre not much given to metaphor, the verb *enedreuesthai* stands out: it is, as a commentator says, "a powerful image, the more so for its use in relation to νόμοι [*nomoi*]."[21] But it is more startling still in relation to the argumentative structure of the case, for it evokes precisely what Euphiletus hopes to deny, the prosecution's claim that he had lured Eratosthenes into his house to ambush him there. It is hard to see why Eratosthenes would have wished to remind a jury in his closing statement of a counter-narrative he has worked so hard to refute or why he would attribute to the laws, whose humble agent he claims to be, the precise act of which he himself stands accused. The metaphor resists explanation within a functionalist hermeneutic of persuasion. Even in this exceedingly polished and artful speech, the speaker seems not to fully control his own words. Instead, for this moment his speech speaks against him. The rhetoric that the oration had tried to render invisible – presenting itself not as the carefully forged words of a prominent logographer but as the simple account of a simple man – suddenly comes into focus, reorienting our entire perspective on the speech. Rhetoric assumes a substance and texture that make it difficult to take it as the transparent vehicle of symbolic communication – what does this metaphor communicate? – and to read through it to a meaning beyond it. Instead, such moments of rhetorical opacity invite us to seek meaning precisely within the rhetorical structure of the text, in its contradictions

[21] Carey 1989: 86 *ad* 49. Porter 1997 argues that the literary qualities of this speech, and in particular its use of comic motifs, suggest that it was a rhetorical exercise, not intended for delivery in court. Gagarin 2003a shows, however, that sophisticated narrative techniques are a seminal feature of court cases, ancient and modern. See also Davis 1987 on the "fictionality" of sixteenth-century French letters of remission and its implications for their use as historical documents: "the artifice of fiction did not necessarily lend falsity to an account; it might well bring verisimilitude or a moral truth" (4).

and overdeterminations, condensations and displacements, errant images and unexpected metaphors.

This book reads juridical discourse in and as the rhetoric of forensic oratory: the substance of the speeches' jurisprudential thought is contained in and constituted by the complex dynamics of its linguistic form. I read the texts not only for the persuasive strategies of the individual speakers, but also for what in the text entraps or ambushes those strategies. Methodologically, these readings are thus literary, even deconstructive. My focus is on those moments when forensic language turns against itself and bespeaks something more than just the manifest talking points of the litigant. Those moments, I suggest, expose the jurisprudential engine of the rhetorical machine. For this reason, it is obviously dangerous to extract and collate statements from across various texts: statements, ideas, images take on full meaning only within the context of the specific forensic argument, against the backdrop of everything a speech is trying to say and not to say. When I do survey scattered passages (as I unavoidably will in places to provide context), it will be with a certain suspension of belief in the conclusions, which will stand or fall with the full readings of individual orations.

Suspension of belief is a general methodological imperative when dealing with forensic oratory. A litigant could be dissembling at any given moment about any given thing, so one must attempt (an exercise more difficult than it may sound) to maintain a radical skepticism about everything a speaker says without simply hypostatizing its opposite as the (lost) truth of his opponent's argument. This is a discourse structured by an inverse form of the koan "I am lying": it is never possible to know whether a speaker is lying or is not lying when he says he is not lying, and thus the best truth we can hope for is that which emerges in the play between these different partial claims. That is to say once again that the full depth of forensic oratory's jurisprudential thought, and thus the full complexity of Athenian juridical discourse, emerge only at the shifting and unstable rhetorical surface of the texts.

The pages that follow substantiate this theoretical claim and illustrate the methodology it entails. They thus constitute a sustained argument, though not a unilinear one. The book aims to elucidate Athens' legal cosmos: it begins by tracing its discursive boundaries and ends by considering its attempt (and ultimate failure) to seal those boundaries through legal codification. The chapters in between fill in the details of this juridical universe, scrutinizing its subjects, logic, and temporality. In principle, these chapters could be read in any order and could also be multiplied: the role of desire, the theatrics of the body, the philosophy of truth, and the concrete politics of juridical discourse, for example, could each have constituted a separate chapter, as could the ways in which that discourse appropriates or excludes other modes of thought. The aim was not to be exhaustive – with such a topic and such a corpus it would hardly be possible – but instead to propose and demonstrate a new way of reading these often refractory texts and of understanding the intricate cosmos of Athenian law.

The first two chapters of *Law's Cosmos* trace the boundaries of Athenian juridical discourse. The first, which is the most synoptic in the book, deals with strategies by which forensic speeches construct a juridical world and an authoritative foundation for it. It argues that juridical discourse stakes its claim to authority not, as many scholars argue, on "popular sovereignty" or "the rule of law" but on its own ability to bring these two vital principles into productive alignment. But it effects this alignment, and thus authorizes itself, only by effacing the constructive force of its own rhetoric. The desire to render the rhetoric of forensic oratory transparent which we see in modern historiography thus has its roots in forensic oratory itself, as it seeks to deny its own status as a self-interested and potentially deceitful *logos*. This self-contradictory denial is never fully successful, of course, and the repudiation of rhetoric leaves awkward remainders within the text, destabilizing by-products of the speech's strategies of self-authorization. In this chapter, rhetoric emerges as an instability within the very juridical world it constructs. The chapters that follow unfold within that space of instability that rhetoric opens within a legal discourse that aims for closure and hermetic self-legitimation.

Chapter 2 examines the relation between law's intrinsic force and the criminal violence beyond its border, a distinction crucial to maintaining both the legitimacy of the law and its intimate connection to justice. This distinction troubles all legal systems, but in this case is exacerbated by the voluntarism of Athenian law, which made the courts an arena for pursuing private feuds. The law was complicit in a social violence that it ostensibly aimed to curtail: it not only legitimized private violence but relied on it for its own forceful execution. This complicity gives rise to a simultaneous acknowledgment and denial of the law's (metaphorical and literal) violence, a dynamic illustrated in the institution of the *basanos*, the torture of slaves for evidence. In this cruel practice, law's violence is displaced onto the body of a slave, where it becomes unrecognizable as violence. But the brutality thus disavowed returns dramatically in the rhetoric of the speeches, which are unable to maintain the necessary distinction between those whose pain matters and those whose doesn't and thus vividly expose the violent exclusions – the violence of exclusion and the exclusion of violence – by which the law seeks to secure its discursive boundaries. The victims of that unrecognized violence haunt juridical discourse, undermining its claim to justice as well as its authority to pass a verdict on the legitimacy of its own inherent force. At the same time, I suggest, their ghostly presence within the rhetoric of the speeches, precisely by exposing the gap between law and justice, points toward a horizon of fuller justice beyond the specific historical limits of the fifth- and fourth-century Athenian legal system.

Chapters 3 and 4 deal with the legal subject. What sort of subject does Athenian juridical discourse assume or posit? The law tries deeds but it can only try them in the person of a doer. Chapter 3 examines that elementary extrapolation of a legal agent from the liable act; it tracks the emergence and traces the outlines of Athenian law's most familiar fictional persons, the intentional, probable, and typical subject. These are the protagonists of Antiphon's *Tetralogies*, a series of abstract, theoretical cases that feature the most abstract and theoretical of legal agents. Each "case" posits a hypothetical legal scenario, the first an unwitnessed homicide, the second an accidental death, the third a murder resulting from a drunken brawl. In playing out these scenarios, the texts construct a legal world governed by particular rules of probability, possibility, and psychology and posit subjects – probable (*Tetralogy I*), intentional (*Tetralogy II*), and typical (*Tetralogy III*) – who act and think in accordance with these rules. In each case, the fictional agent is little more than a rhetorical extension of a specific mode of legal argumentation, the doer of its hypothetical deed. But in their very abstraction, these figures embody and enact the particular metaphysics of the world they inhabit and expose the extent to which the legal world is secured by its fictional subjects. Their subjective qualities, such as they are, thus lay bare the subjective structure of Athenian juridical discourse itself.

If these figures expose the subjective structure of juridical discourse, the characters examined in Chapter 4 expose the profound imbrication of the subjective and the rhetorical in legal discourse. This chapter reads the courtroom speech as a form of biography or life story, a *logos biou*. Each speaker labors to present his own life as a coherent and straightforward account: he is a good man and his entire biography proves it. But these *logoi* are not as simple as they claim, and their subjects' biographies are complicated not only by the counter-arguments of their opponents but also by their own rhetoric, the tropes and strategies that they deploy but don't fully control. This chapter reads the juridical subject through these rhetorical tropes: homonymy (in Demosthenes 39); metaphor (in Demosthenes 48); and metonymy (in Demosthenes 21 and Lysias 24). By these tropes, juridical discourse seeks not only to write a *bios* but also to define itself as a *logos*, a coherent symbolic order. And yet these tropes are by their very nature unstable: they name ambiguously, define through difference, and displace the meaning they seek to fix. To the extent that its own *logos* is predicated on the *bios* of its subjects, then, juridical discourse is riven by the same rhetorical ambiguities and tropic instabilities as the subject whose biography it writes.

The next two chapters look into the past and the future. In Chapter 5, I consider the way juridical discourse remembers the past, in particular the tyranny of the "Thirty" and the civil war of 404–403 BCE. This brief but bloody conflict ended with an amnesty in which every Athenian citizen swore not to hold a grudge – literally, "not to remember evils" (*mē mnēsikakein*). This legal agreement to forget imposed amnesia upon the political traumas of this period. In so doing, it forced civic memory into the courts, where the past and its forgetting were obsessively recalled in the trials of the early fourth century. But what does this injunction to forget do to the law, which is by its very nature a prosecutorial remembering of past crimes? How can the law forget the violence of the past without merely repressing it or, conversely, remember without repeating it? The trials this chapter analyzes (Andocides 1, Lysias 12, Lysias 13) show the legal institution assuming the role of civic archive, as the law remembers political conflict so that the city won't have to. But they also suggest that juridical discourse has a temporality of its own, and that its stake in the amnesty and its modes of remembering and forgetting may be different from those of the city. Thus even as the courts become the site of a displaced civic remembering, these speeches seek ways to forget a civic breach that disrupted the law's own temporal unity between past crime, present trial, and future justice.

This ideal of temporal unity means that in remembering (or forgetting) the past the law is always imagining its own, as well as the city's, future. The sixth chapter looks at another idiom in which legal discourse imagines its future: genealogical reproduction. It focuses on the inheritance speeches of Isaeus and argues that they reproduce not just a normative familial and social structure but, simultaneously, juridical discourse itself. These speeches imagine the family as a frail and faulty structure, in perpetual danger of extermination and therefore in need of legal intervention. Men die intestate; wills are forged; bastards worm their way into the family tree and mistresses are passed off as wives. Each saga of genealogical chaos recounts the genealogy of law's power over the family and its members. These legal speeches thus stage a family drama in which the law itself is a key player: it alone can distinguish legitimate from illegitimate, or provide an heir for a man who died childless. These narratives, moreover, extend the reach of legal discourse into both the past (as it reads the will and reconstructs the intent of the dead) and the future (by determining the legitimacy of wives and their children). In this way they grant the law not only authority over the family and its reproduction, but a power over death and hence over life itself. Law becomes a bio-power and juridical discourse becomes anthropology in the broadest sense of the word.

The book closes with forensic oratory's imagination of the lawcode and its dream of a perfect legal system. This brief final chapter forms a pair with the opening chapter: the destabilizing force of rhetoric examined there is answered here by the stability of the written laws, and the discursive totalization rendered impossible (as I argue in Chapter 1) by the speeches' own rhetoricity is sought in the monumental fixity of the lawcode. In this concluding chapter a judicial notion that might seem to be the ideational cornerstone of the legal cosmos (and therefore to belong in the first chapter) instead appears, in light of the previous chapters, as the site of its most intense internal negotiations. The conclusion thus reopens the guiding questions of the book as a whole: the relation not only between law and rhetoric but also, more broadly, between forensic oratory and juridical discourse. This chapter examines the ambivalence of forensic oratory toward the notion of legal codification, its simultaneous longing for the unity, fixity, and coherence of a legal code and its anxiety about both the possibility and desirability of such a code. Can codification really protect the law's integrity, fixing its legality for all time? And if it does, will the very code that preserves the law's letter kill its spirit? This chapter proposes that in the course of meditating on these questions, forensic oratory reflects upon the systematicity – the limits or limitlessness, fixity or flexibility – of the larger discourse to which it belongs and contributes. The ambivalence of this self-reflection, forensic oratory's simultaneous desire for and wariness of discursive totalization, is not resolved, but instead rhetorically transformed into a positive juridical paradigm in a parable about the law of the Locrians (Demosthenes 24). This rhetorical exemplum is a self-conscious fantasy of a legal code that is stable but not static, inscribed but alive. With exemplary vividness, it reveals forensic oratory in the process of constructing its own ideal world, a legal universe structured by a symmetry that is at once just and beautiful.

This final paradigm resolves the aesthetic and the jurisprudential into a perfect harmony. Here the two meanings of *kosmos* coincide: rhetorical adornment is juridical order. This scene thus exemplifies the double nature of Athenian forensic oratory as both a mode of legal thought and a genre of literary language. The two disciplines that the law and literature movement seeks to unite are here already in intimate symbiosis; they can neither be segregated nor opposed in a hierarchy of style and substance: literary form is a kind of legal matter.[22] Recognizing that symbiosis allows us to see the ways in which the forensic and the rhetorical work together to generate, define, authorize, and reproduce a juridical world. It also, and perhaps more interestingly, lets us see those moments in which the two strain against one another, exposing the tensions inherent in this process of discursive cosmogony and the contradictions within the jurisprudential cosmos it produces. These moments suggest that the critical perspective which many in the law and literature movement hope literature will lend the law is in Athens built into it from the start.[23] Writing about modern law, Shoshana Felman argues that there is something in every trial that will elude legal consciousness, a surplus that the law, by its very nature as a practice that works toward resolution, will necessarily fail to capture. She suggests that literature can convey this legal remainder and express what the trial must repress in order to reach its verdict.[24] In Athens that surplus inheres within the ordinary language of the law, simultaneously repressed and expressed by texts that are always both legal and literary. *Law's Cosmos* reads these texts for that contradictory and complementary dynamic. It argues that in Athenian forensic oratory law *is* literature, and only by understanding it as both at once can we appreciate the sophistication of its thought, the subtlety of its elaboration, and the richness and intricacy of the juridical *kosmos* it creates.

[22] The reverse is also true: we will see literary *hulē* take on legal *morphē* as multivalent narratives are reworked as forensic polarities or complex characterization is recast as criminal intent and culpable agency.

[23] E.g. Goodrich 1998: 114–15: "Literature . . . presents an image of a beyond of law, a justice that exists like equity beyond the letter of legal rule. Literary method provides subtle and, in political terms, non-obvious critical tools for analyzing the felicity – the justice – of legal speech acts. Just speech, at least in an ontological sense, is speech that approximates most closely to the eloquence – the imagination of identity and lifestyle – that literature conjures as its law."

[24] Felman 2002, esp. 86–100 and 131–66.

PART I

The Boundaries of Legal Discourse

CHAPTER I

The world of law: oratory and authority

Once understood in the context of the narratives that give it meaning, law becomes not merely a system of rules to be observed, but a world in which we live.

Cover 1993: 96

We are *foreigners* on the inside – *but there is no outside.*

De Certeau 1984: 13–14

Rhetoric names the textures of relation that make external situations and contexts internal to the truth of law.

Ryan 1989: 155

ON THE INSIDE

Juridical discourse constructs a world of its own, a world of law. That legal world was, of course, embedded within the broader landscape of the polis: *nomos* means "norm" as well as "law" in Greek, and the courts were a central arena for the reproduction and negotiation of Athens' normative values and beliefs, as much recent scholarship has shown. But if the law was enmeshed in the fabric of Athenian society and ideology, it also had a discursive specificity of its own. In the *dikastēria* (courts), the Athenians developed a juridical way of looking at life, social relations, the past and the future; they also reflected self-consciously on the law itself, on its discursive boundaries, its institutional force, its internal rules and regularities. This juridical mode of thought was not, needless to say, isolated or idiosyncratic; if it were, it would have been incomprehensible. Rather the law, as Steven Johnstone has argued, was a "semiautonomous field."[1] Like the theater

[1] Johnstone 1999: 126–31. Bourdieu 1987 theorizes law's relation to the larger social field. See also the essays by Deggau, Lempert, and Nelken in Teubner 1988. Luhmann's distinction between cognitive openness and operational closure is useful in thinking about the autonomy of legal discourse. For him "closure" does not mean that a system has no interaction with its external environment (which would be virtually inconceivable) but instead that all operations, including that of distinguishing

(to which it is often compared), forensic oratory was both a stage for the performance of Athenian social dramas and simultaneously a world of its own, with its own customs, topographies, and inhabitants.

One of the most striking characteristics of this legal world is its internal consistency. Legal agents act, speak, and think in predictable ways. The ubiquitous arguments from *ēthos* (character) define legal subjects as recognizable types, not as unique individuals: a speaker claims that he is not the type of man to have done what he is accused of or, alternately, that his opponent is the type of man to have done that and more. When speakers do profess to reveal their inner thoughts their psyches are discernibly legalistic: crises of conscience are described as if they were court cases and internal monologues are carried on in the very terms of the speech that recounts them.[2] Legal arguments, too, tend to be extremely predictable, following a conventional order of exposition and ringing the changes on a number of familiar topoi; even arguments that strike us as bizarre (and there will be many in the pages that follow) adhere to generic rules of logic and presentation. Metaphysically, as well as psychologically and rhetorically, the legal world is internally consistent. Athenian litigants often based their cases on probability (*eikos*): if I had meant to kill a man, is it likely that I would have done so in broad daylight, in front of witnesses? Would I not rather have waited for night or led him to a secluded spot? This hypothetical argument presupposes that everyone thinks like the law: criminals commit their crimes with an eye toward the defense they will make in court. As we will see in Chapter 3, it also posits a set of physical and logical principles – cause and effect, intention and action – that is coherent within itself and consonant with the rhetoric and logic of legal argumentation. The entire world works like the law.

Even the gods think juridically. In Andocides 1, for instance, the prosecutors propose that the gods saved Andocides from a shipwreck expressly so that he could stand trial in Athens and be put to death for impiety (137). Andocides counters with an argument from probability: if the gods thought I had wronged them, they would never have let me go when they

internal from external, are internally motivated and validated: see 1988: 1420, 1425, 1429–31; 1990: 229–30. I take it for granted that Athenian legal discourse had vital relations with other cultural discourses (i.e. cognitive openness); the point is, though, that it itself defined those relations and determined the boundary between inside and outside (operational closure).

2 Andocides 1.48–60 is a good example. Andocides recounts the moment, more than a decade before the trial in which he delivers this defense speech, when he had to decide whether to inform on his companions in the affair of the Mysteries and the Herms. His internal struggle over the decision (51–53) is described in terms that neatly prefigure the speech he is making in court: the juridical *krisis* is projected or introjected as a personal crisis and his defense today retrojected onto his decision then (59).

had me in the greatest possible peril – on a ship in pirate-infested waters during the winter storms – but would have punished me then and there (137–38). In fact, he tells the jurors, if we are going to speculate about the gods' intentions, I think they would be extremely angry if they saw you put to death a man they had saved (139).[3] The gods do not look down on the trial from above, but instead the divine will exists within the rhetoric of the speech, the product of its improbable logic of probability. Appeals to the divine are not unique to judicial discourse, of course, no more than arguments concerning character (*ēthos*) or probability (*eikos*). What is distinctive, rather, is the way each of these elements mirrors the logic of a forensic brief. Like any discourse, legal discourse is a fractal universe in which each part reiterates the structure of the whole. Just as tragic gods enjoin wisdom through suffering and comic gods are preoccupied by food and sex, the orators' gods think like litigants: when a god appears *ex machina*, he is generated by the machine of forensic oratory.

Indeed, not only the gods but everything that crosses the forensic stage is the product of the law's rhetorical machinery. A case may involve the terms of a contract, for example, but the actual contract is not produced or read out in court; instead, its provisions will be tendentiously paraphrased by litigants who vehemently disagree not only on the text and interpretation of the contract, but in some cases on whether there even was a contract in the first place. Likewise, in a case that rests on the legitimacy of a certain woman, the two litigants will construct competing narratives about her character and life; the jury must then decide whether she was a wife or a mistress, and sometimes whether she even existed at all. Since women could not speak for themselves in court, beyond the speaker's rhetoric the woman does not exist. Even when the orators conjure objects as explicitly extralegal, they turn out to be internal to the rhetoric of the case. Chapter 2 will examine the institution of the *basanos*, the torture of slaves for testimony. Speakers represent this as an independent source of infallible truth – if only their opponent had agreed to hand over his slaves for interrogation. In practice, it seems that the *basanos* was virtually never carried out; instead, it functions within the speeches as part of a rhetoric of dares and challenges that follows the rules of legal probability: why would

[3] Cf. And. 1.113–14. Lysias 6 is a speech for the prosecution in this same case. The prosecutor makes the argument Andocides alludes to (19) and adds that the very fact that Andocides dared to hazard a sea voyage after committing impiety is a sign of his shamelessness (20). The lead tablets discussed by Versnel 1991 may apply the same jurisprudential logic. These texts seem to contain prayers for "divine 'legal aid'" (Versnel 1991: 74) in specific court cases, and their language shows a marked forensic influence; cf. Eidinow 2007: 59–60, 62–64.

I have proposed a *basanos* unless I wanted to uncover the truth, and why would my opponent have refused unless he had something to hide? Thus forensic oratory imagines a truth beyond itself only to subsume it immediately back within its own terms.[4] The same can be said of everything these speeches represent as existing before or beyond themselves, including the characters and biographies of the two litigants, the history of their dispute, the criminal event and all its attendant circumstances and proofs. In this sense juridical discourse is a text with no *hors-texte*, and it constructs a world with no outside.[5]

This means that the sources of authority for juridical discourse – the legitimating foundations upon which individual litigants seek to ground their own claims and upon which the legal system as a whole predicates its power to sentence and to punish – are immanent to the discourse itself, generated within forensic oratory and subject to its discursive regularities. Forensic oratory has infrequent recourse to theology, but when it does (as Andocides' defense shows) divine law is the creation of human law and its human orators. So, too, we will see in the next section that when speakers appeal to the laws of the polis as a legitimating mandate, those laws are the self-interested product of legal speech. For instance, speakers frequently interpret the laws in their own favor by citing the intention of the original lawmaker, Solon or Draco, but often the legislation they attribute to these venerable lawmakers post-dates them by a century and the intention they imagine behind the statute is demonstrably fictional. The laws are interpreted with the same flexibility and according to the same logic of juridical probability as divine will in Andocides' speech. Every external ground of authority to which forensic oratory appeals proves to lie already within its own discursive terrain.

This chapter examines the ways in which Athenian forensic oratory constructs and authorizes its judicial world. The first section looks at two principles that are individually often taken as the authorizing mandate for the Athenian legal system, "popular sovereignty" and "rule of law." These two principles feature prominently in forensic oratory but they appear less as the source than as the effect of the law's authority. Juridical discourse

[4] Johnstone 1999: 70–92. Demosthenes 47 will provide a dizzying example in Chapter 2: in this false-witnessing case concerning testimony in a prior case about a *basanos* proposal and its refusal, the slave interrogation that (the speaker claims) would have resolved the prior suit instead becomes the object of the false testimony at issue in this suit, which itself could be resolved by the interrogation of the same slave, if his opponents were not blocking it. The imagined external resolution of the trial is always absorbed right back into the agonistic rhetoric of the trial.

[5] See Derrida 1976: 157–64, 1988: 136–37. Cf. de Certeau 1984: 8–14, with the quotation at the head of this chapter.

generates its authority, I argue, by situating itself as the medium of a necessary and beneficial convergence between the sovereign demos and the rule of law. The trial makes the people just and the laws democratic, and this happy convergence defines the unique jurisdiction of the law.

This union of law and demos, justice and polis is effected by means of rhetoric, "the textures of relation that make external situations and contexts internal to the truth of law," as Michael Ryan puts it in a quotation that serves as one of the epigrams to this chapter. But if juridical discourse authorizes itself through rhetoric, it does so only by effacing that rhetoric, by pretending, for instance, that popular sovereignty and the rule of law converge serendipitously within the course of the trial, and not through the careful manipulations of a self-interested speaker. Juridical oratory thus takes up a contradictory relation to itself, in which authorizing the juridical often entails denying the rhetorical. The second section of this chapter examines the ambivalence within forensic oratory to its own rhetoricity, an ambivalence expressed not only through bifurcation between the honest, transparent oratory of the speaker and the deceitful oratory of his opponent, but also, more interestingly, in the form of a self-repudiation in which the speaker, in order to deny that he is deceitful, denies that he is a *rhētōr* or that his speech is rhetorical.

This repudiation of rhetoric creates unexpected rhetorical effects within the text, as speakers deny what they are and become what they are not. These effects will be traced in detail in one speech, Demosthenes 25 *Against Aristogeiton*, in the final section of the chapter. That speech constructs an orderly legal cosmos, encircling it with rhetorical chains beyond which it seeks to banish the defendant, Aristogeiton. But in the process of creating this nomic structure it also creates various rhetorical by-products that are not so easily exiled. The rhetoric that produces and authorizes this world of law also renders it unstable.

This destabilizing effect is important. The boundless boundedness of legal discourse, in which every outside is already inside the law, risks depriving it of any ground at all: it risks enclosing law within a hermetic circle of self-reference in which "the law is the law" and there is no justice beyond the given decision of a jury in a given trial. Likewise, if within the homogenous landscape of juridical discourse everything works like the law, then there is no internal standpoint from which to critique the law. But rhetoric, I propose, offers such a standpoint, for the very language with which legal discourse hopes to authorize itself exposes the contingency and constructedness of that authority. Rhetoric, which oratory seeks to banish from the courthouse, always necessarily dwells inside it and this paradox exposes the mechanisms by which juridical discourse imposes and enforces the boundaries between inside and outside. This simultaneous repudiation and persistence – its persistence in the form of something repudiated – makes rhetoric a point of heterogeneity within the homogenous world of law, a point of vacillation between the natural and artificial and between the legitimate and illegitimate, that deconstructs that world's coherence and authority. Rhetoric is a "privileged instability" within judicial discourse that allows us to question, as the following chapters will, the law's violence and exclusions, its amnesias and desires, its genealogy and self-relation.[6] This first chapter paves the way for these critiques by examining not only the law's discursive strategies of authorization but also, and more importantly, how those strategies necessarily fail to achieve the fixity they aim for and how that failure itself becomes the paradoxical foundation of Athens' juridical cosmos.[7]

NOMOS, DEMOS, POLIS

There are two primary sources of authority cited in Athenian forensic oratory: "the laws" (i.e. the written statutes) and the jurors as representatives of the demos. Litigants appeal to each as the decisive foundation of justice, sometimes even within the same speech. The speaker in Antiphon 6 refers to the homicide laws as "by universal agreement the most excellent of all laws and the holiest; they happen to be the most ancient laws in this land and they have always been the same and dealt with the same issues, which is the greatest sign of a well-established law." Therefore, he concludes, "you must not learn from the prosecutors' speeches about the laws and whether or not they were well established but you must learn from the laws about their speeches and whether they are instructing you rightly and lawfully or not" (6.2 = 5.14). But in the next sentence he emphasizes the effective

6 The phrase "privileged instability" comes from Derrida 1992a: 21, where it describes the aporetic gap between law and justice.

7 My discussion of the law's self-authorization in this chapter parallels Steven Johnstone's excellent study (1999). He argues that forensic oratory attempts "to overcome the indeterminacy of rhetorical language and to stabilize the relationship constituted through that language" (3) by appealing to seemingly external sources of authority and truth, but that these are in fact always determined by the rhetoric of the litigants and thus are actually the desired effect, not the precondition of the trial. His book analyzes well the strategies by which speakers seek to surmount the instability of rhetoric, but does not examine that instability itself (which in places appears to be merely an effect of the impersonal relation between speakers and jurors, 2, 90), nor does he explore its lingering effects within the speech. My discussion shifts the focus from the rhetorical strategies for securing authority in the face of linguistic indeterminacy to the way that indeterminacy persistently destabilizes law's authorizing strategies and structures.

power of the jurors' verdict, for there is only one vote, he says, and "if the jury reaches the wrong decision it is stronger than justice and truth" (6.3 = 5.87). If a defendant is found guilty, he explains, he must abide by the sentence even if he is innocent, "for he must obey the verdict even if it goes against the truth" (6.5 = 5.87). On the one hand, the laws are the sole basis for justice in the case; on the other hand, the jurors' decision, even if it is wrong, is final and authoritative.

"The laws" (*hoi nomoi*) occupy a prominent place in Athenian forensic oratory, which draws upon and exemplifies the "enormous reservoir of respect for *nomos*" in Athenian culture.[8] Speakers frequently cite written laws and claim that these laws support their case or, alternately, that their case supports the laws. They have the text of a statute read out by the court secretary for the benefit of the jurors, for "there is nothing like hearing from the law itself" (Dem. 21.46).[9] They call upon the jurors to uphold the laws, appealing frequently to the dikastic oath sworn by every juror at the start of his year of service, and in particular to the jurors' pledge to "vote in accordance with the laws and the decrees of the demos of the Athenians and the Council."[10] Numerous speeches culminate in a rousing ode on this theme: "By the gods and spirits I beg you, jurors, do not allow the victim to be insulted, but remember the law and the oath you swore and what has been said about the matter, and vote according to the laws, in conformity with justice and your oath" (Is. 2.47).[11] When the jurors vote, as they have sworn to do, in accordance with the laws, justice is done.

The generality of this injunction to "vote according to the laws" suggests that the laws functioned in forensic oratory not just as a series of specific regulations but as a broader regulatory ideal.[12] An opponent who has transgressed a single – and sometimes quite technical – statute will be accused of "trying to overthrow the laws." For example, Lycurgus, prosecuting Leocrates for treason because he had fled Athens after news of its defeat

[8] Carey 1996: 36. See also Sealey 1987: 50–52, 146–48; Harris 1994a: 133–37. Harris 2004: 21–34 examines the definition of *nomos* in Athens.

[9] The laws quoted in modern texts and translations of the speeches are generally later additions (usually extrapolated from the surrounding text) and are considered spurious except where confirmed by external evidence: see Todd 1993: 44–45. De Brauw 2001–02 analyzes citation of laws as part of a rhetoric of *ēthos*.

[10] This was the first clause of the oath and is the one most often alluded to. The text of the oath cited at Dem. 24.149–51 is probably not authentic, but this first clause at least seems to be relatively secure. For discussion of the oath, see Cronin 1936; Bonner and Smith 1938: 152–56; Todd 1993: 54–55; Johnstone 1999: 33–42, 60–62; Mirhady 2007. Harris 1994a: 149 nn. 6–7 provides a list of references.

[11] See also Ant. 5.96; Aesch. 3.257; Dem. 27.68, 39.41, 45.87; Is. 4.31.

[12] Todd 1993: 18; Carey 1996: 44–46.

at Chaeroneia, suggests that a transgression against any particular law is a transgression against legality in general (64–67). He refers to the intent of the original lawmaker, a fiction employed throughout forensic oratory to conceptualize the laws as a fixed, traditional, and coherent code.[13] The lawmaker did not differentiate between different degrees of illegality but only asked whether a certain act would harm society if it became widespread. Imagine, he continues, that someone entered the Metroön, the public building where copies of the statutes were kept, and erased a single statute, arguing that there's no harm in deleting just that one (66). In the same way Leocrates, by breaking this one law, has assaulted the very idea of law. "The laws" in this passage signify both a discrete set of legal regulations, the work of a single venerable lawmaker enshrined in the Metroön, and the concept of law as an abstract and universal principle.

Such rhetoric, with its strategic slippage between the concrete and the abstract, has led some scholars to posit that Athenian legal practice was grounded upon the theoretical credo of "the rule of law," an adherence not only to the specific *nomoi* of the polis but to *nomos* as a general principle.[14] More recently, however, a number of students of Athenian law have challenged this view, questioning the role of both "the laws" as a foundation of authority and "the rule of law" as a guiding tenet of Athenian forensic practice.[15] They point out that Aristotle, in his discussion of rhetorical strategies for use in the courts, lists the laws in the category of "artless proofs" (*atekhnoi pisteis*) along with witness testimony, oaths, and contracts.[16] This suggests that in his view the laws had persuasive not determinative force, that citing a law could strengthen your case (just as supplying witnesses or a written document could) but would not in itself prove decisive for the verdict.[17]

[13] On "the lawmaker," see R. Thomas 1994; Farenga 2006: 267–310; and Johnstone 1999: 25–33, who argues that this fiction allowed three interpretive strategies: "nonliteral reading, reading in conformity with other laws, and reading of laws as fundamentally democratic" (26).

[14] See especially Meyer-Laurin 1965; Hansen 1974: 18, 48; Sealey 1982, 1987; Ostwald 1986: 497–524. Their case rests in general not on the language of the forensic speeches but on external facts of legal history, like the revision of the lawcode in 403–399 BCE and procedures like the *graphē paranomōn*, which tried the legality of new decrees. This position has come under a good deal of fire in recent decades, but has been reasserted in a more nuanced form by Harris 1994a: 133–37, 2000, 2004, 2006: 3–25 (and cf. xviii–xxii); Carey 1996; D. Cohen 2005. See the brief but useful discussion of the issue at Todd 1993: 298–300.

[15] Gernet 1955: 61–81; Ober 1989a: 299–304, 1989b; Todd 1993: 54–63, 299–300; Lane Fox 1994; R. Thomas 1994; D. Cohen 1995a: 52–57, 1995b; Johnstone 1999: 21–45; Allen 2000a: 174–96; Lanni 2006 (esp. 64–74).

[16] Arist. *Rhet.* 1375a–b. Carey 1996, however, shows that Aristotle's prescriptions did not always accord with forensic practice; cf. Carey 1994b; Trevett 1996.

[17] Todd 1993: 60: "Laws, like other forms of evidence, served to persuade rather than to bind an Athenian court." Cf. Gernet 1955: 67; Todd 1990b: 32; Carey 1994b: 101–02; Allen 2000a: 174–75;

This "persuasive" use of the laws often looks to modern eyes simultaneously too sweeping and too limited. In his prosecution of Leocrates, for example, Lycurgus insists upon the sanctity of "the laws" and the primacy of law as a principle, but the precise legal charge behind his case is vague and, in fact, rather suspect. The case is technically an *eisangelia*, a procedure used for impeaching individuals, generally public officials, for serious crimes against the polis, including treason.[18] Leocrates is expected to argue that the charge cannot be applied to him because he was a private citizen (59) who left Athens for purposes not of treason but of trade (55). Prosecuting him under this law is a stretch, as Lycurgus himself tacitly acknowledges when he urges the jurors to act "not just as judges (*dikastas*) of this crime but also as lawmakers" (*nomothetas*, 9). It is easy to prosecute someone who commits an act expressly prohibited by a law, he explains, "but when the law does not encompass all related offenses and call them by a single name, and when a man has committed a crime worse than any of these, he is liable under all the laws equally" (9). The bulk of his speech is therefore devoted not to proving that the defendant actually did break the specific provisions of the law against treason but to showing that Leocrates was in every respect a bad citizen. To support this claim Lycurgus quotes from the ephebic oath taken by all citizen youths and from the epitaphs of the dead at Marathon and Thermopylae; he recites extended passages from Homer, Euripides, and the poet Tyrtaeus; he has read out decrees concerning various cases of treason from the previous century and the Spartan edict on military desertion. In short, he quotes everything but the specific regulation under which he is prosecuting Leocrates. "The laws" are simultaneously fundamental in this case – one of the "greatest guardians" of democracy (3) – and in a strict sense irrelevant and insufficient. A speaker need not prove that the defendant broke a specific law in order to win his case (Lycurgus lost his by a single vote, according to Aeschines 3.252) nor can he argue a case based on the law alone.

Thus while speakers appeal to "the laws" as if they were an autonomous source of authority, those laws were in fact subject to extensive interpretation and manipulation within the speeches. Indeed, they invited such interpretation. Athenian legislation was generally procedural not substantive, so statutes would name a remedy or penalty for a crime without

Gagarin 2008: 191–92, 201–04. Bateman 1958 goes further, arguing that Lysias' representation of the laws he cites was fundamentally sophistical.

[18] On this procedure see Bonner and Smith 1930: 294–309; Harrison 1971: 50–59; Hansen 1975; Todd 1993: 113–15.

necessarily defining the crime itself.[19] The law of *hubris*, to take the most infamous example, nowhere specifies what actions constitute *hubris*. Speakers thus have to interpret the text of the law and have broad scope for doing so. From this perspective Lycurgus is not so much trying to deceive the jurors about the law on treason (although he is almost certainly doing that as well) as he is asking them to approve his interpretation of this law's meaning and application, an interpretation allowed and even required by the imprecise language of the statute.[20] The latitude for interpretation of laws was further extended by the amateurism of the Athenian legal system. Although literate individuals could consult the laws in written form – either as inscribed on stone stelai throughout the city or later gathered in the archive at the Metroön – the citizens who sat on Athens' large juries were not expected to have detailed technical knowledge of specific legal provisions.[21] What they knew (and to a large extent what we know today) about the laws they learned from the two litigants, themselves more or less amateurs, who were responsible for selecting, interpreting, and presenting the provisions relevant to their case. It was apparently illegal and punishable by death to cite a non-existent law (Dem. 26.24). Short of that, however, the laws that the jurors heard and according to which they swore to judge were heavily filtered – selectively excerpted or creatively combined, loosely interpreted and tendentiously applied – by the litigants themselves.

"The laws," then, were a privileged marker of authority in forensic oratory, but their authority is immanent and interested, not autonomous or absolute: it is, as Johnstone has stressed, the product of a litigant's

[19] Todd 1993: 65–67. Gernet 1955: 67: "En fait, les juges interprètent la loi – d'où résulte que, dans les conditions les plus défavorables à la constitution d'une jurisprudence, une certaine jurisprudence s'est tout de même constituée."

[20] As Todd 1993: 31 remarks, jurors must decide both the facts and the law in each case; cf. 61–62; Johnstone 1999: 22–25, 33, 42–45; Carey 2004: 112–13; Gagarin 2004: 19–21; Mirhady 2007. Harris, by contrast, stresses the limits on novel interpretations of the laws and notes jurors' apparent preference for "the standard meaning of legal provisions" (2000: 67). For a particularly egregious example of a self-serving reconstruction of "the laws," see Aesch. 1.6–36 and Ford 1999: 241–49; Fisher 2001: 125–64. The role of judicial hermeneutics is no less active in modern law, as Goodrich 1986: 126–67 shows.

[21] Todd 1993: 54–60 notes the practical difficulties of consulting the laws; cf. Christ 1998a: 199. Others posit that consultation was fairly common in the fourth century: Sickinger 1999: 95–96, 160–70; Gagarin 2008: 180–82. Harris 1994a: 135 argues that the frequency of jury duty – the average Athenian citizen, he conjectures, would have served as a juror once every five years and heard roughly twenty cases during his term – meant that jurors were relatively knowledgeable about the law. Cf. Hansen 1991: 186–88. Litigants often speak as though the jurors were familiar with the laws, but this is more a rhetorical appeal to the laws as a communal norm ("you all know") than a presumption of specific legal expertise.

persuasive speech, not an independent validation of it.[22] And while speakers cite the laws on their own behalf as though they had an inherent truth beyond the rhetoric of their own speech, they also acknowledge that in less scrupulous hands the laws are vulnerable to manipulation and self-serving misinterpretation.[23] Forensic oratory thus tacitly admits that the laws to which it appeals are always, to a greater or lesser extent, constructs of the partisan rhetoric of the litigants.

At the same time as they quietly concede their own role in producing the laws, speakers loudly celebrate the role of the jurors, declaring that the laws exist only as actualized in the vote of the democratic jury. The jurors are "guardians" of the laws, reaffirming them in principle and in practice every time they reach a correct verdict.[24] Jurors swore to vote according to the laws, but another clause of the dikastic oath may have stipulated that "concerning matters on which there are no laws I will vote using my own fairest judgment" (*gnōmēi tēi dikaiotatēi*).[25] Jurors are often called upon to exercise that judgment actively: they are asked not only to stand as guardians of the original lawmaker's intent, but to act as lawmakers themselves by casting a verdict that will become law for future juries.[26]

If in its appeals to "the laws" Athenian jurisprudence resembles modern civil-law systems, in which a comprehensive statutory code is the supreme jurisprudential authority, in this notion of the jurors as both guardians and givers of the laws, Athenian legal thought seems closer to modern common-law systems, which rely primarily on the precedent of judgments in previous cases. That latter analogy is complicated, however, by the fact that Athenian law had no formal system of precedent. As Stephen Todd points out, there were no published judicial opinions (and could

[22] Johnstone 1999: 21–45; cf. Gagarin 1997: 21. See also Fish 1991: 207: law is "in the business of producing the very authority it retroactively invokes."

[23] E.g. Dem. 18.121. Carey 1996: 41; Christ 1998a: 198, 201–02.

[24] E.g. Dem. 21.30; cf. Dem. 18.6: "Solon believed that the laws must be authoritative (*kurious*) not only through his writing them down but also through the jurors' oath." For the jurors as guardians of the laws, see, e.g., Aesch. 1.7, 3.7; Dem. 21.34, 76, 177; 22.57; 24.36–37; 25.6; Din. 3.16.

[25] Dem. 20.118, 39.40; cf. 23.96. This clause is much less commonly cited than the clause binding jurors to vote according to the laws, and it is uncertain whether it was ever a formal part of the oath. See Meyer-Laurin 1965: 28–31; Biscardi 1970; Scafuro 1997: 50–55; Johnstone 1999: 41 and nn. 102–03; Mirhady 2007. Based partly on this clause, Ruschenbusch (1957) advanced a "theory of gaps," positing that Athenian law was not a unified or exhaustive code, but a series of discrete statutes with considerable gray areas where judgment fell to the dikasts' discretion; cf. Sealey 1994: 51–58.

[26] The jurors are compared to lawmakers at Aesch. 3.14; Lys. 14.4, 15.9; Lyc. 1.9; Dem. 19.232, 20.94, 56.48. Farenga 2006: 329–45 suggests that the jurors' identification with the lawmaker was a cognitive prerequisite of the concept of the sovereignty of law. On the trope, see further Hansen 1971–80, Rubinstein 2007: 366–67.

not have been, given the size and diversity of Athenian juries) and since jurors did not give reasons for their decisions, their verdicts, unlike those in modern common law, "did not deliver a clear ruling on a point of law."[27] The jurors in any given case thus followed or set precedent only in a figurative sense, and the figurative language of precedent served to magnify their authority: the trope of "guarding the law" did not bind them literally to past decisions, while the trope of "making the law" figured their present decision as notionally binding in the future. This rhetoric suggests a jurisprudential philosophy in which legal authority lay less in the written statutes than in the vote of the jury – or, rather, in the former only to the extent that they were effectuated in the latter. Thus speakers can imagine jurors deciding the case even in the absence of a law – "since you have sworn to use your fairest judgment where there are no laws, even if there were no law established in this case you would be right to cast your vote for me" (Dem. 39.40) – and often suggest that their verdict in and of itself constitutes justice.

These frequent appeals to the vote of the jurors have led a number of scholars to conclude that the ultimate foundation of authority in the Athenian courts was not in fact the rule of law but rather the sovereignty of the demos, the ideological credo of Athenian democracy.[28] In the courts, they suggest, the *kratos* (authority) of the demos was supreme, as hundreds of average citizens selected by lot collectively decided questions fundamental to Athens' social order and civic well-being. Danielle Allen puts it succinctly: "Athenian courts were ruled by the judgments of the jurors."[29] This view has a long history: the Aristotelian *Athenaion Politeia* lists the establishment of the courts as one of Solon's "most populist" (*dēmotikōtata*) reforms, "since the demos' sovereignty over the verdict made it sovereign over the state" (*kurios gar ōn ho dēmos tēs psēphou kurios gignetai tēs politeias*, 9.1). The author notes that the ambiguity of the written laws meant that many issues had to be referred to the courts and says that some people believe (mistakenly, in his view) that Solon made the laws unclear on purpose "so that the demos might be sovereign over the decision" (9.2).

The extant forensic speeches seem to bear out this theory, missing few opportunities to remind the jurors of their power over the outcome of the case. The jurors are treated as representatives of the demos as a whole:

[27] Todd 1993: 61. He offers a clear synopsis of the similarities and differences between Athenian law and both civil and common law at 1993: 49–63. On the issue of precedent, see Lanni 2004, 2006: 118–28; Rubinstein 2007.

[28] Ober 1989a: 299–304, 332–39; D. Cohen 1995a: 52–57, 183–95; Christ 1998a: 20–25; Allen 2000a: 168–96; Roisman 2005: 130–62; Lanni 2006: 139–42.

[29] Allen 2000a: 177. Cf. Yunis 2005: 197: "The law was an instrument of democratic rule."

speakers will refer, for instance, to the "decrees you [the jurors] passed" in the Ecclesia, assimilating these jurors to the entire body of voting citizens.[30] Indeed, the courts did operate much like the Assembly, where a large and untrained populace, relying on its own "fairest judgment" (*gnōmēi tēi dikaiotatēi*) cast immediate and binding verdicts on speakers' proposals. Thus when litigants urge the jurors to vote in their own interests, as they frequently do, those interests are assumed to be identical with the city's. This identity of the particular jury with the Athenian citizen body as a whole may also lie behind the imprecise use of precedent: it is not specific judgments or strict legal reasoning that provides continuity from one case to the next, but the enduring democratic spirit of the Athenian demos, and the jurors must guard the "precedent" of that spirit as enacted in prior decisions and pass it down as a binding "law" for future jurors in their own just decision.[31] Every verdict thus reaffirms the supremacy of the demos and the democracy, and this is presented as the ultimate stake of every case. So Lycurgus ends his speech against Leocrates by pointing to the two urns into which the jurors will cast their votes for conviction or acquittal: one urn, he says, is for treason and destroying the city; the other for ensuring its safety and prosperity (149–50). "Imagine that the country and its trees supplicate you, that the harbors, shipyards, and city walls beseech you, that the temples and shrines beg your help. Remember the charges I have brought, and make Leocrates proof that pity and tears do not carry more weight with you than the salvation of the laws and the demos" (150).

But just as the laws are effective only when actualized in the form of the jury's vote, so the jury's *gnōmē* is only *dikaiotatē* when it accords with the laws. The demos' decision is always authoritative: this is the fundamental tenet of *dēmokratia*. But that authoritative decision is sometimes wrong. There are several notorious examples of misguided – but sovereign – votes in the Ecclesia: in fact, at one point the demos even voted itself out of power, a democratic decision that ushered in the oligarchic regime of the Four Hundred.[32] Forensic orators also allude to misguided votes in the *dikastēria*, instances where the jurors reached the wrong decision and

30 See Ober 1989a: 145–47 for references and discussion. Hansen's argument for a clear distinction between the jury and the demos (1974: 19–21, 1978, 1987: 101–7, 1989; cf. Sinclair 1988: 123–27) has met with little agreement; see Ostwald 1986: 34–35, Ober 1989b and the intelligent discussion in Blanshard 2004, who notes the self-interested artifice involved in speakers' conflation of jury and demos.

31 Rubinstein 2007: 366–67, 371.

32 Thuc. 8.67–70. Another paradigmatic example is the demos' decision after the Battle of Arginusae to sentence to death the generals who, though victorious, were held responsible for heavy losses: see Xen. *Hell.* 1.7; Ostwald 1986: 431–45; Sinclair 1988: 171–72; Munn 2000: 181–87. This vote may have contributed to Athens' defeat in the Peloponnesian War, and is represented in contemporary sources as a symbol of democracy run amok.

voted against justice, their own interests, and the good of the polis.[33] Since every speaker represents a vote against himself as just such a travesty of justice, the possibility of an unjust verdict haunts every speech. The remedy to this danger is the laws: "Although the demos of the Athenians is the highest sovereign power (*kuriōtatos*) over everything in the polis and can do whatever it wants . . . it has established laws for itself" (Dem. 59.88). This is why jurors are so frequently reminded of their oath to vote according to the laws and exhorted to put the laws before persuasive speeches (meaning the opponent's, of course, not the speaker's own). Aeschines, in a passage to which we will return in the next section, tells the jurors that if they reach the right verdict the laws will be good and sovereign, *kaloi kai kurioi*; if they reach the wrong decision, however, the laws will still be good (*kaloi*) but they will no longer be sovereign (*kurioi*, 1.36). The reverse might be said of the jury's vote: if it is right it will be *kalon kai kurion*; if it is wrong it will still be *kurion*, but it will no longer be *kalon*.

This intersection between *kaloi nomoi* and the *kurios demos* is precisely where juridical discourse stakes its claim to authority, for it is in the trial that laws and jury come together in mutual consummation. Juridical discourse thus finds its mandate, I suggest, not in "popular sovereignty" nor in the "rule of law" alone, but in its own ability to unite the two. Ideally, the jurors' judgment accords perfectly with the laws, and the two clauses of the dikastic oath are in harmony.[34] Ideally, the verdict aligns the sovereign will of the demos, the good of the polis, the sanctity of the laws, and the goal of justice. But if that ideal is realized, it is thanks to the forensic process: the trial itself and particularly the speeches, with their persuasive rhetoric of legality and democracy. Only through this process is the abstract "rule of law" actualized in the form of a verdict and "popular sovereignty" converted into *eunomia*.

Lycurgus theorizes that

> three things above all guard and preserve the democracy and the city's prosperity: first, the system of the laws; second, the vote of the jurors; and third, the trial (*krisis*) that hands crimes over to them. For the law proclaims what one must not do; the prosecutor denounces those who are liable to the punishments specified by the laws; and the juror punishes those whom they reveal to him. Thus neither the law nor the vote of the jurors has force without a prosecutor who will hand over criminals to them. (1.3–4)

[33] E.g. Is. 5.8; Dem. 18.132–34; 19.23–26; 20.2–4; 23.97, 206; 37.45; 43.28; 45.6; 51.15. The *locus classicus* for this critique is Aristophanes' *Wasps*. See further Roisman 2004: 272–73 (= 2005: 156–59).

[34] Carey 1996: 37; Johnstone 1999: 41–42.

The theory is self-serving, as Lycurgus is attempting to justify his own public prosecution of Leocrates.[35] But it encapsulates well the way juridical discourse situates itself – in the form of the trial (*krisis*) – as the medium of convergence and mutual realization for its two primary authorizing principles, and derives its authority from that mediating role. On the one hand, forensic oratory represents both *nomoi* and demos as powers external to itself – secure, eternal, and truly existing – and their alignment as natural and inevitable (for in Athens' imagination, as Nicole Loraux has shown, the ideal is never far from reality).[36] On the other hand, it represents this ideal alignment of laws and demos as precarious and requiring the vigilant attention of litigants and jurors alike: speakers picture the whole world standing outside the courthouse awaiting the verdict and what it will reveal about Athens: are its laws potent? Is its demos just? The innate lawfulness and *eunomia* of the democratic polis is thus in perpetual crisis and is secured only through the *krisis*, the trial and its proper judgment.

The clearest example of this harmonious alignment of *nomos*, demos, polis, and justice comes at the end of Demosthenes 21 *Against Meidias*. Demosthenes has been punched in the face by his enemy and rival, Meidias. If the jurors exonerate such behavior, he argues, then every one of them will likewise be at risk of assault from his own enemies. Why is it, he asks in the final sections of the speech, that each of you when he leaves the courthouse does not go in fear that he will be jumped and insulted and beaten up?

> If you wish to think about this and really examine it, what makes those of you who are serving as jurors strong and sovereign over everything in the city (*iskhuroi kai kurioi tōn en tēi polei pantōn*), whether there are two hundred of you or a thousand, or however many the city appoints? It isn't because you are the only citizens arrayed in arms or because you are physically strongest or youngest or anything like that, but because your strength lies in the laws (*alla tōi tois nomois iskhuein*). And what is the strength (*iskhus*) of the laws? If one of you is attacked and cries out, will they come running to help? No, they are just written texts and they couldn't do that. What is their power (*dunamis*), then? You – if you secure them and make them valid (*kurious*) for anyone who asks. The strength of the laws lies in you and your strength lies in the laws (*oukoun hoi nomoi te humin eisin iskhuroi kai humeis tois nomois*). (223–24)

[35] Allen 2000a: 157–60; cf. Allen 2000b. She considers this speech unusual in that Lycurgus, instead of stressing his personal stake in the prosecution, puts forward a disinterested vision of the public good (with Platonic resonances). The speech's ideas about prosecution seem to me not so much heterodox as an isolation and exaggeration of a theme implicit in other orations.

[36] Loraux 1986: 263–327.

He concludes: therefore you must aid the laws as you would yourself if you were assaulted and punish the man who has transgressed them.

This passage is often read in the same way that ancient orators read the laws: it is excerpted selectively and taken as testimony for one position or the other. Some cite the first half as proof that the Athenian legal system was predicated on the rule of law; others quote the second half as evidence that popular sovereignty was the true legitimating ground of Athenian jurisprudence.[37] But what is most striking about this passage is the mutual dependence of jurors and laws. Each is strong (*iskhuein*) only through the other. Without the jurors, the laws are lifeless, inert texts: they gain force (*dunamis*) only when enacted in the just verdict of the jury in a specific trial. Likewise, without the laws, the jurors would be weak and vulnerable, unable to defend themselves, always looking over their shoulder in fear of attack (220–22; cf. 140). Neither is *kurios* – legitimate, authoritative, sovereign – without the other.

This famous passage gives particularly vivid expression to an idea that is ubiquitous throughout forensic oratory: it is invoked every time a litigant pleads his case (as virtually all do) "on behalf of myself and you and the laws" (e.g. Dem. 21.20, 40, 213, 222). The addition of "myself" reminds us that this equation of laws and jurors is not a neutral statement of a preexistent truth, but a self-interested rhetorical construct. Every speaker works to forge a chain of authority between demos and *nomoi* in which he himself is the crucial link: by supporting him the jurors will support the laws; by protecting him the laws will protect each of the jurors. In Demosthenes 21, as we will see in Chapter 4, this equation is part of a broader strategy designed to make Demosthenes' body metonymically interchangeable with the citizen body and to represent an assault upon the former as a violence against the latter. The success of that strategy and of his case as a whole rests upon his claim that "the strength of the laws lies in you and your strength lies in the laws" and his ability to appropriate that combined strength for himself by making it depend on a verdict in his favor. Like everything else in forensic oratory, "popular sovereignty" and "the rule of law" exist only within the weave of a speaker's rhetoric, a weave always cut on the bias. Skillfully harmonized, they lend authority to the very rhetoric from which they derive authority.

[37] Popular sovereignty: Ober 1989a: 300, 1994: 103; D. Cohen 1995a: 56 (= 1995b: 240–41); Christ 1998a: 23; Roisman 2004: 262–63 (= 2005: 132). Rule of law: Harris 1994a: 133; Carey 1996: 45 n. 50 (although he also notes the paradoxical weakness of the laws, 46).

But if this equation of laws and jurors is part of the rhetorical strategy of every individual litigant, it is also key to the self-authorization of the discourse as a whole. Juridical discourse offers itself as the neutral medium for the beneficial fusion of laws and demos, and the catalyst for their explosive production of legitimacy and strength. In any given case, Demosthenes might win or Meidias might win, but every time a speaker self-servingly appeals to the jurors "on behalf of myself and you and the laws," the law – as a discourse, a system, a practice – wins. Every verdict is a verdict in its favor, a vote of confidence in its power to convert dead statutes into the vitality of democratic *eunomia* and individual citizens into the sovereign agents of the just city. In this way, juridical discourse finds its own strength (*iskhus*) in a chain of authority that it itself forges by linking the legitimacy of the laws and the sovereignty of the demos. The power (*dunamis*) it borrows turns out to be its own, a power it lends in turn to the demos, the city, and the laws.

RHETORIC'S UNHAPPY CONSCIOUSNESS (AESCHINES 1)

In order for this chain of authority to hold, though, another key element has to be erased: *logos*. If forensic oratory is going to appear as a neutral catalyst for the spontaneous union of laws and demos, it must efface the rhetorical labor by which it constructs each of these terms and effects the synthesis between them. The authority of any given speech and of the discourse as a whole rests as much on this erasure of rhetoric as it does on the positive terms this negation highlights. This means that the very process of self-authorization turns forensic oratory against itself, for it purchases its legitimacy at the cost of its own essence, its rhetoricity. This unhappy consciousness, as we shall see, is part of the fundamental structure of juridical discourse, a contradictory self-relation that prevents it from ever securing the authority it generates for itself.

When a speaker like Demosthenes represents the laws and the demos as uniting naturally in support of his case, he seeks to avoid any impression that these terms were manipulated or forced into alignment through the pressure of his own self-interested oratory. Demosthenes anticipates this accusation. "Perhaps Meidias will say, 'He is an orator (*rhētōr*),' pointing to me" (21.189). What does it mean for one forensic orator to call another a *rhētōr*? Demosthenes' defense against the charge suggests that it implies, first, that he speaks for his own advantage not for the good of the demos. "If a *rhētōr* is one who gives you counsel he believes will benefit you and does this without being annoying or overbearing, then I would not evade or deny that title. If, however, a *rhētōr* is like some of the speakers you and I see shamelessly profiting off you, then I would not be one" (189). A true *rhētōr* is a good democrat; Demosthenes is a *rhētōr* only in this sense. But there is more to the accusation. "Perhaps he will say this: that I am now making a speech that has been carefully considered and prepared" (191). Meidias will charge that Demosthenes is not only a self-interested speaker but also a skilled one, implying that he uses that skill to mislead the jurors. Demosthenes concedes that he has put some thought into the speech. If it is well written, however, the fault is Meidias' not his own: "It was Meidias who wrote this speech for me. Since he provided the deeds that my speech is about, he should rightly bear the responsibility for it, not I who have exerted thought and effort to speak justly now" (191–92). Meidias' criminal deeds wrote Demosthenes' forensic words, and Demosthenes is no longer the author of his own (carefully written) speech. He may be a *rhētōr*, but his rhetoric appears only to disappear. It becomes translucent in the light of Meidias' glaring criminality.

Demosthenes' denial is illustrative of forensic oratory's general discomfort with its own rhetoricity, its status as a *logos* artfully crafted to persuade. Whether they bought the speech from a professional logographer or, like Demosthenes, wrote it themselves, speakers seek to obscure not only the process of its composition, but the very fact of its composedness. This repudiation fits with a broader suspicion of rhetoric in Athens. Athenian democracy stood on a foundation of words: policy decisions were made based on the persuasive speeches of prominent politicians, who in the fourth century were often referred to simply as *rhētores*.[38] Individual political power and the communal good of the polis were both attained through public speech, and the Athenians were aware that the stakes were as precarious as they were high. Speakers can deceive; the demos can be misled by speeches that are persuasive but not beneficial.[39] "When a political system is based on *logoi*, how can it be governed safely if the *logoi* are not true?" Demosthenes asks (19.184), but he and his fellow citizens knew how hard it was to verify their veracity. Anxiety about the uncertainty of rhetoric was heightened toward the end of the fifth century by the emergence of the

[38] Ober translates *rhētōr* as "expert politician" (1989a: 105–12; cf. Perlman 1963: 328–33; Hansen 1991: 268–72; Connor 1992: 116–17). For recent scholarship on public speech and political leadership in Athens, see especially Harding 1987; Sinclair 1988: 136–61; Ober 1989a: 104–55, 314–27; 1994; Yunis 1996; Hesk 1999, 2000: 202–41; McGlew 2002: 86–111; Balot 2004; Roisman 2004, 2005: 130–62.

[39] Hesk 1999, 2000: 202–91 analyzes the "rhetoric of anti-rhetoric" in Athens. On the mistrust of rhetoric, see also Dover 1974: 25–28; Ober 1989a: 165–77; Detienne 1996: 69–88, 107–34; Johnstone 1999: 87–92, 101.

sophists, teachers of rhetoric who were reputed to teach their students how to make the weaker argument the stronger. Forensic oratory came into its own at about this same time and it is not surprising that the courts became a central arena for Athenian ambivalence toward oratory.

To some extent, as Demosthenes' definition of *rhētōr* at 21.189 suggests, the debates over the status of rhetoric in the courts are a continuation of a struggle over political leadership. Prominent *rhētores* like Demosthenes and Aeschines used the courts to press their own claims to political hegemony and to undercut their opponent's. Thus when Aeschines calls Demosthenes a "man wholly composed of words" or a "pirate who sails through politics on a ship of words" or when Demosthenes calls Aeschines "a tragic monkey and counterfeit orator" or a "scrap-picking gossip, a marketplace pettifogger, a damned secretary," the attack on the opponent's courtroom oratory is a proxy for an assault on his political program and claim to political authority.[40] But the charge of deceptive or damaging speech also circulated among lower profile litigants in private cases, and the way these speakers talk about *logos* reveals not just a displaced political contest but also an ambivalence within juridical discourse toward its own rhetorical nature.

The problem, of course, is never with the speaker's own *logos*. The usual fact that his speech was written for money by an anonymous logographer with no personal investment in the truth of the case – a perfect recipe for deceptive speech – is never mentioned: the speaker talks as though his words were his own. Those words, moreover, are presented as naively straightforward, artless and ingenuous. The speaker generally professes to be an average citizen with no particular rhetorical skills or ambitions who was cheerfully minding his own business until forced by his opponent's unwarranted assault to defend himself by speaking in court. His rhetorical inexperience is one of the oldest clichés in the book, and one often deployed with a good deal of rhetorical skill and confidence.[41] This denial of expertise allows the speaker to present himself (with varying degrees of plausibility) as no different from the jurors and to ward off the kind of insinuations Meidias is expected to make of rhetorical trickery or unfair advantage. The speech he reluctantly delivers is consequently represented as sincere

[40] Aesch. 3.229, 253; Dem. 18.127, 242. Halliwell 2004: 117–30 and Worman 2004 (cf. 2008: 213–74) offer smart analyses of such abuse.

[41] Dem. 58 makes particularly full use of the trope of inexperience; see also, e.g., Ant. 5.1–7; Lys. 17.1, 19.2; Lateiner 1982; L. B. Carter 1986: 99–130. On the bias against rhetorical or legal expertise, see Dover 1974: 25–28, 188–90; Humphreys 1988: 474–77; Ober 1989a: 174–77; Todd 1996; Christ 1998a: 203–08; Montiglio 2000: 118–22; Schloemann 2002: 139–46; Gagarin 2008: 207–09.

and spontaneous, a candid explication of "the truth of the matter" (*hē tōn pragmatōn alētheia*); in forensic oratory's ubiquitous play on *logoi* and *erga*, words and deeds, his speech is an unmediated communication of the raw facts of the case.[42] Ideally the self-effacing speaker effaces his speech altogether, leaving the laws or the lawmaker to speak for him. Aeschines concludes a speech by conjuring Solon to the speaker's podium to beg the jurors to remember their oaths and the laws (3.257). The speaker in Demosthenes 59 asks the jurors to imagine that it isn't him up on the podium speaking to them but the laws themselves (115).[43] Through this fiction the speaker hopes to render his own speech invisible, a pure ether in which (as Lycurgus puts it) "justice is simple, truth easy, and proof succinct" (1.33).

Unsurprisingly, *logos* becomes much more opaque and obtrusive when it is the opponent's. While the speaker is an average citizen forced to speak out – artlessly but truthfully – for his own good and that of the city, the opponent is a speaker by trade. He is not only a *rhētōr*, but a logographer, a sophist, a magician.[44] Delivering an elaborately prepared speech (something suspect enough in itself), he is a craftsman of words invariably designed to mislead the jury. One speech after another warns the jurors not to be taken in by the opponent's clever and deceitful *logos* nor to vote against their oath, the city's advantage, and justice. The jurors must learn to differentiate between a just speech and a clever one, says one litigant, for the laws and the jurors should not depend upon the words of the speaker, but vice versa.[45] Aeschines warns that his opponents have discovered *logoi* stronger than the laws (3.11), but he will save the jurors from their sophistical tricks (3.37, 193): "I will set your law against their words" (3.14). The jurors, too, must marshal (*antitattein*) the law against the shamelessness of his opponents and

> put it to them that you do not accept a criminal sophist who thinks he will undermine the laws by his phrases (*rhēmasi*), but that you will be even more enraged if a man introducing an illegal measure should speak well. For the *rhētōr* and the law should say the same thing, jurors, and when the law speaks with one voice and the *rhētōr* with another, you must vote for the justice of the law not the shamelessness of the speaker. (3.16)

42 E.g. Ant. 5.1–7. Johnstone 1999: 87–92 has an interesting discussion and further references.

43 Cf. Dem. 21.46. Aeschines refers to the laws as his supporting speakers (*sunēgorous*, 3.37). Demosthenes in *Against Meidias* asks the jury to imagine that the laws and the dikastic oath stand by his side (as Meidias' children do by his) begging the jurors to vote for them (188).

44 On these slurs and for references see Ober 1989a: 170–74; Hesk 1999: 211–14, 2000: 209–19.

45 Dem. 58.41, 62: *rhētores* who speak well but unjustly, he continues, insult the demos and diminish the polis (62–65). See further Dem. 35.40–43.

Aeschines begs the jurors to reject the arguments of his opponents, which are designed to "deceive the listeners, harm the city, and undermine the democracy" (3.200). Deceitful *logos* threatens to insinuate itself between the *nomoi*, the *dikastai*, and the polis and to rupture their ideal unity, undermining the stability of the laws, the sovereignty of the demos, and thus the welfare of the city. Indeed, in general this is the only thing forensic oratory can imagine causing such a rupture: all other threats to juridical discourse's lawful and democratic kingdom – oligarchic conspiracy, rampant crime, Philip of Macedon – are the inevitable result of the opponent's argument, and the jurors who forcefully resist his lies are soldiers on the front lines of the war for the city's future.[46] The greatest danger to the world of forensic oratory is thus forensic oratory itself, in the deceitful, illegitimate, and anti-democratic form in which the opponent delivers it.

This negative potential of forensic oratory is embodied in the sykophant, a seminal figure within the Athenian juridical imagination.[47] This derogatory label seems to have referred primarily to litigants who brought cases maliciously, either for their own profit (through shakedowns or settlements) or to harass innocent citizens. But the term refers less to a category of actual individuals than to a negative conceptualization of legal action: the sykophant is, broadly, someone who abuses legal procedure and legal speech in order to further his personal advantage; in the process he perverts the laws, misleads the demos, and undermines the good of the polis. He is forensic oratory's fantasy of its own negative inversion, a vision of itself as the point of rupture, not consolidation, between the laws, the demos, the city, and justice. But this negative figure also serves a positive function within juridical discourse, for he offers the hope that harmful legal rhetoric can be identified and localized within a single malevolent individual or class of individuals. Then it can be contained and cast out like a *pharmakos*, a scapegoat whose exile purifies the community.[48] Behind the nightmare of

[46] For the jurors as soldiers, see Lys. 14.14–15; Lyc. 1.47–51, 76–79; Aesch. 3.7; Balot 2004: 253.

[47] The sykophant is much discussed and there is disagreement as to the precise semantic range of the label and the activities of those to whom it was attached. See Bonner and Smith 1938: 39–74; Adkins 1976; MacDowell 1978: 62–66; Osborne 1990, 2000: 75–78; Harvey 1990; Rubinstein 2000: 198–212; Allen 2000a: 156–67; and the nuanced and insightful study of Christ 1998a, esp. 48–71. I agree with those who argue that there was no professional class of "sykophants" in Athens and that, as Adkins puts it (1976: 308), the word could describe "any behaviour which the writer regards as scoundrelly in a legal context." A full list of passages where the word or concept occurs is provided by Harvey 1990: 119–21; see also Osborne's analysis of their distribution (1990: 92–93). Frivolous or malicious lawsuits were discouraged by penalties imposed on a litigant who failed to gain one-fifth of the jurors' votes. It seems that it was possible to prosecute a man for sykophancy (Isoc. 15.313–14) but in practice it must have been extremely hard to prove such a case.

[48] On the sykophant as scapegoat, see Christ 1998a: 51–52, 67–71; Allen 2000a: 160.

the sykophant, then, is the dream of the trial as a catharsis both for the community and for juridical discourse itself. The courts will be cleansed of deceitful, pernicious speech, leaving forensic oratory pure, its *logos* a pellucid medium through which dikasts commune directly with the laws in a sublimity of democratic justice.

But of course this dream is only a dream: the sykophant can never be fully eliminated from the world of law, nor can the *pharmakos* of deceptive speech be banished from the language of the courts. Every speaker who calls his opponent a sykophant is equally liable to be called one in return, and since the charge of sykophancy rests upon imputations of motive and attitude, it is almost impossible to prove or disprove. This accusation lies behind Demosthenes' defense against Meidias' imagined charge that he is a *rhētōr*: when Demosthenes distinguishes between the speaker who benefits the jurors and the one who profits off them, he tries to draw a solid line between the *rhētōr* and the sykophant, but in the process also marks how easily the one can shade over into the other.[49] Every forensic speaker is a potential sykophant, even as he asserts the transparency of his own rhetoric by contrast to the suspiciously clever speech of his opponent.

This formalized game of *tu quoque* – my opponent will say I am a *rhētōr*, but he is the *rhētōr* – is fundamental to the agonistic structure of the trial. In this dialectic of denial and projection, the two litigants take up a mirroring relationship in which everything one says about his opponent can be turned back against himself and the truth of each man's speech lies in the speech made by or attributed to the other. Moreover, the reciprocal definition of the two litigants is reproduced in a contradictory self-relationship within the speech of each litigant. "My opponent will say I am a *rhētōr*" expresses not only an agonistic alterity but also a negative reflexivity, what Hegel calls "unhappy consciousness."[50] The speaker secretly is what he reviles in his opponent; his own speech is always already infected by the very qualities he hopes to quarantine by projecting them onto his sykophantic

49 Cf. Dem. 59.43: "He was not yet a *rhētōr* but still a sykophant, one of those who shouts from the rostrum and proposes decrees for pay and brings indictments and gets his name on other people's proposals." At Dem. 58.62 sykophants are a subset of *rhētores*.

50 Hegel 1977 [1807]: 119–38 and see the discussion in Butler 1997a: 31–62. She characterizes unhappy consciousness as "an explicit form of ethical reflexivity" (45) that "takes itself as its own object of scorn" (46). This unhappy self-relation is reproduced in rhetorical theory, ancient and modern, as Gunderson 2000: 223–30 shows. The epigram to George Kennedy's seminal book on ancient rhetoric, to take only one example, is a quote from classicist Paul Shorey: "We are freed from rhetoric only by the study of its history" (Kennedy 1963: 2). One studies rhetoric to escape it, but since "wherever persuasion is the end, rhetoric is present" (7), that project is not only futile but (to the extent that Kennedy's study aims to persuade) self-refuting and self-defeating.

antagonist and is defined by that in itself which it denies. Divided against itself, forensic oratory berates its own essence, its rhetoricity.

To see the effects of this unhappy self-relation we might look at one of the most self-consciously "rhetorical" orations in the corpus, Aeschines 1 *Against Timarchus*. This case deals explicitly with the issue of public speech and the question (legal, ethical, and political) of who should speak, and it does so in a speech full of artful touches, including extensive quotation from Homer, Hesiod, and Euripides. The defendant, Timarchus, had accused Aeschines of misconduct during an embassy to Macedonia; Aeschines responded with this prosecution, charging that Timarchus is legally prohibited from speaking in public because he had prostituted himself as a youth. While prostitution was not illegal per se in Athens, it carried the penalty of *atimia*, a loss of certain citizen rights, including the right to speak in the Assembly and courts.[51] The case seeks to enforce that *atimia*, and apparently it was successful and Timarchus was subsequently barred from public speech.[52] But in making his argument against his opponent's oratory, Aeschines must be particularly careful about his own, and in the end he repudiates not only immodest speech, not only deceitful speech, but forensic speech altogether: his speech is not his speech and the trial is not a trial.

Aeschines situates his case within the nexus of laws, demos, and polis that we examined in the last section. Democracies, unlike oligarchies or tyrannies, "are governed by the established laws" (5). The rule of law is stated as an abstract principle and its virtues extolled: the laws "preserve the persons of democratic citizens and the constitution;" "this will be the source of your strength (*iskhusete*), when you observe the laws (*eunomēsthe*) and are not subverted by those who break them" (5). Laws are the strength of the demos and the democracy. At the same time, the democratic jurors are the guardians (*phulakes*, 7) of the laws, and their verdict alone makes them authoritative: "You have heard the laws, jurors, and I know that you consider them good. As to whether they will be useful or useless, however, that is up to you. If you punish those who do wrong, the laws will be both good and sovereign (*kaloi kai kurioi*); if you let them off, the laws will be good (*kaloi*), but they will no longer be sovereign" (*kurioi*, 36).

[51] On *atimia* see Harrison 1971: 169–76; Hansen 1976: 55–90; Todd 1993: 142–43. The sexual politics of this speech have been much discussed: see especially Dover 1978: 19–109; Halperin 1990: 88–112; Sissa 1999; Fisher 2001: 25–53; Fredal 2006: 157–81; Lape 2006.

[52] Dem. 19.284. Fisher 2001: 53–67 analyzes Aeschines' winning strategies. The real target of Aeschines' prosecution is probably Demosthenes, Timarchus' co-speaker (*sunēgoros*) both in this case and in the prior charge against Aeschines. Rubinstein 2000 studies the role of the *sunēgoros* in Athenian litigation: see esp. 24–75, 185–98. On the political background to this case, see Fisher 2001: 2–6.

As in Demosthenes 21, the trial is presented as the natural medium of convergence between just laws and sovereign demos, and the authority of the speech and speaker is the product of that harmonious union.

Aeschines reiterates these jurisprudential principles later in the speech and also introduces the greatest threat to them: deceitful *logoi*. If you convict, the laws will be good and sovereign, he repeats; if you acquit, they will be good but not sovereign (177). What makes the laws so good? The fact that they were enacted by the demos in the interests of justice and the civic good, for "being naturally more clever than others, you of course make the best laws" (178). Too often, however, both in the Assembly and in the courts that same demos is "led astray by deceit and bombast." You allow yourselves to be distracted from the real issues and as a result, "the laws are invalidated and the democracy corrupted" (179). Deceitful arguments intervene between the jurors and the laws they so wisely established. Forensic speech, with its capacity for untruth, divides what the trial should unite, and the jurors, instead of protecting the laws, become the instrument of their dissolution and of the democracy's.

The specific "deceitful and bombastic" argument that splits *nomoi* and *dikastai* here sounds, unsurprisingly, like that Aeschines attributes to his opponents (166–76). "The laws are invalidated and the democracy corrupted" because sometimes the jurors are "too ready to accept a speech without a good life to back it up" (*logon aneu khrēstou biou*, 179). This, of course, is the case against Timarchus in a nutshell. He speaks in the Ecclesia and offers the demos advice, but his private life is one long saga of depravity. And it is not only Timarchus who threatens the laws and democracy, but also his supporter and co-speaker – and Aeschines' arch-rival – Demosthenes. Aeschines anticipates that Demosthenes will drag in diversionary arguments and labored metaphors, "defiling the justice of the city" and making a mockery of the jury (166–67). A "sophist" (125, 175) and "technician of words" (170), he aims to "mislead you with deceitful reasoning and rob the city of its advantage" (117). And like Timarchus', Demosthenes' shameful rhetoric bespeaks a shameful life: he may not have been a prostitute but he, too, is a degenerate (*kinaidos*, 181).[53]

The danger that "a speech without a good life" (179) will insinuate itself between *nomoi* and *dikastai* animates the speech's insistent correlation

[53] Aeschines puts it tersely at 3.174: Demosthenes is "clever in his speech, wretched in his life" (*deinos legein, kakos biōnai*). On the *kinaidos*, see Winkler 1990b: 45–70; Davidson 1997: 167–82. Demosthenes returns the compliment at 18.242. Cf. Aesch. 1.194–95 on the wretched lives and moral characters of Timarchus' other *sunēgoroi*. Gunderson 2000 analyzes the articulation of ethics and rhetorical style in ancient oratorical theory: see esp. 87–110 on rhetorical and ethical self-mastery.

between rhetorical decorum, moral probity, and political leadership. This is a common correlation in Greek thought, but Aeschines transforms it into law. The speech begins with a discussion of the "Solonian laws" designed to produce good citizens and good speakers (9–36): these are the *kaloi nomoi* that the jurors must make *kurioi* by their just verdict. Through selective quotation and tendentious interpretation Aeschines fashions out of a patchwork of provisions on a variety of topics – ranging from the time of day a free boy should go to school to the penalty for *hubris* against a slave – an artificially coherent body of legislation on civic decorum (22) and the decorum of public speakers (34). The lawmaker

> did not believe it possible for a man to be debased (*ponēron*) in his private life but good (*khrēston*) in public life, nor did he think an orator should mount the rostrum having worked on his speech but not on his life. He thought that the words of a good man (*andros kalou kai agathou*) are useful (*khrēsima*) for his audience, even if they are poorly and simply phrased, but that those of an abominable man (*bdelurou*) . . . would carry no benefit for his listeners even if they were well spoken. (30–31)

In this passage heavily loaded with the traditional moral vocabulary of Athenian political discourse, Aeschines legislates an equation between rhetoric and ethics that would in effect outlaw "speech without a good life." This moralization of oratory is lent the venerable authority of Solon's name and is protected by the provision allowing "anyone who wishes" to initiate a legal proceeding against those "wanton sykophants" who speak in public when their immoral life disbars them (32).[54]

Given this insistence on the correlation between the speaker's words and his moral character, Aeschines must be especially careful to display decorum in his own speech. His rhetorical self-presentation throughout emphasizes his cultivation and self-restraint as a speaker: unlike his opponents', his *logos* is "straight-forward, as befits a free man" (*haploun kai eleutherion*, 120); it is "noble and just" (*kalon kai dikaion*, 121). Aeschines contrasts the decorum of the public speakers of yore with the obscene gesticulations of Timarchus at the podium. He points to the statue (*eikōn*) of Solon on Salamis, which shows Solon with his hand inside his robe, as "a reminder and representation" (*hupomnēma kai mimēma*) of Solon's decency when he addressed the demos (25).[55] That *eikōn* is iconic for this speech as a whole,

[54] See Ford 1999: 241–49 for the "disingenuous glossing" (237) in this section, "an artificial synthesis of laws and interpretations designed to add up to an ideal ('Solonian') prescription" (242). See also Fisher 2001: 125–64; De Brauw 2001–02: 170–73.

[55] This passage is singled out for ridicule at Dem. 19.251–52. Ford (1999: 247 n. 58) points out that Aeschines is probably misreading this statue; cf. Fisher 2001: 151–52; Farenga 2006: 334–36; Fredal

which self-effacingly presents itself as a "reminder and representation" of the lawmaker's providential will. "I wish to make my speech to you now in the same manner as the lawmaker made his laws" (8), says Aeschines. Not only will the order of his discussion follow the order of Solon's laws (as he reconstructs them), but his case will prosecute the very acts that Solon, with uncanny foresight, anticipated. Solon established his laws on the education of children to prevent them from growing up to be the kind of citizen Timarchus is (11), and his laws on the behavior of young men were "addressed to no one other than Timarchus himself" (18).[56] Aeschines' speech thus merely ventriloquizes the will of the excellent nomothete, a "reminder and representation" of the latter's moral legislation and an icon of Aeschines' own restraint as a speaker.

But it is hard to speak decorously when you're speaking about prostitution, as Aeschines is the first to remind us. He makes much throughout the speech of his fear that in discussing Timarchus' repulsive deeds he will himself be participating in them. "I would rather die if I even mentioned explicitly in my speech (*logōi*) those acts that he was not ashamed to commit in fact (*ergōi*)" (55). Aeschines dreads that he "will be led to speak more explicitly than is in my nature" (70), but if he is, the fault lies not with him but with Timarchus:

> I beg of you, jurors, to forgive me, if I am compelled to speak about practices that are unpleasant in nature but that this man engaged in nonetheless, and if I am led to speak some word that resembles the deeds of Timarchus. For it isn't right that you blame me if I should speak explicitly in the attempt to inform you, but rather you ought to blame him since it happens that he has lived so shamefully that it's impossible for someone explicating his deeds to speak as he wishes unless he utters some phrases of that sort. I will be as careful as I can not to do so. (37–38)

As in Demosthenes 21, the opponent's deeds are author of the speaker's words. The speaker denies responsibility for his speech by making it a mere "reminder and representation" of the sorry truth of the opponent's actions. This tactic allows Aeschines to be explicit even as he is being decorously euphemistic.[57] In one way, he says, Timarchus' notoriety has made his job easier, since everyone already knows all about him, and his own speech

2006: 167–72. Sissa 1999: 160 aptly dubs the statue "a monumental anti-Timarchus." See Gunderson 2000: 59–86 on the orator's body, and particularly his hands (73–76), as an index of decorum.

56 On Aeschines' anachronistic reasoning, see Ford 1999: 242–43; Fisher 2001: 134–35, 143–44.

57 Note also Aeschines' frequent expostulations: "By Dionysus, I don't know how I can keep it [Timarchus' prostitution] under wraps all day" (52); "By Olympian Zeus, I would not dare speak this [his crimes] before you" (55); "By Olympian Zeus, I don't know how to put it more euphemistically" (76). On the conventions of euphemism in the courts see Biraud 1991: 339; Montiglio 2000: 116–57; Fisher 2001: 166–67.

need only remind them (*anamnēsai*, 44; cf. 116). I didn't create the rumor (*phēmē*) about Timarchus, Aeschines protests. He made it for himself and I am just passing it on (48).

Rumor, *phēmē*, plays a central part in Aeschines' case – unjustly, his opponents will claim, "for nothing is more unjust than rumor" (125).[58] But Aeschines defends rumor as the detective of hidden character (128) and prophet of future actions (127). He proposes that a man's ethical qualities are revealed not only in his own speech but in that of others about him. Nicknames like "Timarchus the whore" reveal the truth, as the demi-goddess Phēmē herself is called upon to testify (130). This testimony simultaneously asserts the power of speech and displaces it onto the abstract and authorless Phēmē, who "undeceiving, wanders by herself (*automatou*) through the city" (127). Autonomous or automatic, it is speech without a speaker. Aeschines' own *logos* merely echoes that wandering rumor. By referring his case to Phēmē, that "immortal prosecutor" (129), he denies both the authorship and the prosecutorial performativity of his own *logos*, its legal power to name Timarchus a whore and thus to name him *atimos*.

Phēmē displaces not only the forensic *logos*, moreover, but the entire case. Aeschines claims his speech is merely a rehearsal of things "you all already know." He will deliver that speech and go through the bother of citing laws and calling witnesses only as a concession to the occasion – "since we are here in the courtroom" (45, 65) – but all this forensic rigamarole is superfluous, he suggests, because the case has already been argued and won in the court of public opinion. Forensic *logoi* are irrelevant and unnecessary: if there were a law forbidding speeches of prosecution or defense, Aeschines speculates, and the herald called on the jurors to vote, they would surely convict on the spot (79). The trial was essentially over before it began. As proof of that assertion, Aeschines reminds them of a meeting of the Ecclesia in which a proposal of Timarchus' was being discussed and the demos repeatedly burst into laughter at the obscene double entendres they detected in the speech (mention of "cisterns and foundations," for instance, was taken as an allusion to sodomy). "I take this as the testimony offered to you by the Athenian demos, which cannot rightly be convicted of perjury. Wouldn't it be strange, jurors, if with me not saying a word you all cried out the name of the deeds which you knew he committed, but now that I am saying it you have forgotten it?" (85). The jurors are simultaneously judges of and witnesses to his case (*dikastai kai martures este tōn logōn*),

[58] For the role of rumor and the deployment of communal knowledge in forensic oratory, see Hunter 1990 (= 1994: 96–119); Ober 1989a: 148–51; Allen 2000a: 168–79.

and his only job is to remind them (*anamimnēiskein*) of their own prior judgment against Timarchus (89).

That the jurors "all already know" is a hackneyed trope, as the orators themselves acknowledged, used to manufacture consent.[59] But Aeschines uses it not to support his case so much as to disown it. The trial has already taken place, he asserts, and a verdict has been reached. His own speech is superfluous, as is that of his opponent; there might as well be a decree against judicial orations (79), since a successful verdict has nothing to do with a good speech or a good case. Just look at the Areopagus, he says, the most august court in the land. Often men who have weak speeches and no witnesses win their case, while those who speak well and provide witnesses are convicted. This is because the jurors judge not only by the speech or the witness testimony but from what they already know and have themselves examined (92). The jurors in this case, he continues, should follow this example, and consider nothing more persuasive than what they already knew about Timarchus before the trial began. "For the words (*logoi*) said about Timarchus and his activities in the past were spoken for the sake of the truth, but those that will be spoken today are spoken for the sake of the trial in order to deceive you" (93). By this Aeschines presumably means the speech of his sophistic opponent and not his own; but the Greek does not specify this, and the effect is to place all forensic *logoi* alike in opposition to a truth the jurors already know, the autonomous truth of *phēmē*.[60]

The appeal to the jurors' knowledge is Aeschines' attempt to solve the problem of his own speech: how to talk decorously about acts it is indecorous to talk about, how to split the difference between polite euphemism and prosecutorial explicitness. But in effacing his own speech, he also effaces the entire trial as a process of persuasive argumentation. The demos already knows the truth and has already passed judgment. Deceitful speech and immodest speech are together banished from the courtroom, but so, too, are forensic speech in general and the forensic process as a whole.

[59] Arist. *Rhet.* 1408a34: if a speaker claims that "everyone knows" something, audience members will agree in order to seem to know what everyone else knows. Cf. Dem. 40.53–54: a speaker uses it when he can't provide witnesses. See further Ober 1989a: 149–50; Hesk 2000: 227–31. For the trope of jurors as witnesses, see also Dem. 18.229, 21.217; Din. 3.15; Lys. 10.1. Cf. Dem. 21.18: "One must consider those *logoi* to be most just which the speaker's audience can testify (*marturōsin*) are true."

[60] Cf. Dem. 19.215–16: "Since the birth of man and the beginning of trials, no one has ever been convicted by confessing to his crime, but they are shameless, they deny, lie, make excuses, do everything so as not to pay the penalty. You must not be misled by these tactics today, but judge the issues based on what you yourselves know and do not pay attention to my words or those of my opponent, nor to the witnesses."

Of course, this is all "just rhetoric." Indeed, Aeschines' speech is nowhere more artful than when he pretends not to be its author. In order to prove that "what I say is manifest and not fabricated" (*enarges esti kai ou peplasmenon*, 128), he cites verses from Homer and Hesiod. Not only are these lines heavily manipulated to make them support his point, but this ostentatious show of *paideia* reveals him to be part of the very elite world he rails against.[61] He, too, he confesses, has written erotic poetry and had love affairs and fought over boys (135). And although he goes to great lengths to differentiate his upright sexual and literary activity from the licentiousness of Timarchus and his friends, the difference appears in this light as one of degree not kind. As he recites these verses, moreover, it is hard not to remember Demosthenes' ridicule of Aeschines' career as an actor whose powerful voice resounds to the disadvantage of the Athenians, and who takes on new court cases as easily as he does new dramatic roles.[62] As an actor, Aeschines is the exemplar of "speech without a good life," of verbal artifice and persuasive words divorced from truth. The literary quotations that Aeschines hopes will prove his *logos* "manifest and not fabricated" instead call to mind his career in the quintessential profession of fabricated speech.

From there it is just a short step to sykophancy. Demosthenes picked up on Aeschines' discussion of *phēmē* in his speech *On the False Embassy* (Dem. 19) and quoted the same two lines of Hesiod back at Aeschines, asserting that the very god whose veracity and power Aeschines had affirmed indicts him for taking bribes from Philip (19.243–44). Aeschines answers this riposte in his speech *On the False Embassy* (Aesch. 2) by drawing a distinction between *phēmē* and *sykophantia* (2.145). The contrast is clearly designed to differentiate his speech about Timarchus (which merely repeats a universally recognized *phēmē*) and Demosthenes' speech about himself (which is one individual's intentional malice), but in the process it shows how fine the line is between his own speech and what he labels *sykophantia*. His *logos* evokes theatricality and sykophancy, then, precisely at the moment when it tries to efface itself behind authorless rumor and communal knowledge. He

61 On the misuse of Homer and Hesiod, see Ford 1999: 250; Fisher 2001: 268–70. For instance, Aeschines quotes Hesiod to the effect that Phēmē is a god (*Erga* 763–64), but omits the prior three lines in which it is characterized as harmful and evil. For the complex sociological self-positioning of Aeschines' poetry recitation, see Ober 1989a: 177–82; Ober and Strauss 1990: 250–55; Ford 1999: 251–53, and on oratory's use of poetry more generally, Perlman 1964; P. Wilson 1996.

62 Dem. 18.129, 262, 313; 19.337–40, 246–50. On the orator as actor, see Easterling 1999 (esp. 159–60 on acting and artifice); P. Wilson 1996: 321–24; Gunderson 2000: 111–48; Hesk 2000: 207 n. 15; Duncan 2006: 58–89; and on the trial as performance, Bers 1985; Hall 1995; Lanni 1997; Fredal 2001, 2006.

conjures *phēmē* to speak for him, but he cannot prevent it from speaking against him, naming him a sykophant where he claims not even to be an orator.

Aeschines, like all forensic speakers, works to intensify the binaristic structure of law and to distinguish his own lawful and moderate speech from the vile, sykophantic words of his opponent. But that binarism – prosecution vs. defense – conceals another dialectic in which each side is defined by the other and speaks words the other puts in his mouth. The opponent's imputation of dishonesty is part of the fabric of the speaker's own speech and the rhetoric of his self-presentation, and thus even in the course of denying it, he will have to speak *in propria persona* the argument against himself: I am (not) a *rhētōr*. Aeschines, Timarchus, Demosthenes, Meidias – these *rhētores* can call each other a *rhētōr* and a sykophant and accuse one another of speaking to deceive. But they cannot thereby banish deceit or rhetoric from their own speech, and their reciprocal accusations merely act out the self-berating reflexivity of forensic oratory as a whole, which is always potentially deceptive and always necessarily rhetorical.

"Forensic oratory" thus becomes a tautology. The two terms function both in tandem and in tension, as the rhetorical, even as it creates and sustains the forensic, also renders it internally unstable. That tension between "forensic" and "oratory" permeates the entire juridical world forensic oratory creates. When a forensic orator like Aeschines repudiates not only his own speech but even its forensic setting, legal discourse is turned against itself. In its attempt to secure its discursive authority it eviscerates its own institutional being: there has been no speech; there might as well be no trial. Hermetic autopoiesis – the discourse's construction of its own legitimating mandate – becomes an unhappy self-elision, as the very words that authorize the case declare it closed before a single word is spoken.

THE IRON CHAIN OF LAW (DEMOSTHENES 25)

Demosthenes 25 *Against Aristogeiton* illustrates with particular clarity the dynamics by which forensic oratory's paradoxical repudiation of rhetoric undermines the juridical cosmos it is designed to authorize. This speech constructs a world of law grounded not, it claims, on the speaker's words but on the jurors' innate nature. It banishes *logos* from this world along with the outlaw Aristogeiton. But the attempt to banish rhetoric generates unanticipated side-effects within the text, rhetorical remainders that disturb its carefully wrought jurisprudential structures and thwart its desire for closure.

In many ways this is an atypical speech. As the hypothesis notes, it is unusually philosophical and periodic (*philosophōteron . . . kai periodikōs*), developing an elaborate theory of law upon which it predicates an entire legal anthropology and cosmology. Its rhetorical pitch throughout is also particularly high and the language uncommonly metaphorical and "purple." Many scholars have doubted its authenticity as a work of Demosthenes or even of the fourth century.[63] But even if the text is a later pastiche, nearly every trope, image, and argument in it can be attested in other fourth-century forensic orations, and its rhetorical strategies are all typical of the genre. Likewise, its jurisprudential metaphysics – the way it structures its juridical cosmos – is indeed unusually "philosophical," but in its basic principles is implicit in virtually every forensic speech. Thus this extraordinary speech allows us to see in high relief textual dynamics that are ubiquitous, albeit in more muted form, throughout the corpus as a whole.

Like Aeschines 1, this case deals with *atimia*. Aristogeiton had apparently fallen into debt to the state and as a result was legally *atimos* and barred from public speech. Demosthenes and his co-counsel Lycurgus charge that while under *atimia* Aristogeiton brought numerous lawsuits (including eight malicious suits against Demosthenes himself) and spoke publicly in the Ecclesia (37). As in most *atimia* cases, the real goal of this prosecution was probably less to disenfranchise a hardened criminal than to discredit a political rival (36–42). But again like other *atimia* cases, the competition between rival *rhētores* plays out in court as a game of all or nothing, as Demosthenes sues not only to silence Aristogeiton but to banish him from human society altogether. Public speech and civic belonging are closely correlated here, as throughout Athenian political discourse: citizens are defined by their *parrhēsia*, the right to speak publicly, and non-citizens, including the disenfranchised, are branded by their legal silence.[64] Speech thus marks the boundaries of the civic and civilized universe. When Demosthenes tells

[63] Sealey 1967 thinks it is the work of a later rhetorician, citing inaccuracies and inconsistencies with Dinarchus 2, which also prosecutes Aristogeiton; cf. Sealey 1993: 237–39. Allen 2000a: 182 notes the speech's anomalous ideas on the purpose of punishment, but Worman 2008: 230–32 emphasizes its similarities to other Demosthenic speeches. The consensus at the moment seems to be that the speech is classical, if not authentically Demosthenic: see de Romilly 1971: 155–58; Hansen 1976: 144–50; Christ 1998a: 56; Rubinstein 2000: 30–32. A passing comment at Din. 2.13 suggests that Demosthenes and Lycurgus won this case.

[64] Allen 2000a: 230–32 discusses *atimia* as public silencing and cites the case of Straton, a man condemned to *atimia* on a charge brought by Meidias, and whom Demosthenes calls as a silent witness to his opponent's *hubris* (Dem. 21.93). See also Dem. 59.26–27 and on *parrhēsia*, Sinclair 1988: 32–34; Monoson 1994; Montiglio 2000: 116–17; Foucault 2001; the essays in Sluiter and Rosen 2004 (esp. Raaflaub, Carter, Wallace, Balot, Roisman); Saxonhouse 2006.

the jurors early in the speech that he will speak the truth "with all intimacy" (*meta pasēs oikeiotētos*, 13), this rhetorical *oikeiotēs* connotes common kinship both in the polis – which is analogized to a household (*oikos*, 88–90) – and in the civilized world (*hē oikoumenē*). It draws the boundaries of an intimate legal universe from which, Demosthenes argues, Aristogeiton's *atimia* disenfranchises him.

As in Aeschines 1, speaking against an opponent's illegal speech puts the status of one's own speech in question, and the oration opens by denying that its case rests in any way on rhetoric. It is not the speech (*logous*) already made by his co-counsel Lycurgus that secures the justice of their case, says Demosthenes, nor the one he himself is about to make, but instead "how each of you jurors is disposed in regard to permitting crime or objecting to it" (1):

> I suppose that I must make my prosecution and present a mass of words (*to tōn logōn plēthos*) for you to listen to, as is habitual (*ethous heneka*), but the matter has already long been decided by each of your innate nature (*tēs hekastou phuseōs oikothen*). If there are more of you today who are well disposed toward criminals and inclined to save them then I will have declaimed (*errhapsōidēkotas*) for nothing, but if there are more who detest them then – god willing – Aristogeiton will pay the penalty. (2)

A verdict will be reached in this case not through the opposing speeches of the two litigants, but through the predisposition of each juror. Oratory appears to be just a matter of "habit" (*ethous*), an incidental by-product of the forensic situation. *Logoi* are secondary and irrelevant, either superfluous (if the jurors already hate crime) or ineffectual (if they don't). They are mere recitations (*errhapsōidēkotas*), empty declamations, useless "rhapsodies." Here as in *Against Meidias*, Demosthenes accepts the label of *rhētōr*: he is a public speaker who has made frequent appearances in the Ecclesia and *dikastēria* (38). But he denies that this case depends on his oratory: "don't look at my speech (*logon*) but at the general habits (*ethē*) of men" (34); "judge not from my argument (*logou*), jurors, but by what you actually (*ergōi*) experienced" (42).[65]

Justice lies not in this "mass of words," but in the *phusis oikothen* of each juror, his inner or intimate nature. As in Aeschines 1, the trial is over before it begins, the case already long decided in the heart of each individual dikast. The "natural law" of the sovereign juror is both psychologized

[65] Cf. 4: the jurors are also prosecutors since they already know the facts of the case better than Demosthenes himself does; 20: "I say nothing new or unusual or unique but what you all know as well as I do."

and theologized by being placed under the aegis of the trial's patron gods, Eunomia (Good Governance) and Dikē (Justice). Demosthenes urges every juror to "cast his vote knowing that Dikē is looking at each individual, and to watch out and guard against shaming her, whose name each of you bears [i.e. as *dikastēs*]" (11). A just verdict will be reached when each juror imagines Dikē watching him personally, when Dikē is installed as a juridical super-ego, as it were, within each juror, urging him to do justice, *ta dikaia*. Dikē is simultaneously a deity presiding over the forensic proceedings from her place beside Zeus's throne (11) and a principle of justice that has made its home (*oikos*) in the individual juror's *phusis oikothen*. If the jurors vote in accordance with this inner divinity, the verdict will please not only Dikē but also the goddess Eunomia, for they are not only eponymous subjects of the former but also the guardians of the latter: "on this day you have received a sworn trust from the laws and the democracy and the fatherland to guard everything that is good and just and beneficial" (11). *Dikē* and *eunomia* converge in the *phusis* of the individual juror.[66] Meanwhile, the *logos* that effects this holy convergence asks to be forgotten.

Where there is *phusis*, *nomos* cannot be far behind.[67]

> All human life, jurors, whether one dwells in a great city or a small one, is governed (*dioikeitai*) by nature (*phusei*) and laws (*nomois*). Of these two, nature is disorderly (*atakton*) and inconsistent, differing according to the individual who bears it, but the laws are universal and ordered (*tetagmenon*) and the same for all. Nature, if it is base, often desires (*bouletai*) despicable objects, and as a result you will find that such men commit crimes. But the laws desire (*boulontai*) what is just and good and beneficial, and they seek this out, and when they find it, they reveal it as a common commandment (*prostagma*), equal and the same for all, and this is what law is. (15–16)

Nomos enters the scene as an active, autonomous force, ordering the disorder of *phusis*, imposing unity and coherence on human life, pursuing its desire and imposing its command. Every *nomos*, Demosthenes goes on,

[66] Cf. 34–35: Dikē, Eunomia, and Aidōs (Shame) have altars in sacred precincts, where they can be worshipped by all alike, but their most beautiful and holy altars are in the heart (*psukhē*) and nature (*phusis*) of each individual. De Romilly 1971: 155–78 examines the relation of law to nature in this speech and stresses the speech's defense of law as a natural order valuable in and of itself. See also Farenga 2006: 542–47.

[67] The antithesis between *nomos* and *phusis* was associated with sophistic thought and is one of the "more philosophical" (*philosophōteron*) elements of this speech, which develops the polarity to a degree uncommon in forensic oratory. But if the motif is philosophical the uses to which it is put are typical of forensic thought: e.g. the ordering force of *nomos*, the location of a just verdict in the jurors' character or nature, the positing of a criminal or chaotic natural state beyond the law. For the influence of the sophistic *nomos/phusis* debate on the classical understanding of law, see de Romilly 1971, Farenga 2006: 439–70.

is "the gift of the gods, the opinion of wise men, the corrector of errors, and the shared contract of the city, according to which all those in the city should live" (16). It is divine and human, metaphysical and political. In a move with both Platonic and Kantian resonances, law is both the desire for the good and the instantiation of that desire as a categorical imperative (*prostagma*).

This law is the governing principle of human life and the only thing that distinguishes it from the life of the beasts (20). It is also the "shared contract" (*sunthēkē koinē*, 16) of political life and in particular of democratic life.[68] It is the laws, Demosthenes asserts, that make the Boule meet and the demos assemble in the Ecclesia, that fill the lawcourts and control the succession of magistrates (20). *Nomos* regulates the administrative mechanisms of democracy. It is the cause of everything that governs (*oikeitai*) and preserves the democratic polis; along with the gods, it saves the city (21). In this jurisprudential cosmology, *dikē* is *eunomia*, and the jurors are the suture between the two. The agents of the law's commandment (15), they "keep watch over the laws and make them strong with their judgments" (24; cf. 99). Laws and jurors work together to aid the good in the constant battle between virtue and vice (24), a battle Demosthenes would like us to see dramatically enacted in this trial.

This theory of law governs a "cosmos of the city and the laws" (*ho tēs poleōs kai tōn nomōn kosmos*, 19). *Kosmos* in Greek indicates a state of order, and indeed order is the key attribute of the speech's legal universe: "Is it necessary to remark that everything is ordered (*kosmeitai*) by the laws and by obedience to them?" (27). In §15, the laws are both ordered (*tetagmenon*) – as opposed to the disorder (*atakton*) of nature – and ordering, as their desire for the good is revealed as a universal order (*prostagma*; cf. 22). They preserve good order (*eutaxia*, 24) and the social order (*to tetagmenon*, 26), differentiating magistrates from laymen, young from old, and base citizens from the elite (24–26). But that social taxonomy is only one aspect of the cosmos the laws organize (*oikeitai*, 20; *oikeisthai*, 26), which at its broadest is equivalent to *hē oikoumenē*, the entire civilized world. Here *nomos* comes close to its original meaning (*nemein*, to divide or distribute), as it allots to everyone his proper place in the world and organizes the world around that neat allotment. Finally, this bounded and orderly world is sealed by

[68] The law is said to work like an *eranos* (21), a loan raised by contributions from club members, a familiar Demosthenic metaphor for collaborative communal activity (cf. Dem. 21.101, 184). By obeying the laws himself and punishing those who don't obey them, each citizen is contributing to the welfare of the fatherland.

its exclusions, for if Aristogeiton is acquitted, "all is unloosed, laid open, and confounded" (25).

The "cosmos of the city and the laws" is both a metaphorical and a literal space. One of the benefits of everyone obeying the laws, says Demosthenes, is the physical sanctity of the institutions of democratic governance. When the Boule meets, it maintains confidentiality by barring the entry of non-members with a wicker fence (*kigklis*); likewise, the Areopagus ropes off (*periskhoinisētai*) the Stoa Basileios when it is in session so it can deliberate in peace, and all allotted magistrates require the removal of strangers so that they can perform their duties without fear of disturbance (23). Aristogeiton has broken through all barriers, Demosthenes claims, and has entered into public places from which his *atimia* disbars him:

> Foulest of all living mortals, although you are barred from public speech (*parrhēsia*) not by wicker barriers or doors which someone might open, but by these heavy debts of yours which are recorded in the temple of Athena, nonetheless you force your way inside (*eis to entos toutōn*) and approach those things from which the laws drive you away. You are roped off (*apeskhoinismenos*) by all justice in the city, by the decision of three courts, by the debtors' list of the magistrates and the tax collectors, by the verdict in the case you brought for wrongful inclusion on the debtors' list – by everything but an iron chain (*halusei sidērai*). And yet you sneak by and break through these things, and by contriving pretexts and composing false charges you think you will overturn all common justice. (28)

In this speech, as in many, the metaphorical register maps closely onto the literal issues of the case: Aristogeiton's legal exclusion from *parrhēsia* – which is the speech's premise and also the thesis it hopes to prove – is a literal exclusion from the sites of Athenian public speech and a figurative exclusion from civic belonging. The literal barriers and ropes become metaphorical as the bureaucratic mechanisms of the democracy lock him out of their inner sanctum (*to entos toutōn*). These mechanisms are the instruments of law's *eutaxia*: law itself is the iron chain that bars him. Law functions as a boundary stone (*horos*, 70), again both literal (since a debtor's property would by law be marked for mortgage with a boundary stone) and metaphorical (as the law of *atimia* marks a figurative boundary separating Aristogeiton from other citizens). Sliding cannily between the physical and the metaphorical, the speech forges the law as an iron chain around the juridical world, securing it within and dividing it from the chaos of crime beyond.

That beyond is Aristogeiton's haunt. Bereft of legal defenses, he wanders a wilderness of "cliffs, crevasses, and pits" (*apokrēmna, pharangas, barathra*, 76): it is no coincidence that this topography of lawlessness culminates in a *barathron*, which in Athens referred to the pit where the bodies of executed criminals were dumped.[69] He shares no common ground with other people. All the other twenty thousand Athenian citizens go around the agora taking care of their own and the city's business; he alone has never in his life engaged in public service, a trade, farming, manufacturing, friendship, or companionship (51). Unlike others, he does not hang out at the perfume shop or the barber's; he is unsociable (*ameiktos*, 52, 58, 63), with no friends or allies except his twin brother, also his twin in debasement and crime (79). Having struck his mother and denied his father burial, he breaks not only the laws of the polis but the "law of nature," laid down for men and beasts alike, to love their parents (65). Alone in his criminal desolation, he shows no *philanthrōpia* toward others and should receive none from the jurors (76). Far from being the "best neighbor" (*aristos geitōn*) Aristogeiton is the worst.[70]

He is a bad neighbor even in a bad neighborhood. Two lurid anecdotes detail his exclusion from even the most marginal communities. The first tells how, after breaking out of debtors' prison, Aristogeiton sought refuge with a woman, probably a foreign prostitute, named Zobia (56–59). She hid him while the authorities were searching for him and then gave him some money to skip town. But later when she sought recompense for the favor she had done him, he tried to have her sold into slavery. This scandalous incident reflects poorly on Aristogeiton in numerous ways, but Demosthenes highlights in particular the shameless ingratitude it illustrates: he betrayed the woman who saved his life (58). This breach of reciprocity chimes with the speech's insistence on Aristogeiton's *akharistia* (ingratitude), which is listed along with sykophancy and perjury among his crimes (35; cf. 52). It reiterates in a debased and humiliating form his failure of reciprocity with the city: having shown nothing but bitterness and ingratitude to others, that is all he deserves in return (81–84).

The second anecdote recounts Aristogeiton's behavior while in prison for non-payment of his debts (60–63). While there, he stole the notebook of another inmate, and when confronted, got into a fight. Since the other man was getting the better of him, Aristogeiton bit off his nose and ate it (61, 62). As a result of this act, the prisoners passed a resolution (*psēphizontai*) "that no one would share fire, light, food or drink

[69] Allen 2000a: 218. Execution by precipitation into the *barathron* was probably obsolete by the mid-fifth century: see Todd 2000b: 36–38.

[70] Cf. 82: "May the earth bear him no fruit nor welcome his corpse when he dies." Should they vote to acquit the jurors, too, will be barred from the civic spaces: they will be too ashamed to go to the Metroön and consult laws they have betrayed, or to pray on the Acropolis where the defendant's name is still inscribed on the debtors' list (99).

with him or give him anything or receive anything from him" (61).[71] They form a rudimentary political body expressly so they can vote to excommunicate him from it. Demosthenes has the court secretary read out the jailhouse resolution and calls as a witness Aristogeiton's noseless victim. Then he draws the inevitable conclusion: if men like this considered him too criminal to have anything to do with him "will you allow him to mingle among yourselves, even though the laws have driven him out of the state?" (63).

This scene dramatizes a primitive form of *atimia*. It also suggests ritual pollution: it recalls the Athenian festival of the Anthesterion, at which every person drank at his own table in silence in memory of the reception in Athens of the polluted matricide Orestes. Aristogeiton is polluted by his own criminality and threatens to contaminate any who communicate with him. He is defiled (*miaros*, 32, 41, 54, 58, 62, 81), thrice-accursed (*triskataratos*, 82), the most defiled of all living mortals (*miarōtate pantōn tōn ontōn anthrōpōn*, 28). Like his evil twin brother, who is a pestilence (*loimos*) and a *pharmakos* (80), Aristogeiton is a polluted scapegoat who must be exiled not only from the community of citizens, not only from the community of prisoners, but from the community of mankind.[72] The scene of nasophagy thus brings to a climax a point Demosthenes has been hammering throughout the speech: Aristogeiton is not even human. He is a beast (*thērion*, 8, 31, 58, 95; cf. Din. 2.10), a serpent or scorpion (52), a rabid watchdog who devours the flocks he claims to protect (40), a snake and a spider (96).

Moreover, what makes him a (figurative) animal is the same thing that makes him a (literal) criminal: his savage mouth. Following the testimony of the noseless man, Demosthenes comments sarcastically: "What fine deeds this *rhētōr* has invented for you! Surely it is worthwhile to hear arguments (*logon*) and advice (*sumboulēn*) from the mouth that has done such things!" (62). Cannibalism is just the most disgusting use to which he has put that demagogic mouth, from which every speech stirs up war and civil conflict (42) and every word is in violation of the law and the public good. It is little

[71] Din. 2.9–10 also relates this anecdote; he includes the theft and shunning but not the nose-eating. Rosenbloom 2003: 112: "The jailhouse narrative measures his *ponēria* against the lowest possible standard, realizing Aristogeiton's moniker as '*ponērotatos* of all who exist'." Christ 1998a: 57–59 discusses the jailhouse narrative and its social implications.

[72] On the criminal as a *pharmakos*, see Allen 2000a: 84–86, 204–05, 210–13; Rosenbloom 2003, 2004: 336–39, 342 and cf. above on the sykophant as *pharmakos*. The story of Aristogeiton's twin mirrors his own. He is a charlatan and magician with children by the slave girl of a Lemnian witch: a distributor of *pharmaka* (drugs, poison) he is himself a *pharmakos*. See Rosenbloom 2003: 111.

surprise that Aristogeiton is labeled a sykophant.[73] His "bitter" (*pikros*, 45, 83, 84, 96) and "savage" (*ōmos*, 63, 83, 84) mouth spouts false accusations against innocent citizens, perverting the legal system when it should not even be speaking in the first place. He is one of the monsters (*thēria*) who enter the Ecclesia to bring false accusations and commit sykophancy and prevail over the laws, the magistrates, *eukosmia*, and all that is good in the polis (9). He goes around the agora like a scorpion, looking for people to intimidate and extort (52); he is "a sykophant, a man with the poisonous nature of a snake" (96), who should be killed before he bites again.

We should remember what Aristogeiton is actually accused of: he has spoken in public while his name is still on the debtors' list. But in Demosthenes' equation of the sykophant with the snake or scorpion, criminality becomes bestiality and illegality inhumanity. The human cosmos is a legal cosmos and vice versa: excluded from that cosmos, Aristogeiton is neither citizen nor human being. He is a cancerous tumor on the citizen body: he can't be cured, only amputated, burned off or cut out, banished from the boundaries of the state, hurled from the city, driven out (95) – the metaphors trip over themselves in their zeal to expel him. His exclusion will heal the civic body and repair the order of the political and legal cosmos that his illegitimate speech has disrupted. Indeed, his exclusion is the founding act of this cosmos, which Demosthenes first names as such in describing the devastating effect of Aristogeiton's crime upon it: "I believe I can show you clearly, jurors, that the entire *kosmos* of the city and the laws is corrupted and thrown into confusion as far as this man is concerned" (19). Just as the prisoners come together as a political body, however debased, to banish Aristogeiton, the legal *kosmos* comes into being in response to his criminality. His is the disorderly *phusis* upon which the laws impose their organization (15); his attempt to break into the inner sanctum of democracy defines the boundary between inside and outside and justifies the iron chain between them. The outlaw seals the limits of the law and defines the order he threatens to destroy.

Law needs an outlaw, but so, too, does legal oratory, for the beauty and order (*kosmos*) of this vision of law is also the beauty and order of

[73] The term is named at 9, 19, 35, 37, 39, 41, 45, 46, 48, 49, 63, 83, 96, 97, but it is implicit in many other places. On the association of sykophancy with bestiality in particular and all varieties of *ponēria* in general, see Harvey 1990: 108–09; Christ 1998a: 50–59. Note also the charge, elaborated in detail (36–42), that Aristogeiton does not speak against other *rhētores* but only against private citizens who cannot defend themselves. On the distinction, see Rubinstein 1998. Worman 2008: 32, 37–40, 49–50, 230–31 draws the link between speech and cannibalism.

the speech itself. Demosthenes' case is effective only to the extent that he can erect a solid edifice of civic and legal order upon his vilification of Aristogeiton. The order of his legal speech is thus at stake in the order of the legal world it depicts, and its authority is only as strong as the iron chain of law forged by its own rhetoric. At the same time, of course, the legal cosmos depends upon the rhetorical *kosmos* of which it is the product. But neither cosmos is as secure as Demosthenes would like. In its attempt to create a nomic order, this speech tries to subject everything to law's organizing command. But this rhetorical structuring leaves inconvenient remainders, objects that can be neither assimilated into its *eutaxia* nor expelled along with the outlaw Aristogeiton. These awkward products of the speech's rhetorical order linger within the legal world it creates. Disturbing its inner taxonomy and its iron division between inside and outside, they "corrupt it and throw it into confusion" (19) from within its own gates.

One such remainder is *phusis*, nature. *Phusis* is an original element of human existence, along with *nomos*: "all human life . . . is governed by nature (*phusei*) and laws (*nomois*)" (15). Civic life, on the other hand, "is governed and preserved" by law alone (20). What becomes of *phusis* in this shift from anthropology to politics? *Phusis* initially appears as unruly matter in need of the law's ordering. "Disorderly and inconsistent, differing according to the individual who bears it" (*atakton kai anōmalon kai kat' andr' idion tou ekhontos*), it is the source of difference and disharmony within the city: *phusis* is sometimes base (*ponēra*) and desires despicable objects (*pollakis phaula bouletai*), leading it to crime (15). This disorderly and potentially felonious *phusis* is placed under the beneficial rule of the law. But for all that it doesn't disappear, but instead persists as a weak link in the rhetorical and legal chain the speech labors to forge.

As we might expect given its antithetical relation to *nomos*, *phusis* is closely associated in the speech with criminality in general and Aristogeiton in particular. "Do you not see that his nature and politics (*tēs phuseōs autou kai politeias*) contain no rationality nor sense of shame, but are led by madness?" (32). His irrational nature, a product of "paradox and accident" (32), is the opposite of those happy natures in which Dikē and Eunomia have their altars (35). This *phusis* is what makes him a snake and a sykophant by nature (*tēn phusin*, 96) and a natural enemy to all good citizens (*ek phuseōs*, 48). He was "born (*pephukōs*) entirely to the detriment of everything" (50).

Demosthenes cannot simply banish *phusis*, however, for in its positive form it represents the possibility of justice in the case: "the matter has long been decided by each of your innate nature" (*phusis oikothen*, 2). That dikastic nature is characterized, in contrast to Aristogeiton's misanthropy (51), by its *philanthrōpia*, its humanity, benevolence, or sense of fellow-feeling. Demosthenes praises the jurors for "the common *philanthrōpia* which you possess by nature" (*tēn koinēn philanthrōpian hēn humeis ekhet' ek phuseōs*, 87) and "the *philanthrōpia* of your nature" (*tēi tēs phuseōs . . . philanthrōpiai*, 87).[74] But this philanthropic spirit also poses the risk that the very juridical nature that should execute justice will instead undermine it by acquitting Aristogeiton:

> What recourse remains for him, jurors? The one that your nature (*phuseōs*) makes available to all litigants, and which no defendant provides for himself but each of you brings into court from home (*oikothen*), that is, pity, forgiveness, human sympathy (*philanthrōpian*). But it is neither holy (*hosion*) nor right (*themis*) for this foul man to receive these things. Why? Because it is just that each man receive in return the law (*nomon*) that he holds in his nature (*tēi phusēi*) toward others. What law (*nomos*) or what purpose (*boulēsin*) does Aristogeiton seem to you to hold in regard to everyone else? (81–82)

Nomos should govern *phusis*, with its wayward desires. But in this passage *phusis* seems, on the one hand, to contain a *nomos* of its own and, on the other, to require the ordering intervention of a higher form of law, the divine *themis* that declares the jury's pity unholy. The notion that the Athenian jurors are by nature charitable and empathetic is a cliché in Athenian forensic oratory, as is the prosecutor's warning against extending their pity to the undeserving defendant.[75] In this speech, the trope seems to function to unite *nomos* and *phusis* in the lawful souls of the individual jurors, where Eunomia and Dikē reign (35). The jurors embody the *phusis* of *nomos*, its living spirit and forgiving heart; they also represent the *nomos* of *phusis*, manifesting by their vote their innate sense of lawfulness. But at the same time, this passage imagines this "natural law" as a source of possible injustice, a possibility that must be checked on appeal to an authority

74 This common feeling binds the city together, like a happy *oikos* in which differences are accommodated without conflict and individuals can do "whatever their natures incline them to" and "everything is fine" (88). This unanimity in difference, which is "fixed in your nature and characters" (90), is threatened by Aristogeiton, the embodiment of a difference that cannot be assimilated or ignored. Sternberg 2006: 14–15 discusses the emergence and semantic range of the term *philanthrōpia*.

75 Johnstone 1999: 109–25. Cf. 12: "if you sit here with your accustomed good nature I am afraid that the case will be reversed and we who seem to accuse Aristogeiton will also turn out to be condemning you."

beyond *nomos* itself. Without the intervention of *themis*, would the law of *phusis* trump the law of *nomos* and exceed its ordering force? *Nomos* alone is inadequate to guarantee that it does not.

The jurors' philanthropic *phusis* also threatens *nomos* and the speech's nomic order in another way, for *philanthrōpia* is listed as one reason why an otherwise upstanding citizen might find himself in debt (86) and why others might look the other way and pretend not to notice his pecuniary misfortune (89). Demosthenes acknowledges that some of the jurors might have friends and acquaintances who are in debt for this reason, and engages in some lengthy special pleading to differentiate these fine Athenians from Aristogeiton, whose debts arose from sykophancy and not beneficence, and thus deserve no pity. From a philanthropic perspective, Aristogeiton's crimes no longer look quite so uniquely monstrous; they are, Demosthenes concedes, different only in degree from the kinds of crimes jurors routinely and rightly forgive (90).[76] Thus the jurors' *phusis* proves to be a precarious foundation for the enactment of justice, as their innate benevolence threatens to corrode the iron boundaries Demosthenes so carefully constructs around his cosmos of law.

Another rejected term also lingers to disturb the tranquil order of this speech's legal and rhetorical universe. In the oration's legal anthropology, the polarity between law's order and nature's disorder was articulated as a difference of desire.[77] Nature's base wants (*phaula bouletai*) are the origin of crime. By contrast, "the laws desire (*boulontai*) what is just and good and beneficial, and they seek this out, and when they find it, they reveal it as a common commandment, equal and the same for all, and this is what law is" (16). Law's command embodies its desire or will. This legal will, law as desire for the good, must govern and guide the unruly impulses of nature. Aristogeiton is an example of what would happen if that governance failed: "if everyone in the city had the shameless audacity of Aristogeiton and agreed with him that in a democracy one can do and say whatever one wants (*boulētai*)," the democracy would be thrown into confusion and "everyone would drive all order (*pan to tetagmenon*) from his life and consider his own wants (*boulēsin*) to be his law, magistracy, everything" (25–26). "If the laws are dissolved and liberty granted to everyone to do whatever he wants (*ho ti bouletai*), not only is the constitution destroyed but our life is no different from the beasts'" (20). This alarmist vision is reminiscent of Plato's

[76] Rosenbloom 2003: 104: "For Aristogeiton to be similar to the Athenians is to admit all the goods the laws represent – religious, social, economic, and political – have been corrupted."

[77] The verb used throughout is *boulomai*, with the related nouns *boulēsis* and *boulēma*. These words indicate not erotic desire but will, want, wish. Cf. below, Chapter 3.

critique of democracy as a chaotic constitution of multiple and conflicting desires. Here the only thing that prevents this dystopic devolution is the law, instantiated in a verdict to convict Aristogeiton. *Kosmos* requires the imposition of law's desire upon the diverse and inferior wants of individual *phusis*.

This jurisprudence of desire would seem to be replicated at the level of rhetorical practice in Demosthenes' claim that he did not want to prosecute (*ouk eboulomēn*, 13). Trials in Athens were divided between *dikai*, private cases prosecuted by the injured party or his family, and *graphai*, public suits involving crimes against the state, which could legally be prosecuted by "anyone who wishes" (*tōi boulomenōi*).[78] This case falls into the latter category: Demosthenes is a "voluntary prosecutor" (*ho boulomenos*), his legal role defined by his prosecutorial will. But just as forensic orators frequently deny their rhetorical proficiency, voluntary prosecutors, anxious to counter the imputation of sykophancy, will deny their personal volition, claiming that they really did not want to bring the case and did so reluctantly only to protect the communal good.[79] So Demosthenes denies his own litigious desire by displacing it onto the jurors: I did not want to litigate, he tells them, "but nonetheless I knew that it was necessary to obey your wishes" (*tois humeterois boulēmasin*, 13). The case is a result of the jurors' will not his own.

But what do the jurors want? Dikastic desire is, in fact, offered as the prime example of law's necessary regulation of the democracy's diverse wishes. Every Athenian citizen was a potential member of the jury pool for this trial and every one, Demosthenes asserts, wanted to be allotted to this court (*pantōn . . . boulomenōn eis touto lakhein to dikastērion*). But you alone can judge the case, he tells the jurors, because you alone were selected by lot and assigned to the case. "That's what the laws say" (27). The jurors themselves illustrate the principles of the speech's legal order. The laws limit the wishes of the citizens – in this case the wish to sit on this scandalous trial – through the democratic mechanisms of sortition and jury allotment. This is *eutaxia* and *eunomia* in action. "Then will you who have entered the court in accordance with the law acquit this

78 [Arist.] *Ath. Pol.* 9.1. For the differences between *graphai* and *dikai* and the various procedures for initiating each, see Harrison 1971: 74–82; Osborne 1985; Todd 1993: 99–112; Allen 2000a: 39–49, 190–96. In practice it seems that *graphai* were virtually never prosecuted by individuals with no personal interest in the case. On the voluntary prosecutor, see Todd 1993: 91–92; Christ 1998a: 26–32, 118–59; Allen 2000a: 151–65; and the discussion in Chapter 3 below. Technically this case is an *endeixis*, an extraordinary procedure involving summary arrest, but it was prosecuted like a *graphē*. See Harrison 1971: 221–32; Hansen 1976: 9–24; Todd 1993: 112–19.

79 E.g. Aesch. 1.1–2; Lys. 22.1–4; Lyc. 1.3–6; Dem. 24.8. Cf. Christ 1998a: 148–50.

man who has been caught speaking and acting in violent transgression of the law?" (27). The jurors who themselves embody the laws' constraint of desire must impose the same constraint upon Aristogeiton's criminal desire.

But just as with *phusis*, there is the danger that the jurors' *boulēsis* might lead them to the wrong verdict. When Demosthenes sees Aristogeiton, whom the laws debar from public speech, harassing other citizens,

> I wonder what you think "upside down" means. Does it mean if the earth were up and the stars down? That is impossible, and I hope it never happens. But when your will (*tōn humeterōn boulēseōn*) allows someone to do something that the laws forbid, when vice is honored and virtue banished, when justice and benefit are subordinated to envy, then one must believe that everything has been turned upside down. (75)

If the jurors' will (*boulēsis*) allows what the laws prevent and grants rights to those the laws disenfranchise – if, in other words, the jurors acquit Aristogeiton – then the entire legal cosmos is thrown upside down. This chaos is presented as an *adunaton*, a warning not to acquit couched as an imagination of the unimaginable consequences that would follow. And yet even in the form of an impossibility this fantasy opens a gulf between the jurors' wishes and the law's commanding will. The possibility that the jurors will not uphold the laws is imagined as an inversion of the cosmic order and an undoing of the carefully regulated and bounded legal universe that the speech has created. Pursuing this desire, the jurors would join forces with Aristogeiton. "You must watch over the laws and make them strong by your judgments. For in that way good citizens will prevail over bad. But if you don't, everything will be set loose, burst open, confounded, and the city will belong to the most shameless criminals" (24–25). The jurors themselves have the power to unbind Demosthenes' iron chain of law and to decompose his rhetorical "cosmos of the city and the laws."

This speaker tries to authorize his speech by locating justice not in his own words but in the *phusis* and *boulēsis* of the jurors. But that is a dangerous displacement: neither can be counted upon to preserve the legal order the speech constructs. Demosthenes had repudiated his own speech as a superfluous and futile declamation (*errhapsōidēkotas*, 2), but his words turn out to be more necessary than he admits, for only his own rhetoric can ensure that the *phusis oikothen* of the jurors will turn against Aristogeiton and their *boulēmata* fall in line with the laws' desire. That is to say, it is his persuasive *logos* and not (as his jurisprudential philosophy would have it) *nomos*, that governs human nature and that orders and preserves the city. The *kosmos* of the juridical cosmos is the work not of the law itself but of Demosthenes' rhetorical "rhapsodies" upon it.

Thus forensic oratory succeeds by failing. It is because its strategies of self-authorization are never fail-proof and its rhetorical boundaries never finally sealed – because some errant term, some nature or desire, will always escape its jurisprudential ordering – that the speaker's words are necessary. If the law's command really did create the fixed cosmic and social order that Demosthenes imagines, he would have nothing to talk about, and (as Aeschines put it) there might as well be a law against legal oratory. But in fact, *nomos* requires *logos* no less than, in Demosthenes 25, *phusis* requires *nomos*: it needs forensic rhetoric in order to sustain its orderly nature and to execute its ordering will. *Logos* is by its nature never fixed or final, though, and it insinuates difference – *phusis*, *boulēsis* – within *nomos*' clear divisions and taxonomic distributions, blurring its defining distinction between inside and outside, and always threatening to break the chain of authority within which juridical discourse tries to encircle itself.

In this chapter rhetoric has thus emerged as the key point both of consolidation and of instability within Athens' juridical cosmos. We have seen how forensic orators construct that cosmos as what Niklas Luhmann calls an autopoietic system, a system that is self-structuring, self-legitimating, self-bounding, and self-replicating.[80] Indeed, the speeches illustrate the process of autopoiesis in action. They show how Athenian juridical discourse fills itself with fractal elements that replicate its own systemic logic; how it generates its own grounding mandate and defines its boundaries in such a way that the legal becomes coterminous with the human. This process threatens to render legal discourse inaccessible to analysis: sealed within the circle of its own self-justification, it seems to allow no internal or external standpoint from which to question its jurisdiction or to challenge its self-serving definitions of legality or justice.[81] But I have suggested that rhetoric opens a space of potential critique within the very world it helps to build. A study of forensic rhetoric exposes the labor of cosmogony by which this juridical order was generated and secured, revealing the precarious circularity of its self-authorization and the unhappy contradictions it entails. It troubles the iron boundaries of this order, uncovering repudiated terms (including the term "rhetoric" itself) within the structure predicated

80 Luhmann 1988, 1990: 1–20, 227–45. See also the essays in Teubner 1988.

81 Drucilla Cornell has repeatedly posed this criticism of closed systems of jurisprudence like Luhmann's (1992a: 116–54; 1992c: 85–87; 1995a: 232, 247).

on their exclusion and thereby undermining its aspiration to closure and self-consistency. If Athenian law is an autopoietic system, then, it is one in which rhetoric's *poiēsis* continually disrupts the solipsistic homogeneity of the *auto*. The chapters that follow examine some such moments of disruption, when forensic rhetoric, instead of securing a world of law, becomes its weakest link.

CHAPTER 2

Legal violence and the limit of justice

> The law is a calculated and relentless pleasure, delight in the promised blood, which permits the perpetual instigation of new dominations and the staging of meticulously repeated scenes of violence. The desire for peace, the serenity of compromise, and the tacit acceptance of the law, far from representing a major moral conversion or a utilitarian calculation that gave rise to the law, are but its result and, in point of fact, its perversion . . . Humanity does not gradually progress from combat to combat until it arrives at universal reciprocity, where the rule of law finally replaces warfare; humanity installs each of its violences in a system of rules and thus proceeds from domination to domination.
>
> Foucault 1977b: 151

LAW IN A FIELD OF PAIN AND DEATH

The law, as Robert Cover famously put it, "takes place in a field of pain and death." As a result of a jury's ruling, an individual may lose his or her savings, family, freedom, or even life.[1] The exercise of law implies and, indeed, demands a kind of violence. Legal judgments must be enforceable and therefore require force; force is interior to the law.[2] How does legal discourse legitimate that interior force and distinguish it from the violence beyond law's borders? Can it even make this distinction? Is the legitimacy of law's force decidable within the terms of the law itself? If it is, legal discourse risks falling into a self-justifying hermeticism: law's force is legitimate because it is the law. If not, then how does the law sustain its own authority and coherence and its right to pass judgment?[3] To study the law's force is

[1] Cover 1986: 1601. On Cover and legal violence see especially Sarat and Kearns 1991, 1992.

[2] Derrida 1992a: 5–6, 11. See also Benjamin 1978 [1921] on "law-preserving violence."

[3] Benjamin 1978 [1921] and Derrida 1992a are meditations on these questions; see also LaCapra 1990. Fish 1989: 503–24 argues for the law's self-legitimation; Cornell 1992a: 155–69 offers a sharp critique of his position.

to ask about legal discourse's representation of its own boundaries and its relation, on the one side, to the lawless violence of the streets and, on the other, to the ideal of justice, since the law's claim to justice is predicated on the legitimacy of its use of force.

This chapter examines how Athenian forensic oratory negotiates the question of law and violence. Beyond the walls of the court, forensic orators conjure a vision of pervasive and escalating violence. The law responds vigorously to this threat: it defends the city and itself through the use of its own legitimate force. Forensic speakers recognize the law's judgment as a form of violence: the jurors kill by their verdict as surely as the criminal does by his hand (Ant. 5.92). Indeed, the law itself kills: "It is not I who kills you," the litigant Euphiletus, on trial for the murder of Eratosthenes, reports having proclaimed as he stabbed his victim to death, "but the law of the city, which you have transgressed" (Lys. 1.26). The law redresses criminal violence by means of legitimate violence, but the two are not easily kept apart. The killing that Euphiletus represents as the law's own righteous blow is for Eratosthenes' relatives a criminal homicide. Forensic oratory works to secure rhetorically a distinction that is ontologically unstable yet crucial both for the individual litigant like Euphiletus (whose life depends on proving that his killing was lawful) and also for the law itself, which premises the legitimacy of its own violence partly on its ability to judge the legitimacy of the violent acts on trial before it: if Euphiletus is convicted and put to death, the jury's determination that his act was lawless murder is what prevents his execution from itself being a lawless murder. Thus, as Danielle Allen (2000a) has argued, the law's authority rests in part on the faith that its punishments are not mere brutality by other means.

This faith was complicated, as Allen shows, by the role of private initiative in Athenian law. Whether the case was a *dikē* or a *graphē*, individual litigants were responsible not only for initiating and prosecuting cases but also, in many instances, for proposing a penalty and carrying out the judgment.[4] With certain crimes like adultery, treason, or temple-robbery, an individual could himself kill a criminal caught in the act: this is how Euphiletus justifies his murder of Eratosthenes, whom he claims to have caught in bed with his wife, and represents it as the execution of a legal judgment before the fact. Private initiative risks turning the law into a sword in the grip of a vengeful individual. As an instrument, as well as

[4] Allen 2000a, esp. 39–40, 45–49, 99–107, 122–46, with further bibliography on procedure at 345 nn. 37–41. See also Hunter 1994: 120–53; Christ 1998a: 26–39.

arena, for the feuds that structured Athens' agonistic social life, the legal system comes to participate in and contribute to the social violence it ostensibly curtails. Indeed, it thrives on this covert complicity. Individuals often executed legal judgments with a zeal that generated further lawsuits. More violence means more litigation which in turn means more violence. The law thus proliferates by way of a violence carried out in its name. In the process, the law sustains extralegal violence, borrowing power from it and lending legitimate force to it. Demosthenes 54 *Against Conon* will illustrate how forensic oratory negotiates this tense collaboration between social violence and the law: even as it denies their complicity and thereby works to euphemize the law's force, the speech tacitly underwrites Athens' social agonism and suborns it for the purposes of the law.

Athenian jurisprudence also colluded with another form of social violence: the cruel hierarchy of citizen over slave. The abstract force of law was enacted all too concretely in the *basanos*, the practice of torturing slaves for interrogation. Through this practice Athenian law simultaneously acknowledged its intrinsic violence and denied it by displacing it onto the body of a slave, which was so natural an object of violence that violence against it became invisible, transmuted into "truth." The *basanos* produced almost no discernible unease: orators challenge the results of particular interrogations but never question the ethics of the practice in principle. Thus what to our eyes is the most visible and horrific example of legal violence was for the Athenians a way of denying that their law took place in a field of pain and death, since it was not the pain or death of a citizen. But the simultaneous admission and denial that the *basanos* holds together in its spectacular display of unrecognized cruelty frays and splits in the speeches, where it proves hard to maintain the necessary division between those whose pain matters and those whose doesn't. We will see the effects in Antiphon 1 *Against the Stepmother*. There the violence disavowed in the *basanos* returns in the rhetoric of the speech, and the slave's painful truth, instead of legitimating legal violence, declares it tragic and unjust.

That injustice in turn reveals another. The *basanos* requires a rigid distinction between legal persons and non-persons: the pain and death of a slave are not injurious. Thus the *basanos*' disavowal of legal violence rests upon a prior foreclosure of certain people's pain. That foreclosure is itself a form – the best concealed form – of legal violence, as we shall see in Demosthenes 47 *Against Euergus and Mnesibulus*. In that case the brutal agonism of elite citizens moves in and out of the courts; legal force is both justified as part of the machinery of the democracy and denied, as the reciprocal exchange of violence between citizens is represented as necessary and painless. But that bloodless competition is grounded on a prior sacrifice, the vicious beating and death of the speaker's old nurse. This speech reveals in startling clarity the violent exclusions by which Athenian legal discourse secures its boundaries, but it also shows that discourse haunted by what it would eliminate. The legal authorities forbid prosecution of the nurse's death, placing her outside the limits of the law. But the speech itself chafes against this decision and laments a death the law refuses to acknowledge, much less to mourn. In so doing it exposes a gap between this specific law and justice: it shows how expanded possibilities of legal meaning are sacrificed to maintain legal order, both the order of a coherent and authoritative juridical discourse and the hierarchical social order in which the law participates.[5] But by including in its rhetoric precisely what it represents as excluded by the law, the speech points toward an alternate definition of justice beyond this legal order, an open horizon that prevents the law from fully sealing its boundaries (*horoi*) or passing a final verdict on the legitimacy of its own intrinsic force.

This case suggests that the question of legal force is intimately connected to the possibility of justice: because the legitimacy of law's force cannot be taken for granted it must be decided anew in each case by appeal to an ideal of justice.[6] The indeterminacy of legal force is thus productive, even as it is problematic. To preserve this productive indeterminacy requires accepting a certain slippage in the diction of law's force or violence. To call law's force "violence" risks minimizing the very real difference for the individual and the community between the pain or death imposed through due legal process and the lawless brutality of violent crime, as well as that between the symbolic violence of legal discourse and the literal violence of physical assault.[7] To call law's violence "force," however, is to risk uncritically accepting a legal system's own self-justifying definitions and thereby occluding the rhetorical and institutional means by which legal discourse itself attempts to secure the distinction – so vital to its own

[5] Cover 1986: 1628–29 identifies a fundamental tension between law as the generation of meaning and law as the maintenance of social order; cf. Cover 1993: 112; Sarat and Kearns 1992.

[6] Cornell 1992a: 116–69, drawing on Derrida 1992a: 16–29. Cf. Cornell 1995a; Douzinas and Warrington 1995; Sarat 2001: 3–9; McVeigh, Rush, and Young 2001.

[7] Sarat 2001: 4. Without denying the real experiential difference between symbolic and literal violence (on which see Scarry 1985: 27–59), I stress the continuity between the two in order to highlight the euphemized forms of violence in which the law deals and the real consequences for its victims. Indeed, as Foucault hypothesizes (see the epigram to this chapter), the legal system itself may be the most insidious form of euphemized violence.

authority – between illegal violence and legitimate force.[8] Thus the echoes of the one word, "force" or "violence," must always be heard in the other. A second slippage involves historical perspective. Violence is, of course, a culturally specific phenomenon. What counts as violence varies across cultures and over time; we should be wary of hypostasizing violence as an invariable category and imposing modern judgments under the guise of the universal. On the other hand, a culturally relativistic stance toward violence risks condoning it in its specific manifestations and conceding too much to a culture's own strategies of justification, which can themselves become a superadded form of violence. The *basanos* will provide a glaring example, as a violence not culturally recognized as such. A hermeneutic double-vision is needed in order to analyze the cultural logic of the *basanos* as a historically situated practice without accepting, along with the Athenians, that violence against slaves was not violence and thereby turning a blind eye to the cultural blind spots that enabled (and were perpetuated by) the practice.

These oscillations in diction and perspective are not only inevitable but necessary if we are to avoid falling in with the law's own self-legitimating rhetoric and equating (as that rhetoric encourages us to do) the decrees and verdicts of a specific legal system with justice. The non-identity of the laws with justice was a concern for classical Athenian thinkers across genres, from Sophocles' opposition in *Antigone* between the laws of the polis and the justice of the gods, to Thucydides' meditation on justice and power in the Melian Dialogue, to the proposition of the personified Nomoi in Plato's *Crito* that the city's laws must be obeyed even when they are unjust, and that justice consists in such absolute obedience.[9] In each of these instances, the potential for harm perpetrated under the banner of legality opens a gulf between the law and a broader ideal of justice. Forensic oratory offers a particularly nuanced contribution to this cultural discussion of legal violence and the limit of justice. Even as the genre works to naturalize law's force and thus to close the fissure between law and justice,

[8] Sarat and Kearns 1992: 212–13. The generic word for violence in Greek, *bia*, can bear either sense, and the ambiguity of its meaning is often in play: in Aeschylus' *Prometheus Bound*, for instance, the pairing of Kratos and Bia as Zeus's henchmen (and Prometheus' jailers) is an equivocal commentary on the force of sovereign authority. In forensic oratory, however, *bia* mostly signifies illegitimate violence. Omitowoju 2002: 51–56 traces the semantic range of the word.

[9] The bibliography on the topic is vast, but for general discussions see, e.g., Havelock 1978: 281–95; Ostwald 1986: 250–73, 305–12; Garner 1987: 1–30; de Romilly 1971: 97–201. Plato, in particular, returns repeatedly to this question; see especially *Hippias Major* 283e–285b, *Gorgias* 482e–484c, *Republic* 338c–354b, *Minos*, and, of course, the *Laws*. Cf. Xen. *Mem.* 4.4, where *to dikaion* is defined as *to nomimon*.

that fissure is persistently reopened in the rhetoric of the speeches, which record a sympathy for the forgotten victims of legitimate force and thus amplify the muted echo of violence within it. This reminder of the law's intrinsic violence – not least the discursive violence by which it defines itself as law – marks the limits of Athenian legal discourse's aspirations to justice. And yet by refusing the equation of the law with justice, forensic rhetoric preserves the hope of an alternate justice, a hope that belies the pessimistic fatalism exemplified by the quotation from Foucault that serves as the epigram to this chapter. Rhetoric itself thus acts as a force for justice within Athenian juridical discourse, as the horizons of possibility that Athenian jurisprudence denies in its drive toward self-authorizing closure reappear like a mirage within the language of the speeches, the indistinct vision of an expanded justice at and as the limit of the law.[10]

LEGAL VIOLENCE AND SOCIAL VIOLENCE (DEMOSTHENES 54)

Demosthenes 54 *Against Conon* is about an act of violence and about the law's relation to violence. The plaintiff, Ariston, claims he was assaulted by Conon and his son Ctesias. A series of increasingly hostile encounters between them culminated, as Ariston tells it, in a violent attack in the agora: Conon and his gang held him down and stripped him of his cloak; they jumped on him and threw him in the mud, split his lip and closed his eye. Humiliating insult was added to physical injury: after they knocked him down, Conon stood over him crowing and flapping his arms like a victorious fighting cock. Ariston was left naked and bleeding, unable to speak or get up, on the threshold of death (8–9).

This episode is set against a backdrop of pervasive societal violence. Gangs of youths roam Athens trading insults and blows. Enemies seek to humiliate one another on the streets or in the courtroom. The speech depicts a society in which citizens compete in protracted and often bloody contests over status and reputation. David Cohen has studied this Athenian culture of agonism and proposes that litigation played a seminal role within it as a means not of resolving disputes but of pursuing them, of triumphing over one's enemies and affirming one's own honor at their expense.[11] Cohen sees Demosthenes 54 as "part of the dynamic of insult and revenge which

10 Cornell 1992a deploys the hermeneutic tools of deconstruction, which she renames "the philosophy of the limit," to analyze justice "as the limit to any system of positive law" (2). See esp. 1992a: 155–69 on violence and the possibility of justice, and cf. 1992b, 1992c.

11 D. Cohen 1995a, esp. 61–142. See also Christ 1998a: 160–92; Allen 2000a: 59–62; Osborne 2000, and the critiques of Kurihara 2003; Harris 2006: 405–22.

characterizes feuding behavior": the trial, in his view, is just the latest bout in the ongoing feud between Ariston and Conon.[12] Cohen's vision of Athenian society has recently come under attack by Gabriel Herman, who argues that, compared to true feuding cultures, Athenian society was in fact remarkably peaceful and harmonious.[13] Whereas Cohen foregrounds the speech's depiction of physical violence as a pervasive, normal, and (within limits) acceptable part of daily reality in Athens, Herman stresses the mildness of Ariston's response to his opponents' provocation and takes it as exemplifying an Athenian ideology of moderation and self-restraint.[14]

While these two scholars, from their opposite perspectives, read Demosthenes 54 for the light it casts on the violence of Athenian society, my focus is rather on the way the speech uses its imagination of social violence to work through the problem of legal violence. The speech represents social violence as external and antithetical to the legal system and works to secure a distinction between that extralegal violence and law's legitimate force, marking the boundary between them with a gruesome vision of the citizen body in pain. Even as it does so, however, it tacitly acknowledges the law's complicity with the brutality beyond its borders and the intimate connection between legal and extralegal violence. In its simultaneous attempt and failure to maintain an antithesis between peaceful legality and social conflict, the speech offers support for both Cohen's and Herman's vision of Athens. But its rhetorical investment in each side of this antithesis makes it problematic evidence for either, and thus both the culture of agonism and the ethics of moderation should be understood not as a preexisting context for the speech but instead as its rhetorical effect.

The central rhetorical strategy of the speech is the clear-cut opposition between the unbridled violence of Conon and his sons and the lawful

[12] D. Cohen 1995a: 119–30. The quotation is on p. 138. Rubinstein 2000: 172–84, 232 notes that this model of individual agonism works better for private suits than for public actions, which often involved team efforts on both sides.

[13] See esp. Herman 2006: 155–214. Cf. Herman 1994, 1995, and the reviews of Herman 2006 by Christ 2007 (with response by Herman 2007) and Balot 2008. Herman's polemic against Cohen (2006: 199–203; cf. Herman 1996) seems misplaced, since Cohen does not deny that self-restraint was a normative virtue in Athens, but rather sees it as one among others (including the virtues of vengeance and macho competition), the tensions between which forensic orators had to mediate. Since my argument concerns law's relation to social violence in general – and all societies are, to some extent or another, violent – it makes little difference whether Athens was an exceptionally violent place.

[14] Herman 2006: 153, 155–59, 199, 283–85. Fisher 1999 and Lanni 2006: 27–31 also stress the relatively peaceful and cooperative nature of Athens compared to other pre-industrial societies. Fisher 1998 emphasizes the tension between the Athenian ideals of honor and self-restraint; cf. D. Cohen 1991a: 160–61, 1995a: 123; Herman 1993, 1995; Christ 1998a: 160–92; Roisman 2005: 20, 71–79.

restraint of the speaker Ariston.[15] This distinction bolsters another, between the lethality of Athenian society and the non-violence of the law. Violence is represented as something that happens elsewhere, beyond the confines of the courtroom, in the streets and camps and agora. The problems began, as Ariston tells it, two years earlier when he was on guard duty with Conon's sons: drunk and rowdy, they insulted Ariston and beat up his slaves, urinating on them and overturning chamber-pots (4). Ariston was justifiably upset, but instead of retaliating in kind he merely joined his messmates in reporting them to the general (4). When they returned to Athens, he resolved not to take action, legal or physical, but simply to avoid the obnoxious young men (6). This prudent course proves impossible: a chance encounter in the streets escalates, culminating in the assault, with its bloodshed, obscene insults, and humiliating cock's crow (8–9). But Ariston responds even to this outrage with restraint: he defends himself against their brutal physical violence with the legitimate force of legal action.

Ariston anticipates that Conon will try to laugh the whole thing off as a trivial private matter. "Diverting the issue from the violent insult (*hubris)* of the act, he will try to turn it into a ridiculous joke" (13). He will say that many elite young men in the city form gangs, calling themselves the "Erections" (*Ithuphalloi*) or the "Lamp Holders" (*Autolēkuthoi*), and fight with one another over courtesans, and "that this is what young men do" (14).[16] Ariston concedes that "boys will be boys" (though he points out that Conon is hardly a boy, 21), but refuses to accept that the outrage is a laughing matter:

> If Conon says "We are a gang of *Ithuphalloi* and we fall in love and beat up and choke whomever we want" are you going to laugh and let him off? I don't think so. For none of you would have laughed if you happened to be present when I was dragged and stripped and insulted (*hubrizomēn*); when I left the house healthy and came home on a stretcher; when my mother ran out and the women were crying and lamenting as if someone had died, so that the neighbors sent round to see what had happened. Surely it is not right for you to grant an excuse or immunity to anyone to commit abuse *(hubrizein*). (20–21)

[15] E.g. 3, 6, 15–17, 24. On *ēthos* in this speech, see especially Morford 1966; De Brauw 2001–02: 163–65.

[16] The names of the gangs connote sexual and social transgression. *Ithuphallos* means "erect penis" and may evoke fertility rituals. *Autolēkuthos* means "holding one's own oil flask." This may have an onanistic connotation or may, as Carey and Reid 1985: 87 *ad* 14 suggest, express "contempt for social norms" by mimicking behavior associated with slaves or the poor; cf. Henderson 1972: 141–43. Fisher 1999 discusses the activity of gangs in Athens and notes the particular anxiety about their legal abuses; cf. Murray 1990b. Halliwell 1991: 287–96 analyzes the cultural attitude toward laughter reflected in this case, and Roisman 2005: 17–21 its reliance on stereotypes of youth. See also Ober 1989a: 257–59 on the class politics of the speech.

Conon's expected trivialization of the incident and Ariston's outraged response are part of a debate over the limits of socially acceptable violence, as Cohen has shown.[17] Ariston seeks to clarify that limit and place Conon on its far side. He draws a clear boundary between legitimate and illegitimate violence and marks that boundary with his own battered body.

That notional boundary stone is not just a physical body, naked and bloodied, but a citizen body. Throughout the speech, Ariston insists that Conon's crime was not merely battery (*aikeia*) but *hubris*: indeed, the first word of the speech – Ariston's justification for bringing this case – is *hubris* (*hubristheis*, 1).[18] While the precise meaning of this term is disputed, it seems to have indicated an act, as N. R. E. Fisher puts it, "deliberately intended to bring major and improper dishonour or shame on others."[19] A crime against a man's status, as well as his person or property, *hubris* operates within the same agonistic sociality as the feud between Ariston and Conon. It functions in Ariston's argument as a shorthand for that feud and indicates its most damaging and antisocial effects. Legally, *hubris* constituted a public injury: it was prosecuted not by a private suit (*dikē*) but by the higher-risk, higher-stakes *graphē* used for crimes that affected the city as a whole. By calling Conon's act *hubris*, Ariston suggests that it was more than an assault on himself as an individual; it was an assault on his status as a citizen and therefore on the sanctity and sovereignty of the entire citizen body.[20] Thus he calls on every citizen of the jury to hate Conon as if he himself had been his victim (42). It is just by chance, he says, that this happened to me not to you (43), and if Conon could do this to me, he could – and would – do it to any citizen.

And yet despite his repeated insistence that Conon's crime constituted *hubris*, Ariston decided to bring a *dikē* for *aikeia* not a *graphē* for *hubris*.[21]

[17] D. Cohen 1995a: 126–28. Cf. Fisher 1998: 75–77 on the "acceptable face" of male violence.

[18] "They jumped me and committed *hubris* against me (8); Conon's crow is "a sign and proof that the whole affair was a result of his *hubris*" (9). Cf. 10, 13, 15, 17, 20, 21, 24, 25, 28, 32, 33, 40, 41, 43, 44.

[19] Fisher 1998: 78. There are two "laws against *hubris*" preserved at Dem. 21.47 and Aesch. 1.16; on the former see MacDowell 1976b: 24–29, 1990: 263–65 ad loc; on the latter, Fisher 2001: 138–40 ad loc. On the debate over the meaning of *hubris* see Gernet 1917: 1–33, 179–211, 389–424; Fisher 1976; 1990; 1992: 36–150; 2001: 138–40; MacDowell 1976b, 1990: 263–65; Gagarin 1979a; Carey and Reid 1985: 75–76; Murray 1990a; P. Wilson 1991; D. Cohen 1991b; 1995a: 120–26, 143–62; Ober 1994; Cairns 1996; Omitowoju 2002: 29–50; Farenga 2006: 186–88.

[20] Halperin 1990: 96–98; Fisher 1992: 62–68. This is a key rhetorical strategy in Dem. 21, discussed below in Chapter 4.

[21] On the difference between a *graphē hubreōs* and a *dikē aikeias*, see Gagarin 1979a: 232–36; Carey and Reid 1985: 75–76; Osborne 1985: 50–51; Fisher 1990, 1992: 36–68, 1998: 84–85; Todd 1993: 270–71; Christ 1998a: 130–33; Carey 2004: 116–19; Rubinstein 2005. A third legal procedure was available to Ariston: he could have had Conon summarily arrested for cloak-snatching (*apagōgē tōn lōpodutōn*, 1, 24). On the variety of legal options in bringing a case, see Dem. 22.25–27; Osborne 1985; Allen 2000a: 122–28; and Carey 2004, who stresses the limitations on procedural flexibility.

"Having been insulted (*hubristheis*), jurors, and suffering at Conon's hands such things that for a long time neither my friends nor any of the doctors expected me to survive, when I unexpectedly recovered and was restored to health I brought this case of battery (*dikēn aikeias*) against him" (1). He wanted to bring a *graphē hubreōs*, he says, and Conon's acts certainly warranted one. But his friends advised him against it, warning him "not to bring upon myself more trouble than I was able to handle or to prosecute the crime against me in a way that seems inappropriate for my youth" (1; cf. 13, 24). This explanation, with its calculation of relative status and power, assimilates the *graphē hubreōs* to *hubris* itself. If *hubris* is, in the words of one scholar, "thinking big," Ariston represents his procedural option as a deliberate choice to "think small."[22] In responding to Conon's physical attack, Ariston eschews not only physical violence but even legal violence. In this way, Ariston explicitly repudiates the idea that David Cohen sees implicitly at work in the speech, the idea of the law as an extension and vehicle of social agonism. In differentiating his own *ēthos* from Conon's, Ariston also differentiates the ethos of the courts from that of the streets: the former has no part in the hubristic violence of the latter.

That distinction forms the basis for a broader jurisprudential and sociological theory. The speech conjures a vision of social violence out of control, a Hobbesian world in which social agonism escalates inexorably to murder:

> The laws anticipated even excuses of necessity, so that things don't escalate. Take cases of slander (*dikai kakēgorias*), for example . . . They say that slander cases exist so that insults don't lead to blows. Likewise, cases of battery (*dikai aikeias*): I hear that these cases exist so that the man who is at a disadvantage does not defend himself with a rock, but waits for the punishment provided by law. Again, there are cases for wounding (*graphai traumatos*) so that victims of wounding don't turn to murder. The least offense, slander, has been provided against to prevent it from becoming the most serious and extreme, murder, and to prevent the gradual escalation from slander to blows, from blows to wounds, from wounds to death. There is a procedure (*dikē*) in the laws for each of these so that they are not judged merely by the anger and will of whoever happens to be involved. (17–19)

Ariston conjures up a savage existence in which seemingly trivial violence – like that Conon claims he and his son engaged in – automatically escalates to its logical conclusion, murder. This nightmare of intensifying violence and retributive self-help is prevented only by law, which by taking seriously even the least offense, places a brake on this cycle of escalating brutality. Conon may try to laugh away his crime as something harmless, but in this theory of jurisprudence there is no such thing.

22 Cairns 1996.

This dystopic vision is the justification for the legal system.[23] The passage offers a cosmogonic myth in which the law is both the divine creator, anticipating and controlling the natural cycle of violence, and the entity newly created, as the chaos is gradually populated with one *dikē* (case) after another. These procedures come into being as a result of this preexisting violence and its innate entropic tendency. In this jurisprudential genealogy violence exists outside of and prior to the law, which is conceived as a secondary response and remedy to it. Legal procedure (*dikē*) is the antithesis of natural violence, its negating supplement and peaceful substitute.

This juridical cosmogony elaborates at a theoretical level the speech's distinction between Conon's brutality and Ariston's restraint. But if Ariston's jurisprudential theory sets law as the antithesis and exterior supplement to violence, the juridical practice of the case suggests a more complicit relation between the two. *Dikai* are put in place to prevent escalating violence, but there is a danger that they will become the mechanism of that escalation. Ariston anticipates that Conon will put his friends on the stand, as he did during arbitration, to swear to the truth of his own account. But Conon's witnesses are all liars, Ariston asserts; they are his drinking buddies and colleagues in crime and have lied for him on the stand before (33). This *hetaireia* (social club) of liars is another incarnation of the violent gangs of *Ithuphalloi* and *Autolēkuthoi* with whom Conon and his sons associate. Their "illustrious youthful activities" (35) include bearing false witness for one another. "Won't we testify for one another? Isn't that what friends and companions do? What dreadful charge will he bring against you? Someone says he witnessed him being beaten? We will testify that he wasn't even touched" (35). When they were younger, Ariston continues, Conon and his cronies formed a gang called the *Triballoi*, after the barbarous Thracian tribe. They would get together and feast on the pigs' testicles left at the crossroads as offerings to Hecate "and would casually swear oaths and break oaths and things like that" (39). The false oath Ariston predicts Conon will swear during the trial today continues their perverse and impious collusion. The violence of the streets will follow Conon into court.

If the trial is a continuation of the crime, Ariston fears that the jurors will join in the assault. "Jurors, I have trouble bearing what I have suffered and I would be no less aggrieved and consider myself no less insulted (*hubristhai*), if I may put it that way, if you believe that Conon speaks the

[23] A similar genealogy is articulated at Dem. 21.76; Isoc. 20.8–9. On legal redress as the alternative to violent self-help, see further Gernet 1917: 136–78; Gustafsson 1998: 167–68 n. 12; Weisberg 1992; Herman 1993: 417–19, 1994: 107–17, 1995, 2006: 184–215; Fisher 1998: 80–92; D. Cohen 2005. The quotation from Foucault at the head of this chapter is a critique of this genealogy.

truth about me" (15). The jurors, too, have the power to inflict *hubris*: a verdict against Ariston would amplify the *hubris* he has already suffered at Conon's hands. It would constitute an added *hubris* (*proshubristheis*, 43; cf. 40) against his person and reputation. Hence Ariston's anxiety that the jurors will not take the assault seriously and, instead of punishing Conon, will join him in laughing at his now doubly humiliated opponent. In Ariston's pessimistic vision, passive spectators turn into eager participants, urging on the fight. He insists that Conon should be held liable even if, as he claims, he was present at the melee but didn't take part, "for if bystanders, rather than preventing men who are trying to commit a crime, whether through drunkenness or anger or any other cause, instead urge them on, there is no hope of salvation for victims of uncontrolled violence, but they will be abused (*hubrizesthai*) until the perpetrators run out of strength" (25). So too the jurors, if they acquit Conon, will become co-conspirators in his crime, encouraging him and others like him to greater violence (43).[24]

Against Conon's anticipated claim that a certain level of conflict is normal and innocuous, Ariston imagines a bleak scenario in which social violence is ubiquitous, uncontrolled, and ever intensifying, in which everyone – spectators as well as perpetrators – shares the "will and anger" (25) that generate violence and every dispute eventually ends in death. More importantly, he imagines the law, which should act as a brake on this violence, instead condoning it, augmenting it (*proshubrizein*), urging it on. This is the world Conon's acquittal will create, and it will be a world of the law's own making.

This nightmarish state of unchecked savagery is, as often in forensic oratory, the imagined result of the opponent's acquittal. Just as a correct verdict maintains justice and order in the world, a wrong verdict (from the speaker's perspective) creates violence and chaos. Inasmuch as it is a result of a judicial injustice, then, this outcome is an aberration. But this case suggests that even in the normal course of its execution the law contains a potential violence. Ariston makes much of his decision to prosecute Conon with a *dikē* for *aikeia* not a *graphē* for *hubris*. His disingenuous procedural choice – disingenuous because he continues to call Conon's act *hubris* throughout the speech and even has the clerk read out the law on *hubris* under which he is not prosecuting (24) – is represented as a deliberate rejection of judicial *hubris:* he will not display the arrogant superiority

[24] This inverts the trope that cast jurors as bystanders to a "crime" unfolding in the courtroom and called upon them to come to the aid of the defendant and the community: Christ (in press b).

in prosecuting Conon's crime that Conon displayed in committing it. Ariston's forensic moderation would seem the practical instantiation of his jurisprudential theory: legal procedure – a *dikē* for each crime – will check the escalating violence of the streets. Indeed, Ariston's suit de-escalates, answering a greater violence with a lesser: "suffering the ultimate through the *hubris* and profligacy of these men, I brought a charge much less serious than was warranted" (13).

But even as Ariston magnanimously refrains from using the law as a weapon of *hubris* he shows that the law can become such a weapon, and not only through the unfortunate anomaly of an unjust verdict but in the course of its normal procedure. It is perhaps not accidental that the *graphē hubreōs* is not mentioned in the jurisprudential theory at §§17–19. In that passage's direct correspondence between crime and prosecution, each *dikē* – slander, battery, wounding – fixes its crime in place, preventing its escalating slide. But the charge of *hubris* is inflammatory by nature: it places a surcharge of malicious insult upon slander, battery, or wounding. A prosecution for *hubris* magnifies the crime: it becomes a supplementary *hubris* (*proshubrizein*).[25] The omission of *hubris* and its *graphē* from this theory of legal restraint thus denies the possibility that legal procedure can exacerbate the cycle of violence it is created to mitigate. It rejects the possibility, both acknowledged and denied by Ariston's ostentatious procedural decision, that *dikai* might impel, not halt, the slide from insult to battery to murder.

It is, in fact, murder that is at stake. One difference between a *dikē aikeias* and a *graphē hubreōs* is that whereas the former was generally punished by a fine, the latter could carry a death sentence. Ariston wanted to bring a *graphē hubreōs*, he says, because he "would have been most happy to have Conon sentenced to death" (1). "For what would be a worthy punishment for the acts he has committed? Not even death is enough in my opinion" (22). While from Ariston's perspective this death would be, not murder, but lawful execution, that distinction has already been blurred by the speech's admission that legal procedure can be used as an instrument of social aggression or retaliation: if a court case is the functional equivalent of a punch, then a death sentence is euphemized murder. The legitimate juridical force that one citizen employs to prosecute his enmity against

[25] Perhaps for this reason, *hubris* cases seem to have been very rare. None survives in the extant speeches, and where a *hubris* charge is mentioned (e.g. Din. 1.23; Dem. 21.36–39, 45.4; Is. 8.41), there is no indication that it was actually brought to trial or resulted in a conviction. See MacDowell 1976b: 29; Osborne 1985: 50–51; Fisher 1992: 43.

another is, in the extreme case, homicidal. The *graphē hubreōs* could be such an extreme case, and by rejecting this procedure, Ariston acknowledges the law's power to kill even as he refuses to deploy that power.

Lethal violence does not stand outside of and opposed to the law, then. Instead, Ariston implies, it exists as a latent potential within the law. The only thing that prevents that dangerous potential from being actualized, as he represents it, is Ariston himself in his decision not to kill his opponent by means of the trial. By curbing his own murderous desire he curbs the law's potentially murderous force; by knowing his own limits he sets limits on the law. In this way he himself becomes the sole check on the legal procedures that were created as the sole check on social violence. One man's personal virtue, in other words, is all that separates law from the violence it was supposed to curtail. And as proof of that virtue, we have only Ariston's word.

Thus the speech's representation of its own judicial practice undercuts its jurisprudential theory, undoing the latter's distinction between social violence and its legal remedy. The speech attempts to resecure that theoretical distinction, as we have seen, with the graphic image of Ariston's battered body. The scene of the assault, described twice in detail, shows us that body as victim both of the symbolic violence of *hubris* and of an excruciatingly literal violence:

> Afterward the doctor said he wasn't too concerned about the swelling and cuts on my face, but a constant fever followed and terrible pains over my whole body, and especially around my ribs and stomach. I was unable to eat, and the doctor said that if I had not spontaneously expelled a large amount of blood when I was already in tremendous pain and despair the festering wound would have killed me. The loss of blood saved my life. (11–12)

With a precision of medical detail virtually unparalleled in forensic oratory, Ariston offers up the spectacle of his brutalized body as physical evidence of Conon's crime. The realism of the scene is presented as indisputable proof: his lacerations and bruises speak for themselves, and they bespeak not only Conon's savagery but also Ariston's truthfulness. In a sense, this citizen performs a *basanos*, an interrogation by torture, upon himself, subjecting his body to narrative torment in order to prove the veracity of his account. In the *basanos*, as we will see in the next section, the tortured slave body seems to contain an absolute truth beyond the rhetorical manipulations of the trial. So here, Ariston's visceral description aims to give an unmediated experience of the crime, to transport the jurors from the courtroom to the crime scene and to make them feel his actual suffering. There is no arguing with the reality of pain.[26]

Ariston attempts to make that pain real within the courtroom by affirming its exteriority to the law. The real injury took place beyond the walls of the *dikastērion*: the law is called to the scene only after the damage is done. This description of the incident follows the spatio-temporal logic of Ariston's jurisprudential theory: violence exists before and outside the law. In this way the legal system is purified of its own potential violence: the threat of death that is eliminated from the law with Ariston's decision not to bring a *graphē hubreōs* is relocated in the world beyond the law in the near-fatal effects of the assault. Conon kills, the law does not. The trial takes place within a framework of potential death, both Ariston's and Conon's, but is not itself the agent of death. By situating his own battered body on the boundary between the law and its violent outside, Ariston denies that the law itself operates (in Cover's words) in a field of pain and death. This denial is important enough to his case that he sacrifices his own body and honor to it, rhetorically reenacting his humiliating pain in order to offer himself as a touchstone (*basanos*) to both the guilt of Conon and the innocence of the law.

And yet the very vividness of his description of this extralegal violence underscores the euphemized brutality at work within the courts. It is entirely possible, after all, that Ariston is fabricating this episode. As Carey and Reid point out, he provides no witnesses to the incident: his only witnesses arrived on the scene after Conon and Ctesias had fled and cannot testify as to who actually took part in the assault.[27] He may be making up the whole story: there are other cases where speakers accuse their opponents of bringing a case based on self-inflicted wounds (Aesch. 2.93; 3.51, 212; Dem. 40.32; cf. Lys. 4.9). Even if he is not faking his injuries, Ariston is no doubt putting his own spin on events. When we return to the scene of the wounding (7–9) with that in mind, we notice how artfully it is staged. The military metaphors (*exanastēsas*, 7; *anemeikhthēmen*, 8) recall Ctesias' bad behavior on guard duty, as well as highlighting the seriousness of the engagement. A series of forceful participles (*prospesontes*, *huposkelisantes*,

[26] Scarry 1985: 3–23. Her study of pain is the starting point for Cover's discussion of legal violence (1986: 1602–3). Ariston's account resembles the modern "victim impact statement." These testimonials are often excluded from the courtroom on the grounds that they are too prejudicial and elicit an emotional, not a reasoned response from the jury (Gewirtz 1996: 137–49; cf. Brooks 2000: 130–39). This, of course, is exactly what Ariston is hoping for.

[27] Carey and Reid 1985: 70–72. They note that the pluperfect in §9 (*ōikhonto*) and tense of the participles in §32 suggest that Conon and his gang were already gone by the time Ariston's witnesses arrived; contra, Christ (in press a).

rhaxantes, *enallomenoi*, *hubrizontes*) culminates in the physical violence of the split lip and the closed eye (8). The insults and slanders they uttered over his prostrate body – "some of which I would be ashamed even to name in front of you" (9) – as well as the "song" of Conon's crowing cock are carefully focalized from Ariston's own semi-conscious perspective: he hears them as he lies there, unable to rise or to speak (8). The chorus of wailing women (9, 20) puts the finishing touches on this dramatic description. Similarly, the brief reiteration of the scene later in the speech is a tiny masterpiece of forensic narrative, with its tricolon crescendo ("I was dragged and stripped and insulted," *heilkomēn kai exeduomēn kai hubrizomēn*) and its sharp antithesis between his carefree departure and miserable homecoming ("leaving the house healthy I came home on a stretcher," 20).[28]

To note the artistry of these descriptions is to make an obvious point, but one the speech does not encourage us to make: the brutality of this episode, which Ariston represents as occurring prior and external to the law, is the creation of the forensic speech and the forensic context. Whatever actually happened out there on the street, this theatrical staging of the violent scene takes place within the courtroom and follows its rules of evidence and narrative. Its visceral realism is a product of the speech's rhetorical artifice, and merely to recognize this fact is to unsettle the dichotomy that artifice was deployed to naturalize between the violence of the streets and the legitimate force of the courts.

Likewise, the citizen body in pain that calls for and justifies the law's forceful remedy is also a product of the forensic argument. Indeed, as a victim of *hubris*, that body is not just a rhetorical object but more precisely a legal object: it owes its integrity to concrete laws of citizenship and a legal distinction (upheld by, among others, the law of *hubris*) between the slave body, always vulnerable to violence, and the inviolability of the free citizen. The body attacked in this scene exists not in a state of nature but within the law itself. Law was already there, then, at the scene of the crime: it preexists the crime that, in Ariston's jurisprudential cosmogony, it is created to remedy. Furthermore, if law exists at the scene of criminal violence, violence also exists within the law, for Ariston's injured body becomes a lethal rhetorical and legal weapon to deploy against his opponent. If he had his way, his near-death would seal Conon's death-sentence.

[28] Carey and Reid 1985: 91 ad loc; they also note the strong verb *exepepēdēkei* and the detail that the women wailed "as if someone had died" (20).

Ariston's body thus itself undermines the distinction it was intended to secure, the distinction between law and outlaw, between the law's non-violence and the illegitimate violence beyond its borders. The law is not a pure and later addition to a brutal sociality but part of its very working. The legal system not only tolerates social violence but in fact requires it in order to justify its existence and to legitimate its own forceful interventions. Thus even as the law serves (as Cohen argues) as a vehicle for social conflict, social conflict is also a vehicle for the law, which thrives on it and reproduces itself through it: this is not the first time Conon has been in court nor will it likely be the last. Demosthenes 54 works hard to deny any connection between the legitimate force of the courts and the violence of the streets. But in the very process it sustains this secret collaboration between them, a collaboration that works to the benefit of each and also of forensic oratory itself, which can represent itself as the medium of a pure and peaceable legality, all the while wielding the dissimulated power of a retaliatory punch in the face.

TOUCHSTONE OF VIOLENCE (ANTIPHON 1)

Demosthenes 54 sets the citizen's battered body on the borderline between the law and the violent world beyond it. But there are other wounded bodies inside that border, within the legal system itself. The question of Athenian law's internal violence is most intensely negotiated around the *basanos*, the practice of torturing slaves for evidence. Slaves were often witnesses to the domestic and business dealings of their masters, but they could not testify in person in court and their testimony could be introduced only if produced under torture.[29] The theory was that torture would correct the slave's natural biases regarding his or her master; the practical backdrop was the pervasive abuse of slaves in Athens.[30] Typically one litigant would challenge the other to hand over his slaves for interrogation. The details were arranged by the two litigants beforehand: the questions to be asked,

[29] Hunter 1994: 70–95; Todd 1993: 96, 184–94. The exception to this rule was the procedure of *mēnusis*, on which see Osborne 2000. The *basanos* is one of the most discussed aspects of Athenian law. The definitive treatment is Thür 1977: see esp. 287–319. See further Bushala 1968; Dorjahn 1971; Harrison 1971: 147–50; Carey 1988; Todd 1990b: 33–35; duBois 1991: 35–68; Hunter 1994: 89–95; Gagarin 1996; Mirhady 1996, 2000b; Thür 1996; Johnstone 1999: 70–92; Sternberg 2006: 146–73; Bassi (in press).

[30] On the practice and ideology of slavery in Athens, Hunter 1992 and duBois 2003 are particularly relevant to this discussion. Citizens were almost certainly immune from judicial torture (except perhaps in the case of crimes against the state): see Carey 1988, a persuasive answer to Bushala 1968. See further Gernet 1955: 151–72, Hunter 2000: 5–15 on the legal status of slaves.

the length and mode of torture, who was to do the questioning and who was to be present for it, the consequences that would follow upon the information obtained, and who would pay for any damage to the slave. The procedure could be used to settle the dispute and prevent a trial but it could also, at least in theory, produce evidence that might be presented in court if the dispute did go to trial.

Forensic orators speak frequently of the *basanos* and generally speak of it as a means of access to an absolute and unimpeachable truth. No slave has ever lied under torture, says Demosthenes:

> In both public and private affairs, you consider the *basanos* the most accurate of all proofs, and wherever slaves and free men are both present and some question must be investigated, you do not use the free men as witnesses but instead you torture (*basanizontes*) the slaves and in this way you seek to discover the truth (*alētheian*). This is reasonable, jurors. For some witnesses have been found in the past to have borne false testimony (*ou t'alēthē marturēsai*). But no one investigated under torture (*tōn basanisthentōn oudenes*) has ever been proved to have spoken something untrue (*ouk alēthē*) under investigation (*ek tēs basanou*). (30.37)

The same confident assertion is repeated nearly verbatim in Isaeus (8.12) and Isocrates (17.53). The *basanos* is praised by Lycurgus as "most just and most democratic" (1.29), a fail-safe method of uncovering "the whole truth about all the crimes committed" (1.32). The speaker of Lysias 7 considers it a stronger proof than his opponents' words and even his own deeds (7.34). Most speakers seem to agree that the *basanos* provides "the most exacting proof" for revealing "the truth of the matter" (*tēn alētheian tōn pepragmenōn*, Dem. 29.5).

Orators maintain this faith in the *basanos*' absolute veracity even as they admit that slaves can and sometimes do lie under torture. The speaker in Antiphon 5, accused falsely (he claims) of murder on the basis of a *basanos*, criticizes the procedure as inherently unreliable. Slaves will lie in the hope of obtaining their freedom or simply to end the torture (31; cf. 40–41, 49). The answers one extracts depend on who is doing the questioning and who is present when it is done; slaves will say what the interrogators want to hear and often testify falsely against those who aren't present (32). The speaker in Isocrates 17, immediately after praising the *basanos* as a means of getting at the truth – "you consider nothing more reliable and true than a *basanos*" (54) – remarks that his opponent should not resist subjecting his slave to torture since he is much more likely to speak in support of his master and be rewarded with freedom than to speak against him and "suffer for this most miserably for the rest of his days" (17.55; cf. Lys. 4.16).

The speaker in Lysias 7 imagines the opposite probability: since slaves are by nature inimical to their masters, it seems unlikely they would choose to bear the pain of torture when they could escape it by speaking against them (7.35).

Aristotle, in his discussion of the *basanos*, breaks it down along strategic lines: those whose case will profit from the testimony of the *basanos* should assert its unimpeachable truth; those to whom the *basanos* evidence is disadvantageous should discredit the entire procedure (*Rhet.* 1376b31–1377a7). But if we consider the *basanos* at the level not of the individual speaker and his tactical advantage but of Athenian juridical discourse as a whole, the persistent contradiction between the assertions of truth and the acknowledgments of non-truth requires further explanation. Throughout forensic oratory, the *basanos* is articulated in the double form of a disavowal, which acknowledges an unpleasant fact in the very process of denying it: "I know very well, but just the same . . . ".[31] I know very well that slaves will lie under torture in order to end their suffering; I know that they might lie out of hatred for their masters or in the hope of earning their freedom. But just the same, "there is nothing more reliable and true than a *basanos*;" no one has ever lied under torture; the *basanos* always elicits the truth. This contradiction expresses juridical discourse's uneasy relation not only to the truth but also to the violence by which it is obtained. What truth about legal violence does the *basanos* simultaneously recognize (I know very well . . .) and deny (but all the same . . .)?

Page duBois locates the *basanos* within a Western philosophical tradition that views truth as "always elsewhere, always outside the realm of ordinary human experience" and retrievable only through violence.[32] In forensic oratory, the *basanos* is represented as access to a "truth of the matter" outside of and otherwise inaccessible to the law: the truth of the original criminal event. In Antiphon 5, for example, the crime is consistently described as unknowable. A man has been killed and the corpse has vanished without a trace (*ēphanisthē*, 26), "neither any visible blood nor any sign of it on land or on the boat" (45; cf. 27). The murderer has also vanished. The prosecution's strongest argument against him, says the accused, is the fact that the man who actually committed the murder is unknown (*aphanēs*, 64; cf. 66). I

[31] The paraphrase is Octave Mannoni's (1969: 9–33). Freud associates disavowal closely with the fetish, which both acknowledges and denies the woman's lack of a penis: Freud 1961 [1927]; cf. Žižek 1991: 241–53; Copjec 2002: 222. DuBois 2003: 10 remarks on the disavowal and fetishism at work in scholarly discussions of ancient slavery; cf. 118. See also Bassi (in press), who sees in the ancient ambivalence toward the *basanos* an illustration of the "incoherent logic" that makes pain the price of information.

[32] DuBois 1991: 105–6; cf. 49.

can guess his identity no better than you jurors, he says, since I am no more guilty of the crime than you and "it is difficult for the man who didn't do it to offer guesses about unknowns" (*tōn aphanōn*, 65). If you want the truth, he continues, ask the perpetrator himself (65), for only the criminal knows the truth about the crime. All others – the speaker, his opponent, the jurors – must rely on *sēmeia* (signs) and *tekmēria* (evidence) to lead them back to that invisible crime scene. Among these signs is the *basanos* of the slave who supposedly assisted in the murder – or, rather, it would be a sign had his opponents not extracted false testimony from the slave and then killed him, making both him and the truth he might have told "disappear" (*ēphanisan*, 38). Despite this malicious miscarriage of justice, the speaker implies that when properly executed the *basanos* can reveal the invisible truth of the unwitnessed event. That truth both requires and justifies violence. The defendant rails against the "lawless violence" (*biaiotēs kai paranomia*, 8) of his opponents in killing the slave, but only because in so doing they have made him inaccessible to the normal, lawful violence of interrogation.[33]

Forensic oratory marks the truth of the *basanos* as external to the law: it is located in the body of a legal non-person and extracted outside of the courtroom.[34] It is also explicitly contrasted to juridical discourse's two other primary modes of truth-production: *logoi* (speeches) and *martures* (the testimony of free witnesses). In oratory's ubiquitous contrast between *erga* (deeds) and *logoi* (words), the *basanos* is arrayed with the former against the latter. Lycurgus equates the examination of slaves with "trusting in *erga* more than *logoi*" (1.29). Unlike jurors, who are easily seduced by emotional arguments, slaves on the rack cannot be "led astray by clever manipulations of the argument" (1.32). Likewise, Demosthenes charges that his opponent Aphobus buries the truth through his speeches and refuses to uncover it through a *basanos* (29.5): the *basanos* would reveal what *logoi* conceal.[35] The *basanos* is also regularly contrasted to the testimony of free witnesses.[36]

[33] The *biaiotēs* he refers to in §8 is actually the summary arrest his opponents used against him. But the theme is picked up later in the claim that by murdering the slave, they took the law into their own hands, usurping the rights of the court and the vote of the city (47). On the *basanos* in this case, see Thür 1977: 48–57; Gagarin 1989: 57–78.

[34] Dem. 45.16: it is not possible to *basanizein* in front of you. Aesch. 2.126, where Aeschines offers to hand over his slaves to a public official who will torture them "in front of you," is taken by Mirhady (1996: 121) as a "mock challenge" (and one that his opponent, of course, refuses). Contra, Thür 1977: 190–92.

[35] Cf. Dem. 30.35: "not only *logoi* but *basanoi*"; Lys. 7.34: "a proof stronger than his words or my deeds." Johnstone 1999: 87–91; Mirhady 2000b: 67.

[36] Mirhady 1996: 124–26, 2000b: 65–66; cf. Thür 1977: 209–11. Thür 2005 offers a useful synopsis of the role of witnesses in Athenian law.

It is an open secret in forensic speeches that witnesses may lie on the stand to support a friend or harm an enemy. Speakers frequently admit the general principle while denying its validity in their own case, and the admission is institutionalized in the form of the *dikē pseudomarturiōn*, the prosecution for false witnessing.[37] But whereas witnesses may lie to help a friend, the *basanos* does not lie. When you really want to get to the truth of a matter, says Demosthenes (in a passage quoted above), you don't rely on the testimony of free men but on the *basanos* of slaves. "For some witnesses have been found in the past to have borne false testimony. But no one investigated under torture has ever been proved to have spoken something untrue under investigation" (Dem. 30.37; cf. Is. 8.12).

Oratory thus situates the truth of the *basanos* outside of its own discursive boundaries and sets its truth against that produced by and within the trial. In this vein, we might imagine the violence of the *basanos* as a labor of self-transcendent will-to-knowledge, the painful exertion by which the law reaches for a truth beyond itself, its violence justified by the purity of the truth obtained. It is not clear, however, that that truth ever actually was obtained. The *basanos* is always treated in the counterfactual mode, as a truth that would have been produced, that would have been unimpeachable, if only the opponent had accepted the challenge. But the opponent never does accept the challenge. In fact, we know of no undisputed case in which a *basanos* was actually carried out. It is possible that this is just because in those instances the dispute did not come to trial. But it is also possible that the challenge was actually designed to be refused. Thus Michael Gagarin views the *basanos* as a "legal fiction" designed not to obtain evidence but to allow a litigant to shape the issues to his own advantage and to introduce the evidence of slaves, otherwise inadmissible, into the court.[38] In a similar vein, Steven Johnstone argues that the most important elements of the *basanos* were precisely the challenge and its refusal and their rhetorical manipulation in court. The representation of the *basanos* as the source of an extra-discursive truth, of *erga* not *logoi*, is thus disingenuous, a misrecognition (in Johnstone's word) of an immanent truth produced by the trial itself as "an effect of its discussion in the rhetorical context of litigation."[39]

[37] Ant. 6.28; Dem. 29.22–23, 47.8; Is. 4.12–14, 9.8; Scafuro 1994; D. Cohen 1995a: 107–12. As Humphreys 1985b: 350–56 has shown, the purpose of witnesses in Athenian law was not to establish an objective truth but to show that the litigant has the support of his family and community; thus "witnesses were expected to be partisan" (351). Cf. Gernet 1955: 83–102.

[38] Gagarin 1996; see also Gagarin 1997: 22; Thür 1977: 205–32; Hunter 1994: 71.

[39] Johnstone 1999: 70–92. The quotation is on p. 85. See also Thür 1977: 233–61; Carey 1989: 137 *ad* Lys. 7.35; Mirhady 1996; Allen 2000a: 104–5.

Pursuing this productive line of reasoning, we might see in the violence of the *basanos* not a will-to-knowledge but, on the contrary, a will-to-ignorance, law's repression or negation of its own mechanisms of truth production and the violence they entail. In the *basanos*, violence mediates law's relation to truth. But truth also mediates law's relation to violence, as the law's internal force is legitimated by a triple displacement: first, onto a sanctioned object (the body of a slave); second, out of the courts (as the *basanos* is always represented as occurring elsewhere); and third, into the fantasmatic sphere of the non-event, an event much imagined but never manifestly enacted. This overdetermined denial is then sealed with a final transformation: legal violence now goes under the name of pure and inaccessible truth.

Through the *basanos*' fetishized truth juridical discourse repudiates (and, in the contradictory idiom of disavowal, also admits) the force of its own rhetoric (*logoi*) and sociality (*martures*). The contrast between the *basanos* and *logos* denies the force of rhetoric itself, a source of perpetual anxiety for the Athenians. Gorgias, the first teacher of rhetoric in Athens, figures *logos* as analogous to *bia* (force) and its persuasive effect on its listeners as a kind of compulsion (*anankē*).[40] This concern about rhetorical compulsion recurs throughout forensic oratory: the jurors are urged to resist the pressure of the opponent's words, not to be subjugated by his arguments or cowed by the vigor of his speech.[41] In the *basanos*, the violence of rhetorical persuasion – the compulsion of citizens under the aegis of the law – is displaced onto the body of a slave, a natural and legitimate object of *anankē* and *bia*. In Lycurgus' contrast between the *basanos* and forensic *logoi*, slaves' truth is incontrovertible because they, unlike the jurors, cannot be led astray (*paragagein*) by a clever argument or charmed (*psukhagōgēsai*) by words (1.32–33). Truth is the result not of persuasive coercion of free citizen jurors (we know very well that happens, but all the same . . .) but, much less problematically, of the physical torture of slaves.

If the *basanos*' contrast to *logoi* allows juridical discourse to disavow the violence of its own rhetoric, the contrast to *martures* denies the law's complicity with social violence. The dishonesty of witnesses, as we saw in the previous section, is part of the broader social agonism in which

[40] *Encomium to Helen* 12. Persuasive rhetoric was imagined as enslaving its audience (e.g. Thuc. 3.38.5–7); in Greek, to be persuaded is to obey (*peithesthai*) and to listen is to be subordinate (*hupēkoos*). See Hesk 2000: 202–91; Wohl 2002: 73–123. Roisman 2004 discusses the relation between speaker and audience as a power struggle; cf. Wallace 2004: 223–27; Balot 2004: 242–46.

[41] Aesch. 3.206, for instance, compares the trial to a boxing match between speaker and audience. Defendants sometimes represent the prosecution as a form of violence against them comparable to the crime itself: see Johnstone 1999: 111–13; Christ (in press b).

the courts participated: in Demosthenes 54 the concerted false testimony of Conon's *hetaireia* threatens to import their brutal criminality into the trial.[42] The law tries to forestall this by binding witnesses with oaths that call down destruction on them and their families if they lie. Antiphon suggests that the oath is to a free man what the *basanos* is to a slave, a form of *anankē* compelling him to tell the truth (6.25). But the necessity of the oath is self-imposed and its terms set by the litigant himself (thus Ariston can argue that Conon and his gang make and break oaths so casually that the oath avows nothing but his shameless dishonesty, Dem. 54.40). The only one who can force a citizen to speak the truth is himself, whereas slaves tell the truth even if they will die for it, as Antiphon remarks, "for a present compulsion (*anankē*) is more forceful than an anticipated one" (6.25). In the *basanos*, then, law's *anankē* finds its proper object, a body that can legitimately be compelled.[43]

Like the original *basanos* – a touchstone used to distinguish genuine from counterfeit metal – the juridical *basanos* functions as a touchstone for legal violence, vouching for its validity and legitimacy and repudiating its base imperfections. At the same time, though, it also functions as a philosopher's stone, transmuting the denied violence of law into the familiar and sanctioned brutality of master against slave. Law's force is turned to the socially useful end of reinforcing the all-important distinction between slave and free.[44] Conversely, that oppressive hierarchy – the everyday violence of a social system that licensed some men to own, exploit, and torture others – is suborned to authorize and naturalize the violence of the legal system. Law's internal violence is in this way magically transformed into the pure gold of a socially unquestionable truth.

Finally, this alchemy allows juridical discourse to deny its own power to define and impose the truth, including the truth as to what counts as violence. What is perhaps most disturbing to modern readers about the *basanos* is how little the ancient texts seem to be disturbed by it. They debate

42 Fisher 1999: 82–83; D. Cohen 1995a: 111–12, 129. Cf. Dem. 21.139 on Meidias' "mercenaries" and "*hetaireia* of witnesses." In Dem. 47.53, the same brother and brother-in-law who bear false witness for Theophemus (according to the speaker) also assist him in his violent and lawless collection of the settlement from the case. The speaker in Lysias 30 claims that the defendant's co-litigants have barged into the court in order to deceive the jurors and seize the opportunity to do whatever they want in the future (34). See also Dem. 58.7, where the witnesses are threatened by the defense and compelled by the prosecution.

43 Mirhady 2000b: 65–66 suggests that one assumption underlying the contrast between the torture of slaves and evidence under oath of free witnesses was that "while a free person valued his own future and that of his family, a slave could value only his body, and only for the moment" (66).

44 DuBois 1991: 41, 2003: 105–6; Hunter 1992. Gagarin 1996: 17 remarks that even if the *basanos* was a legal fiction it still had the ideological impact of "reminding slaves that their bodies were always available for the physical domination of their masters."

its veracity and reliability, but they never debate its ethics. In general, it is simply not considered a problem.[45] Indeed, the *basanos* seems not even to be recognized as violence. The *basanos* as a fetish of truth thus occludes the violence that the *basanos* as a practice (real or imaginary) enacts, the violence by which juridical discourse decides whose pain matters. The double action of disavowal both acknowledges that violence (I know the law operates in a field of pain and death) and represses it (but all the same, it is merely the pain and death of a slave). The casual cruelty of the *basanos* – which is all the more striking if it was never actually enacted – expresses the force of that denial, the exertion of holding together two contradictory beliefs about legal violence, united in the body of a slave under the counterfeit name of pure truth.

*

The *basanos* represents an attempt to purify the law of its violence by displacing it onto the body of a slave, where it no longer appears as violence. Its contradictory logic makes what to us is the most obviously brutal practice in Athenian law into a sign of that law's non-violence. But this contradiction proves hard to maintain in practice. The violence repressed in the *basanos* returns in forensic oratory, creating textual fissures around the question of legal violence and its victims. The remainder of this section examines one such instance, Antiphon 1 (*Against the Stepmother*). The speaker's father was killed when he was just a boy, poisoned, he claims, by his stepmother; now he has reached adulthood and is prosecuting her for murder. His opponents are his half-brothers. The speaker's case rests on two acts of torture: a challenge to interrogate the family slaves (which his opponents refuse) and the torture of a concubine who administered the drug on the stepmother's instructions and whose testimony may have formed the basis of the speaker's narrative. The first is handled in the casual, matter-of-fact manner typical of forensic oratory's treatment of the *basanos*. The latter, however, receives unexpected elaboration. The speaker shares with this concubine an unacknowledged bond of sympathy that makes it difficult for the text to naturalize her pain and death as an unexceptional part of legal procedure. Pity for the victim in turn dissolves the distinctions upon which the *basanos*, the speech, and indeed Athenian law itself are built, the distinction between free and slave and between legal persons and non-persons. The speaker, it turns out, may have more at risk than he recognizes in the torture he so casually proposes.

[45] Sternberg 2006: 146–73.

The speech opens with the trope of legal compulsion. The young speaker is on the horns of a dilemma: either he must disregard his father's dying command to avenge his murder or he must go to court against his own relatives, "the last people I should quarrel with" (1). The speech dramatizes this choice in an explicitly tragic mode. The speaker calls his stepmother a "Clytemnestra" (17). This allusion to the *Oresteia* makes the speaker an Orestes who, under the yoke of necessity, must kill his (step)mother to avenge his father. His vengeance is executed with a legal prosecution not a sword, but the case hints at the tragic effect of even such legitimate violence and leaves it uncertain whether this Orestes, like his tragic model, will find justice in an Athenian court of law.[46]

The speaker has a double burden of proof. He must show, first, that even though his stepmother did not herself administer the drug, as the mastermind behind the act she is liable for its results and, second, that she knew those results would be fatal. The defense will probably concede that the stepmother did plan the administering of the drug, but will argue that she thought it was a love potion, and therefore the death was unintentional. The Aristotelian *Magna Moralia* mentions a similar case in which the woman was acquitted because she thought the poison was a love potion and therefore did not kill her husband deliberately (1188b29–38). But the speaker here disallows this defense, claiming that the stepmother killed his father deliberately and voluntarily, "by plotting and planning" (*ex epiboulēs kai proboulēs*, 3). Her active agency is contrasted to the passivity of her accomplice, the concubine who "followed the instructions of Clytemnestra, my opponent's mother" (*Klutaimēstras tēs toutou mētros*, 17). It is also contrasted to the "involuntary" death of her victim. "He died involuntarily (*akousiōs*) by malice aforethought (*ek proboulēs*); she killed intentionally (*hekousiōs*) and deliberately (*ek pronoias*)" (5).[47] This imprecise theory of liability, which conveniently obscures the distinction between volition and

[46] That the reference to Clytemnestra is tragic and not just mythic is suggested by the tragic language and thought that peppers the speech, e.g. the image of *dikē* as a helmsman (13), the irony of a prayer that was to remain unfulfilled (19), and phrases like *atheōs kai akleōs* ("impiously and infamously," 21). Due 1980: 20–21 notes further tragic echoes in the speech; cf. Bers 1994: 189, Gagarin 2002: 147. There were many tragic versions of this myth, of course, but since Aeschylus' *Oresteia* is paradigmatic for all of them – and since it explicitly situates the myth in a judicial context – I take it as paradigmatic here, too. I explore Antiphon 1's tragic allusions in Wohl (in press).

[47] Cf. 26: "She killed intentionally (*hekousiōs*) and planned his death (*bouleusasa ton thanaton*); he died involuntarily (*akousiōs*) and violently (*biaiōs*)." On the complex question of liability in this case see MacDowell 1963: 62–63; Carawan 1998: 216–50. Gagarin 2002: 146–52 argues that the issue is not intent but planning, that is, agency not state of mind. Cf. Carawan 2000, esp. 211–15, who proposes that knowledge of lethal effect, and not the intent to kill, determined liability in Athenian law. In this case, knowledge, agency and intent are (purposely) hard to disentangle. I return to the problem of intentionality in Athenian legal discourse in Chapter 3.

premeditation, is clarified by the tragic allusion. When the speaker calls his stepmother Clytemnestra he evokes the deliberate scheming and unapologetic intent of Aeschylus' anti-heroine, as well as the ignominious suffering of her unsuspecting victim. He also appeals to the precedent of a prior judgment: Orestes' conviction and summary execution of his mother, and his ultimate acquittal for this act in the mythic court of the Areopagus.

This charge of "plotting and planning" is supported by a *basanos* – or would have been, had his opponents accepted his challenge. The speaker has demanded the family slaves for torture and represents their evidence as hard proof of his case, as they would have testified to a prior instance in which the stepmother had been caught drugging his father (9). But, as is so often true, the refusal of the *basanos* offers the speaker more ammunition than the *basanos* itself ever could. Not only does it allow the speaker to introduce his (unsupported) claim that the stepmother had tried to poison his father before and to explain away his lack of evidence for that claim. It also allows him to insinuate that his half-brother is aware of his mother's guilt. His opponent has sworn that he knows for sure that his mother is innocent (6, 8, 28). But his refusal of the *basanos* obviously refutes his oath. "Since he was not willing to conduct an examination of the facts, how is it possible for him to know about things he was not willing to find out about?" (7; cf. 6, 8). Through the speaker's manipulation of the *basanos*, the half-brother's asserted knowledge that his mother did not kill his father becomes a non-knowledge that she did kill him, a non-knowledge sustained not by a non-event but by a will not-to-know. That will is in turn proof that his half-brothers care more about exonerating their murderous mother than avenging their father's death (5, 21, 23): indeed, in defending his murderer they themselves become his murderer (2, 4). Conversely, his own proposal of the interrogation, he says, "is just proof that I am pursuing my father's murderer properly and justly" (*orthōs kai dikaiōs*, 10). In this family drama, the *basanos* is a touchstone of legitimacy: it is a sure sign of this Orestes' filial devotion and proof that he is the better son to their dead father.[48]

Like all forensic oratory, this speech treats the *basanos* as a simple matter of truth and the will to reveal it: pain plays no part. The only force the

[48] Gagarin proposes that the case, brought long after the murder, when the speaker had grown to adulthood (30), may have been motivated by an inheritance dispute (1997: 106, 2002: 152). Cf. Carawan 1998: 220–21, 228–29. The speaker invites the jurors to join him in his act of filial piety, for by avenging his dead father, they will be avenging "your laws, which you inherited from the gods and your forefathers" (3; cf. 24). They will also themselves become part of the speaker's family (4), replacing the treacherous half-brothers.

speaker recognizes in this process is that imposed upon himself, compelled to bring this suit against his will (*ēnankasan*, 2; *anankaiōs ekhei*, 1), and upon his opponents, who would be forced by the *basanos* to stick to accusations that are true (*hē basanos anankazoi ta gegonota katēgorein*, 10). Indeed, the speaker even denies that the tortured slaves would be under compulsion from him. He proposed writing down his questions and letting others ask them so that the slaves "would not be forced (*anankazomenoi*) to say what I asked them" (10). But the violence that is denied in this *basanos* is undeniable in another, the torture of the concubine for information about or as punishment for the poisoning. If the torture of the family slaves would have proved the stepmother's knowledge of the drug's effect, the torture of the concubine will prove her liability: although the stepmother did not administer the drug, she "planned and plotted" the crime.[49]

The narrative portion of the speech sets the scene. The speaker's father was entertaining a friend named Philoneus, who had with him his concubine (*pallakē*), whom he was about to abandon and send to a brothel (14). While the two gentlemen dined, the stepmother befriended the *pallakē*. As the speaker tells it, the stepmother took advantage of the girl's desperate situation, getting her to administer the lethal drug on the promise that it would secure them both the love of their men. He reports the conversation between the two women and the concubine's agreement to perform the deed: the stepmother "said that she had discovered a way and her [the *pallakē*'s] job was to to carry it out. Then she asked her if she was willing to serve her, and she promised she would" (15). The stepmother is convicted by her own (reported) words of having plotted the deed that killed her husband. The *pallakē*, who is probably a slave, is merely the assistant: she performs a "service" for the stepmother and ministers to her commands (*hupēretēma*, 15; *diakonēsai*, 16; *diakonousan*, 17).[50]

49 Gagarin 1990b shows convincingly that there was no separate legal category of *bouleusis* (planning), and that those who planned a murder were charged simply with *phonos*, homicide: "planning is treated simply as one way of committing homicide, like poisoning, and it is considered just as serious as the actual killing" (92). Hence the setting of this case in the Areopagus, which heard cases of intentional homicide. On planning and the rhetoric of conspiracy in the speech, see also Roisman 2006: 11–13.

50 Gagarin 1997: 115 *ad* 16 notes that the stepmother is the subject of all the main verbs in this narrative, and the *pallakē* either the object or subject of subordinate verbs. "This reinforces the impression that the stepmother is the primary agent, the *pallakē* her subordinate." The status of this *pallakē* is disputed, but I assume she is a slave. Bushala's (1969) argument that she is a free woman is disputed by Carey 1988. Even if, as Bushala claims, many *pallakai* were free non-citizens, it is unlikely that a free woman would be sold to a brothel. Cf. Din. 1.23.7, where an individual is sentenced to death for putting a (presumably free) Olynthian woman in a brothel. On the place of the *pallakē* in the Athenian family, see Mossé 1991; Patterson 1991.

The speaker's source for this crucial conversation – if he is not merely inventing it – may be the *pallakē* herself, who after Philoneus' death was tortured and then handed over to the public executioner (*tōi dēmokoinōi trokhistheisa paredothē*, 20). This torture is probably not, strictly speaking, a *basanos*. The speaker mentions no challenge or procedural negotiations and thus is likely imagining the torture not as interrogation of the *pallakē* as a witness but as her punishment as an accomplice.[51] Still, if the *pallakē* is the source for the women's conversation her penal torture becomes a de facto *basanos*. This narrative, moreover, contains precisely the sort of information the speaker expected to procure through torture of his stepmother's slaves: information about the private affairs inside the *oikos*, overheard conversations, admissions of motive (9). If she is the source of the narrative, then the *pallakē* is a tool of the speaker no less than of his stepmother, performing an indispensable service for his forensic argument.

The speaker uses her, then swiftly disposes of her. After the deaths of Philoneus and his father,

> the woman who assisted in them got the rewards she deserved, although she was not responsible (*hē men diakonēsasa ekhei ta epikheira hōn axia ēn, ouden aitia ousa*): she was tortured on the wheel (*trokhistheisa*) and then handed over to the executioner. But the woman who is responsible (*aitia*), who devised the plan and executed it, will soon get hers too, if you and the gods are willing. (20)

The account of the *pallakē*'s death is brief and unsentimental. The torture – described in a single passive participle – is doubly motivated at the level of the event (by her participation in the crime) and of the narrative (by the information she provides). Likewise, execution would be the normal fate of a slave implicated in the murder of her master. At the same time, her death serves as an argument a fortiori against the stepmother: if the mere assistant, who "was not responsible," deserved death, so much more does the woman who planned it and "is responsible." The *pallakē*'s torture and death are thus a fitting end to the role she plays in the speaker's argument. She exits the stage with little fanfare and no choral lament.

And yet this death scene is perhaps not as straightforward as it at first seems. Its very compression creates a striking contradiction: the woman "got the rewards she deserved although she was not responsible" (*hē men diakonēsasa ekhei ta epikheira hōn axia ēn, ouden aitia ousa*, 20). On the one hand, this sentence is legible within the terms of the speaker's argument. The *pallakē* is not responsible because the stepmother is; nonetheless she

[51] There is disagreement on this point: see Thür 1977: 21 n. 42; Hunter 1992: 283.

deserved death as the agent – however subordinate or unwitting – of a murder. On the other hand, the juxtaposition of innocence (*ouden aitia*) and deserved punishment (*epikheira . . . axia*) is jarring, almost paradoxical. In its compression, this sentence takes on the doubleness of disavowal, the logic of the *basanos*. I know she was not responsible, but all the same she deserved to be tortured and killed.

The discordance of this passage is a direct product of the forensic argument. In order to make his stepmother bear sole responsibility, the speaker is forced to kill a woman whom he represents as not responsible. Further, if the speaker's narrative of the preliminaries to the poisoning – the conversation between the two women and the dominant role of the stepmother – is based on the testimony of the *pallakē*, then his brief also requires her torture. He requires her both to be innocent and to be tortured, and these contradictory argumentative pressures result in the paradox of the undeserving *pallakē*'s deserved death. The contradiction is sustained by the compression of the account and also by the woman's status. Deserved or not, the torture and death of a slave do not merit comment or arouse pity.

What makes this death scene so remarkable, though, is precisely that the *pallakē* does arouse pity. Occasional sympathetic glimpses into her thinking humanize her. Being placed in a brothel was a horrifying proposition compared to the relatively comfortable and secure life of a *pallakē*; the stepmother calls it an injustice (*adikeisthai*, 15).[52] Therefore when the plan was proposed to her, the speaker says, the girl agreed "immediately, I think" (*takhista hōs oimai*, 16). This aside, as Gagarin notes, suggests "sympathy for the poor *pallakē*" by imagining the desperation of her situation and her gratitude for what she thinks is a means of salvation.[53] Her delusion is the source of further pathos: when she poured the drug into the men's drinks, she gave more to Philoneus, "thinking she was being clever because the more she gave him the more he would love her. For she didn't yet know that she had been deceived by my stepmother, until she was already in trouble" (19). The girl's simple reasoning becomes a tragic blindness: she will understand what she has done only too late, and her wisdom will come through suffering. These hints of sympathetic focalization resonate in the death scene's execution of an innocent woman. If the logic of the speaker's argument requires that the *pallakē* be *ouden aitia* and Athenian homicide law requires that she be punished nonetheless, her sympathetic

[52] Davidson 1997: 83–91 paints a vivid picture of life in the brothels and suggests that Philoneus' *pallakē* murdered him to avoid this dire fate. Cf. duBois 2003: 112, who sees in the murder "traces of ingenious resistance."

[53] Gagarin 1997: 115 *ad* 16.

portrayal adds a tragic pathos to the collision of these opposing necessities and makes it difficult to accept the violence of her death as blithely as the text depicts it.

That violence becomes all the more disturbing if, as seems probable, the speaker is himself the son of a *pallakē*. As Gagarin observes, the half-brothers are older than him and (since their mother was still married to his father at the time of the murder) he must therefore be the child of his father's concubine, presumably a free non-citizen, although it is impossible to know.[54] This concubine, the speaker's mother, may herself be obliquely involved in the erotic tragedy the case reports. In her conversation with Philoneus' *pallakē* preceding the poisoning, the stepmother sympathizes with the wrong (*adikia*) the *pallakē* was about to suffer at Philoneus' hand and says that "she too had been wronged (*adikoito*) by our father" (15). Gagarin suggests that the *adikia* she suffered, and for which she now takes revenge, is the affair with the speaker's mother.[55] The speaker never mentions his mother. He presents himself as an Orestes avenging his father by killing his stepmother. In the process, though, he also "kills" his own mother, who is silently erased from his text. In this way he erases his personal investment in the erotic designs of his stepmother and in the tragedy of Philoneus' *pallakē* who (if we accept this reconstruction) executes the stepmother's vengeance for that other *pallakē*, thereby becoming the immediate cause for a murder of which the speaker's own mother is the remote cause.

This suppressed maternal legacy implicates the speaker more deeply than he can admit in the feminine drama that culminates in his father's death and complicates the speech's construction of guilt and innocence through an unacknowledged bond of sympathy. Like the *Oresteia*, its tragic paradigm, this speech tries to reduce a complex domestic drama to a black and white vote between the father and the mother.[56] Near the end of the speech, the speaker recasts the issues of the case as a straightforward alternative: "whom should one pity more, the dead man or the murderer?" (25). The answer, he says, is obvious. The stepmother deserves no pity from the jurors because she killed her husband without pity. "It is more appropriate to have pity for involuntary suffering (*tois akousiois pathēmasi*) than for crimes and injustices committed intentionally and with forethought" (27). Through this strict allocation of juridical pity, the speaker reduces the case to a simple choice with a simple answer. The dead father deserves

[54] Gagarin 1997: 104. [55] Gagarin 1997: 114 *ad* 15. See also Carawan 1998: 220–21.
[56] See especially Zeitlin 1984.

the jury's pity; the stepmother does not.[57] But where does this leave the *pallakē*, whose "involuntary suffering" earns a quiet sympathy in the speech? Like the father, she was an unwitting victim of the stepmother. Both are described as tragic figures who "do not know anything until they are in the midst of the evil itself, and only then understand the disaster they are in" (29; cf. 19). The speaker sympathizes with this concubine but can make no positive space for that sympathy within the parameters he sets on judicial pity. Instead his sympathy comes out in the compressed and conflicted account of her death. In this trial's catharsis of pity and fear, the "involuntary suffering" of a *pallakē*'s death constitutes a minor tragedy of its own. Even Orestes hesitated before striking the breast that nursed him.

What wisdom might be gained from the concubine's suffering? If the jurors' pity is extended to her, the entire case looks very different. For example, we might revisit the conversation between the concubine and the stepmother, a conversation used to establish the latter's guilt and perhaps discovered through the former's torture. In this conversation, the stepmother uses the language of law to win over the concubine: she "perceived that the *pallakē* was about to be wronged (*adikeisthai*) by Philoneus" and told her "that she too had been wronged (*adikoito*) by our father" (15). This language transports us to a fantasmatic counter-jurisdiction, a notional "court of love" where women can sue for erotic betrayal.[58] Here the father and his friend are tried for their *adikia* against these women and found guilty. The women, meanwhile, are acquitted on all counts: theirs is not a cold-blooded murder but an act of erotic self-help gone awry. In this courtroom, the stepmother is not a Clytemnestra but a Deianira, the sympathetic tragic heroine who poisons her husband Heracles with the drug she hopes will restore his love, and kills herself when she discovers her lethal error. Or even if she is a Clytemnestra, this jury will remember that Clytemnestra, too, had her reasons – among them her husband's *pallakē* – and represented her crime as an act of justice. Needless to say, this is not the court in which this case is tried. Yet this alternate juridical universe becomes imaginable, I think, once we recognize the speaker's maternal connection to the erotic drama that unfolds there.

57 On the appeal for juridical pity, see Johnstone 1999: 109–25 (who stresses its differences from tragic pity). Konstan 2001: 27–48 argues convincingly that the Greeks reserved pity for undeserved suffering. See further Konstan 2000, and Sternberg 2006, for whom the *basanos* marks the limit of Athenian empathy.

58 Goodrich 1996 studies the medieval "courts of love" as a "minor jurisprudence," a rejected mode of legal knowledge that forms part of an alternate genealogy of law. See also Goodrich 2002. Johnstone 1998, 1999: 53–54 shows how in Athens disputes between husband and wife (or disputes involving other individuals excluded from legal competency) had to be represented as disputes between citizens in order to be brought to court.

The speaker's repressed maternal genealogy also opens up another possible juridical horizon, for if the jurors can pity the torture of an innocent concubine, can they also pity the "involuntary suffering" of those other potential victims of torture, the family slaves? The speaker, as we have seen, makes the *basanos* a touchstone of his own legitimacy and proof that he is carrying out his father's final injunction to avenge him. He returns to this theme at the end of the speech where he describes the deathbed scene (29–30). Victims of violent crime, he says, call their friends and relatives to them before they die, if they are able, telling them who was responsible and exhorting them to avenge the crime; so his father did with him when he was a child (or because he was his son, *k'amoi paidi onti*, 30). Those who don't have time to do this write down what they know and call their slaves as witnesses, showing them the murderer. My father, the speaker repeats, showed me and laid his command on me, not on his slaves (30). The speaker offers two genealogies of vengeance, one a legacy from father to son, the other transmitted through slaves who would reveal that information under torture. His knowledge of his stepmother's guilt is his paternal inheritance and he describes it as the antithesis of a *basanos*: my father told me, his son (*pais*), not his slave (*pais*).[59]

This oddly insistent contrast between son and slave again makes the slave's truth – now the truth the slave doesn't know – a proof of the speaker's legitimacy. But that contrast looks rather too insistent if the speaker is the son of a *pallakē*. Which sort of *pais* does that make him? Legally, of course, he must be a free man, or else he could not bring this case. And yet his maternal lineage introduces a fundamental uncertainty about his status. Some *pallakai* were slaves, like Philoneus' *pallakē* in this speech, and only one step removed from a common prostitute. Others were free, possibly even citizens, and lived lives virtually indistinguishable from those of legitimate wives. The ambiguous status of the *pallakē* posed the danger that the son of a non-citizen mother, in the worst case even a slave mother, might pass for an Athenian citizen.[60] While there is no suggestion that this is the situation in Antiphon 1 – if his opponents were leveling such serious accusations the speaker would surely counter them – the speaker's

[59] Carawan 1998: 241 suggests that this pointed contrast alludes to a *basanos* challenge by his opponents to ascertain what his dying father said and to whom, a challenge he clearly declined.

[60] The status of the children of *pallakai* is much disputed: see Sealey 1984a; Mossé 1991; Patterson 1991; Ogden 1996: 157–63; and cf. the discussion in Chapter 6 below. It is possible that they were barred from full citizen status but were able to claim an inheritance. Roisman 2005: 39 lists cases where children of *pallakai* claim inheritances. It is also possible that Pericles' Citizenship Law of 451/0, which made citizenship depend upon the citizen status of both parents, was relaxed at the end of the fifth century (when this speech was probably written) in response to the Peloponnesian War's depletion of the citizen population.

maternity means that his own civic status is not above question. But if the speaker cannot confidently maintain the difference between a *pais* and a *pais* then the servile bodies he wants tortured in order to prove his filial piety are not so clearly different from his own. And once the possibility of this distant kinship is admitted then it is no longer possible to take for granted the legitimacy of either the speaker or the *basanos*.

In this speech the contradictions that the *basanos* holds together threaten to come apart, splitting both the speech and the speaker and turning the argument against itself.[61] The *basanos*' logic of disavowal prevents this text from asking the sort of questions I have put to it, questions about the speaker's maternal connection to the crime he prosecutes and the difference between a slave and a son, about the limits of juridical pity and the legitimacy of legal violence. But these questions are latent, I think, in the paradox of the undeserving *pallakē*'s deserved death. In that death the *pallakē* becomes a tragic Cassandra, the locus of truths the speech – and judicial discourse – cannot or will not hear. Indeed, the speech's allusions to tragedy, a genre that routinely evoked pity for "involuntary suffering," obliquely highlight that juridical deafness and gesture toward an alternate jurisdiction in which the miserable fate of tortured slaves or a dead concubine might elicit at least sympathy, if not recompense. The *pallakē*'s contradictory death thus exposes the parameters Athenian jurisprudence placed on justice. It enacts Athenian law's disavowal of its internal violence, its refusal of the ethical challenge of the *basanos* and rejection of the difficult truth it might otherwise reveal: that the violence the law disowns through the torture of slaves may turn out to be (as the speaker puts it, 13) "an evil in its own house."

AT THE LIMITS OF THE LAW (DEMOSTHENES 47)

The *basanos*, I argued, serves to disavow law's violence, not least its power to define what counts as violence. But the *basanos*' logic of disavowal obviously requires a prior negation, the foreclosure of certain people from legal personhood.[62] This is perhaps the least visible, but in some

[61] Copjec (2002: 222–24) posits that in fetishism the subject tries to sustain the unity and coherence of the law by taking its divisions upon him or herself. This speech suggests such a dynamic: the contradictions that surround the torture of the concubine – I know she was not responsible but all the same she deserved her fate – allow it to maintain its faith in the legitimacy of law's violence, but at the cost of the speaker's and the speech's coherence.

[62] "Disavowal" translates Freud's Verneinung (negation), which indicates a repression of an intellectually conceivable idea from conscious thought; "foreclosure" translates Verwerfung, the repudiation of an idea from the symbolic order altogether. See Hyppolite 1988; Lacan 1993: 12–13. Goodrich 1995 and Felman 2002 offer particularly illuminating analyses of law's repressions and their return within legal discourse.

ways the most pernicious cruelty perpetrated by the law. Demosthenes 47 *Against Euergus and Mnesibulus for Bearing False Witness* illustrates that foreclosure. Like Demosthenes 54, this case depicts the law as an arena for feuding citizens, but unlike that speech, this one also acknowledges the terrible cruelty upon which this social agonism is founded, a cruelty perpetrated not against the body and honor of the citizen, but against victims not even recognized as such. This speech is an exegetical text: in it the legal authorities themselves lay down the boundaries of the law and mandate the foreclosure that grounds legal discourse as a whole. It is also a haunted text, in which the ghostly presence of those the law excludes lingers in the rhetoric of the case, frustrating the law's desire for closure and marking the limit of its aspiration to justice.

The speaker, as he tells it, was selected to serve as trierarch, a liturgy (a special public duty imposed on wealthy Athenians) that made him responsible for outfitting naval vessels. As part of his office, he had to retrieve equipment removed from the shipyard by a previous trierarch, Theophemus. The speaker went to Theophemus' house to obtain either an inventory of the equipment or securities against its return, and in the course of events he and Theophemus came to blows. Theophemus subsequently brought a suit for *aikeia* (battery) against the speaker – outrageously, the speaker says, since Theophemus threw the first punch. In that trial, Theophemus claimed that the speaker had refused his offer to torture a slave woman who had witnessed the fight, and he called his brother and brother-in-law, Euergus and Mnesibulus, as witnesses to the offer and refusal. Theophemus won that prior suit and was adjudicated a large settlement. When the speaker asked for a few days' extension in paying Theophemus agreed, only to break into his house and seize all his property as security for the payment. This case prosecutes Euergus and Mnesibulus for giving false testimony about the *basanos*: in reality, the speaker asserts, he himself demanded the woman for torture but Theophemus would not hand her over. Like many *pseudomarturiōn* trials, this one is actually a pretext for retrying the previous case, as the speaker himself acknowledges: he asks the jurors "to adjudicate concerning the truth of the testimony and at the same time to examine the entire affair from the beginning" (46). It is also an indirect prosecution of the violence Theophemus committed in collecting the penalty from that case. Thus this trial, like the case against Conon, illustrates the symbiotic relation between legitimate and illegitimate violence in a society where personal feuds were pursued in court and in a legal system that relied upon individuals to carry out its verdicts.

This speaker, like many, legitimates the violence of his actions by emphasizing the civic dimensions of the case. This is not just a private matter, he asserts. He did not enter Theophemus' house as a result of some love affair or a drunken dispute. It was not the prospect of gain or the enticement of pleasure that motivated him but "the decrees of the demos and the Boule and the command of the law" (19). Everything he did, he did "in service to the city" (42). He represents himself as a reluctant agent, compelled by the decrees of the polis. Driven by "urgent necessity" (*pollē . . . anankē*, 25), he "was forced (*ēnankazomēn*) according to the decrees and the laws to receive the debtors' list" (23).[63] He documents this institutional *anankē* in great detail, listing and quoting the laws and decrees, explicating the various duties of a trierarch and the bureaucratic procedures for recovering debts, and even subpoenaing the law and decrees as "witnesses" (*humin marturas parexomai to te psēphisma kai ton nomon*, 24).

The meticulous procedural detail is an important feature of the speaker's case and of the way he presents himself in it. Theophemus failed to pay what he owed but made no attempt to claim a legal exemption; he delayed and lied and perjured himself. The speaker, by contrast, is punctilious about protocol. He does what his official position demands of him and does it to the letter. At every stage, he secures the mandate of the Boule (33); he makes sure to issue the proper summons in front of the proper magistrates (26) and to work through the proper legal channels (28). Even during the altercation at Theophemus' house he was following correct procedure: he went there under a valid decree of the Boule (34) and took with him an assistant provided by the magistrate (35); he politely asked for an inventory of the equipment and showed Theophemus a copy of the decree (36); when Theophemus refused he called for citizen witnesses and offered him a choice of pursuing the matter in court or giving securities (37). Everything, as he presents it, was done by the book. At the same time he was scrupulous about social proprieties: before entering Theophemus' house, he says, he made sure that he was not married (so his entry into the house would not insult a wife's modesty), that the property he was about to seize really belonged to him, and that he would be at home during the process (38, 80). This procedural decorum is in sharp contrast to the

[63] One law "compelled and commanded" (*ēnankazen kai prosetatten*) trierarchs to receive a list of those who owed naval equipment to the state; another democratic decree compelled (*ēnankaze*) them to recover that equipment (21). As trierarch "it was a matter of necessity" for him (*ex anankēs oun ēn moi*) to proceed against Theophemus (23). "Who was the criminal, then, I who was forced (*ho anankazomenos*) to recover from Theophemus what he owed or Theophemus who owed the equipment to the city for so long and would not return it?" (25).

way Theophemus took securities from him, breaking into his house when he wasn't there, bursting in on his wife and son as they lunched in the courtyard, seizing over his wife's protestations property that was part of her dowry, and assaulting his old nurse (52–59) – all this after he had agreed to an extension on the debt and while the speaker was trying to get him to accept payment (49–52).

The speaker's emphasis on his own procedural correctness obviously works to legitimate his actions. Since he has ruled out personal motives – he is impelled not by profit or pleasure but by the laws (19) – the technical details of the bureaucratic process stand in for plausible psychological motivation in his narrative. At the same time, the administrative detail of his account legitimates the violence of the conflict by situating it within the context of democratic institutions like the trierarchy, liturgies, Boule, and courts. Breaking and entering, battery and seizure of property all become a matter simply of (correct or incorrect) protocol. Social agonism becomes a branch of democratic government.

In this way the speaker justifies not only his violence against Theophemus, but also Theophemus' against him. This may seem counter-intuitive, as the speaker spends much of his time railing against Theophemus' unprecedented villainy. For instance, he represents Theophemus' taking of securities as a military assault upon his house. Theophemus and his gang first seized his flocks and shepherd and a slave boy carrying a pricey borrowed vessel. "But this did not satisfy them" (52). They then proceeded to his farm; they rushed at (*ēixan*) the household slaves, sending them fleeing, they broke down (*ekbalontes*) the garden gate and entered the house, invading the privacy of his wife and assaulting his nurse (53). "They leap in upon (*epeispēdōsin*) them and seize the women and snatch the furniture; meanwhile the other slave girls, who were in the tower (*purgōi*) where they live, when they heard the tumult (*kraugēs*), lock the tower so the men could not enter there, but they carried off the furniture from the rest of the house" (56). His house is plundered (*tēn oikian porthoumenēn tēn emēn*, 60) and his son nearly led off as a slave, as if from a conquered city (61).

But even as he represents this assault upon his house as violence beyond the pale, the speaker also legitimates it in principle on procedural grounds. He is particularly outraged that Euergus and Mnesibulus entered his house "although I owed them no settlement and they had no right to touch my property" (53; cf. 63, 65). This implies that Theophemus, to whom the speaker did owe a settlement, did have a right to seize his property. Likewise his chronological argument – that Theophemus seized the securities even while he was trying to repay the debt – suggests that Theophemus would have been within his rights to seize the property if the speaker had not yet repaid the debt.[64] More tellingly, the neighbors just stand by and watch as all his property is carried off.[65] They inform the speaker of what has happened, but seem not to have intervened in the action except to point out that one of the "slaves" being led away was actually the speaker's son (61).

Thus the same procedural argument that justifies his own entry into Theophemus' house also justifies, at least in principle, Theophemus' entry into his. The same arguments the speaker raises in his defense here were probably all used by Theophemus in his defense in the previous case, a case that Theophemus won. This speech assumes that a certain degree of violence is mandated in the execution of the trierarchy: the Boule (in a decree that the speaker reads aloud in court) authorized the speaker to recover the equipment "in whatever way he was able" (33). Likewise, a certain violence is licensed in the execution of the court's verdict. As always in Athenian law, it is up to the individual who wins a case to collect the settlement. The speaker claims, of course, that Theophemus went beyond the bounds of legality in carrying out the judgment of the court, but his objection is one of degree not of principle. The procedural details of the speech thus legitimate social violence as a legal necessity – what Walter Benjamin calls "law-preserving violence"[66] – and also deflect the law's own violence, its ability to enforce its judgments, onto the extralegal world of social agonism. As in Demosthenes 54, so here law and society each borrow the other's violence and lend the other legitimacy.

One central element of this procedural legitimation of violence is the *basanos* of the slave woman who answered Theophemus' door when the speaker came for the naval equipment and witnessed their fight. Both

64 The speaker claims that he had already collected the money to repay the debt and had already asked Theophemus to accompany him to the bank to receive the money when the assault took place (51), and that they continued to steal his property even as the debt was being paid (63–66). But the timeline is suspect. The former claim seems to be supported only by probability (if I hadn't collected the money before the attack, how could I pay it so soon afterward?, 66) and the assurance of his wife based on what she had heard from him (57). He calls witnesses to the fact that he invited Theophemus to the bank, but they cannot say what he would have found there had he gone.

65 At least some of the neighbors presumably testify at §61, but we don't know who or what they said. Rhodes 1998: 148 notes that the fact that the speaker did not try to prosecute Theophemus for this violent entry into his house suggests that "Theophemus and his relatives were technically within their rights in entering the property when the speaker's payment was overdue." Legal self-help on private property was not uncommon, as Christ 1998b shows, but the Athenians were wary of its abuse and therefore careful about how they presented it in court. On the proprieties as represented in this speech, see Christ 1998b: 536–41, and on the role of bystanders in the conflict, Christ (in press a).

66 Benjamin 1978 [1921]: 284–89.

sides agree that the evidence from her interrogation would end the case (5). Each accuses the other of refusing it. The inaccessible truth of the *basanos* is presented as an alternative and antithesis to the false testimony of Euergus and Mnesibulus, but that truth is quickly subsumed within the manipulations of the trial. The refusal of the *basanos* becomes evidence of false witnessing, an *ergon* that proves the falseness of the false *logos*: "they bear witness to lies in speech and do not hand over the woman in deed" (10). Instead of offering an external truth that might resolve their conflict, the *basanos* is a means of continuing the fight.

This *basanos* reveals the ritualized nature of the *agōn* as it is pursued both in and out of the courts. Each man says he offered the woman for torture and that the other refused. This parallelism is sustained through a series of reciprocal exchanges or non-exchanges. In addition to the offering or not offering and accepting or not accepting of the woman for torture, there is also the speaker's demand of the naval equipment and Theophemus' refusal to give it, the speaker's legal debt and his delay in repaying it, the speaker's seizure of securities and Theophemus' seizure of securities. Then, too, there is the reciprocal exchange of break-ins and assaults, punches and lawsuits. Even the description of the physical confrontation that prompted the *aikeia* case has a kabuki quality: Theophemus punches the speaker in the mouth; the speaker calls witnesses and then returns the blow (38). The fight follows a formal legal and rhetorical choreography – punch-witness-punch – that renders the exchange of violence not only structurally balanced but also seemingly bloodless and painless: the speaker shows his bruises to the Boule (which takes them as a *hubris* against itself and the law, 41) but not to the listeners of this speech. In contrast to Demosthenes 54, here the contest of reputation seems not a matter of life and death, but a ritualized game.

But if this *agōn* seems bloodless for the competitors, there are other victims. The men's dance of honor revolves around two women who occupy structurally parallel positions in the case and the speech. The first is Theophemus' slave (*hē anthrōpos*), who is demanded (and refused) for interrogation (5–17). A weapon in the men's rhetorical conflict, she is also a victim of their physical conflict: when Theophemus refused to turn over the naval equipment, the speaker, announcing that he was going to collect securities, took hold of her (37–38). Theophemus makes him release her, but her near-seizure anticipates her role as an object of hostile exchanges in the *basanos*. This woman's threatened seizure and torture are described without comment by the speaker: they are just part of the procedure of a conflict represented, I have argued, as legitimate and normal.

Things are different when Theophemus comes to the speaker's house to collect the settlement from the previous trial. There, too, a woman (*hē anthrōpos*, 55) is a victim of the men's reciprocal violence, the speaker's old nurse, who is eating with his wife and son when Theophemus and his gang break in and is badly battered by the men in their attempt to seize every last piece of the speaker's property.[67] Structurally the speaker's nurse is equivalent to Theophemus' slave woman. But whereas the latter is an anonymous body (*sōma*, 6) passed between the two men as part of their game of legal one-upmanship, the old nurse is granted a prominence in the speech that unbalances the reciprocal relationship between the two men and delegitimates the violence that the speech has worked to naturalize:

> My wife and children happened to be eating lunch in the courtyard, jurors, and with them was an old woman who had been my nurse, a kindly and loyal creature (*anthrōpos eunous kai pistē*) who had been freed by my father. She lived with her husband after she was freed, but when he died she was an old woman and had no one to care for her, so she returned to my house. It was necessary (*anankaion*) not to allow my nurse . . . to live in need. Then too, as trierarch I was often away on sea voyages and my wife wanted me to leave someone like this with her to watch the house. (55–56)

In this speech dominated by administrative protocol, the nurse is spoken of with notable warmth. Her relationship to the speaker is emotional on both sides: she is well disposed and faithful to him; he feels a moral obligation toward her. Formerly a slave, she is now virtually a part of the family.[68] Not only does she eat inside the house with his wife and children, but the speaker's sense of obligation to her mirrors that of a male head of household to his female kin: like a daughter, she returns to him after her marriage ends; like a mother, she asks his support in her old age. The necessity (*anankaion*) that makes him care for her is not legal, though: as a free woman not related to him by birth, marriage, or adoption she has no legal connection to or claim on him. Instead, their bond is represented as one of personal affection: he cares for her because he cares about her.

The savage assault on this old woman is the emotional climax of the speech. When she saw the men inside the house, she took the cup she

[67] The speaker's wife is also insulted (though not physically harmed) by the men's break-in. But the wife occupies a very different place in the structure of the case and the feud than the nurse. She is the speaker's agent within the household, protecting (as well as symbolizing) his property, negotiating with the intruders and reporting to them what her husband had told her about repayment of the debt (57). As his proxy, she has a stake in the feud and the trial that the two slave women do not have, and the harm done to her is an extension of the harm done to the speaker.

[68] Hunter 1994: 86–87; Cox 1998: 192.

had been drinking from and hid it in her bosom so they would not get it. But Theophemus and Euergus noticed and snatched the cup from her so roughly

> that her arms and wrists were bloodied (*huphaimoi*) as they twisted her hands behind her and dragged her around in their attempt to get the little cup (*kumbion*). Her neck was bruised from being choked and her chest was black and blue (*pelion*). And they went so far in their criminality that they did not stop choking and beating the old woman until they had grabbed the little cup from her bosom. (59)

This assault upon the nurse is described with a degree of physiological detail that is rare in forensic oratory: the assault on Conon in Demosthenes 54 is perhaps the closest parallel.[69] Its vividness and corporeal detail also stand out against the procedural background of the case, with its decrees and magistracies, settlements and securities, and against the formalized agonism of the two opponents, in which even a punch in the face leaves scars more legal than physical. The pain that is mostly absent in the narrative of the conflict is concentrated here in the brutal battery of an old woman. Five days later she dies of her wounds.

This graphic scene is designed to illustrate Theophemus' meanness and greed: he is not satisfied until he has seized every last possession and kills an innocent old woman for the sake of one little cup (68, 81). The reciprocal exchange of violence between the men that structures the speech up to this point is now unbalanced by the pathos of the scene: Theophemus has gone beyond the bounds of acceptable social or legal agonism. So the speaker claims and he pushes that claim. Summoning witnesses to the nurse's sickbed and, finally, her deathbed, he prepares her bruised body as evidence in his case against Theophemus. In a sense, he subjects her to a posthumous *basanos*, using her brutalized body in the same way as he would have liked to use that of Theophemus' slave woman. If the nurse's death functions as a sort of *basanos* in the case, however, it exceeds its probative purpose, for her body testifies not only against Theophemus but also against the speaker himself, who likewise seized hold of a woman and but for Theophemus' intervention might have subjected her to the same fate. The nurse is a victim not just of Theophemus' unprecedented criminality, as the speaker would have it, but of the feud between the two men, and the pathos of her death testifies to the brutality of that feud

[69] Several words in the passage are found elsewhere primarily in medical texts. *Huphaimos*: Hipp. *Aph.* 5.23; Sor. 1.19, 3.43.2; Gal. 18 (2).301; *pelios*: Hipp. *Prog.* 2.9, *Morb.* 2.68. Biraud 1991: 343 notes the unusual realism of this episode in a genre that generally shies away from corporeal description.

and undoes the speech's attempt to legitimate it as a routine part of the administrative and judicial business of the city.

Furthermore, the nurse is also a victim of the law itself. After her death, the speaker goes to the exegetes (*exēgētai*) "to learn what I should do about this" (68). These officials are obscure; they are mentioned only one other time in classical Greek literature and their actual role may have been limited to expounding ritual procedure in homicide cases.[70] Within this case, though, they function as authoritative representatives – virtual embodiments – of the law. After consulting with them the speaker confirms their response by going to read the official text of Draco's homicide law inscribed on a stele near the Stoa Basileios in the agora (71). These consultations of the law in its official instantiations – as a set of rules inscribed in stone or revealed by a body of experts – are offered as another example of the speaker's procedural scrupulousness: he wants to know the law so that he can act, as he always does, accordingly.

He inquires of the law what he should do, and the law replies: there is nothing you can do. The exegetes both expound the religious law (*ta nomima*) and advise him as to his own advantage (*to sumphoron*, 69), and on both counts their response is the same. Because the nurse is neither his kin nor his slave, the laws do not command him to prosecute her murder (70). Under these circumstances, the exegetes say, it is not legal for him (*oude gar en tōi nomōi esti soi*, 70) to bring a homicide case before the arkhon.[71] It is also inadvisable, since he has only the testimony of his wife and child to go on (69) and if he prosecuted he would have to swear an oath on their lives that would expose him, if he lost, to the risk of perjury and, even if he won, to the contempt of others (70). Therefore, they counsel him, "bear

[70] On the exegetes see Von Fritz 1940, esp. 96–100; Oliver 1950; MacDowell 1963: 11–16; Todd 1993: 31–32; Tulin 1996: 23; Gagarin 2008: 207–08; and the idiosyncratic discussion of Svenbro 1993: 116–22. The other reference is at Pl. *Euth.* 3e7–5d7 (on which see Tulin 1996: 55–100). The exegetes here expound (*exēgēsometha*) on ritual but merely advise (*parainesomen*) on matters of law (69), as MacDowell 1963: 16 stresses. It is not clear what jurisdiction they have over the latter, since the speaker also consults with his friends. But since all the sources he consults – exegetes, the laws of Draco, his friends – give the same answer, the exegetes' response takes on the weight of legal authority in the rhetorical context. Tulin 1996: 21–54 offers an exhaustive and persuasive account of this passage.

[71] This echoes the text of Draco's homicide law (*IG* I^3 104), but there is considerable debate about how restrictive the clause is: were only family obliged to prosecute or only family allowed to prosecute? See MacDowell 1963: 11–19, 94–96; Evjen 1971; Gagarin 1979b: 302–13, 1981: 56–57; Tulin 1996; Rhodes 1998: 149: "here we seem to come up against a grey area in Athenian law." This speaker hedges the issue in implying that legal obstacles prevented him from prosecuting the nurse's death, despite his desire to do so. He may, of course, be exaggerating the legal difficulties in order to justify his failure to bring a case. Johnstone 1999: 63 notes that it was a common rhetorical strategy to represent the law as foreclosing choices.

the misfortune (*sumphoran*) as easily as you can and get vengeance in some other way, if you wish" (70).

The response of the exegetes acknowledges that his loss is a *sumphora*, a misfortune, but it also announces the law's indifference to that misfortune. There is nothing he can do about it: *oude gar en tōi nomōi esti soi*, "It is not (possible) within the law for you (to bring a case)" (70). And if revenge is not "within the law" for him, neither is the old woman. By denying his right to avenge her, the law declares their relationship legally meaningless. The disconnection between the close affective bond he describes and the legal interpretation of relatedness is felt in his paraphrase of the exegetes' response: "Jurors, the law commands relatives as far as the first cousin once-removed to prosecute a homicide (and it specifies in the oath what 'relatives' means), and if the victim is a slave, that there be a prosecution for that. But the woman was not related to me by birth – except inasmuch as she was my nurse – nor was she my slave" (72). To him, she is a virtual member of the family, all but related to him "inasmuch as she was my nurse." But the law does not recognize this affective relationship, nor does it care about her kindness and loyalty or his sense of obligation to her. Legally she is unconnected to him: she is not "within the law" in relation to him, *oude gar en tōi nomōi esti soi*. Furthermore, with no husband, master, or kinsman to serve as her legal guardian, she has no formal legal standing at all. She effectively does not exist within the law: *oude gar en tōi nomōi esti*.[72]

This scene of legal consultation comes up against the limits of Athenian jurisprudence and dramatizes the violent foreclosure by which it secures those limits. In the *basanos* we saw the law's disavowal of its own violence, its simultaneous recognition and denial of the pain and death it causes. But in this speech we see a prior and more profound violence: the cruel exclusion by which the law refuses to recognize not only the nurse's suffering but her very existence. This foreclosure, this violent preclusion, grounds the coherence of *nomos* both as a set of rules (formally inscribed and expounded) and as a social practice. The exegetes explain *ta nomima* but also advise *ta sumphora* (69), warning the speaker that if he did bring a case he would earn contempt and enmity: "many will think worse of

[72] The argument in this paragraph rests on three possible readings of the phrase *oude gar en tōi nomōi esti soi*. First, "it is not possible for you (to bring a case) within the law" (reading *esti* as *exesti*); second, "she is not within the law for you" (taking the nurse as the subject of *esti*); and third, "she does not exist within the law" (existential *esti* and *soi* as a weak ethical dative). The exegetes do provide a mechanism for the prosecution of her murder "if she has any (male) relation" (69), but there is no indication in the speech that she does. See Tulin 1996: 44.

you;" "people will resent you" (70). This advice situates the law within the same contests over reputation that drive the feud between Theophemus and the speaker. The law's exclusion of the nurse enables that feud by constructing a world in which only citizens and the violence against them legally matters. This kind, loyal old woman must be barred from the domain of law and the speaker's bond with her legally severed in order for his contest, with its *basanos* challenges and seizures of slave women, to continue. The connection between these two levels of legal violence is particularly disturbing if we believe the speaker to be disingenuous in the concern he expresses for the nurse and see him as cynically exploiting her death to gain the upper hand against Theophemus. But even if he is sincere, the legally sanctioned ritual of violence exchanged between these two citizens requires and conceals this prior violence of foreclosure, the law's decision that certain people are legally non-existent and therefore that their deaths, though perhaps unfortunate, are not legally actionable.

The speaker accepts the exegetes' advice and "bears the misfortune as easily as he can." But he does so, as he tells it, reluctantly: "I did what was fitting for me to do on behalf of my household and what the exegetes told me to do. Concerning those legal matters which no longer pertained to me, I kept silent" (71). The speaker resigns himself to silence, but his speech narrates that silence. The case thus becomes a sort of obituary for the nurse, recording her kindness and the speaker's affection for her, and forcing the jurors to recognize the "misfortune" (*sumphoran*, 70) of her death. Through this memorialization she is incorporated into legal discourse even as she is excluded from it and, more exactly, incorporated into it precisely as excluded from it. She becomes a "ghost in the house of justice," a haunting reminder of what must remain unspoken within legal discourse in order for that discourse to maintain its coherence and authority.[73] But her vital presence in the narrative, I will suggest, challenges that authority, exposing the violence of the law's grounding exclusions and refuting its claim to justice.

More than just a lament, the speech is a demand for legal reckoning. We might even imagine it as that "other form of vengeance" that the exegetes recommended the speaker pursue ("if you wish," 70). Though technically a prosecution of Euergus and Mnesibulus' false witnessing, the speech solicits

[73] I take the phrase from Felman 2002; the chapter that goes under this title offers a moving reading of the testimony of K-Zetnik during the Eichmann trial (131–66). Derrida, too, sees the law as haunted: since every legal decision is made, in the instant when it is made, in uncertainty about its ultimate justness, a "ghost of the undecidable" resides in the very deliberative process of law, deconstructing its certitude (1992a: 24–26).

a verdict on Theophemus' criminality. When the nurse's fate is attributed to that criminality, the trial becomes a displaced prosecution for her murder as well. If the speaker succeeds in evoking pity for the old woman's suffering, then, and in conveying his own distress at this "misfortune," he stands to gain from the jurors precisely what he was refused by the exegetes, the posthumous justice of a legal judgment against her killers. This strategy is, to be sure, self-interested, and the interests are narrow: the speaker uses the nurse, a victim of his feud with Theophemus, as a rhetorical weapon in that feud. And yet, by inviting the jurors to consider the nurse's fate when the exegetes would not, the speech also evokes a justice that exceeds the strict exegesis of the law.[74] With his detailed and emotional narrative, the speaker asks the jurors to go beyond, and indeed vote against, the verdict of the exegetes, to make a space within their legal judgment for an individual the legal authorities decreed had no formal existence "within the law." In the narrative, that callous decree compounds the pathos of the nurse's suffering: the injustice against her was perpetrated not only by Theophemus but by the legal system itself. This trial thus becomes an appeal of the exegetes' verdict and a hearing on the justice of the law.

When the exegetes declared the nurse beyond the limits of the law, they also set a limit on that law's aspiration to justice. The law responds to injustice: that is part of its very raison d'être. But the law itself defines what counts as injustice. Athenian law set depressingly narrow parameters on that definition, and declared itself just by ignoring "misfortunes" that fell outside those parameters. Demosthenes 47 asks the jurors to look beyond this narrow judicial limit, to see the suffering of those the law renders invisible, and in this way to envision the potential for an alternate or expanded definition of justice. That potential was obviously never realized within the historical context of classical Athens, whatever may have been the verdict in this case. But by suggesting that there is a gap between the exegetes' law and the justice the nurse deserved and, further, by asking the jurors to acknowledge that gap and affirm it with their vote, this speech keeps open the horizon of a potential justice beyond the cramped parameters set by the legal authorities in this case. If, as Robert Cover says, "law may be viewed as a system of tension or a bridge linking a concept

[74] This justice beyond the law is not easily conflated with Aristotle's notion of equity (*to epieikes*) as "justice, but not justice according to the law but a correction of legal justice" (*NE* 1137b11–13). Equity's correction involves more precise application of general rules and does not look beyond the bounds of law. Moreover, since Aristotle conceptualizes justice in terms of reciprocity, he necessarily restricts it to social equals; thus for him "there is no absolute injustice towards one's own property," including slaves (1134b9–10).

of a reality to an imagined alternative," it is that imagined "alternity" – the possibility of a justice to which Athenian law could not do justice – that the speech preserves in its sympathetic account of a kind old woman's death.[75]

To say this is to suggest that the speech can imagine a different sort of justice as a work of literature than it does as a legal action, for it is precisely through its artful narration that the speech generates that vision of an alternate justice.[76] The narrative, with its pathos and suspense, its visual detail and deft characterization, gives the nurse's death the force it carries in the speaker's brief, a force, I have argued, that exceeds not only the speaker's immediate forensic purpose but even the bounds of justice set by the fourth-century Athenian legal system. From the domestic scene of his family eating lunch in the courtyard before the assault (55), through the graphic account of the assault itself (59), to the bitter brevity of the eventual death (67), the episode is elaborated in a vivid narrative style that stands out in this often technical and bureaucratic speech.[77] Through the artistry of the scene, this forensic oration lays claim as rhetorical *logos* to a justice that it foregoes as forensic *ergon*: its judicial action complies with the exegetes' limited definition of justice (this is a prosecution for false witnessing, after all, not for the nurse's homicide), but its judicial rhetoric

[75] Cover 1993: 101. Cornell, following Derrida, elaborates the same idea in temporal terms; the possibility of justice for her is not merely an imagined alternative but, more optimistically, a potential future, "the not yet of the never has been" (Cornell 1992a: 128–54; 1995a: 242–51). Cf. Derrida 1992a: 27: "Justice remains, is yet, to come, *à venir*, it has an, it is *à-venir*, the very dimension of events irreducibly to come."

[76] For Cover, narrative provides the bridge between nomic reality and imagined alternatives, between "the 'is,' the 'ought,' and the 'what might be'" (1993: 102). Violence, however, threatens that bridge, unyoking nomos from narrative and revealing the crucial difference between legal and literary interpretation (1986: 1606–7; cf. 1609–10, 1616–18). Felman 2002 juxtaposes literary and legal justice, arguing that literature reopens historical wounds that the law covers over (8–9, 94–96), and asks, "Can literature be viewed precisely as the *record* of what has remained *out of the legal records*?" (100). The opposed forces she associates with law and literature I see working simultaneously within the legal-literary text of Athenian forensic oratory.

[77] One might note, for example, the word *kumbion* for the "little cup" Theophemus and his men seize from the nurse, a diminutive carefully chosen for its pathetic effect (58, 59). The nurse is first introduced in a few brief sentences that emphasize not only her kindness and loyalty, but also her advanced age and long relationship with the speaker and his house; this description is set off by ring composition (*aristōsa en tēi aulēi*, 55; *aristōntōn de en tēi aulēi*, 56). In the long sentence describing the assault (59), word order foregrounds the words *huphaimoi* ("bloodied"), *amukhas* ("bruises"), and *pelion* ("black and blue") in a tricolon of increasing brevity and intensity, while references to the nurse's bosom (*kolpos*, 58, 59) and allusions to her age (*graun*, 59) add pathos. At §67 the doctor informs the speaker, in a locution common in tragedy, that the nurse is "done for" (*ouden eti eiē*); the denouement is swift and alliterative (*eteleutēsen hē titthē*). The key rhetorical points are reiterated in the compressed report of the incident to the exegetes: "I told them about everything that had happened: about the men's arrival and the loyalty of the woman, and why I had her in my house, and how she died on account of a little cup, because she would not hand it over" (68; cf. 81).

exceeds that limit and gestures (if only for its own local purposes) toward a more expansive definition of justice. To put it this way is not to try to separate facets of the speech that are actually inseparable but instead to identify a tension internal to this speech and to juridical discourse as a whole inasmuch as it is comprised of both *logoi* and *erga*.

This tension inters the dead nurse as a ghostly presence within legal discourse. What is repressed by the law is mournfully expressed within the rhetoric of the speech, as is the act of repression itself and the suffering it inflicts. Rhetorically, if not judicially, then, the nurse does exist "within the law" (*en tōi nomōi esti*). This rhetorical return of the repressed, this haunting of the law by what is beyond the law, destabilizes its discursive boundaries and refuses the self-authorizing closure that would equate law with justice and legitimate law's violence on the simple grounds that it is the law. Thus even as forensic oratory works to construct, authorize, and delimit a judicial world, securing the boundaries between inside and outside, it also preserves a trace of that outside within: not only the echo of outlaw violence within legitimate force but also the specter of an alternate justice implicit, though never fully realized or realizable, "within the law."

This chapter has examined both of these traces – violence and justice – within Athenian legal discourse. It has shown how forensic oratory labors to differentiate law's legitimate force from the violence of the streets but also tacitly acknowledges (and uses to its own ends) the collusion of the legal system with the manifold brutalities of Athens' agonistic and hierarchical society. It has examined the scene of physical violence in the practice (whether real or fictional) of the *basanos* – a scene staged as a drama of disavowal, with torture masquerading as truth – and has suggested that this disavowal constitutes a cruelty in itself, a symbolic violence superadded to the physical violence of torture. This symbolic violence takes the general form of repression: disavowal, foreclosure, or merely the callous indifference to the suffering of law's unrecognized victims, be it a murdered nurse, an executed concubine, or the countless slaves demanded or offered for torture. But this chapter has also argued that these victims are not entirely forgotten, and their silent presence in the texts of forensic oratory is a haunting reminder both of the law's violence and of its willful blindness to that violence. The law seeks to forget its own cruelties, but forensic oratory preserves an archive of its ruthlessness. In its double role as law and literature, it conjures and sustains the limits of Athenian jurisprudence but also strains against them, lamenting, among its other sacrificial victims, the law's sacrifice of its own claim to justice. And yet precisely by marking this loss – this gap between the law, embedded as it is in a particular historical society with all its violence and iniquity, and justice – forensic oratory preserves the possibility of a fuller justice beyond the law. This possibility, I have suggested, inheres within the rhetorical language of the speeches, in the tragic pity for a tortured concubine or the narrative of a kind old nurse's pain and death. Rhetoric itself thus functions as a potential agent of justice within legal discourse, encrypting the hope of justice at the exact spot where it shows the law to be most violent and unjust.

PART II

The Legal Subject

CHAPTER 3

Legal fictions: subjects probable and improbable

> One might say that this is probable: that many improbable things happen to mortals.
>
> Aristotle, quoting the tragedian Agathon (*Rhetoric* 1402a12–13)

THE LEGAL SUBJECT

Among the law's many fictions, none is more vital than the legal subject, the implied subject of legal action. The law tries deeds, but it can only try them in the person of their doer. Every act requires an agent to explain it, motivate it, bear witness to it, or simply represent it in court. But those agents are always to a greater or lesser extent fictions, from the shibboleth of the corporation as individual to the good-faith fabrications of a victim who imaginatively reconstructs the emotions of a traumatic event many months or years later. How forensic speeches construct their subjects, when they conjure them into being, why, and how, is the topic of this chapter and the next.

Act and agent are mutually determining in Athenian juridical discourse. The criminal's presumed state of mind defines the crime, as well as its presentation in court. Whether the crime is voluntary or involuntary will dictate where the case is judged, how it is argued, what punishments are meted out – in short, the whole shape of the case. The difference we saw in Demosthenes 54, for example, between a private suit for *aikeia* (resulting in a fine) and a public suit for *hubris* (which could warrant the death penalty) was what modern law calls *mens rea*, culpable mentality. What were the perpetrator's intent and motive when he struck the victim? What was he thinking?[1]

[1] Arist. *Rhet.* 1374a13–15; Dem. 21.42–46. Farenga 2006: 310–45 explores the cognitive challenge jurors faced in reconstructing the hypothetical mental state and intention of the litigants. For a history of *mens rea* in English common law see Sayre 1931–32.

A psychology of the doer is thus everywhere implicit in the law's trial of deeds. The legal subject begins his life, as it were, as a grammatical function: a proper noun attached to a criminal verb. *Ēthos*, character, is a fundamental building block of a persuasive legal argument, but it functions in forensic oratory much as Aristotle proposes it does in tragedy.[2] Tragedy, Aristotle writes, is an imitation of an action (*praxeōs mimēsis*) but since actions are performed by agents, the ethical quality of the action can best be judged by considering the character and intent (*ēthos* and *dianoia*) of those agents (*Poet.* 1449b36–1450a20, 1450b8–12). *Ēthos* is thus like coloring that fills in the lines drawn by the action (*Poet.* 1450a38–b3).[3] Sometimes that coloring, in forensic oratory as in tragedy, is intricate and subtle, and *ēthos* becomes an argument in and of itself. The following chapter will look at several such cases in examining how forensic oratory writes a biography for its agents. In that chapter, *ēthos* will appear as the product of colorful fictions with a complex rhetorical structure of their own.

The focus in this chapter is more preliminary. Here I attempt to isolate the legal agent in its first emergence from the liable act. Ancient Greek did not need to express a grammatical subject; the subject was implicit in the verb form (*prattei* is "he/she/it acts") and was expressed separately only in order to foreground the agent or differentiate one possible agent from another. Linguistically, then, Greek starts with an action and adds an agent adverbially, as it were, in order to clarify or specify the source of that action. The same process, I am suggesting, operates within the Athenian legal system. First there is an event, a crime. But the law can punish only individuals, not events. Therefore if the crime is to become legally actionable, there must be a criminal. That criminal is at first just a grammatical subject, a nominal placeholder for liability. But in the course of prosecuting the deed, of examining the circumstances, motives, intentions, and results, the case begins to qualify and color in the bare outlines of this fictional being.

One rudimentary but seminal incarnation of the legal subject is the voluntary prosecutor, *ho boulomenos*. Any citizen who was personally wronged

[2] Arist. *Rhet.* 1388b31–1391b6; cf. 1356a1–13, 1373b25–1374a17, 1408a. On *ēthos* in oratory, see further Sattler 1947; Pearson 1976: 75–119; Russell 1990; Johnstone 1999: 93–108; Lanni 2006: 59–64. Eden 1986 studies the cross-pollination between Aristotle's philosophy of law and his philosophy of literature: see esp. 25–61. Cf. Goodrich 1987: 190–91 on the legal subject as an epiphenomenon of legal discourse. The notion of the doer as "a fiction added to the deed" is derived from Nietzsche *On the Genealogy of Morals* 1.13.

[3] On Aristotle's theory of tragic character, see Jones 1962; Halliwell 1986: 138–67; Goldhill 1990: 118–22. The homologies between courts and theater are explored by Dover 1974: 23–33; Garner 1987: 95–130; Ober 1989a: 152–55; Ober and Strauss 1990; Halliwell 1991: 294; P. Wilson 1991: 175–80, 1996; Bers 1994: 189–91; Hall 1995; Lanni 1997; Scafuro 1997.

could bring a private suit (*dikē*) to seek redress. But in the higher stakes and higher profile public cases (*graphai*), where the crime was perceived to affect the city as a whole, a law attributed to Solon decreed that the case could be prosecuted by "anyone who wished" (*ho boulomenos*).[4] This Solonic law gives a name to an idealized subject – one might even say a subjective embodiment – of Athenian jurisprudence. *Ho boulomenos* is a legal subject characterized by a sustained will (*boulomenos* is the present participle of *boulesthai*, to will or want) and masculine autonomy (the article *ho* marks masculinity and singularity). A vigorous agent and defender of both his own and the city's integrity, he is also the ideal subject of Athens' direct democracy: meetings of the Assembly opened with the herald's invitation to "anyone who wants" (*ho boulomenos*) to come forward and speak his opinion.[5] Athens' council, the Boule, enacted that will (*boulē*) as law. Voluntary prosecution is thus akin to engaged citizenship; it is an exercise of democratic free speech (*parrhēsia*) and an individual contribution to the *eunomia* of the city. The prosecutorial will is a civic and democratic will, as the prosecutor never fails to remind the jurors.

That will is converted unerringly into action. *Ho boulomenos* describes not those who contemplate prosecution but those who carry it through. This was no small commitment, as we saw in the last chapter: the prosecutor in Athens not only filed a charge but was himself normally responsible for summoning or arresting the accused, gathering witnesses and material evidence, delivering his own speech in court, and seeing that the sentence was carried out. While there were in practice various procedural alternatives available to those unable to shoulder this burden, in theory prosecutorial intent manifests itself in vigorous action.[6] Both intention and action, moreover, take the law as their object. *Boulēsis* is an appetitive impulse, a "reaching" (*orexis*), as Aristotle has it, in the same category as passion and desire (*thumos* and *epithumia*).[7] *Ho boulomenos* reaches toward litigation. Defined solely by his prosecutorial passion, he has no other relevant desires beside prosecution and the civic good it represents. And if the object of

4 [Arist.] *Ath. Pol.* 9.1 lists this law among Solon's most populist (*dēmotikōtata*) innovations. Cf. Plut. *Solon* 18; Osborne 1985; Christ 1998a: 119–22. The voluntary prosecutor is often viewed as a practical necessity: Athens had no public prosecutor so there would be no public cases if not for individual initiative. But the Athenians could presumably have instituted a public prosecutor had they wished, and the voluntary prosecutor is better analyzed for what he reveals about the Athenian imagination of judicial agency. On this, see especially Christ 1998a: 118–59; Rubinstein 1998; Allen 2000a: 39–72.

5 E.g. Aesch. 1.23, 1.27, 3.220; Dem. 18.170. The grammatical singularity of *ho boulomenos* belies the complexity of litigational practice in which, as Rubinstein (2000: 91–111, 186–98) has shown, prosecutions in public cases were often group efforts.

6 MacDowell 1978: 53–54, 235–59; Osborne 1985; Todd 1993: 123–29, 147–63; Allen 2000a: 45–47.

7 Arist. *MA* 700b22–24.

this aggressive *boulēsis* is the law, so too is its implied subject: the voluntary prosecutor's will-to-law is the law's own prosecutorial will embodied. That is to say, this fictional legal person personifies the law itself and enacts a vision of the law's agency.[8]

Over against this legal fiction stands another, his opposite and twin, *ho epibouleuōn*. The verb *epibouleuein*, which means "to plot against," is one of the most common ways of speaking about a crime in Greek. Cognate with *boulesthai*, it too connotes a purposeful mental state directed toward action. Its root verb, *bouleuein* ("to deliberate," "plan," "determine"), expresses cognitive activity at its most energetic; it drives into motion the *boulē* that is the result of *boulesthai*'s willing.[9] Like the voluntary prosecutor, the criminal mastermind is an autonomous agent defined by a focused intention that he translates invariably into action (or else he would not be a criminal). But here the two cognates diverge: the prefix *epi-* suggests the malicious direction of the criminal's planning. His will is directed against someone: against his victim, in the first instance; against the civic good; and ultimately against his legal nemesis, *ho boulomenos*. The trial is a clash of wills between these two fictional characters, characters who exist only as substantive forms of that aggressive legal intent. These two figures emerge out of the legal *agōn* and embody juridical discourse's fantasy of the law as autonomous, energetic, and purposeful. Both in its positive form (as righteous prosecutor) and in its negative (as plotting criminal), the law projects a vigorous agency, a will-to-law (or, its inverse, a will-to-crime) that acts deliberately and achieves its intent.

This chapter explores the personification of legal will, focusing on three figures: the intentional subject, the probable subject, and the generic subject. It examines the emergence and the qualities of these subjects and, since they tend to be men largely without qualities, attempts to theorize their subjective emptiness. This chapter thus does not look at the many vivid characters who populate Athenian forensic oratory (some of whom will appear in the next chapter), but instead it approaches these colorless legal

[8] This explains why defendants so often level the charge of sykophancy against prosecutors. The sykophant shares a good deal of his DNA with *ho boulomenos*: he, too, is driven by a will-to-law; he too enacts private will as public prosecution. Only the motive behind that will is different: private vendetta and personal profit not civic justice. On the sykophant as the inverse of the voluntary prosecutor, see MacDowell 1978: 62–66; Todd 1993: 93; Christ 1998a: 118–59.

[9] Chantraine 1968: 1.189: *bouleuein* is the denominative verb from *boulē* (will, plan, council, decision), itself derived from *boulomai*. Vernant 1988: 66 notes an oscillation in this word group "between the spontaneous tendency of a desire and intelligent premeditated calculation." There was a type of crime termed *bouleusis*, planning, but as Gagarin 1990b shows, it had a very narrow range in practice. See further Maschke 1968: 83–92, 101–09. Needless to say, neither word, *boulesthai* or *epibouleuein*, was unique to legal discourse.

subjects as abstractions produced by juridical discourse in the elementary process of attaching an agent to an act.

No text offers a better perspective for viewing the legal subject in the abstract than the uniquely abstract cases of Antiphon's *Tetralogies*. This strange text consists of three "cases" with four paired speeches each (hence the title). Each *Tetralogy* imagines a different scenario and pursues a different mode of legal argument. The first is a case of unwitnessed homicide; the argument here is focused on questions of probability. In the second *Tetralogy* a boy has been killed accidentally during javelin practice and the central question is the liability of unintended actions. The third *Tetralogy* tries a homicide resulting from a drunken brawl; its legal strategy is more diverse than in the other two but rests in part on ethical typology.

These speeches were clearly not intended for delivery: the situations are too sketchy and devoid of concrete details; they lack the narratives that dominate most speeches; the arguments don't conform in every instance to contemporary Athenian law. Most scholars assume these were display pieces intended for teaching rhetorical principles or analyzing different types of forensic argument and see them as part of the intellectual movement surrounding the sophists in the last third of the fifth century.[10] They occupy a unique position both in Athenian literature and on the continuum between forensic practice and legal theory. Reflecting on arguments used in actual court cases, taking a single line of legal reasoning and pushing it to its logical conclusion in order to expose its possibilities and limitations, the *Tetralogies* are not practical texts: they neither try real crimes nor provide particularly useful training for would-be litigants. Their relation to law is theoretical and analytical. But it is not distant; they don't develop a metatheory of forensic practice (in the way, for example, Aristotle does). They locate their analysis within the courts, using common legal language and deploying common legal strategies. Thus we could say that they offer a theoretical *mimēsis* of legal *praxis*. They are not real cases but they imitate the form and reflect the concerns of real cases. In their staged scenarios we can watch the play of contemporary legal thought.[11]

These artificial dramas are not big on characterization. Their hypothetical crimes have no real-life victims or perpetrators and the speeches make

[10] On the purpose and nature of the *Tetralogies*, see Dover 1950: 56–59; Decleva Caizzi 1969: 11–83; Gagarin 1997: 8–9, 2002: 52–62, 103–09, 133–34; Carawan 1998: 171–215. Carawan (1993, 1998: 171–215) stresses the *Tetralogies*' divergences from both Athenian law and forensic speeches designed for delivery; see also Sealey 1984b.

[11] The *Tetralogies* might be imagined as a proto-form of declamation, on which see Gunderson 2003.

little effort to "color in" these positions. The speakers, likewise, are lifeless and lacking individuation. We hear nothing of their magnanimous liturgies or of their opponent's shameful personal failings. We don't even learn their names. As fictions, they remain generic and one-dimensional, mere subjective extensions of the legal argument put in their mouths. But this subjective emptiness is precisely what makes these characters valuable. My claim in this chapter is that the *Tetralogies*' abstract legal persons, though almost completely devoid of any individual subjectivity in themselves, reveal in its barest outlines the subjectivity of Athenian juridical discourse, that is, the motives and desires, preoccupations and patterns of thought that constitute the subjective structure of the juridical world.

The first section looks at the intentional subject (*Tetralogy II*). Volition or intention (the diction is equivocal) is the minimal ligature between a culpable act and a liable agent, and thus the intentional actor represents the most elementary stage in the evolution of the legal subject. *Tetralogy II* imagines a legal world so purposeful that intention can be found even in accident; the tortured logic of the case bespeaks juridical discourse's commitment to the efficacious intent that animates such vital fictions as the voluntary prosecutor. The second section deals with the probable subject (*Tetralogy I*), an *ēthos* constructed wholly through *eikos*, probability. This hypothetical subject embodies the subjective hypotheses that underpin Athenian law: he thinks like the law; his motives derive from it and his desires lead back to it. In this case, the law's probable subject is set against a "real" subject only to show that reality to be another fiction of legal discourse, operating according to the same probabilities. The third section, examining the *Third Tetralogy*, also deals in likelihoods. This *Tetralogy* advances an argument from probability based on ethical type. Typology is the essence of characterization in forensic oratory: here it is also the cornerstone of the legal universe the case constructs, and the generic probabilities of the agent's psychology ground a legal metaphysics. The high stakes of this relation are revealed when, at the end of the case, the defendant unexpectedly flees. This seemingly atypical behavior threatens to disrupt the fundamental logic of the case's legal world; in the process, it exposes the fictionality of that world and the crucial role of the legal subject in maintaining it. The subjects in these cases are hardly colorful: they have only barely emerged from the acts on trial. But even in their barest outline they sketch a vision of law embodied, and the very emptiness of the individual legal subject will reveal the fullness of the law's own subjectivity.

THE INTENTIONAL SUBJECT (*TETRALOGY II*)

The three *Tetralogies* do not build a sustained argument, and thus can presumably be read in any order. I start with the second because it deals with the most basic relation between doer and deed, and therefore lets us see the legal subject in its most elementary form. The primary suture between a criminal deed and its doer is volition or intention. This is what makes an agent ethically and legally (and not just physically or mechanically) responsible for his actions. But intention is a notoriously slippery concept.[12] Greek, like English, conceived of it as a blurry continuum between deliberate premeditation (*dianoia*, *pronoia*) at one end and compulsion (*anankē*) or sheer accident (*atukhia*) at the other. The middle ground between these two extremes (the terrain of most court cases) was covered by the term *hekōn* or *hekousios* and its antonym *akōn*/*akousios*. These words describe the doer's attitude toward the deed, his commitment to or detachment from it.[13] The precise semantic range of these words was diffuse, covering both intention and volition; sometimes *hekōn* is translated "deliberately," sometimes "voluntarily." Their imprecision is partly what makes these terms so useful to Antiphon in this *Tetralogy*, as it allows him mobility among varying degrees of agency and responsibility, from minimal volition to willful intent.

Intent played a central role in Athenian law. As early as the lawcode of Draco (dated to c. 620 BCE and truly venerable in Athenian eyes) intentional homicide seems to be differentiated from unintentional: in the course of assigning them the same penalties, the code distinguishes between committing murder with and without malice aforethought (*pronoia*) and between planning and perpetrating a crime.[14] These distinctions were formally institutionalized in legal practice, where there were different courts corresponding to different degrees of intent and liability. Intentional killing

[12] See especially Arist. *MM* 1188b25–38; *NE* 1109b30–1111b3, 1135a15–1136a9. L. Wilson 2000: 25–67 offers a fine discussion of intention in Renaissance English law. See also B. Williams 1993: 50–74 on the notion of responsibility in antiquity, and Brooks 2000: 65–87 on the problem of voluntariness in modern legal thought.

[13] This is the conclusion of Rickert's (1989) exhaustive study of the word group; cf. Gernet 1917: 350–88; Vernant 1988: 60–61, 63–64. Awkwardly there is no noun form corresponding to these adjectives. The closest equivalents (*bouleusis* and *dianoia* on the *hekōn* side, *anankē* on the *akōn* side) are much stronger. I will use "intention" and "volition" as the context dictates. On the vocabulary of will in classical antiquity, see Maschke 1968: 69–170; Dihle 1982: 20–31; Vernant 1988: 53–69.

[14] For the text of this law, see *IG* I³104 and Stroud 1968: 1–18. For various interpretations of the place of intention in Draco's law and subsequent Athenian homicide law, see Gernet 1917: 310–88; MacDowell 1963: 44–47, 117–25; Maschke 1968: 28–110; Stroud 1968: 34–40; Loomis 1972; Gagarin 1981: 30–37, 65–79; Carawan 1998: 33–83, 2000. The notion that Draco's law prescribed death for all crimes (the origin of the epithet "draconian") is late and probably mistaken: see Plut. *Solon* 17.2–4.

or wounding and poisoning where the accused administered the poison himself were tried in the Areopagus; unintentional killing and murder through an intermediary were tried in the Palladion; justifiable homicide, where the accused admits to the murder but claims it was legal, was tried in the Delphinion; when the cause of death was an animal or inanimate object, the case was heard in the Prytaneion.[15]

Tetralogy II deals with the second type of case, involuntary (*akousion*) homicide, a particularly difficult case for Athenian legal thought. If volition connects the doer legally to the deed, involuntary or unintentional crime opens a theoretical gap between the two. On the one hand, it leaves a criminal act with no liable agent, and therefore yields an act that is inaccessible to litigation. On the other, it posits an agent who acts against the law yet without legal responsibility. How does the law parse such a sentence fragment?

In *Tetralogy II* a youth practicing javelin-throwing has accidentally struck and killed a boy who ran out on the field to collect the javelins.[16] The plaintiff and the defendant, fathers of the dead boy and the youth respectively, agree on the facts but not on the "truth of the event" (*tēn alētheian tōn prakhthentōn*, 3.3, cf. 2.3). In order to get to that truth, the event must be "interpreted" (*hermēneusai*, 2.1), submitted to a hermeneutics that will situate it on the continuum between volition, action, and result. The *Tetralogy* rules out intentional homicide: both parties concur that the youth did not strike the boy *hekōn*, intentionally. Both also agree that he threw the javelin by which the boy was killed. Antiphon toys with various ways of splitting the difference: he raises the possibility of shared responsibility (3.10) or of blaming the trainer who called the boy (3.6, 4.4) but grants neither much argumentative weight. The text is concerned not to resolve the question of liability – in these fake cases there is neither jury nor verdict – but instead to use this scenario to dismantle, inspect, and reassemble the various links in the chain of legal liability. The very language of the scenario bespeaks the complexities of this causal chain. The verb *ballein*, which expresses the key action of the event, means both to throw and to strike. Antiphon relishes the ironies: the youth threw but did not strike (2.3–5, 4.4), the strike was

[15] [Arist.] *Ath. Pol.* 57.3–4; Dem. 23.22–99; MacDowell 1963: 39–89, 1978: 117–18; Sealey 1987: 70–77; Carawan 1998: 6–20, 84–135. There was also a court (off-shore at Phreatto) for cases of homicide brought against someone already in exile for homicide, presumably designed to offer redress to the victim's family without incurring pollution by recalling the murderer to Athens.

[16] Plutarch reports that "When a pentathlete accidentally struck Epitimios the Pharsalian with a javelin and killed him, Pericles spent the whole day debating with Protagoras whether the most correct argument should assign liability for the death to the javelin, the thrower, or the organizer of the games" (Plut. *Per.* 36.3). Carawan 1998: 180–81 believes the *Tetralogy* was inspired by this same case.

fatal even if the throw was not (3.5), the throw was intentional even if the strike was not (3.6). The case's rhetorical playing field is bounded by these verbal ambiguities. It suspends the javelin in mid-flight and between the youth's hand and the boy's body tries to locate a culpable agent of the accident. But will its hermeneutics hit the mark?

The plaintiff, the dead boy's father, tries to close the gap between throw and strike, to fuse action and result and exclude intention altogether. For him the ethics of agency can be reduced to a physics of causality. His one-paragraph opening speech has the brevity of common-sense: his son was killed by the javelin thrown by his opponent's son. He recognizes that the youth did not mean to kill his son, but that, he says, does not change the result or lessen his own grief (1.2). For this father, the deed is defined by its result and causality entails culpability. The strike killed his son, and the agent of the deed is necessarily liable for its results, whatever his intent. He presents this interpretation as obvious and needing no elaboration. There was a deed. Here is the doer. *Akōn* or *hekōn*, the doer is liable for the deed and its consequences. Case closed.

The plaintiff will later be said to regret having wasted his first speech by assuming the issue was so clear-cut (3.2), and the case will go on to challenge this seemingly straightforward relation between agent and act. But the plaintiff's position is not totally naive. In fact, it is supported by the notion of religious pollution so prominent in this and the other two *Tetralogies*. In Greek religious thought bloodshed created a pollution or *miasma*, a moral stain that attached to the murderer until the crime was expiated and could be passed on like a disease to anyone who came into contact with him.[17] Thus the boy's father tells the jurors that if they do not convict the youth the divine stain of pollution will fall upon them (3.11) and the whole city will become polluted (1.2).

While *miasma* theory plays only a small part in real forensic oratory, it dominates the *Tetralogies*, opening or closing (and in some instances both) ten of the twelve total speeches. Scholars have seen its anomalous prominence as evidence of the text's artificiality, and this is no doubt right.[18]

[17] Parker 1983, esp. 104–43. On the pollution from homicide, see also Moulinier 1952: 81–87, 176–212; Adkins 1960: 86–115; MacDowell 1963: 3–5, 141–50; Gagarin 1981: 164–67; Sealey 1984b: 74–75; Arnaoutoglou 1993; Carawan 1998: 17–19, 192–97; Bendlin 2007: 185–88.

[18] Parker 1983: 130: "It seems that the author of the *Tetralogies* has taken the doctrine of pollution to a theoretical extreme some way beyond the level of unease that in practice it created." Carawan 1998: 197: "the author's archaizing piety is a purely formal posture – his evocative language is learned in large part from the [*sic*] drama." On Antiphon's treatment of *miasma*, see further Decleva Caizzi 1969: 25–31; Parker 1983: 104–10; B. Williams 1993: 60–63; Carawan 1993: 249–54, 1998: 192–98; Gagarin 2002: 109–12; Bendlin 2007: 185.

But *miasma* also allows the text to posit an alternate jurisprudential logic to its own imaginary jurisprudence. In each case pollution is woven into the key issues of the trial and offers an ideal solution to problems that human law cannot easily resolve. In the first *Tetralogy* (as we shall see) it offers a theological foundation for the case's legal probabilities; in the third, it represents a mechanical justice that answers every crime with an equal punishment.

Here in the second *Tetralogy*, religious culpability cuts the legal knot of intentionality. Pollution caused by a violent deed adheres to its doer and can be erased only by his punishment. As a theory of justice, then, pollution functions according to the same presuppositions as govern the plaintiff's first speech: every act has an agent; liability for the act rests with the agent; the wrong of the act can be righted only by punishing the agent. *Miasma* cares no more for motive or intention than does this plaintiff.[19] This is why pollution is imagined as transferable. Though embodied it is impersonal and non-subjective – so much so, in fact, that it may have even been transferable to inanimate objects.[20] In this sense it captures one of the paradoxes of this *Tetralogy*: its simultaneous need for a liable agent and lack of interest in an individualized subject.

The plaintiff takes for granted the immediate and straightforward connection between the criminal act and its liable agent (1.1). For this speaker, liability lies wholly on the side of the outcome. The defendant's son caused that outcome – if only in the most literal causal sense – and is thus liable: between throw and strike, intention is ellipsed. The defendant, the father of the javelin-throwing youth, likewise argues for strict liability and a strong connection between intention, action, and result. But he will give this connection a surprising twist, as he warns us when he asks the jurors' forgiveness if he speaks "more subtly than is usual" (*akribesteron*, 2.2; cf. 4.2 *lepta kai akribē*).[21] Both sides agree that the death was unintentional,

[19] It does apparently care about legality, though. In the fourth century justifiable homicides seem to have been considered ritually clean (Parker 1983: 117, 366–69). Parker points out that pollution in the *Tetralogies* is less epidemiological than in other contemporary literature: it does not spread indiscriminately via contagion, but adheres to any who fail to attain justice for the victim; in the *Tetralogies*, he concludes, "pollution appears as a stern and discriminating upholder of the moral order" (1983: 110).

[20] Homicide cases involving inanimate objects were tried in the Prytaneion. They may have reflected *miasma* theory or may (as MacDowell 1963: 89, 1978: 118 suggests) merely have been a way of officially registering the cause of death. Cf. Aesch. 3.244; W. Hyde 1917: 171–75; and the ritual of the Bouphonia, discussed below.

[21] For *akribeia* ("precision") meaning "subtlety" see Gagarin 1997: 16, 148, who suggests that the word had sophistic connotations. Cf. Christ 1998a: 200, 204; and Ar. *Nub.* 130.

he begins. Therefore the responsibility rests with the agent whose unintentional action resulted in the death. That was not his son, since he intended to throw the javelin at the target and did so. It would be different, he says, if his son had hit the boy while throwing outside the prescribed boundaries; then he would have no defense. But in fact the boy ran into the course of the javelin – accidentally (*hamartontos*, 2.3) but of his own free will (*hekousiōs*, 2.5) – and is thus himself responsible for his own death. The father defends his son on the grounds not that he acted unintentionally (yes, he hit the boy but he didn't intend to) but that he acted intentionally (he meant to hit the target and would have, had the boy not got in the way). While the plaintiff views the act from the standpoint of its results (my son is dead whether the act was intentional or not) the defendant judges it only in relation to its intent, uncoupling it from the unfortunate consequences. His son intended to throw his javelin at the target and he did. He did not intend to kill the boy and thus he did not kill him. A subtle argument indeed.

For the other father intent meant nothing. For this one it means everything. This father, instead of using intention to loosen the bond of liability between doer and deed, makes it an adamantine ligature between the two. In the end he will go even further and make willed action innocent and involuntary action culpable. He explains his theory of agency in defending his son's innocence: "doing everything exactly as he intended he did nothing involuntary" (*alla panta orthōs hōs epenoei drōn edrase men ouden akousion*, 2.7). Where we might have expected an apologia for involition and a meditation on chance and human error we meet instead the willful, autonomous, intending agent, *ho boulomenos*. The proper (*orthos*) subject of action is the man whose action directly (*orthōs*) enacts his intention (*panta orthōs hōs epenoei drōn*). For this man, every decision to throw results in a bull's-eye. Against the plaintiff's rather mechanical conceptualization of agency (in which the agent is the person physically responsible for the fatal act) the defendant offers a model of agency governed by the fiction of a willful and efficacious subject – a fiction applicable in this case only if we overlook the "wretched and bitter target" (as the bereaved father puts it, 3.6) that he actually hit. The defendant implies that the law requires this fiction of an intentional agent to try even an unintentional crime. He salvages that subject from the scene of the accident by rediscovering agency in an unexpected location.

If the youth merely achieved his intention on the practice range, who then is responsible for the death? Who bears liability for an involuntary action?

> Those who fail (*hamartanontes*) to accomplish something they intend (*epinoēsōsi*) are the agents of unintentional (*akousiōn*) acts. Those who do or experience something involuntarily (*akousion*) are responsible for their suffering. The youth committed no mistake (*hēmarten*) concerning anyone. He was practicing what he was told, not anything prohibited; he threw the javelin in the javelin range and not where the boys were exercising. He didn't hit the boy by missing (*hamartōn*) the target and throwing toward the sidelines. Instead, doing everything exactly as he intended, he did nothing involuntary (*alla panta orthōs hōs epenoei drōn edrase men ouden akousion*), and he suffered because he was prevented from hitting the target. The boy, wanting (*boulomenos*) to run out but mistaking the proper moment (*diamartōn tou kairou*) to run without getting hit, ended up with results he didn't want (*ouk ēthelen*). He erred unintentionally toward himself (*akousiōs de hamartōn eis heauton*) and brought on his own suffering. He has thus paid the penalty (*ekhei tēn dikēn*), avenging himself for his error (*hamartias*), though I wish it weren't so and I grieve for him. But since the error (*hamartias*) occurred to him, the deed belongs not to us but to the one who committed the error (*exhamartontos*). The suffering that comes to the agent clears us of liability, and has punished the doer justly at the very moment of his error (*hamartiai*). (2.6–8)

The same logic of intentionality that makes his son innocent makes the dead boy guilty of his own murder. If the death is defined as an unintended act, then the agent who acted unintentionally must bear responsibility. Criminal liability is shifted from agent to victim. The boy acted of his own free will; like the youth he began with an intention (*boulomenos*), but he mistook the proper moment (*tou kairou diamartōn*) and ended up with a result he did not want (*ouk ēthelen*). The model of agency is the same in both cases, but in one case intention flies straight, in the other it misses its mark. In this strained and unnatural line of argument, involition is redefined as a fatal failure to enact intent (*akousiōs de hamartōn*). The adverb "unwilling" is reparsed as a new verb "to err." That error is then construed as an active agency bearing liability for the consequences. The unintentionality that might have been expected to exculpate the defendant's son in fact condemns the plaintiff's son. The dead boy is his own murderer and he has paid the price for that death with his life.

"Erring unintentionally (*hamartōn*) . . . he has avenged himself for his error (*hamartias*)" (2.8). At the heart of this schema of unintentional agency lies *hamartia*. *Hamartia* is the common Greek term for a mistake or error of judgment. Aristotle defines it as a culpable action committed in ignorance of its object or effect: his example is hitting (*ballein*) the wrong person or with the wrong weapon or with unintended results. Unlike mere accident (*atukhēma*), the effects of a *hamartia* are foreseeable, and therefore it is culpable; unlike a crime (*adikēma*), however, it is performed without evil intent and causes the agent regret.[22] *Hamartia* thus names the gap between the agent's intention and the act's results.

In itself the word *hamartia* does not specify the source of the error or the psychology behind it. Speculating upon these questions is one of the central preoccupations of Athenian tragedy, the genre par excellence of *hamartia* and one that lurks in the background of this case, as we shall see. There *hamartia* is yoked variously to a blindness sent by the gods (*atē*), to the uncertainties of communication and the schism between appearance and reality, or to the plight of mortals in a universe that exceeds their understanding and control (and often to all at once). The notion of *hamartia*, in short, opens onto tragedy's most profound ethical, psychological, and theological concerns. In *Tetralogy II*, by contrast, *hamartia* is understood in its most literal sense. The root meaning of *hamartanō* (the verbal form of *hamartia*) is "to miss the mark."[23] This case is thus about *hamartia* at both the literal level (in the scenario of the missed target) and at a figurative level (in the theme of unintentional action). The case is a metaphor for itself.

This collapsing of the literal and figurative yields a particular and particularly limited understanding of *hamartia*. The case's paradigmatic error is purely mechanical, a mismatch between throw and strike. The defendant transfers the physical model of the javelin to the mistaken behavior of the boy. But these two actions are incommensurate. The reasons why, in the absence of malice, a javelin may fail to hit its target (a poor throw, a tired arm, bad eyesight, a gust of wind, or in this case an obstruction) do not exhaust the reasons why individuals act in error, either ancient reasons (*hubris, atē, akrasia*) or modern (unconscious desire, internal conflict). Freud famously argued that there are no mistakes.[24] This is not to suggest that the boy ran in front of the javelins out of some death wish or to act out an unconscious fantasy. It is merely to notice that by tying metaphorical *hamartia* to its literal meaning, by framing it in terms of mechanical failure, the second *Tetralogy* strips error of all the psychological complexity and moral meaning it bears, for example, in tragedy.

[22] Arist. *NE* 1135b11–25; cf. *NE* 1109b30–1115a24, *Rhet.* 1374b6–9. On *hamartia* in Aristotle, see Bremer 1969: 4–24, 52–57; Stinton 1975; Kenny 1979: 59–63; Sorabji 1980: 278–81; Dihle 1982: 54–60; Halliwell 1986: 215–37; Vernant 1988: 62, 64–65; Rickert 1989: 93–126. Gernet discusses the role of *hamartia* in the development of Greek legal thought (1917: 305–48). See further Ant. 5.92: "An unintentional error is a matter of bad luck; an intentional one a matter of choice (*gnōmēs*). What could be more intentional than if someone immediately accomplishes what he plans?"

[23] For instances of this usage, see Bremer 1969: 30–59.

[24] Freud 1960 [1901], esp. 162–216.

Indeed, it strips it of any significance at all. On the human level *hamartia* is just carelessness (*aphulaxia*, 4.7). At the theological level it is explicitly contrasted to the gods' involvement in human affairs: either the accident was the result of divine intervention (*epimeleia*) or it was pure error, *hamartia* (3.8). Meaningless in itself, error serves only to block the path of efficacious agency. *Hamartia* intervenes between the boy's desire to act (*boulomenos prodramein*) and the desired results (*periepesen hois ouk ēthelen*, 2.8). It obstructs the boy's intention in the same way that the boy physically obstructs the javelin-thrower's intention: both cause a temporary break in an otherwise smooth and predictable chain of causality. This extension of the literal meaning of *hamartia* to the error of the boy thus paradoxically works to preserve the intending subject. *Hamartia* becomes the empty but essential link between intention and result and the very ground of legal liability. To that extent, it less describes than simply replaces the subject of accidental action. In short, error erred. But the case does not explore this interesting tautology: it has a different target. Thus while the law takes aim at the errant deed, it misses the mark of the erring subject. The result is less an instance of "case closed" than it is one of "case never opened."

Literalization of the metaphor of error allows the case to save intention from accident, to link deed to doer and hence to make the event available to litigation. But it also creates a circularity within the legal reasoning of the case. Instead of working through the difficult issues of responsibility and intention, the case merely enacts them. The literal becomes a metaphor for the metaphoric. Metaphors explain by comparison: they reveal something about the term they modify by carrying it over (*meta-pherein*) into a different register. But this metaphor doesn't carry the issue anywhere except back to itself. The legal thinking, in other words, is unable to escape the parameters of the imagined scenario and as a result is unable to clarify that scenario. Mis-hits proliferate within the arguments of each side. By dying, says the defendant, the dead boy has struck (*prosebalen*) his son with a guilt he does not deserve (2.4); he begs the jurors to acquit his son and not to strike (*peribalēte*) them both with untimely disaster (2.12; cf. *embalēte*, 4.10). The plaintiff uses the same metaphor to pathetic effect, referring to the "wretched and bitter target" (*athlion kai pikron skopon*) that his son became (3.6) and asking the jurors not to obstruct with their vote the gods' assault (*tas theias prosbolas*) against his murderer (3.8). The rhetoric of the case replicates the metaphor of the accident and the error. The case that cannot be resolved can only be repeated.

Circling around the accident without ever making sense of it, the legal arguments in this case stall out in a dead end of bad alternatives. The plaintiff puts them starkly. My opponent claims that his son did not strike or kill my son. "I believe I could more plausibly claim that he killed him intentionally . . . He did not kill him intentionally, but it is more true that he killed him intentionally than that he didn't strike and kill him at all" (3.5–6). Either the youth killed the boy intentionally or the boy was responsible for his own death. The former option is agreed by both sides to be false. The latter, argued strenuously by the defense, is characterized by the plaintiff as shameless and reckless (*anaidēs* and *tolmēros*, 3.1; cf. 3.5), a "depraved subtlety of argument" (*ponēras logōn akribeias*, 3.3).[25] On the one side we have the callous logic that makes the dead boy the criminal and the javelin-thrower his victim; on the other an admitted falsehood. The case never escapes from this argumentative double-bind. In its commitment to the intending subject the case is unable either to theorize or to exculpate unintentional action. As a result it is trapped between all and nothing: either the youth threw intentionally or he didn't throw at all. As a forensic metaphor, *hamartia* does not resolve the legal conundrum, it merely names it.

Perhaps this explains why the law is so unhelpful in deciding this case. The defendant invokes "the law which forbids just or unjust homicide" (*mēte adikōs mēte dikaiōs apokteinein,* 2.9; cf. 3.7). This citation has perplexed scholars since, as Michael Gagarin puts it, "a statute prohibiting lawful homicide would be self-contradictory."[26] He takes it as a reference to law in general (*ius*) rather than a specific law (*lex*), but even so it is a strange formulation. Did the Athenians really think "the law" prohibited killing under all circumstances, even "just" ones? If they did, there would be no point in having a special court designated for the defense of justifiable homicide. In fact, ancient sources list numerous instances of lawful homicide, including accidentally killing an opponent in an athletic contest.[27] Perhaps this is an allusion to the pollution that attaches to all murder,

25 The text seems to back up this charge in the aggressive tenor of the defense speeches. Gagarin 1997: 151 ad loc. comments on the "almost mocking tone" of the jingles in 2.8 (*ou sunēdomenōn men oude sunethelontōn hēmōn, sunalgountōn de kai sullupoumenōn*), "particularly in conjunction with the conclusion that the boy's death was just punishment." Similarly, the claim that the boy's death has made the youth into the victim is punctuated by a cruel pun: the boy, by being killed, has "struck us with undeserved guilt" (2.4). If this is, as Gagarin says (1997: 150 ad loc.), a "frivolous touch," it is a heartless one.

26 Gagarin 1997: 151 *ad Tet. II* 2.9; cf. 1997: 24: "more likely [this law] is a product of the sophistic spirit of provocative experimentation that informs the Tetralogies." The same law is cited in *Tetralogy III* in reference to self-defense (2.3, 4.8). See further Decleva Caizzi 1969: 21–44; Gagarin 1978b, 2002: 56–58; Sealey 1984b: 75–76; Carawan 1993: 254–65, 1998: 198–208; Eucken 1996.

27 [Arist.] *Ath. Pol.* 57.3, Dem. 23.53; MacDowell 1963: 73–79, 1978: 113–18; Gagarin 1981: 62–64; Carawan 1998: 92–96, 198–208.

but if so it is remarkably obscure, especially given the frequent overt references to pollution throughout the text. It is equally obscure as support for the issue at hand, *mens rea*. The defendant claims his son is innocent under this law because he killed neither intentionally nor unintentionally (*akousiōs*, *hekōn*, 2.9). He conflates volition and justice, but *adikōs/dikaiōs* (unjust/just), the terms of the law, are not precisely commensurate with *akōn/hekōn* (involuntary/voluntary). The former address the deed's legality, its conformity to *dikē*, not the mentality of its agent. By shifting the terms from volition (agency) to justice (a description of the act) "the law" merely begs the legal questions the case has posed about the relation between the two.

Statutory law proves to be too blunt an instrument to help cut through the case's knots of agency and liability. The plaintiff reinforces this impression when he later uses this same legislation to eliminate intention from the debate:

> He killed my son involuntarily (*akousiōs*) no less than he would have voluntarily (*hekousiōs*), but he altogether denies he killed him and says the law that forbids just or unjust homicide does not apply to him. But who threw the javelin? . . . I think the law is right (*orthōs*) to punish killers, for it is just (*dikaios*) that a man who kills unintentionally (*akōn*) have unintended (*akousiōs*) troubles, but it would be unjust (*adikoit'*) for the victim to go unavenged, since he was destroyed no less by unintentional (*akousiōs*) than intentional (*hekousiōs*) harm. (3.7)

The law that bans all killing, just and unjust, makes all agency, voluntary and involuntary, equally culpable. Justice is a straight throw (*orthōs*) from the deed to its punishment; volition is no obstacle. For the defense, the law against just and unjust killing acquits his son of both voluntary and involuntary homicide; for the plaintiff it condemns the youth, indifferently, on either count. The law that is introduced as if it were an independent source of persuasion is subsumed back into the aporetic arguments of the case, unable even to speak to – much less resolve – the dilemma of intent.

Neither the legal argument nor the law seems able to determine the legal status of an involuntary agent, to legislate the gap between throw and strike, or to parse the grammar of a verb without an intending subject. Instead, the *Tetralogy* defers its verdict elsewhere. Repeatedly throughout the case, the accident itself is referred to in the language of a trial. "Punishing himself for his own error, the boy has his just deserts," says the defendant. "His suffering justly punished the doer at the very moment of his error" (2.8). The boy's death is a death-sentence passed against his self-murder; the jurors must honor "the sanctity and justice of what has happened" (*eusebeian toutōn tōn prakhthentōn kai to dikaion*) and vote to acquit (2.12). The implication is that the gods have already passed a verdict upon the boy's action: his death proves his guilt. The jurors must not "vote against the god" (*enantia tou daimonos gnōte*, 4.10).

The plaintiff concurs that the accident was a trial, but of course disagrees about the verdict and the ramifications for this "appeal." He sees his son's death as a sentence passed unjustly against himself (*thanatōi zēmioumetha*, 3.9). He concedes for the moment the defense's point that the boy is responsible since he ran into the path of the javelin instead of standing still, but argues that if that is true then the youth should share responsibility for throwing the javelin instead of himself standing still (3.10). If the two share the guilt, he concludes, they should receive the same penalty. The boy has punished himself by dying (*tetimōrētai, tethnēke gar*), but his "accomplice and partner in the mistake" has gone unpunished (3.10). The youth's misfortune (*atukhia*) in having struck the boy, far from being a reason to acquit him, is all the more reason to convict, for either it is the result of his own error and he deserves to suffer for it or it is a "divine stain fallen upon the agent who commits impiety" and "it is not right to obstruct the divine onslaught" (3.8). His unfortunate miss, in other words, is either a crime in its own right (and the jury must convict) or divine punishment for some other impious act (and the jury must uphold that conviction). By turning the accident into a divine trial and the death into a verdict, the speeches try to by-pass the case's difficult questions of liability: those questions have already been answered by the "supreme" court. At the same time the intentionality that is so bedeviled in the accident itself is rediscovered in the divine *boulē* behind it, a *boulē* that has always already hit its mark.

If the trope of the accident as a trial deflects the problem of intention, the text's recurring allusions to tragedy defer the issue of unintention, *hamartia*. Tragic diction, frequent throughout Antiphon, is particularly notable in this *Tetralogy*. The boy's death "weighs on the heart" (*enthumion*, 1.2) of his father; the javelin struck a "wretched and bitter target" (*athlion kai pikron skopon emoi*, 3.6); this "harsh necessity" (*sklēras anankēs*, 2.2) has forced the defendant into court.[28] This is language Athenians would have recognized from the tragic stage. More strikingly, the text alludes

[28] *Enthumios*: cf. Soph. *OT* 739, *Trach.* 109; Eur. *HF* 722, *Ion* 1347. *Sklēras anankēs*: cf. Soph. *OC* 774, 1406 and Decleva Caizzi 1969: 215–16 *ad Tet. II* 2.2. *Athlion kai pikron skopon emoi*: it is the use of the metaphor here (plus the pathetic dative) more than the specific vocabulary that evokes tragedy, but compare the juxtaposition of *pikros* and *athlios* at Eur. *Hipp.* 787, *Or.* 952. See also *sullēptōr*, 3.10 (cf. Aes. *Ag.* 1507; Eur. *Or.* 1230); *sklēroti tou daimonos*, 3.4 (cf. Eur. *Alc.* 500–01, Xen. trag. fr. 2.1).

to the classic formulation of tragic responsibility: *drasanta pathein*, the doer suffers (Aes. *Cho.* 313). "Since the error (*hamartias*) occurred to him, the deed belongs not to us but to the one who committed the error (*exhamartontos*). The suffering that comes to the agent (*to te pathos eis ton drasanta elthon*) clears us of liability" (2.8). This allusion invites us to think about *hamartia* in tragic, as well as legal terms. *Hamartia* is a central problematic of tragedy, as I indicated above. This problematic emerges from a view of human action that emphasizes the blindness and ignorance of its motives, the overdetermination of its causes (both divine and human), and the unpredictability of its results. The formula "the doer suffers" denotes in short-hand the tragic justice that is sympathetic toward a character's error while holding him or her fully accountable for its results. In tragedy intention makes no difference (the doer must suffer) and all the difference (for the suffering of the undeserving agent is precisely where tragedy derives its pity and fear). Indeed, to the extent that in tragedy every action brings potential suffering and no mortal can foresee the outcome of any deed, the tragic subject is defined by unintention, by the necessary mismatch between intention, action, and results. It is no coincidence that Aristotle places *hamartia* at the very heart of tragic action (*Poet.* 1452b–1454a).[29]

This *Tetralogy*, by contrast, uses *hamartia* as a way of cementing even unintentional action to an intending subject (mistakes are just mis-hits) and evading the psychological complexities of a subject who acts unintentionally, a subject whose intentions, even when they aren't misguided, rarely hit their mark – precisely the subject of tragic *hamartia*. Antiphon's gestures toward tragedy, I think, both acknowledge and displace – acknowledge by displacing – this unintentional subject. There is no place for him within the law. This *Tetralogy* is tragic not only in its unfortunate scenario but also in its aporetic insolubility; unlike a real case, it is designed precisely not to reach a conclusion. And yet for all the text's own aporia, it figures the law's aim as sure and true. The law will in the end strike its mark, and it is not willing to entertain meditations on its own potential errancy.

This *Tetralogy*, then, shows us the legal subject in his most rudimentary form: as the locus of a volition that links the deed to a doer. In its eagerness to secure that link, this case willfully (*boulomenos*) extrapolates a willful subject even out of an involuntary act. There is a deliberate agent of accident. At the same time, the case also imagines an alternate logic, the jurisprudence of pollution, in which intent is irrelevant and the act itself

[29] Eden 1986: 25–61 studies the place of intent in Aristotle's poetic, rhetorical, and ethical theory. I discuss *hamartia* in Antiphon and tragedy further in Wohl (in press).

guarantees culpable agency. What it is unwilling to imagine is a space between these two alternatives, a space of unintention, of errant will and doer-less deeds. Thus the law itself intends that agents intend. Otherwise it will be forced to admit its own potential for *hamartia*, the tragic possibility that law's *boulē* will fly off-course and fail to hit the aim of justice.

THE PROBABLE SUBJECT (*TETRALOGY I*)

Close cousin to the intentional subject, the probable subject is the hypothetical protagonist of *Tetralogy I*. A man is found dead. His slave had identified the defendant before himself dying, but his testimony has been challenged since it was not given under torture.[30] In the absence of material evidence or valid witnesses, both sides argue the case from probability, *eikos*. The plaintiff argues that the defendant not only did kill the victim but was the most likely person to have killed him; the defendant argues that he didn't in fact kill him, nor was he likely to have done so.

The *eikos* argument had a long history in Greek rhetoric. Found already at the beginning of the fifth century in the *Homeric Hymn to Hermes* (265), it was said to have been developed by Corax, the quasi-mythical inventor of oratory.[31] The noun *eikos* is the substantive form of the participle from the verb *eoika*, "it looks like, seems, seems fitting." On the one hand, then, the word is associated with mere seeming (partly what Plato objected to about the argument[32]). On the other, *eikos* connotes propriety and comes in the classical period to bear the further meaning "what is reasonable, equitable, fair." Although *eikos* is by no means an exclusively legal concept – Aristotle makes it a defining feature of tragedy, which should tell not what actually happened but what might have happened "according to probability or necessity" (*kata to eikos ē to anankaion*, *Poet.* 1451a36–38) – the linguistic slide between appearance and equity marks its close affinity to the law.[33] In the *Tetralogies*, as we shall see, the probable world is an equitable world, a world of law.

30 Cf. Chapter 2 for the practice of torturing slaves for evidence.

31 Arist. *Rhet.* 1402a17–28; Kennedy 1963: 30–32; Gagarin 1994, 1997: 14, 2002: 112. On Corax see Kennedy 1963: 58–61; T. Cole 1991a: 23–27, 82–83; 1991b. Schmitz 2000 is an interesting discussion of *eikos* and the strategies orators used to produce the effect of verisimilitude.

32 He complains at *Phaedrus* 267a that rhetoric honors probability above truth. Cf. Gagarin 1994.

33 *Eikos* arguments are ubiquitous in Athenian literature across genres, and especially prevalent in tragedy (including the paradoxical lines of Agathon quoted in the epigram to this chapter), Thucydides, and the philosophers. This bespeaks the permeation of Athenian literature by rhetorical modes of thought. A full discussion of the word is beyond the scope of this study, but see Westlake 1958; Eden 1986: 18–19, 69–75; O'Sullivan 1995; Schmitz 2000 (with further bibliography). See also Dershowitz 1996 on the improbability of real life in contrast to legal narratives.

The *Tetralogy* opens with a theoretical justification of the method, in which a specific vision of the legal subject is already implicit:

> Crimes planned (*epibouleuetai*) by ordinary people (*tōn epitukhontōn*) are not difficult to prosecute; but if the doer is naturally capable, experienced in action, and at the age of greatest mental strength (*kratistoi phronein*), it is hard to identify and reveal him. Because of the great danger, such men spend a long time considering the safety of their plan (*epibouleuousi skopountes*) and do not undertake (*epikheirousin*) anything before they guard (*phulakēn poiēsōntai*) against all suspicion. You must (*khrē*) bear this in mind, and if you get a probable argument (*eikos*) you must put your faith in it. (1.1–2)

This *Tetralogy*, like the second, starts from the crime and moves to the criminal, but immediately differentiates between two types of criminal. There are crimes committed by "ordinary people" (*tōn epitukhontōn*: literally, "anyone who happens along"); these are easy to prosecute because the criminals leave behind evidence. Then there are the crimes committed by expert criminals: skilled by both nature and experience, at the peak of their rational power (*kratistoi phronein*), they plan the deed (*epibouleuousi*) carefully and calculate (*skopountes*) the risks thoroughly. If we didn't know the context we might think Antiphon was describing a general, setting up look-outs (*skopountes*) and placing guards (*phulakēn*) to assure the safety of his attack (*epikheirousin*).

The argument from probability presupposes this rational and skillful criminal. Indeed, it requires him, for his cautious planning makes it necessary (*khrē*) for the plaintiff to offer an *eikos* argument and the jurors to believe it. The probable argument needs a probable criminal and it creates that criminal in its own likeness (*eikos*). Intent is not the problem for this *Tetralogy* as it was for the second: the intent of the criminal mastermind, *ho epibouleuōn*, is taken for granted. Instead the problem lies in making that intent apparent (*eoika*). The suspicious criminal covers his tracks. *Eikos* will provide clear "tracks of suspicion" (*ta ikhnē tēs hupopsias*, 3.10, cf. 4.10) leading directly back to the scene of the murder and connecting the *logoi* of the trial to the *ergon* of the crime. The *eikos* argument conjures a probable doer out of the deed and makes him appear before the court; it simultaneously makes visible the equity (*eikos*) of the law that tries him.[34]

The plaintiff begins by eliminating other hypothetical suspects, summoning each in turn and judging him according to the standard of the

[34] A similar justification of *eikos* arguments is offered at Aesch. 1.91. See also Antiphon 5, where the probability of the prosecution's case founders on the lack of visible signs (*sēmeia*, 27–28, 43–45): the disappearance of the victim's body (*ephanisthē ho anēr*, 26) and the erasure of any signs of blood (*aphanisai*, 45) are not probable (*eikota*).

expert criminal. The crime couldn't have been committed by a cloak thief. The victim was not robbed of his cloak and no one would risk his life and then fail to take his prize. The murderer couldn't have been a drunk, since his drinking buddies would recognize and identify him. It couldn't have been a brawl over an insult, since those don't happen in a lonely spot in the middle of the night. Nor could he have been killed accidentally by a blow meant for someone else since his slave was killed too (1.4). This survey of crimes and criminals draws on a number of different registers of probability: individual psychology (the deliberations of the cloak thief); social behavior (the cultural practices of drinking and quarreling in Athens); logical argument (if it were an accident the slave wouldn't also have been killed). The probable subject is part of a probable universe that follows predictable patterns.

In this universe there are no irrational acts or actors. No one kills because he is a psychopath; drunkenness is as close as we come, and even that has its own rationality, or at least normativity. The *Tetralogy* as a whole has no time for the criminally insane. In his answer to the plaintiff's argument, the defendant counters that in fact it is quite likely that the murderers killed the man for his cloak, but someone came along before they could strip it off. "They would be sane and not mad (*esōphronoun kai ouk emainonto*) putting their safety before profit" (2.5). The pleonasm underlines the point: the insane criminal is simply impossible; he is by definition a subject who does not follow the rules of probability and thus has no place in the probable world of this case.

The expert criminal's strength is his rationality: he is *kratistos phronein*, a most powerful thinker. That *phronēsis* takes a very particular shape in this *Tetralogy*, though, and one that doesn't seem especially powerful. In fact, the criminal's success as *epibouleuōn* is precisely inverse to his failure as *boulomenos*: his legal failings explain his putative life as an outlaw. After eliminating the other possible (but not, he stresses, probable) suspects, the plaintiff explains why the defendant is the most likely murderer. His motive is a history of legal conflict. The defendant (says his opponent) had been an enemy of the victim for a long time (*ek pollou*, the same phrase used in 1.2 of the criminal's careful planning). He had brought many prosecutions against him but never won a case. The other had in turn brought many charges against him; he was convicted in all of them and had lost much of his property as a result. Recently the man had charged him with theft of sacred property, a very serious offense carrying a stiff fine. "Conscious (*suneidōs*) of his crime and familiar (*empeiros*) with the other man's power, resentful (*mnēsikakōn*) about what had happened in the past, he probably (*eikotōs*) plotted and, defending himself against the enmity of the other, he probably (*eikotōs*) killed the man" (1.6).

The narrative of probable motives is a legal narrative, a story of prosecutions and counter-prosecutions. The bare forensic facts of the narrative are fleshed out by a juridical psychology. A long sentence leads us by a series of participles from the legal history ("bringing prosecutions," "being prosecuted") through psychological reactions ("conscious," "familiar," "resentful") to the probable crime ("he plotted," "he killed").[35] The speaker moves deftly from the actual legal facts to the probable criminal act, suturing the two with his imagination of the probable workings of the probable criminal's mind. In that hypothetical mind, self-consciousness, memory of past experiences, and expectations for the future are all articulated within the framework of the law. The psychology of the probable subject, as the plaintiff reconstructs it, is a specifically legal psychology.[36]

The speaker elaborates this psychology. He goes on to explain. "Desire (*epithumia*) for vengeance made him forgetful of the danger, and fear (*phobos*) of the impending trouble terrified him (*ekplēssōn*) and made him more eager (*thermoteron*) for the attempt" (1.7). Desire and fear, those two primary driving emotions in Greek thought, worked on him. This is as close as the *Tetralogies* get to describing an irrational state of mind: *ekplēssōn* describes a terror verging on blind panic; *thermoteron* literally means "hotter" and may be borrowed from the language of medicine.[37] But the desire and the fear in this case are purely juridical: a desire to win his case and a fear of losing it. These two emotions are supplemented by hope. "He hoped in this way to kill the man without being caught and to be acquitted of the indictment [for theft], since there would be no one to come forward in the prosecution and the case would be won by default. Even if he were caught, he thought it would be more honorable (*kallion*) for him to suffer this and get his revenge than to be destroyed by the indictment like a coward (*anandrōs*), and have taken no action" (1.8). Like his fear and desire, his hope is fully juridical, an optimistic calculation of legal risks and benefits. All psychic life – not just desire and fear, but also honor (*kallion*) and manly shame (*anandrōs*) – is lived within the walls of the law. Law occupies the probable criminal's fears and hopes. Law is at the heart of his self-relationship (*suneidōs men autōi to adikēma*, 1.6), filling both his memory and his expectation. Law makes him hot, or at least "hotter." The

[35] Gagarin 1997: 127 ad loc. offers a good analysis of the structure of this sentence. On Antiphon's style in the *Tetralogies*, see further Zuntz 1939.

[36] Compare Johnstone 1999: 65.

[37] E.g. [Arist.] *Prob.* 869a2–5, 877a30–34, 947b–949a.

probable subject is a legal subject through and through. He is not only the subject of and subject to legal action, the nominative or accusative noun attached to the legal verb. He is also a psychological subject whose psychology is dominated by the subject of the law. Psychology itself then becomes the science of interpreting legal probabilities. Thus the probable psyche of the agent is fitted precisely to the hermeneutic which will render the probable as the visible within a framework of juridical equity.

We might expect that the defendant would counter this prejudicial probability with the reality of his innocence. He begins his first speech, promisingly enough, with the language of poetic woe: "I don't think I'm wrong to consider myself the most unfortunate (*atukhestaton*) of all men. For other unfortunate men, when they labor in the storm get a rest when fair skies return; when they are sick, are saved once they return to health . . . But in my case, alive this man was the ruin of my house and dead, even if I am acquitted, he has afflicted me with pain and care" (2.1–2). Emphasizing his heavy fate (*barudaimonias*, 2.2) he offers a vision of his real suffering self to counterweigh the probable self described by his opponent.[38]

This lamentation soon yields place, though, to the hypothetical him. My enemies have presented an inconsistent picture of me, he says. They claim that my cleverness makes me difficult to prosecute but they also paint me as a fool. "For if I am reasonably (*eikotōs*) the object of your suspicion now because of my tremendous enmity toward the victim, it was more likely (*eikoteron*) that before committing the crime I would have anticipated that suspicion would fall on me and far from doing the deed myself and voluntarily falling under open suspicion, I would even have prevented someone else from doing it, if I knew anyone was plotting against him" (2.3). The defendant does not draw a contrast between the prosecution's probable criminal and his own actual self. Instead he distinguishes between two probable selves. He talks about his own psychology in precisely the same terms that the plaintiff spoke of him and that he later speaks of the motives of other hypothetical suspects (2.6). He doesn't test *eikos* against actuality but only examines it within its own logical terms. In the process he turns himself into a probable subject.

The defendant employs a reverse-*eikos* argument, arguing that the likeliness of him having committed the crime made him less likely to commit the crime. In doing so, he attributes to himself a complex multi-step legal reasoning that approaches the potential deed from the perspective of its

[38] In classical Greek, *barudaimonia* (and its adjectival form) is predominantly poetic: see Alc. fr. 348; Ar. *Eq.* 558, *Ecc.* 1102; Eur. fr. 913, *Alc.* 865, *Tro.* 112. It occurs elsewhere in oratory only at Lys. 4.9.

eventual legal prosecution. Calculating the probabilities of the crime and its aftermath, trying to secure himself against suspicion, he thinks like the criminal mastermind (*ho epibouleuōn*) conjured by the plaintiff (1.1–2): he insists that he himself is *kratistos phronein*. But to the extent that he also thinks about the legal ramifications of the crime – how it will play before a jury – and works in advance to guarantee not only his safety but his eventual criminal defense, he approaches the crime not as a criminal but as a prosecutor, *ho boulomenos*. He presents himself as having worked through all the potential outcomes of facing the indictment for theft: if I was convicted, I knew I would lose my property but I wouldn't risk exile, as I do now. "Unless I was mad (*parephronoun*) I knew that the risk of committing murder was not less than that of the indictment but in fact many times greater" (2.9). The masterful *phronēsis* the defendant here claims for himself – the *phronēsis* of criminal and prosecutor alike – consists in thinking like the law, basing his thought and action on the likelihood of their legal outcome. To think otherwise is to be out of your mind (*paraphronein*). *Sana mens est mens rea.*

This text does recognize the difference between probable people and real. It opens, as we saw, with a distinction between "ordinary people" (*hoi epitukhontes*) and the criminal whose flawless planning necessitates and justifies the *eikos* argument (1.1). The defense insists on the difference between probability and truth (*alētheia*, 2.8) and between probably and actually killing (*eikotōs men ontōs de mē,* 2.10). My opponents claim to convict me from probability, he complains, but they charge that I murdered the man not probably but in actuality (*ouk eikotōs all' ontōs*, 4.10). The *Tetralogy* seems to want to preserve some ontological space for an extralegal, improbable reality. Likewise, in its glancing references to an irrational criminal it seems to preserve space for an improbable subject. But for the most part the text simply isn't interested in the improbable. It is obviously in the defendant's interest to emphasize a distinction between truth and probability, but he does so only to sideline truth. "If anyone thinks probability is equal to truth in the accusation against me, he should consider that I was more likely to . . . " (2.8). He is being tried on probability not truth; that is the premise of the *Tetralogy* and he accepts it.

The improbable truth appears only to be folded back into probability. The defendant objects that although he is being tried on probability, the accusation is real murder. But even while crying foul, he hopes to turn that same confusion of real and probable to his own advantage: "If I killed the man probably but not really, I deserve to be acquitted all the more, since it is clear that I was defending myself against a terrible injustice or else I wouldn't seem likely to have killed him. But you would properly convict those who really kill and not those who have a reason to kill" (2.10). Even as he insists on the difference between really killing and probably killing he suggests that the probable motive would provide adequate justification for actual murder.

The *Tetralogy* acknowledges a distinction between the probable and the real, then, but seems unable (or perhaps unwilling) to sustain it. The speakers segue almost imperceptibly between probability and actuality. The plaintiff's first speech, as we have seen, invokes only to dismiss various hypothetical suspects. These are introduced in a series of implied contrafactual conditions: it wasn't cloak thieves, because if it were his cloak would have been stolen; it wasn't an accident because if it were his slave would not have been killed, and so on (1.4). This parade of contrafactual characters culminates in what seems at first to be a genuine question: "Who is more likely to have attacked him than someone who had suffered great trouble in the past and expected to suffer more in the future?" But the answer shows the question was rhetorical: "That someone is the defendant!" (*esti d' ho diōkomenos houtos*, 1.5). The contrafactuals of probability move through the rhetorical question (who is more likely to have done it than the man who did it?) to the emphatic indicative *esti* (from the verb "to be"). The connective particle *de* ("and", "but") marks both the transition and the tension between the contrafactual and the actual. It *could have been* someone else, but it *is* the defendant.

This syntactical slippage is replicated at another level in the second defense speech when the cloak thieves and other criminals who have served as hypothetical counter-examples throughout the text suddenly become real:

> They say that if someone had happened upon them while they were beating him, he would be more likely to find out the murderers' identity and report it when he got home than to go off and leave them there. But I don't think there is any man so reckless and courageous that if he came across bodies gasping out their last breath in the dead of the night he wouldn't turn around and run away rather than risk his life investigating the perpetrators. Since these men [i.e. the ones who came across the crime in progress] did what was reasonable (*eikos*) [i.e. ran off without learning the identity of the criminals], those who killed them for their cloaks should not reasonably (*eikotōs*) be let off, and I am thus freed from suspicion. (4.4–5)

The logic of this passage is dizzying. In structure it is an argument a fortiori: if the less likely thing is true then the more likely thing must be true. But what is startling here is that both terms are unreal:

neither the passers-by nor the cloak thieves actually exist. As Gagarin explains, "these hypothetical passers-by, who were created to explain why the 'likely' murderers did not steal the victim's cloak, are now spoken of as actual persons . . . as are the hypothetical muggers, whom it would no longer be reasonable to acquit . . . [T]he defendant essentially turns likelihood into fact."[39] And if hypothetical criminals are let off, a fortiori the actual defendant is freed from any suspicion, probable or reasonable.

This confusion of the real and the likely is apparently resolved in the final speech of the *Tetralogy*. At this eleventh hour, after arguing at length why he was unlikely to have committed the murder, the defendant comes out with this surprising claim: not only was I not likely to have committed the crime, but I could not have committed it, since I was at home asleep that night and didn't go out anywhere (4.8). This, he says, is the testimony of fact not probability (*ouk ek tōn eikotōn all' ergōi*). As alibis go this isn't particularly convincing, but he bolsters it with a significant detail: I remember the specific night, he says, because it was the night of the Dipolieia, the festival of Zeus Polieus. And if his opponent doesn't believe it, he offers his slaves for torture.

With this last-minute alibi, the *Tetralogy* seems to invalidate its entire argument from probability.[40] The real subject – sleeping at home in his bed on a specific night – seems to trump the probable. Real slave bodies are offered to prove the probability of this asserted reality. But of course these slaves are no more real than their master. Both are fictional creations of this fictional case. It is as if at the last minute Antiphon tries to salvage a real – living, sleeping – subject of the law, to differentiate firmly – invoking the truth of the *basanos* and the name of Zeus – between probability and fact, *eikos* and *ergon*. But it is too late: the real defendant has already claimed for himself a probable psychology; hypothetical thieves have already been acquitted; the indicative has become hopelessly counterfactual.

It is significant that the alibi is a festival of Zeus or, to put it another way, that a festival of Zeus is offered as the only hard fact in the case, apart from the brute fact of the victim's death. An alibi, as the word suggests, looks elsewhere for its truth.[41] This alibi seeks to ground the case's probabilities on a supreme ontology: reality (*alētheia*, *to on*, *to ergon*) belongs not to the court but to the gods. Zeus's festival is the only actual *ergon* and the only

39 Gagarin 1997: 141 *ad Tet. I* 4.5. See also Decleva Caizzi 1969: 205 ad loc.

40 Gagarin 1997: 142 *ad Tet. I* 4.8 suggests this is why Antiphon waits until the end of the case to introduce it. See also Gagarin 1994: 53; Decleva Caizzi 1969: 206–07 ad loc.

41 Derrida 2002: xvi–xvii.

proof that the defendant really is, *ouk eikotōs all' ontōs,* what he claims, not just a probability but a real man in a real bed. But this reality, too, turns out to be hypothetical. The alibi's gesture toward a theological reality resonates with the theme of pollution that echoes through this *Tetralogy*, as it does through the other two. The pollution of the dead man casts a pall over the case: it will fall on the plaintiff if he prosecutes the wrong man (1.3), and on the jurors and the city as a whole if they fail to punish the murderer (1.10, 2.11); the dead man's spirit seeks revenge (3.10), but murdering an innocent man will fail to appease it and will only cause more pollution (4.11). If *eikos* is the crime's ghostly cause, pollution is its ghostly effect. The dead man's *daimōn* becomes yet another hypothetical character haunting the trial, this time not another hypothetical defendant but a spectral plaintiff, prosecuting his case from beyond the grave.[42] With the reference to the Dipolieia, the case tries to theologize the real. But the gods' justice offers no clearer path to the truth of the matter than does the *eikos* argument. The risk of *miasma* is incentive to "show as clearly as possible" who committed the murder, as the plaintiff says (1.3), but it does not in itself guarantee that clear revelation, and each side can with equal likelihood claim the gods' support for his own probabilities. The alibi seeks a reality elsewhere, beyond the case and its apparent truths, but it finds that reality in the unreal register of the divine, a world of *doxa* not secure *alētheia*.

The Dipolieia, moreover, was no ordinary festival. Even to the Greeks it seemed archaic and odd due to the unusual ritual at its center, the Bouphonia.[43] In this ritual, according to the travel-writer Pausanias, an ox was slaughtered to Zeus Polieus by a priest who then threw down the axe and fled. "The others, as though they don't know who did the deed (*hate ton andra hos edrase to ergon ouk eidotes*), bring the axe to trial" (Paus. 1.24.4; cf. 1.28.10). The late writer Porphyry tells an expanded version in which the guilt for the sacrifice is transferred serially: after the priest flees, blame falls first on the girls who fetched the water used in sharpening the axe; they blame the men who sharpened it, who in turn blame the man who applied the axe, and so on to the axe itself (*De Abst.* 2.10, 2.29–31).

The content of the ritual replicates with surprising fidelity the issues of this *Tetralogy*. There has been a death. A liable agent must be found and punished. But unlike our fictional case, the ritual acknowledges the fictionality of this process and its result. A real killing leads to a pretend

[42] Parker 1983: 116 speaks of pollution as "a kind of shadowy spiritual *Doppelgänger* of the law."

[43] Ar. *Nub.* 983; W. Hyde 1917; Parke 1977: 162–67; Simon 1983: 8–12; Katz 1992b: 254.

prosecution: the witnesses act "as though they don't know who did the deed." Trying the axe is the final act of this communal make-believe. The axe is, in one sense, the most plausible cause of death, the immediate, material, and visible instrument of the bloodshed. But in another sense, of course, an object without autonomous agency cannot bear legal liability. Or rather, it can bear liability only in a fictional sense. The axe is not itself guilty, but we will act "as though" it is. This fake trial does not solve the case, but we will act "as though" it does. This farcical drama shares the impulse of the *Tetralogy* to localize liability in a single, solid agent. But it admits in a way the *Tetralogy* does not that liability is always more or less a convenient fiction and the process of assigning it always involves a certain amount of make-believe. *Mens rea*, the intentional agent, the probable criminal, *ho epibouleuōn*: these are no less fictional than the fiction of a guilty axe, even if we act "as though" they were in order to bring the case to a close. The ritual that was to provide a secure reality for the legal subject is itself an unlikely drama of hypotheticals. The most the defendant can claim on the basis of such an alibi is that it was "as though" he was really home in bed. By the same token, though, the most the plaintiff can claim is that it is "as though" the defendant really committed the murder. Each pretense is equally probable as the other and neither more plausible than a guilty axe.

Moreover, the suspiciously close thematic fit makes this alibi itself seem improbable and reminds us of the fictionality of this text written "as though" it were an actual trial. Perhaps, then, this text's inability to sustain a distinction between the probable subject and the real is simply an effect of its own artificiality. The *Tetralogies* are not, after all, "real" cases; in many ways, they aren't even likely cases. There are no "real" people involved. Even their author, Antiphon, has his own problems of probability. Did he really write the *Tetralogies*? Is the author we know as Antiphon really one man or two different men (Antiphon the Rhetor and Antiphon the Sophist) or even more?[44] For what probable reasons would a man, be he rhetor or sophist, write such an improbable text? Are the *Tetralogies* just the hypothetical double of the real Antiphon's real court cases (and if so

[44] On the identity of Antiphon, see Hermog. *Peri Ideōn* (fr. 87A2 DK); Gagarin 2002: 7, 38–52. Gagarin and most other scholars believe that the character Xenophon (*Mem.* 1.6.1–15) refers to as "Antiphon the Sophist" (presumably author of the sophistical tracts, *On Truth* and *On Concord*) is the same man as Antiphon of Rhamnus, the orator. Cf. Morrison 1961; Decleva Caizzi 1969: 71–83; Avery 1982; Gagarin 1990a; Edwards 1998. The argument against this "unitarian" position is made most forcefully by Pendrick 1987, 1993, 2002: 1–26. I incline toward the former position, although my argument does not depend on it. On the fictionality of the *Tetralogies* in relation to their own logic of probability, see further Schmitz 2000: 54.

would that make the actual law of the courts their alibi)? Or was this all just a sophistic game of semblances (*eikones*) from the beginning?

But if the *Tetralogies* themselves seem improbable, their problems with probability can also be tracked in speeches designed for real cases, where *eikos* arguments are ubiquitous. For the sake of comparison, we can briefly consider Lysias 1, a speech famous for its *ēthopoiia*, its realistic characterization.[45] Euphiletus is on trial for the murder of Eratosthenes. He claims in his defense that Eratosthenes had seduced his wife and that he had killed him justly upon finding him in her bed. Homicide in instances of *moikheia* (adultery or rape) was considered justifiable in Athens and carried no punishment.[46] The plaintiffs, Eratosthenes' relatives, claim that the murder was actually premeditated, that Euphiletus lured Eratosthenes into his house by design so that he could kill him on the pretext of adultery. Euphiletus' defense rests largely on convincing the jurors that he was not the man to hatch such a plot, that he was an innocent cuckold and not a scheming murderer.

Ēthos is thus essential to his case and he devotes the bulk of his speech to a narrative carefully designed to portray it. He tells in first-person of the happy early days of his marriage, sharing with the jurors the intimate arrangements of his home life. He presents himself as a good and conscientious husband, lenient but not negligent toward his wife (6) and solicitous of her comfort (9). His casual mention of past drunken "attempts" on the maid (12) make the picture that much more believable. The split perspective of the narrative – ironically juxtaposing what he knew then and what he later found out, his apparent domestic bliss with his retrospective realization of its hollowness – creates the impression of an ingenuous, even gullible character. He relates incidents which, he says, he made nothing of at the time: a locked door, a squeaky hinge, his wife's made-up face. Only later does he discover the truth and look back over these details "full of suspicion" (17). Until then, he says, he was totally ignorant: "These things went on for some time and I never suspected a thing, but I was such a fool

45 It is generally assumed that this speech (or one very much like it) was composed for actual delivery and not as a show piece. For hesitations, however, see Porter 1997: 434–48. On Lysias' *ēthopoiia*, see Kennedy 1963: 135–38; Morford 1966; Dover 1968: 57–93; D.H. *Lys.* 7–8: "No one who pays attention to Lysias' words is so dull or stupid that he will not feel like . . . he is encountering face-to-face the characters the orator introduces. He will seek no further proof of what the various characters are likely (*eikos*) to do, feel, think, or say. For Lysias was the best of all the orators at observing the nature of men and granting the appropriate feelings, character, and deeds to each."

46 [Arist.] *Ath. Pol.* 57.3; Dem. 23.53. On the semantic and legal meaning of *moikheia* see MacDowell 1978: 124–25; S. G. Cole 1984; D. Cohen 1991a: 98–132, 1991b; Herman 1993; Todd 1993: 276–79; Carey 1995; Kapparis 1996; Omitowoju 2002: 72–115.

that I thought my wife was the most chaste woman in the entire city" (10). His gullibility then sets the stage for his distress at discovering the truth and his righteous self-vindication as protector of his *oikos* and agent of the law (26). All of this narration and all these details of characterization are designed to elicit the identification of the jurors with both his humiliation and his necessary revenge: I would very much wish, he says in the opening sentence, to have jurors who had experienced these things themselves, "for I know that if you had the same attitude toward others as you have toward yourselves, every single one of you would be upset at what has transpired and consider the penalty for this crime too light" (1). *Ēthos*, then, is his central legal strategy, and most readers agree that he makes a superb job of it.[47]

After narrating this plausible tale of his own real experiences and character, though, at the end of the speech he goes back over the same details, this time presenting them in the form of a probable, not an actual narrative. My opponents say I entrapped Eratosthenes (37). But if I were planning to entrap him, do you think I would have invited a friend to dinner on the night I was to execute my plot or that, having invited him, I would let him go home and would face Eratosthenes alone (40)? Wouldn't I have rounded up potential witnesses beforehand, or at a minimum ascertained if my friends were at home, instead of waiting until I discovered him in bed with my wife and then gathering a posse (41)? What had been presented as a factual, indicative account of actual events is now re-narrated in the contrafactual of probability.

This repetition is no doubt a product of forensic oratory's kettle-logic: one argument is never enough. But in this case the probable narrative undermines the plausibility of the "real" narrative. In the course of denying its probability, the speaker admits the possibility of an elaborate frame-job and of a subject capable of pulling it off. A Euphiletus who knows that gathering friends at the last minute makes his deed look unpremeditated could easily have used that knowledge deliberately to stage the scene as unpremeditated. This character, far from the innocent bumbler of the first narrative, looks a good deal like the first *Tetralogy*'s master criminal, who plots his deed with the eye of a prosecutor, planning his defense even as he plans his crime. The *eikos* argument insinuates this character next to the gullible cuckold of the "factual" narrative, and this repudiated probable

47 Usher 1965: 101–05; Edwards and Usher 1985: 221–22; Carey 1989: 62: "Euphiletos is Lysias' most impressive creation." Porter, by contrast, finds the characters too typical to be plausible (1997: 435–40). Even if, as Porter argues, the narrative is structured around a traditional "comic adultery scenario," the impression the speaker strives to give is one of authenticity.

subject makes the real subject, with all his good-natured obtuseness, himself seem rather improbable.

The probable subject is both a necessary and a problematic fiction within forensic oratory, then. *Tetralogy I* presents the *eikos* argument as an evidentiary supplement, employed only when there are no eye-witnesses or material evidence (1.1, 3.8). Positioned at the trial's epistemological limit, the probable subject testifies to the law's limitation, its inability to be eye-witness to the crime. Both defendant and plaintiff in *Tetralogy I* emphasize the stakes: in the absence of material evidence, without the *eikos* argument it would be impossible to convict criminals (1.10, 3.9) or to defend the innocent (4.10). Without clear "tracks of suspicion" (*ta ikhnē tēs hupopsias*, 3.10, 4.10) leading from the crime scene to the criminal, *eikos* is the law's only path, and without it the law is consigned to aporia. The probable subject, like the intentional subject, carries the law down that path and allows it to traverse the epistemological space between the court and the crime scene. The shared psychology, the forceful legal-minded *phronēsis*, that binds *ho boulomenos* and *ho epibouleuōn* allows the law to summon the criminal into court, transforming his probabilities into a manifest and culpable actuality: "that someone is the defendant!" (*esti d' ho diōkomenos houtos*). At the same time, by imagining the probable criminal psyche as a juridical psyche, the law can return to the very scene of the crime and see the event's probabilities as they appear to the eye of the criminal. In a sense, then, the probable subject becomes the law's bodily projection from its own hypothetical, discursive existence into the real world of the event itself, the actual *ergon*.

And yet, as this *Tetralogy* recognizes, that projection is only and always a phantasm and one, moreover, that reveals the fantasmatic quality of the law's very reality. The world within the courtroom, as this *Tetralogy* acknowledges, is an unreal and improbable place inhabited by fictions of the law's own creating, its "real" subjects no less than its probable. Juridical discourse may dream of reaching the extra-discursive reality of the deed itself, of understanding the crime "not probably but actually." It may try to distinguish the real from the probable and to preserve the probability of its own reality. But the *ergon* itself, Antiphon suggests, will always remain elsewhere, *alibi*.

LEGAL ANTHROPOLOGY (*TETRALOGY III*)

Tetralogy III deals with a homicide resulting from a drunken fight. A young man has killed an old man. The victim's relatives argue that the young man is liable, since he struck the fatal blow. The young man argues that the old man struck him first, and that he only hit back in self-defense. This *Tetralogy* is more diffuse than the other two, developing a number of different arguments on each side (including arguments from probability and intention). The scenario is generic. It resembles the paradigm example of the *eikos* argument attributed to Corax in which a strong man has killed a weak man; the plaintiff argues from probability (a strong man is more likely to kill a weak man than the opposite) and the defense from reverse probability (a strong man, knowing he would be the likely suspect, would not kill a weak man).[48] The issue is likewise generic: drunken fights appear in ancient rhetorical and legal theory as test-cases for agency and responsibility.[49] The actors, too, are generic. The Greeks conceived of *ēthos* in general in terms of typology (rather than individuality); in Aristotle's discussion of the various types of *ēthos* found in oratory, young men and old men lead the list.[50] The characters in this *Tetralogy* are not individualized in any way: their only characteristics are those characteristic of their type.

Their typicality is part of a central rhetorical strategy of the *Tetralogy*, an *eikos* argument from typology. The plaintiff argues that "it is more likely for young men to get drunk and start fights than old men" (3.2). He elaborates: "With young men the vanity of their kind (*genos*), the strength of their prime, and inexperience with drinking incite them to indulge their passion; with old men, experience around drunks, the weakness of old age and fear of the force of youth make them restrained" (3.2). The defense counters that many young men are moderate and many older men drunks, and this argument is not conclusive proof for either side (4.2). This typological argument is a refinement of the *eikos* argument we saw in *Tetralogy I*. Ethical type narrows the scope of human probabilities and sharpens the predictive force of the probable. This kind of reasoning is common in forensic speeches. When defendants cite their past liturgies, for example, they draw upon typological logic: the type of man who has served the state so well is not the type to commit a crime against it or its citizens.[51] But whereas in most real cases the typicalities of type are fleshed out with details from an individual life, in this *Tetralogy* the two figures

48 See note 31 above.

49 E.g. Arist. *NE* 1113b30–34, *Rhet.* 1402b10; Dem. 21.73–75. Carawan 1993: 239–40 suggests that all three *Tetralogies* are based on famous or typical cases.

50 *Rhet.* 1389a–1390b. See further Decleva Caizzi 1969: 251 *ad Tet. III* 3.2; Dover 1974: 102–06. For ethical typology, see Arist. *Poet.* 1454a16–b18, *Rhet.* 1413b3–1418b39; Johnstone 1999: 93–108; Worman 2002.

51 Johnstone 1999: 97.

remain unindividualized, merely an old man and a young man. The generic case is peopled by generic agents, agents fully defined by their *genos*.

What is the psychology of a generic subject? A generic psychology. The *Tetralogy* unravels this tautology by a shift of perspective from individual type (*genos*) to the human species (*genos*). *Tetralogy III* opens with a fable about the origins of the human race (*to anthrōpinon phulon*), an anthropology of human *phusis* that becomes the foundation for a larger juridical physics and metaphysics:

> *Nomos* rightly dictates (*nenomistai men orthōs*) that those trying murder cases do their utmost to prosecute and testify in accordance with justice, neither acquitting the guilty nor bringing the innocent to trial. For the god, wishing (*boulomenos*) to make the human race (*to anthrōpinon phulon*), created (*ephusen*) the first-born of us and gave us the land and sea to nurture us so that a lack of daily necessities would not make us die before the end of old age. Since the god judged our lives worthy (*axiōthentos*) of these gifts, anyone who kills someone unlawfully (*anomōs*) is committing impiety toward the gods and is confounding the lawful existence of mortals (*ta nomima tōn anthrōpōn*). For the dead man, robbed of what the god gave (*edōken*) him, likely leaves behind hostile avenging spirits as the god's vengeance. Those who judge or testify unjustly share in the murderer's impiety and introduce into their own homes an alien pollution. We who seek retribution for the dead, if we prosecute the innocent because of an unrelated enmity, will face the terrible avenging spirits of the dead for not avenging the victim and we will ourselves be liable to the wages (*epitimiois*) of murder for unjustly killing innocent men. We will also be responsible for your error if we persuade you to act unlawfully. (1.1–4)

Antiphon here envisions a state of nature, mankind's original *phusis* (*phulon*, *ephusen*).[52] The gift of a benevolent and creative god, this edenic existence is characterized by its order and balance. Mortals lack for none of the necessities; they live their allotted spans and do not die before their designated end. Our *phusis* is a gift of divine deliberation (*boulomenos . . . ephusen*) and is regulated by the equity of divine evaluation (*axiōthentos*). This orderly economy is confounded by murder, which steals the god's gift and leaves a vengeful spirit in exchange.

Law intervenes to repair the idyllic balance disrupted by the murderer's lawless (*anomōs*) crime. By adding (*epithentes*, 1.5) a punishment equivalent to the crime (*axian*, 1.5; cf. 1.7), the jurors will purify the city of pollution. *Nomos* is added to *phusis* in order to restore its lost equilibrium.[53] But if

[52] Such anthropological fables may have been a common topos among the sophists. Cf. Pl. *Prot.* 320d–323c; Kerferd 1981: 125–30, 139–62.

[53] In *On Truth* Antiphon (if it is the same Antiphon) states that law is supplementary (*epitheta*) to *phusis*, which is primary (*anankaia*), and that "most of what is just according to law is hostile to nature" (fr. 44B1–2, following the text of Decleva Caizzi 1989). See Pendrick 2002: 315–50; Gagarin

phusis requires *nomos* for its smooth operation, *nomos* requires *phusis* as its justification: it is because life is a divine gift that *nomos* dictates that homicide cases are prosecuted with particular care (1.2). Not only mutually dependent, *phusis* and *nomos* are at one point virtually equated: the original state confounded by the murderer's lawless act is glossed as *ta nomima tōn anthrōpōn* (1.2). Law stands on both sides of the fall. Its order symbolizes the harmony of this original world, and its prosecution of crime is both an attempt to regain that paradise and an emblem of its loss. *Nomos* thus has a deep stake in this vision of human *phusis* and *to anthrōpinon phulon*.

The disorder introduced by crime is represented in this *Tetralogy* as an economic imbalance: the god's beneficent gift is stolen and replaced with pollution (1.3).[54] In contrast to the generous abundance of our original state, the post-lapsarian world is one of dangerous exchanges, in which jurors who decide unjustly import an alien stain into their own homes (1.4) and crooked prosecutors are liable to the wages of murder (*epitimiois*, 1.4; cf. 1.6, 2.3, 4.7). From then on, exchange and reciprocity are the guiding metaphors of the case. The crime itself is a reciprocal exchange of blows. Even if I had struck him with a rock or stick I would be in the right, says the defendant, "since those who start fights deserve to suffer in return (*antipaskhein*) not the same thing but more and greater. I was struck by his hands. I gave back what I suffered with my hands. How did I do wrong?" (2.2; cf. 2.3, 2.5, 3.3, 4.6). If the fight is a return of blow for blow, justice is the taking of a soul for a soul. The plaintiff urges the jurors to repay the murderer's theft of the victim's soul (1.6) with a punishment worthy (*axiōs*, 1.7) of the crime by "robbing him in exchange of the soul that plotted" the deed (*tēn bouleusasan psukhēn antaphelesthai auton*, 1.7). The defendant counters that if the jurors falsely condemn him they will be robbing him of the life the god gave him (2.7) and will reap a double *miasma* as a result (4.10). The trial continues the reciprocal violence of the fight, as the litigants exchange equal charges (sometimes in identical language, e.g., 1.7, 2.7) in place of blows. Thus the plaintiff complains that the defense's words are equally impious to his deeds (*homoia,* 3.1), while the defendant berates his opponent for equating (*exisoun,* 2.1) the event to the most serious accusations.

2002: 65–73; and Farenga 2006: 445–70. The relation between *nomos* and *phusis* seems to me more harmonious here.

[54] In this Antiphon's anthropology follows Hesiod's, where Prometheus' theft of fire initiates a series of negative exchanges between mortals and gods (Hes. *Th.* 507–616, *Erga* 42–105). Pursuing this analogy, law would play the role in Antiphon's anthropology that woman plays in Hesiod's: both a sign of mortals' separation from the gods and their only hope of regaining what they lost with that separation.

This cadence of exchange regulates the jurisprudential metaphysics of the *Tetralogy*. Causality, liability, agency, subjectivity all follow the metronomic rhythm of punch and counter-punch. Draco's homicide law places legal responsibility for the fight on the man who starts it,[55] but what does it mean to start it? The defense, accused of striking the fatal blow, deflects that blow first backward to the old man's prior blow (2.3) and then forward to the doctor who treated the victim and whose incompetence (the defense claims) caused his death (2.4). His own action is just one reaction in a deadly chain of reactions originating in the old man's drunken punch. In response to the claim that the doctor is responsible, the plaintiff counters that, first, doctors are immune by law and, second, if he did die under the doctor's care, the killer is not the doctor but the person who was responsible for him being sent to the doctor in the first place (3.5). The defense comes back: "If the man who struck is the murderer because his blow forced you to go to the doctor, then the one who struck the first blow is the murderer, since he forced the other man to strike back in self-defense and sent the man who was struck to the doctor" (4.3). As Gagarin notes, the causality here works "like a series of billiard balls."[56] Cause and effect follow mechanically one after the other.

Ethics become physics as this mechanical model of causality turns every action into a reaction. "I was struck by his hands. I gave back (*antidrōn*) what I suffered with my hands. How did I do wrong?" (2.2). The defendant may have struck back harder than he intended, but even his *hamartia* was reactive: "Seeking to do in return (*antidran*) what he suffered, he erred because the old man forced him to" (4.5). His action is not an action: "He defended himself, he did not act" (4.6). Even premeditation is just a reaction, a reciprocal exchange of plan for plan. "The law declares that the man who plots (*epibouleusanta*) the murder is the murderer, but how could I have plotted (*epibouleusaimi*) against him if I were not plotted against (*epebouleuthēn*) by him? Defending myself by the same means and doing the same as I suffered, clearly I plotted the same as I was plotted against (*ta auta epebouleusa kai epebouleuthēn*)" (2.5). Even intentional agency recedes, leaving the willful subject a mere cog in the larger causal machine: criminal liability (*aitia*) is indistinguishable from abstract causality (*aitia*, 2.6). The intentional criminal (*ho epibouleuōn*) becomes purely passive, like the "plotting soul" (*bouleusasan psukhēn*, 1.7) the jurors will take in exchange for the stolen life of the victim.

55 The phrase is *arkhein adikōn kheirōn*, literally "to start the unjust hands." *IG* $I^3$104.33–36; Gagarin 1978a, 1981: 61–62, 1997: 165 *ad Tet. III* 2.1.

56 Gagarin 1997: 171 *ad Tet. III* 4.3. See also Adkins 1960: 104.

It would seem to be in the plaintiff's interest to halt this regression of liability and to insist on both the defendant's active agency and his responsibility. He does this, but his understanding of intention and agency is no less mechanical than his opponent's:

The defendant had the nerve to argue that the one who struck the first blow and not the one who struck the fatal blow is in fact the murderer instead of the man who actually killed him, since he claims that the former is the one who intended (*bouleutēn*) the death. But I say the opposite. For if our hands are the slaves of our intention (*hai kheires ha dianooumetha hekastōi hēmōn hupourgousin*), then the man who struck but did not kill planned (*bouleutēs*) the blow but the man who struck fatally planned the death, since it was a result of his intentional action (*ek gar hōn ekeinos dianoētheis edrasen*) that the man died. (3.4)

This bizarre passage seems to privilege intention as a way of restoring the agency denied by the defendant. Intention (*dianoia*, *boulē*) is master. The hands are his slaves and execute his commands. Their servitude unites intention and action (*dianoētheis edrasan*) and links a deliberative and therefore culpable agency to the act: if they strike fatally, he must have planned a fatal strike. Actions, no longer reducible to mechanical reactions, become signs of culpable intent. Some commentators suggest that there may lurk behind this passage a notion of blaming the weapon for the death it causes.[57] If that notion is invoked, though, it is only to be rejected in favor of the sovereign intention and legal liability of the mind. There is no blaming the axe in this trial.

But the master–slave relation, as all good Hegelians know, is not so straightforward. First, if the hands supplement the mind in this passage, they also supplant it. *Dianoia* can be known only through the works of its servants. Its very existence is just an extrapolation from those works. Second, it's not at all clear in this speech that the hands do in fact loyally serve their master. The plaintiff couches this claim in the conditional, and goes on to acknowledge that intention and results are not always perfectly aligned: "doing more than he wished to do, by his own misfortune (*atukhiai*) he killed one he did not wish to kill" (3.4). Interposing *atukhia* between *dianoia* and the hands, this passage deposes the intending mind it had enthroned as the source of liable agency. Either that sovereign subject of action is irrelevant (since he cannot even master his hands) or else he is a mere extension of his deed and thus is drawn back into the mechanical causality of action and reaction. Either way, the intending subject – *ho*

57 Decleva Caizzi 1969: 252–53 ad loc.; Gagarin 1997: 169 ad loc.

boulomenos, ho bouleutēs – is no longer the autonomous master of his actions. Instead, he becomes just another billiard-ball on the table.

To this mechanized agency corresponds a mechanical jurisprudence, represented through the theme of pollution. The victim, robbed of the gift of his life, leaves behind an avenging spirit that circulates like a poisoned gift in the post-lapsarian economy (1.3). Despite the defendant's claim to be able to direct this hostile force (2.8), it seems to move autonomously, even automatically, along the paths of injustice, transferring itself from the murderer to those who fail to punish him or who wrongly convict an innocent man instead. Relentless and impersonal, pollution figures law as a machine of justice in a mechanical world: crime and punishment follow the same regular beat of action and reaction. Law participates in the fallen economy of hostile blows, but it does so as the agent of the god. The hostility of the victim's spirit is the god's vengeance (*theou timōrian*, 1.3) for the theft of life. The just verdicts that spirit compels mark the god's faded involvement in human affairs. The law itself, then, is a human remainder of that original divine gift. The jurors' deliberate verdict (*boulesthai*, 2.8; *boulomenois*, 3.1) is the human descendant of the god's original deliberate gift of generation (*theos boulomenos . . . ephusen*). *Ta nomima tōn anthrōpinōn*, that happy existence disrupted by murder, is recaptured in the case's just enforcement of *nomos*.

Tetralogy III, then, envisions a divinely automated justice. Both a facet of the natural world's balanced reciprocity and its regulatory mechanism, the law takes on the symmetry of the *Tetralogies* themselves. In these cases speech matches speech; argument balances argument. The *Tetralogies*' form is their content: the abstract nature of the cases preserves their hermetic equilibrium, creating a formal order uncomplicated by witnesses or the reading of testimony. This order has no place for random or improbable acts. Nor does it have a place for unruly subjects. The third *Tetralogy*'s opening fable of human genesis (*tous prōton genomenous ephusen hēmōn*, 1.2) links the *phusis* of *to anthrōpinon phulon* to the *genos* of the typological subject. The typical actions of a young man and an old man are as regular as cause and effect: generic human *phusis* obeys the physical laws of Antiphon's universe. Indeed, *phusis* must be generic for that very reason. This *Tetralogy*'s typical subject, like the probable and intentional subjects of the other *Tetralogies*, is built in the image of the world he inhabits, personifying the orderly and predictable legal universe of which the *Tetralogies* dream.

This dream is harshly broken, however, in the final speech of the *Tetralogy*. Athenian law allowed defendants to go into voluntary exile before their second speech rather than face conviction.[58] This is what has happened in this case: the defendant has run away, and the last speech is delivered in his absence by his relatives. What does the defendant's flight mean? With this unexpected act, does the real individual subject trump the generic subject, or by fleeing is the young man just behaving like a typical young man? Does his flightiness interrupt the *Tetralogy*'s orderly world, or does his relatives' speech, by maintaining the formal symmetry of the text, repair the order of that world? Does he elude the victim's avenging spirit, or by sentencing himself to exile does he satisfy that spirit and erase the stain of the crime? Does this escape throw a wrench in the machine of law, or does it rather show that machine working as it should, rejecting the weaker case and according a just verdict in favor of the stronger?

The defendant's flight and the speech delivered in his absence reopen the question of human *phusis* and its relation to the law:

> It seems to me that the wrong in this case concerns who started the fight. The plaintiff says that the defendant started it, but he uses improbable arguments. For if it were as natural (*kata phusin*) for young men to be aggressive and old men to be restrained as it is to see with our eyes and hear with our ears, then there would be no need for your judgment (*kriseōs*), since young men would be convicted by their age alone. But in fact many young men show self-restraint and many old men get violent when they drink, and this is no more an argument in favor of the plaintiff than the defendant. (4.2)

The opening speech's anthropology predicated *nomos* on a particular vision of *phusis*, an orderly nature of regular juridical and physical laws. This speech unyokes the law from nature by unyoking *genos* from *phusis*. In the typological *eikos* argument, as we have seen, assumptions about human *phusis* form a bridge between the actions of the individual and the typical behavior of the *genos*. Individual young men can be supposed to be aggressive because young men are, as a type, aggressive naturally, *kata phusin*. But this passage denaturalizes that argument by confronting this legal and rhetorical fiction with a different, more fundamental understanding of *phusis*: the physiology of the human being.[59]

The human body, as in *Tetralogy I*, offers a physical bedrock against which to test the legal argument's assumptions about human nature. In *Tetralogy I* the body of the defendant asleep at home on the night of the

[58] Ant. 5.13; Dem. 23.69; MacDowell 1963: 113–15, 1978: 119.

[59] *Phusis* is understood similarly in fr. 44A2 of Antiphon's *On Truth* (as reconstructed by Decleva Caizzi 1989). Challenging the distinction between Greek and barbarian, Antiphon writes: "For we all breathe the air through our mouths and noses and we all laugh when we are happy and cry when we are sad; we take in sounds with our hearing and we see with our vision; we work with our hands and walk with our feet." Cf. fr. 44B3 and Gagarin 2002: 66–69.

crime exposed the unreality of the probable subject of the law. Here the sensory body, *phusis* at its most basic, challenges the plaintiff's typological argument, with its assumption that individuals act inevitably *kata phusin*. It also challenges the text's anthropological vision of *to anthrōpinon phulon* and *ta nomima tōn anthrōpōn* and the clockwork universe predicated upon them. If young men don't necessarily, *kata phusin*, start fights then perhaps hands don't necessarily, *kata phusin*, enact intention; cause does not automatically, *kata phusin*, follow effect; and punishment doesn't inevitably, *kata phusin*, avenge crime. The natural reciprocity of life for life that drives the machine of justice is interrupted. The billiard-game is over.

The possibility that individuals, young and old, may act *para phusin* – unnaturally, atypically – destroys this *Tetralogy*'s dream of a mechanical world and a mechanical law. On the other hand, if the world did work as regularly as this *Tetralogy* imagines and all actions were as predictably "natural" as our basic bodily functions, then there would be no need for law. If it were as inevitable, *kata phusin,* for young men to start fights as it is for our eyes to see and our ears to hear, the speaker says, there would be no need for the jurors' judgment (*krisis*) and the case would be over before it started. The mutual imbrication of law and trial with which the *Tetralogy* begins (*nenomistai orthōs . . . krinontas*) is here unraveled: the same *phusis* that justifies *nomos* as a principle vitiates *nomos* as a practice. The law in fact needs human nature to be erratic and unpredictable or there would be nothing to try.

This final speech preserves the text's formal symmetry in the face of the defendant's unexpected flight, but it does not in the end resolve the tensions it exposes within the case's vision of a "natural" law. Instead, it ends irresolutely with that tension. Factually the killer is in self-imposed exile, and thus legally the victim has been avenged and the ledger of *miasma* has been balanced. But the speaker for the defense does not make that argument. He warns the jurors against convicting an innocent man and thereby doubling the stain of murder (4.10). "Fearing this, consider it your job to free that innocent man from blame. As for the polluted man, give him over to time to reveal and leave him to the victim's kin to avenge. Thus would you act with the greatest justice and piety" (4.11). The final exchange is open-ended: the pollution is passed on and vengeance indefinitely deferred. The reciprocal exchange of life for life is left in a disequilibrium that belies the formal equilibrium of the case – and the text – and its vision of a perfectly balanced jurisprudence.

*

The abstract subjects of these abstract cases stand at the intersection of *nomos* and *phusis*, between legal discourse and the life it imagines beyond it.

Through its subjective fictions, *nomos* goes beyond its theoretical, discursive existence and claims a physical presence in the real world: in the unerring intent or probable motives of its agents the law projects itself bodily into the world in the form of a subject who thinks and acts like the law. Both the psyche of the individual and human nature as a whole are structured by the law's own logic and animated by a judicial will: *phusis* works like *nomos*. And while these abstract cases are, as we have seen, in many ways anomalous within the genre of Athenian forensic oratory, their hypothetical agents offer the skeletal outline of a thesis that can be fleshed out in other speeches, as they show the law mustering various modes of irreality to secure the reality of its own existence and reveal that reality itself to be a rather improbable fiction.

This subjective embodiment creates not only a subject in law's image but also a world. The *Tetralogies* conjure a consistent and orderly cosmos, one in which human nature is predictable and every action has its reaction, in which "clear tracks" lead from deed to doer, all murderers are convicted "actually not probably," and every javelin hits its target. Even as the *Tetralogies* construct this artificial legal world, though, they also theorize its limits. Each case reaches a point beyond which it cannot go. The second *Tetralogy*, caught in the circular logic of its own metaphor, leaves unanswered its most fundamental questions about accidental agency. The first, unable to segregate the real and the probable, defers its ontology elsewhere (*alibi*). The third imagines justice as a natural balance, but leaves its own case open and its relation to nature uncertain. The sketchy individuals who populate these speeches – the intentional, probable, and typological subjects – have no reality, subjective or objective. They don't need to: the machine of justice keeps running even after the real subject is acknowledged to have fled. But as embodiments of legal thought they reveal the subjectivity of Athenian legal discourse itself, with both its dream of a regular and predictable world and its acknowledgment of that world's improbability.

CHAPTER 4

Logos biou: *law's life stories*

> There is no concept "I" that incorporates all the *I*'s that are uttered at every moment in the mouths of all speakers . . . Then, what does *I* refer to? To something very peculiar which is exclusively linguistic: *I* refers to the act of individual discourse in which it is pronounced, and by this it designates the speaker . . . And so it is literally true that the basis of subjectivity is in the exercise of language.
>
> Benveniste 1971: 226

> I am lying.

TROPES OF SUBJECTIVITY

The courtroom speech tells a life story, a *logos biou*. Litigants relate glowing autobiographies of their own lives and vicious exposés of the lives of their opponents. A vision of the subject is always implicit in juridical discourse, and subjective strategies are a vital means by which that discourse produces and secures legal meaning.[1] But what kind of story is law's *logos biou* and what kind of life does it narrate? Legal theorists who put these questions to modern law often conclude that legal discourse in general is unable to embrace a complex subject, whether it is the subject of psychoanalysis, with its unconscious motivations and ambivalent desires, or the decentered and ontologically divided subject of postmodernism.[2] These scholars argue (with various attitudes of regret or approbation) that law both assumes and requires as its ideal subject a unified and unitary, autonomous and rational individual, the conscious initiator of intentional action and the identifiable bearer of legal rights.

[1] Schlag 1991.

[2] See, for example, Wicke 1991; *contra*, Boyle 1991; Frug 1992: 18–23; Barron 1993; Caudill 1997: 66–81. See also the discussions in Ryan 1989: 149–64; Nedelsky 1990; Brooks 2000. The strongest voice urging the law to adopt a more expansive notion of subjectivity is Drucilla Cornell, who offers a compelling vision of what a psychologically complex legal subject would look like. See especially Cornell 1995b, 1995c, 1996, 1998.

This modern legal subject would seem to trace his ancestry back to the protagonists of Athenian forensic oratory. These characters tend to be homogenous and one-dimensional. The speaker is invariably a good man: he performs his civic duties cheerfully, honors his parents piously, and defends his polis bravely. His opponent is invariably a bad man: a malicious sykophant at best and arrogant oligarch at worst. Their stories are often colorful; with their malicious gossip and hyperbolic self-aggrandizement they make for a good read. But as a juridical sub-genre these biographies seem, at least superficially, conventional and generically over-determined, and their subjects neither original nor psychologically profound. Indeed, the speakers work to produce this impression, omitting or distorting details to produce a coherent account of a coherent life.

On closer inspection, though, these biographies are perhaps not as straightforward and their subjects not as simple as they first appear. As the object of juridical *logos*, the individual's life story emerges within the contested and deceitful dialect of Athenian forensic rhetoric: like all the other objects of legal discourse it is mediated by and thoroughly implicated in the slippery rhetoricity of the speech. And if the objects of these *logoi* are problematic, their subjects are no less so. However coherent a story he tells about himself the speaker is always necessarily divided. First there is the gap (more or less obvious) between the speaker of the *logos* and the character depicted in the *logos*: the *autos* within these autobiographies is never quite identical with its author. This gap is widened by the lurking presence of the logographer, the ghostwriter of the litigant's first-person narrative. Finally, there is the discrepancy between the speaker's own version of himself and the version presented in his opponent's speech: that sinister twin cannot be fully banished from the speaker's rosy account of his life, since it emerges every time he alludes to and argues against his opponent. The subject who presents himself in court as unitary is always multiply divided, his life story necessarily partial, agonistic, mediated, and contradictory. The law's *logoi biou* are thus always *dissoi logoi* and the subject cannot simply be identified with any one of the many I's – speaking or spoken, writing or written, positive or negative – who populate them.

These forensic biographies thus offer the possibility of a complex juridical subject, if only we can figure out how to read them. Clearly we cannot take them at face value and simply believe what a speaker says about himself or his opponent. As we have seen, speakers lie about everything, themselves included. But this apparent obstacle may actually prove to be an interpretive in-road. Rather than the transparent account of a knowable life, law's *logos biou* is a kind of liar's paradox. When someone says "I am lying," he splits himself between an enunciating "I" and an enunciated "I," either of whom may or may not be lying.[3] The tension between the two (with neither exactly refuting or supporting the truth of the other's statement) opens a space within the speaking subject, who is never precisely identical with the "I" he says he is. This riddle produces the illusion that, if we ponder all the possibilities long enough, we might catch one "I" or the other in the act of telling the truth about himself. The speeches perpetrate this same frustrating hoax, as if by sorting through the lies of his self-presentation we might catch sight of the "real" Demosthenes or, conversely, by judging the veracity of the real Demosthenes we might verify his account of himself. But the liar's paradox suggests that both "I"s are equally effects of speech. In searching for the subject of forensic oratory, we cannot speak of discursive self-representation as though there were a self outside of and prior to its representation in language: as Benveniste puts it (in the epigram to this chapter), "it is literally true that the basis of subjectivity is in the exercise of language." The legal subject will thus figure in this chapter not as the real narrator of his own true life story nor as the real individual who lived the life narrated, but precisely as a *logos biou*, that is, a creature whose life is (nothing but) *logos*.

If the legal subject is a fiction of juridical discourse, our focus can no longer be the absolute truth or falsity of his *logos biou*: that *logos* is always potentially lying (and thus potentially speaking the truth). Instead, this chapter will read that *logos* rhetorically, concentrating on the rhetorical tropes and strategies through which juridical discourse constructs its subjects.[4] The first section tracks the subject as a signifier within the text of the law. Demosthenes 39 *On the Name* constructs a positivist semiotics in which each individual has his own unique name and the law constitutes a coherent and authoritative symbolic order. The speech defends against the threat of homonymy: nominal ambiguity – two men with the same name – raises the specter of an illegible subject that undermines the coherence of law's semiotics and calls for a new hermeneutics of identity. The second section takes up that challenge by exploring the metaphors by which legal

[3] Lacan 1981: 136–48; cf. Lacan 1977b.

[4] H. White 1978: 2: "tropics is the process by which all discourse *constitutes* the objects which it pretends only to describe realistically and to analyze objectively." Cf. Burke 1945: 503–17. On the force of tropes within legal discourse see Barfield 1962; T. Murphy 1994: 86–91; A. Hyde 1997; and especially Goodrich (1994a, 1995: 181–222), who argues that "rhetoric, which studies the tropes and figures of language simultaneously and necessarily, studies also the unconscious of the institution" (1995: 183).

discourse constructs a self. In Demosthenes 48, a contract case, the contract functions as a metaphor for an idealized legal subject who is rational, coherent, and consistent over time. The contractual metaphor is an attempt to seal the subject's identity and secure it against change. But metaphors themselves are transformational; operating within the uncertain shifts of poetic language, they resist the fixity of the linguistic or legal contract. Thus in this speech, the contractual metaphor is breached by the irrationality it was designed to exclude, an erratic desire metaphorized as a courtesan. The final section moves from metaphor to metonymy and a self elaborated through a metonymic web of politically vital alliances. In Demosthenes 21 *Against Meidias*, Demosthenes defines himself as an ideal metonym of the demos and the polis; this strategy is more problematic, though, in the case of the crippled litigant of Lysias 24 *For the Disabled Man*. The unfortunate speaker in that case forges a metonymic bond to the city only by taking up a viciously ironic relation to himself; through his self-wounding humor he reveals what is at stake in the metonymic strategy of subjectivity for the individual, the city, and the law.

These tropes – metaphor and metonymy, irony and homonymy – are simultaneously rhetorical and psychological, a structure of language elaborated as a structure of subjectivity and vice versa. They constitute a tropology of the self in which we can trace not only the outlines of a legal subject, himself a "rhetorical figure," but also the discursive strategies by which forensic oratory produces, circulates, and secures legal meaning in the person of its subjects. Reading the law's *logoi biou* shows how juridical *logoi* narrate a *bios*. It also suggests how the law uses the *bios* of the individual in order to secure itself as a *logos*, a coherent symbolic system. The stories law tells are ultimately about itself.

AM I THAT NAME? SEMIOTICS OF THE HOMONYM IN DEMOSTHENES 39

Proper names occupy a central place in the language of the law. The individual claims his name – his identity and social being – by appealing to the law, and that name in turn is a signifier of the law's nominating authority, its power to attach words to things and to secure their meaning. Demosthenes 39 is a contest over a name and over legal naming. The speaker Mantitheus is suing his half-brother Boeotus to prevent him from using his name. He supports his suit by detailing the dangers of *homōnumia*, two men sharing the same name or, more broadly, semantic ambiguity, one signifier indicating two different signifieds.[5] The speaker would have us believe that two men named "Mantitheus son of Mantias of Thorikos" disrupts both the unique identity of the individual and the semiotic coherence of the law. Homonymy injects doubleness into both the *bios* and the *logos* of legal discourse, a doubleness that the speaker believes fatal. He argues strenuously for a positivist semiotics of law, in which each man has one name and every word has a single meaning. But this case will prove more ambiguous than it initially appears and will open the possibility that the legal subject and legal semiotics are themselves more homonymic than "Mantitheus son of Mantias of Thorikos" might wish us to believe.

As Mantitheus tells it, he is the legitimate son of Mantias son of Mantitheus, officially registered in his father's deme of Thorikos. His name bears testimony to that identity.[6] Boeotus and his brother Pamphilus are the sons of Mantias' mistress Plangon. She claimed Mantias was the father, but Mantias repudiated the claim. When he reached adulthood, Boeotus sued Mantias to compel him to recognize his legitimacy but Mantias, rather than go to court, made a deal with Plangon that he would challenge her to swear the children were his and she (for a price) would refuse the oath. Plangon agreed to the deal but then broke her promise and instead asserted under oath that the boys were Mantias' sons. His hand forced, Mantias enrolled Boeotus in his phratry under the name of Boeotus, but died before he could enroll him in the deme, the next stage of legitimation. After Mantias' death, Boeotus registered himself in the deme under the name Mantitheus, apparently claiming that his mother was Mantias' legitimate wife and that as the first-born son he had the right to bear his grandfather's name, which (he claims) he had been given by his father and had borne his whole life. Mantitheus disputes that claim, arguing that the name is rightly his and that two men sharing the same name is not only inconvenient but impossible (*adunaton*, 6, 20).[7]

5 The term *homōnumia* comes from the hypothesis to the case: "the speech provides sufficient proof that *homōnumia* is harmful both to the state and to the individual." The word is unattested in classical Attic.

6 Athenian men bore three names, marking their personal identity, paternity, and deme (the administrative region of Athens where their citizenship was registered). Thus the name marks a point of intersection between the individual, family, and city and suggests that identity is incomplete without any one of these elements. On naming and legitimacy, see Golden 1986: 257–67; Ogden 1996: 91–98.

7 Carey and Reid 1985: 160–66 reconstruct the probable facts behind this story. They suggest plausibly that Mantias was married to Plangon and at first recognized Boeotus as his own (naming him Mantitheus), but later came to suspect Plangon's fidelity and divorced her and repudiated Boeotus. "It would appear," they comment, "that both brothers have an equal right to the name" (167). See further Rudhardt 1962; Humphreys 1989; D. Cohen 1995a: 163–67; Roisman 2005: 43–44; Gagarin 2007. On the problem of proving legitimacy, cf. Chapter 6.

This contest may seem strange, as Mantitheus himself acknowledges at the outset (*atopon*, 1). But much is at stake in ownership of the name. Mantitheus does not contest Boeotus' legitimacy (although he does refer incessantly to the devious way in which he obtained it). He does not deny Boeotus an equal share of Mantias' estate (6, 20, 26).[8] But the name is a different matter. I am not such a fool, he says, as to have given him his third of the property and then to go to court over the name "if changing names were not an affront to my status and manliness (*atimian ephere kai anandrian*) and if it were not for many reasons impossible for us to have the same name" (6). The name signifies more than just a claim to the father's estate, Mantitheus implies; it is a claim to the father's recognition – even affection (22) – and the masculine and civic identity it confers. The name these half-brothers contend for is not just Mantitheus but "son," "man," and "citizen."

The name Mantitheus functions as a *sēmeion* (9, 10). It is a signifier of legitimate identity that circulates within a civic and juridical semiotics. These two, the *sēmeion* and the semiotic order, are mutually reaffirming: the name takes its legitimacy and meaning from the symbolic order of law and polis and in turn secures the coherence and authority of that order. Mantitheus stresses the name as a mode of civic interpellation, the address by which the city hails the individual, calling him into being as a citizen-subject. If the two men share one name, he argues, when the city imposes a liturgy upon one of them he can use the ambiguity to evade his public service. In answer to the city's demand, "you will say it names me and I will say you" (7). Conversely, one of them may be named to public office, but "if there is no *sēmeion* on the ballot" neither they nor the demos will know which one has been elected. "He will say he has been and I will say I have" (10). They will be forced to take the matter to court and one of them will be deprived of his "fair and equal right" (*tou men koinou kai isou*, 11) as a democratic citizen to be elected to public office.

Nominal ambiguity will cause the civic address to fail: both may answer the city's call or neither. This will cause a disturbance (*tarakhē*, 9) not just for the individual, Mantitheus predicts, but for the city, too. The homonym will jam the bureaucratic mechanisms of the polis and will jeopardize the

8 The property is in dispute in a later case, though. In Dem. 40, Mantitheus sues Boeotus again to recover his dead mother's dowry from the distribution of Mantias' estate. That speech repeats many of the themes of this one, but with a greater emphasis on the monetary stakes. There Mantitheus suggests that the suit over the name was in fact another attempt on Boeotus' part to deprive him of the dowry (40.18, but compare 40.35), and rehashes the question of their relation to their father in support of his claim to the dowry (40.26).

very ideology of Athens' democracy. On the one hand, the individual citizen may be deprived of his "fair and equal right" to participate directly in the *politeia*; on the other hand, the half-brothers may collude to pool votes for both of them in order to get one of them elected (12). Either way the bad mathematics of the homonym – two men for one name, one office, one vote – skews the calculus of direct democracy, which locates political authority in the individual citizen. The unique name of each citizen is thus a *sēmeion* of the democratic city's coherence and exactitude as a semiotic order.

The name also functions as a birthmark, hailing the subject as "son." That *sēmeion*, however, is not immediately legible. It requires interpretation: what is a son? Boeotus may be Mantias' son; he may even (as a result of his conniving) be a legitimate son. But he is not a true son. A true son tries to please his father and behaves "as he ought" toward his parents (33). He does this, in part, by accepting the name his father gave him. Our father registered you in the phratry as Boeotus and would have registered you as Boeotus in the deme had he lived, Mantitheus declares. By registering yourself as Mantitheus, you disrespected your father's wishes. "Is it not dreadful, Oh earth and gods, that he claims Mantias is his father and then has the audacity to render invalid (*akura*) the measures he took when he was alive!" (21). A true son validates his father's wishes. By rejecting his paternal name and claiming the legal right to name himself, Boeotus has rendered his father's authority invalid (*akuron*). For this, Mantitheus declaims, he deserves "not only to be insulted but to be killed" (33). Mantitheus catches Boeotus in a nominal double bind: in order to prove himself a true son worthy of his father's name, he must accept the detested name that robs him of the status of favored first son.[9] "Come then," says Mantitheus, "wouldn't it seem fair if our father should rise up from the dead and demand that you either keep the name under which he made you his son or else claim some other father? I demand the same things: either enroll yourself under some other father or else keep the name he gave you" (31).

Mantitheus' invocation of his dead father suggests the extent to which the sons' contest over the name reaffirms the father's exclusive power to grant the name "son." The father has the legal authority to "make" (*poiein*)

9 The name Boeotus also connotes foreignness (it means "Boeotian") and possibly bestiality, if the phrase "Boeotian pig" mentioned in Pindar (*Ol.* 6.90) was still in currency. On the "enabling violation" of legal naming, see Butler 1993: 121–24, 143–66, 1997b: 28–38 and, more generally, Riley 1988, from whom the title of this section is borrowed.

his son into a legitimate person.[10] He has the authority to "inscribe" (*engraphein*, 4, 5, 20, 21, 29, 30) the son in the official deme register and thus to establish him as a sign within the significatory systems of the polis. Moreover, the father who made the son can unmake him. In the verbal register of the address, he can disown him by proclamation (*apokēruxai*, 39); in the textual register of the inscription, he can "erase" him (*exaleipsai*, 39).[11]

This power of life and death constitutes the sovereignty not only of the father but of the law itself:

> If he is able to show a law that gives children authority (*kurious*) over their own name, you would be right, jurors, to decide in favor of his argument. But if – and you know as well as I do that this is the case – the law gives parents authority (*kurious*) not only to establish the name to begin with but even to erase it if they wish and publicly disown the child, and if I have shown that our father, who was authorized (*kurios*) by the law, gave him the name Boeotus and me Mantitheus, then how can you fail to cast your verdict for me? (39)

The authority of the father is the authority of the law. The law makes the father *kurios* to name the son, and itself names the son through the father: hence this appeal to the law to confirm the paternal name and the appeal to the paternal name to support the legal brief. The identity of the son is a *sēmeion* of the law's power, its authority to "make" the individual or unmake him, to "inscribe" him in the social text or to erase him.

The sole challenge to this semiotic hegemony – a maternal surname – is raised only to be laughed out of court. If "Mantitheus" is called upon to perform a liturgy, "what sign (*sēmeion*) will there be which of us is meant? Will they add (*prosparagrapsousi*) 'the one born of Plangon,' if they mean you and the name of my mother if they mean me? Who has ever heard of such a thing? Under what law would this addendum (*paragramma*) be added (*prosparagraphoit'*), or anything else beside just the father and the deme?" (9). The mother's name would be at best a later addition (*prosparagraphein*) to a paternal inscription already written and sealed, a marginal scribble on the official document of male identity. This *paragramma* would be a mere supplement and a potentially dangerous one,

10 4, 6, 18, 20, 29–33, 35, 36. On the term, see Rudhardt 1962: 53–64. This is also the terminology of adoption and by using it Mantitheus may be trying to imply that Boeotus was not a natural-born son. In practice, there were legal restrictions on adoption, as we will see in Chapter 6, including laws that prevented men from adopting if they already had natural-born legitimate sons and from adopting their own illegitimate children. But rhetorically this speech represents the father's power as unlimited.

11 In practice it was extremely rare for a child to be disinherited: Rudhardt 1962: 51–52; W. K. Lacey 1968: 125–26; Harrison 1968: 75–76.

linking male citizen identity to the unstable sign of woman. Legally the Athenian woman had no name of her own: Plangon is a pet-name meaning "Doll" and Mantitheus' mother, like most respectable Athenian women, is not named at all. What would it mean to append such an illegible *paragramma* to one's own identity? The prospect is unheard of (41).[12]

The name thus functions as the mark of paternal and legal authority upon the son. By answering to his name, the son affirms that authority, and he must affirm that authority in order to assume his name. But the name he thereby assumes, whether Boeotus or Mantitheus, is a *sēmeion* of his subjection to that denominating authority. The name that makes him a legitimate and legible person also inscribes him within a paternal-juridical semiotics that renders him powerless to name himself. We have already seen how Mantitheus tries to trap Boeotus in this double-bind: either submit to the name Boeotus or relinquish your place as Mantias' son. Boeotus' bid to name himself invalidates his bid for the name. Conversely by litigating under the name Boeotus, he has already accepted that name; if he repudiates it (and the subordinate status it confers) he no longer has a legal name in which to bring his suit (37–38). Trapped between subjectivity through and subjection to his name, Boeotus has (as Mantitheus puts it) "reached a verdict against himself" (38).[13]

But Mantitheus is no less trapped. He, too, tries to co-opt the legal and paternal power of naming: the entire speech is, after all, an attempt to name himself Mantitheus and Boeotus Boeotus. But he can only nominate vicariously, conjuring his father's ghost so as to plead in his name (31). Speaking in the borrowed voice of his father, he affirms his father's posthumous authority even as he seeks to wield it himself. But he can never own that power: as a legal subject he will always be a docile son. Thus his speech ends with an appeal to the jurors:

Who among you has given the same name to two of his children? Which of you who does not yet have children will do this? Surely no one. If you assume this is just in the case of your own children, judge it right in my case too. What I ask of

[12] On Plangon, see Carey and Reid 1985: 175–76 *ad* Dem. 39.9; Glazebrook 2006: 131–32. For Mantitheus' mother, cf. Dem. 40.6. On the anonymity of women in Athenian forensic oratory see below, Chapter 6. Mantitheus further insinuates that Boeotus has already taken his mother's name by staking his legitimacy on his mother's (false) oath that he is Mantias' son. Boeotus' identity is thus rooted in the unrecoverable complexities of his parents' love affair. Even if a man is bitter against the mother, he does not hate the child if he thinks it is really his, Mantitheus postulates; in fact, the reverse is more often the case and shared children reconcile feuding parents (23). Boeotus' name has no more solid foundation than the shifting soil of marital affection. Cf. Dem. 40.27–29.

[13] On this paradox of subjectivity as subjection, see Althusser 1971: 177–83; Foucault 1980: 92–108, 1982; Brown 1995a: 52–76, 96–134; Butler 1997a.

you is just and reasonable in accordance with your own most just judgment and with the laws and your oaths, and in accordance with Boeotus' own admissions. What he asks you is not only unreasonable but unheard of. (40–41)

Mantitheus hails the jurors not as sons who value their own names but as fathers.[14] Just as they hold the paternal authority to name their own sons, as jurors they have the legal authority to name Boeotus and Mantitheus. Positioning himself as their son, Mantitheus affirms their sovereignty over his identity. And by affirming this power and submitting dutifully to it, Mantitheus declares himself the true son of the law, its ideal subject and *sēmeion* of its significatory hegemony.

The *sēmeion* of the name helps us read the semiotics of Athenian law. As a symbolic order, this case suggests, the law rests on a positivist semiotics. One name equals one person. Every signifier indicates one (and only one) signified and every signified has its own unique and proper signifier.[15] This same positivism, I suggested, characterizes the ideology of direct democracy, in which every individual citizen in himself signifies the sovereignty of the citizen body, without the potentially ambiguous doubling of political representation. Both the law and the democracy, then, have a good deal invested in the name of the individual and its direct and stable relation to that which it names.

To this politico-juridical symbolic, the ambiguity of the homonym threatens a double disruption (*tarakhē*, 9). The first is a splitting or doubling of the individual subject. "Yoked" to his half-brother like two oxen in a plough (6), Mantitheus is divided in and from himself by the otherness of this spurious double.[16] Mantitheus worries that if the two share one name, he will be held accountable for the "wholly unpleasant reputation" (*doxa holōs aēdēs*, 16) incurred by Boeotus, who apparently hangs around with a rough crowd and stirs up trouble. "Sharing jointly in Boeotus' reputation and deeds" (18), Mantitheus will become separated from his own proper *doxa*, the public reputation attached to his personal name. The signifier "Mantitheus" will be set loose from its signified; the names "citizen" and "son" will wander "unpleasantly" (*aēdēs*, 16, 20), unmoored from any stable

[14] Cf. Dem. 40.8: "my father raised me and loved me, as all of you love your children." See further Dem. 40.45.

[15] Cf. Goodrich 1984: 188–90; 1986: 186–89; 1987: 63–81; 1990a: 111–48. Stanley Fish is perhaps the most insistent critic of the law's wish for transparent legibility: see, e.g., Fish 1991. See also J. B. White 1999, and my discussion of Lysias 10 in the Conclusion.

[16] Boeotus is represented as variously other in this speech. Not only does his name connote foreignness, but Mantitheus further insinuates that he might be an alien (*xenias*, 18) and that he forced his way into "a family that doesn't belong to him" (*eis allotria*, 34) like an alien arrogating the rights of a citizen (*eisbiazomenōn*, 33).

referent. The *sēmeion* will become meaningless and the subject, divorced from the name that signified his legal and civic being, will properly cease to exist.[17]

The second threat of *homōnumia* is to the symbolic order of law itself. Mantitheus' insistence on the unitary name is also an insistence on law's power to name unambiguously and authoritatively, to produce and circulate legitimate meanings. Homonymy exposes the arbitrariness of those meanings and the power that underwrites them. Law does not speak a natural language in which words bear an innate connection to the things they name.[18] Instead its names are revealed in this case as fictions and their relation to things purely conventional, a matter of *nomos* not *phusis*. Names are given and taken back, adopted and traded, "made" and "erased," through the authority of the courts. Even human life is denaturalized. In his attempt to refute Boeotus' claim to be the older son, Mantitheus briefly suggests – only to immediately reject it as "foolish" (*euēthes*, 27) – a natural semiotics based on physical *sēmata*: he looks younger than me. But age cannot be counted in biological years, he asserts, but instead should be counted from the moment of naming. "None of you knows our age in years, jurors: I say I have more and he'll say he does. But you all know the account of what is just (*ton de tou dikaiou logon*). What is it? To consider (*nomizesthai*) children to exist from the moment the father made them his" (*epoiēsato*, 29). This argument is, as Carey and Reid note, "a splendid red herring," and not even Mantitheus places much weight on it.[19] But this denaturalizing of a life-span follows upon the law's power to "make" an individual by naming and inscribing him. If the name has no fixed or natural connection to the individual, then his whole *bios* becomes just a *logos*, a product of legal *poiēsis* with no reference to *phusis*. The ambiguity of the case's *homōnumia* shows law's *logos biou* to be the unnatural product of a closed and self-referential system in which every name is a *sēmeion* of the law's significatory power.

The speech represents the *tarakhē* of the double name as intolerable, impossible (*adunaton*, 6, 20) for both the subject and the law. Its anxious re-securing of the singular name within a positivist semiotics anticipates

[17] This theme is treated at length in Euripides' *Helen*. Replaced by a phantasmic double in Troy, the real Helen spends the war in Egypt, where she laments the evil reputation she has earned because of the acts of her double. There, too, the doubled name creates semiotic confusion. See especially Menelaus at 483–500: "I don't know what to say. I guess in this great world there are many men who have the same names as other men, women as other women, and cities as other cities" (496–99).

[18] On the fantasy of natural language and the theory of the subject it entails, see Derrida 1976: 16–17, 35–44. See also the discussion of naming in Butler 1993: 208–18.

[19] Carey and Reid 1985: 186 *ad* Dem. 39.29.

the defensive gesture of some modern legal theorists in the face of post-modernism's theoretical *tarakhē*. Such scholars insist that the law requires a single subject and a stable significatory system within which to issue its commands.[20] If anywhere, we might expect such an argument to find support in this suit, where the stakes are so high not only for the individual but also for paternal power, democratic ideology, and the legal symbolic. But the case is not so open and shut. This is one of the rare trials for which we know the verdict: the jurors found for Boeotus (Dem. 40.17–18, 21). Moreover, they did not strip Mantitheus of the name and give it to his half-brother, but instead allowed both men to keep the same name. A contemporary inscription lists the payment of a debt by the heirs of Mantias: Pamphilus of Thorikos, Mantitheus of Thorikos, and Mantitheus of Thorikos.[21] It sets in stone precisely the homonymic ambiguity Mantitheus feared.

This surprising verdict serves as a reminder of the perils of trying to infer jurisprudential thought from any given forensic speech: we know only the arguments the litigants make, not whether and why they were persuasive. We cannot guess why the jury in this case voted for Boeotus and which, if any, of Mantitheus' arguments gave them pause. We can say, however, that this jury, if not Athenian jurisprudence in general, seems to have been less perturbed by the prospect of *homōnumia* than Mantitheus hoped. They, at least, seem to have felt that Athenian legal discourse could inscribe that double *sēmeion* "Mantitheus son of Mantias of Thorikos" without jeopardizing its own legibility or semiotic authority.

Perhaps, then, the legal *logos biou* tells a more subtle and ambiguous story than we might have anticipated. If this is true and Athens' juridical language is not as singular and straightforward as Mantitheus desires, then we cannot just read it literally. An ambiguous legal semiotics requires a more sophisticated hermeneutics. The verdict in Demosthenes 39 invites us to read juridical discourse figuratively, as a poetic and not a positivist language, a language that produces meaning not through the rigid designation of the singular signifier but through homonymic strategies that make every word mean more than one thing and ensure that no subject will ever be fully identical to his legal name.

20 See, e.g., Wicke 1991: 462: "to efface or erase the legal subject, however much predicated on an illusory unity, singularity, intentionality would be an enormous political loss."

21 *IG* II^2 1622.435–43; cf. Carey and Reid 1985: 167.

THE CONTRACT AND THE COURTESAN: METAPHORS OF SELF IN DEMOSTHENES 48

One way in which language calls two things by the same name is metaphor. By substituting one word or concept for another, metaphors attempt to fix identity, both the identity between two different things and the identity of the thing metaphorically described. Jacques Lacan, who insists on the rhetorical structure of the psyche (one of his mantras is "the unconscious is structured like a language"), compares the linguistic dynamics of the metaphor to the psychic dynamics of the symptom. Metaphors fix the deeper meaning of a thing by expressing it in terms of something else; so symptoms express a latent psychic meaning through the symbols – the metaphors – of corporeal affliction.[22] Metaphor is thus a central device for any *logos biou*, equally at home in the grammar of *logos* and of *bios*.

Legal discourse has many metaphors for the subject. Demosthenes 48 presents one of those most familiar from modern jurisprudence, the contract. Contracts assume and express an idealized vision of the subject as a rational and responsible agent, honest in his dealings with others, consistent in himself and over time. They symbolize the deliberate choice (Demosthenes will call it a *prohairesis*) of a lawful and legitimate way of life. To the extent that it documents a commitment to that choice, the contract reiterates the dynamic of metaphor itself, which fixes the identity of a thing by describing its essence. But metaphor fixes identity by introducing difference, carrying over meaning (*meta-pherein*) from elsewhere. So we will see in Demosthenes 48, the metaphor by which the speech tries to consolidate legal meanings and fix them in the idealized figure of the contractual subject instead risks disrupting those meanings by importing or carrying over something different. That difference, metaphorized in the speech as a courtesan, destabilizes the legal subject and becomes the symptom of a latent madness within the contractual rationality of the law.[23]

[22] Lacan 1977a: 166, cf. 1977a: 156–71, 1993: 218–30. On metaphor, see further Burke 1945: 503–17; Jakobson 1956: 90–96; H. White 1973: 34–35; Silverman 1983: 109–22, and the interesting discussion in Lloyd 1987: 172–214 of the invention of metaphor in Greek thought.

[23] On the contract as a subjective metaphor in legal discourse, see Goodrich 1990a: 149–75, 1990b, 1995: 181–222; P. Williams 1991: 146–65, 216–36; Douzinas, Warrington, and McVeigh 1991: 124–35; Caudill 1997: 42–65; L. Wilson 2000: 68–113. For the theory of contract in Athenian law, see Todd 1993: 59–60, 262–68, who argues that the Athenians had an idea of contractual obligation but no formal doctrine of contract; his conclusion, that any agreement could be produced in court but none could have more than persuasive force (268), is supported by my reading of Dem. 48. See further Pringsheim 1950: 13–85; Gernet 1955: 201–36, 1981a: 146–73; Wolff 1957; Maffi 1988: 203–10; Christ 1998a: 218–23; Mirhady 2004; D. Carter 2007; Carawan 2007.

Demosthenes 48 deals with a dispute between two brothers-in-law over a contract (*sunthēkai*). After the death of their relative Comon, Callistratus and Olympiodorus agreed to divide the estate evenly between the two of them and to work together to resist all future claims to the estate on the part of other relatives. They swore an oath "to divide the existing visible property well and justly (*kalōs kai dikaiōs*) and neither to have more of what Comon left than the other; and that we would investigate all the other property together (*koinēi*) and would consult with one another to accomplish whatever should be necessary at the time" (9). They transcribed the oath in a written contract, which they sealed and deposited with a mutual friend, Androkleides. But Olympiodorus has apparently violated the contract and managed, through a series of intricate legal maneuvers, to appropriate the whole estate for himself. Callistratus is therefore suing for damages (*blabē*) and he is the plaintiff in this speech.

From the modern perspective such a case would seem to be relatively open and shut: the contract, a legal document, would be examined and the actions of the two litigants measured against its express terms. But in this case the status of the contract is far from straightforward. For one thing, its precise terms are never disclosed. Callistratus claims that he tried to convince his brother-in-law to enter a copy of the contract as evidence for the trial: he proposed that they go to Androkleides and together, in the presence of witnesses, copy out the contract, sign and seal it again, and deposit copies in the evidence box (48). Olympiodorus apparently refused. Callistratus reissues the challenge in the course of his speech: Androkleides is there in the courtroom and has the contract with him; they could open it and read it to the jurors right then and there (51). Challenges are often designed to be refused, and Callistratus makes the most of the refusal: obviously Olympiodorus doesn't want the jurors to hear the terms of the agreement (49).[24] Yet despite frequent allusion to these terms, he himself never quotes them directly either, nor does he have them read into the testimony. The law governing contracts is read, as is the testimony of Androkleides that the contract was placed with him (11). The oath that the contract presumably records is frequently repeated (18, 19, 22, 44).[25] But the text of the contract itself is never quoted in court.

[24] Johnstone 1999: 70–92.

[25] The oath and contract are presented in hendiadys as the oral and written version of the same agreement (9, 38, 42). The contract is presumed to be simply a transcription of the spoken oath. But are the two actually interchangeable? If the contract merely records the contents of the oath – which are repeated frequently in the speech – then why does Callistratus insist that the contract, too, be read to the jurors? If the oath is still valid, why does the contract need to be resigned and resealed? Carawan 2007 examines the force of the oath in this case.

Perhaps this reticence regarding the contract can be explained in historical terms. Rosalind Thomas notes that written documents (contracts, wills, witness depositions) were still a relatively new addition to legal procedure in the mid-fourth century BCE, and the hazy status of the contract in this case could simply reflect the litigants' mistrust – or their anticipation of the jurors' mistrust – of the evidentiary force of a written document.[26] But this wariness produces a curious effect within the speech, since the contract is simultaneously present and absent, known and unknown: it is physically there in the courtroom, but remains sealed and unread. Odder still, it seems to be simultaneously valid and invalid. Callistratus accuses Olympiodorus of having broken it; Olympiodorus has clearly leveled the same charge against Callistratus (38). Both believe the contract has been breached but neither declares it void. If Olympiodorus thought I had acted against him, says Callistratus, he should have gone to Androkleides with witnesses and invalidated the contract (46). But Callistratus never invalidated the contract either, although he claims that Olympiodorus has been acting against it for years. The agreement to divide the property equally stands even after the property has been divided unequally (22), even after the property has been lost (28–29). Callistratus implies that they are mutually bound by the contract's terms even after both have broken its terms; they are contracted to "act in concert" even as they are suing each other (30). The contract takes on a life of its own, independent of the conditions and the relationship it legally records.

The contract, then, is more than just a disputed document. It functions in the speech less as concrete evidence or a solid point of fact than as a symbolic axis around which each litigant situates himself and his opponent. That is to say, it functions figuratively not literally, as a symbol – a metaphor – of a particular relation to oneself, to others, and to the law. As Callistratus represents it, the contract is more than just a business arrangement or a legal document. It is an ethical commitment. "I chose (*proheilomēn*), jurors, voluntarily to give a share to Olympiodorus rather than to embark on a court case and risk saying something unpleasant to my relative or hearing something inappropriate from him" (8).

The contract is a *prohairesis* (the nominal form of the verb *proheilomēn*). *Prohairesis* is the word philosophy uses for a conscious and deliberate ethical choice (e.g. Arist. *NE* 1111b). In Callistratus' case it is the choice of a lawful way of life, a choice of restrained civility over conflict and

[26] R. Thomas 1989: 40–44. See also Calhoun 1919; Maffi 1988: 201–10; and Gagarin 2008: 188–205 on the use of writing in fourth-century legal procedure and its ambivalent representation in forensic oratory.

"unpleasantness." It is a commitment to being an ethical individual: in swearing to divide the property well and justly (*kalōs kai dikaiōs*, 9, 17, 30), each partner commits himself to being good and just. Indeed, his goodness is measured precisely in relation to his justness: a *kalos anēr* is a *dikaios anēr* and he proves it by his deliberate choice, *prohairesis*, to sign and stick to the contract. The contract thus documents Callistratus' self-proclaimed moderation and propriety (*metria kai prosēkonta*, 4; cf. 5) and its own propriety overwrites the very distinct possibility that Callistratus is lying about his kinship and his right to the estate from the start.[27]

The most obvious and insistently emphasized test of each partner's *prohairesis* is his contractual relation to the other. In theory, that relation is one of perfect equality. When Comon died, his estate was divided clean in half. Each brother-in-law got one house and one shop with its workers, the one a sail-making shop, the other a dye shop (12). "I got half; Olympiodorus got half," Callistratus says, his syntax marking the symmetry of the deal *(to men hēmisu egō elabon, to d' hēmisu houtosi Olympiodōros*, 17). Disagreement is alluded to but then hastily brushed aside in order to maintain that symmetry: "Why should I trouble you and myself, jurors, by recounting the disagreements we had as we were discussing these things? The end result is what you must hear. We mutually determined that each of us would take half of Comon's estate and there would be no further unpleasantness" (7–8). The contract papers over past inequality and documents the resulting equality between the two men.[28]

[27] So the hypothesis: "Callistratus says that the whole estate belongs to him because he is nearest by kinship to Comon. But he is perhaps lying about this and arguing without support." See also Gernet 1957: 227–28. Suspiciously, Callistratus never specifies his precise relation to the dead man nor provides witnesses to it. Moreover, Callistratus' brother (by the same father but a different mother) would seem to have had no more success in his claims to the estate than Callistratus, although their degree of kinship to the testator would probably have been the same.

[28] This equality is precarious from the start, however. Comon had a slave named Moschion, part of the dye works that fell to Olympiodorus' share of the estate, who knew where Comon hid his money and gradually embezzled a good deal of it. The two men suspect the slave and together torture him until he admits to having stolen one thousand drachmas; this money the two partners share *kalōs kai dikaiōs* (17) according to the terms of their agreement. But later Olympiodorus tortures Moschion further on his own and uncovers another seventy mna which he refuses to share with Callistratus (20). Extracted through deceit and violence, this seventy mna unbalances the fair division of the contract and insinuates into the partnership the bad faith that the contract was designed to prevent. Moschion stole the money by and for himself (*autos di' heautou*, 15); his individual action contrasts with the contract's commitment to cooperation (*koinēi*, 9, 10, 18, 22, 28, 41, 42, 48). But Olympiodorus soon imitates the slave: "he tortured him by himself (*autos eph' heautou*) and didn't call me, although he had sworn to examine the property together (*koinēi*) and do everything with me" (18). The suspicion the two men feel toward Moschion (*hupopsia*, 16, 18) will become part of their own relationship as Olympiodorus offers various false pretexts not to share the money (20, 21). The text perhaps hopes to localize deceit in the body of a slave and in this way

At the same time it documents the equity of each, his willingness to be an equal to his equal. For the Athenians such respect for equality was not just an economic virtue, of course, but a political one, connoting a commitment to the egalitarian ideology of democracy. The political resonances of the deal are perhaps heard in the contract's stipulation of *isomoiria*, the equal division of property (19, 32, 38). In political discourse this term denotes the equal distribution of democratic power to all citizens.[29] Likewise, when Callistratus insists that his case is *metria* (moderate, measured) the word also advertises his political moderation: although, he claims (with only a hint of bitterness), he could have sued initially for the entire estate, he seeks only his fair share, *metria kai prosēkonta* (4).

The equality and propriety enshrined in the contract governs not only the behavior of the two signatories toward one another but also their relation to the law. Callistratus wants the contract to be read aloud in court, he says, "so that there will be no suspicion (*hupopsia*), but that you will hear everything well and justly (*kalōs kai dikaiōs*) and can decide as seems most just to you" (48). Callistratus extends the just terms of the contract – *kalōs kai dikaiōs* – to his relation with the jurors. On his part he agrees to tell the truth (e.g. 39). On theirs, they agree to abide by their oath. "Decide as seems most just to you" echoes the dikastic oath sworn by all jurors (cf. 52, 58).[30] It also assimilates that oath to the oath between Callistratus and Olympiodorus "to deliberate as seemed best to both" (9). The jurors, too, are bound by the contract's logic of legality, equality, and fair play.

Whereas Callistratus contracts to deal well and justly with the jurors, Olympiodorus is as untrustworthy in court as he has been (Callistratus claims) in everything else:

> Everything he says, jurors, is just fabricated suspicions and base, unjust pretexts (*huponoiai plastai . . . kai prophaseis adikoi kai ponēriai*) designed to rob me of what he properly ought to give me. But what I will tell you – that he's a liar – won't be a mere suspicion (*huponoia*), but I will show you his shamelessness clearly, offering proofs that are true (*tekmēria . . . alēthina*) and known to everyone, and providing witnesses to everything. (39)

to preserve the ideal of trust and equity between the two citizen subjects of the contract. But the slave's stolen cash resists the contract's equal division and instead persists throughout the case as an economic imbalance and contractual impropriety (27, 32, 34, 37).

29 E.g. Solon fr. 34.9W (= [Arist.] *Ath. Pol.* 12.3); Thuc. 6.16.4, 6.39.2; Plut. *Thes.* 24.2; Xen. *Cyr.* 2.2.21. For the financial sense in which the word is used here, cf. Is. 1.2, 1.35, 6.25, 7.19, 7.22. The term also has a medical meaning (Hipp. *Aer.* 12), to which we will return below.

30 Gernet 1957: 246 *ad* Dem. 48.52. On the dikastic oath, cf. above, Chapter 1.

Olympiodorus insinuates suspicion and pretexts – *huponoiai* and *prophaseis* – into the contractual relations of the courtroom. *Prophasis* puts forward (*pro-*) a false front; *huponoia* secretly (*hupo-*) attributes that same falseness to others. Olympiodorus' "fabricated" words skew the juridical contract by introducing suspicion between the litigant and the jurors. They also introduce a shadow of suspicion within the litigant himself, a schism between his true motives and his words or actions.

This schism suggests a further dimension to the contractual metaphor. Not only the transcript of an idealized relation between legal subjects, the contract also documents an ideal self-relation within the contracting subject. Contracts commit their signatories to self-identity: they are a promise to be what one promises to be. The tautology captures the desired congruence – the rhetorical goal of every litigant – between *ēthos* and action, essence and appearance. Callistratus is a just man; he signed a just contract and his just character is proved by the existence of and his adherence to that contract. To that extent, a contract is an ethical agreement with oneself to be only and always the person who signed the contract. This is the agreement Olympiodorus violates when he stands before the jurors and speaks fabricated pretexts and unjust suspicions. He lies not only about the facts of the case but about himself: in the circular reasoning of the prosecution, his very claim to be the just and reasonable man who signed the contract is a lie that proves that he is not, in fact, that man.

The contract commits its subject to synchronic consistency – to seem what he is and to be what he seems – and also to diachronic consistency. The essence of a written contract is its temporal duration: what is agreed today will last into the future as long as the contract holds. That goes not only for the agreed terms but also for the two signatories themselves, who in effect contract to be the same men tomorrow as they are today. In this speech, the contract is figured as a way of mastering temporal change and fixing the self-identity of the subject over time. Life comes at the individual violently and unpredictably. The need for the contract in the first place is provoked by Olympiodorus' "sudden" claim to the inheritance (*exaiphnēs logon moi prospherei*, 6). This is followed by the "sudden" onslaught of the unexpected and unjust claims of other relatives (*exaiphnēs epipeptōkenai*, 23). These claims produce anger, disputes, and unpleasantness, but the contract shields against such slings and arrows: we agreed "to each take half and have no further unpleasantness" (8). Over the years, events batter the two brothers-in-law, sent by "some chance and deity" (*tukhēn tina kai daimona*, 24). Court cases are won and lost; war breaks out, and Olympiodorus goes on campaign and then returns; the property is seized and later regained. But regardless of what goes on around (and despite) them, "the *sunthēkai* themselves still even now lie with Androkleides" (32). The contract is written, sealed and, in an overdetermined gesture toward its immutability, deposited with a human guarantor whose name, Androkleides, might itself be taken as a "manly lock" upon it.[31]

Of course, the idea that the contract resists all change and masters all events is pure fantasy. Callistratus and Olympiodorus write up the agreement because they foresee challenges to the estate (10), yet when they occur the brothers-in-law are caught unprepared (*aparaskeuoi*, 23). The "further unpleasantness" the contract is meant to eliminate – "saying something unpleasant to my brother-in-law and hearing something inappropriate from him" (8) – might aptly describe this case, as well as the many unpleasant episodes leading up to it. The contract fails to deliver what it promises. But as Callistratus represents it, this is simply because Olympiodorus breaks their deal. While Callistratus figures himself as the ideal contractual subject – rational and restrained, consistent and unchanging – Olympiodorus is the precise opposite. He has broken his contract, both literally and figuratively, by his dishonest dealings with his brother-in-law, the court, and himself.

That breach of contract is played out in the speech as pathological inconsistency. "Olympiodorus never says the same thing, but whatever occurs (*tukhēi*) to him at the moment, and he goes around making strange and suspicious excuses and false accusations (*prophaseis atopous tinas kai huponoias kai aitias pseudeis*) and he is unjust concerning the whole matter" (36). Whereas Callistratus' actions are governed by an unwavering *prohairesis*, Olympiodorus' random words are a result of *tukhē*. He contradicts himself (37), offering first one excuse then another. He tells our friends that I act and speak against him (*hupenantia*, 38, 41), says Callistratus, but in fact he is proven to be speaking against himself (*hupenantia legōn autos hautōi*, 45). The contract Olympiodorus breaks is a commitment to be what he seems, to say what he means, and to be always the same as he is.

Inconsistent in himself, mistrustful toward others, suspect in his relation to the law, Olympiodorus is quite simply mad. He is ruined (*diephthartai*, 52), out of his mind (*paraphronei*, 52, 55, 56), insane (*mainetai*, 53, 54, 55); nothing he says is "healthy" (*hugies*, 51). Callistratus offers a diagnosis,

[31] The name is more likely to mean "Manly fame" (from *kleos*), but in the context an Athenian may also have heard the word *kleis-kleidos* ("key"). The very word for contract, *sunthēkai*, implies its duration: *sunthēkai* are things placed together (*sun* – *tithenai*). The stative verb behind the noun is reiterated in the verb used for their continuing validity: *keisthai*, which functions as the passive of *tithenai*. The contract is put and stays put.

both moral and medical. "Such a man is Olympiodorus. Not only is he unjust, but all our relatives and acquaintances believe he is melancholic (*melankholan*) in his choice of a way of life" (*prohairesei tou biou*, 56).

Melankholē was originally a medical term that referred to an imbalance of black bile within the theory of humors.[32] The late-fourth century Aristotelian *Problemata* remark on the wide range of the disease's psychological and physiological symptoms (953a10–955a40). Summing up his survey of its varied (*pantodapoi*, 954a30) effects the author comments, "the melancholic mixing [of humors] is itself inconsistent (*anōmalos*) and makes those who suffer from it inconsistent (*anōmalous*)" (954b9–10). Men who are physically disposed toward this condition "differ from themselves" (*diapherousi autoi hautōn*, 954b8).[33] *Melankholē* thus appears to be the inverse of *isomoiria*, a term that (in addition to its political and economic meanings) in medical literature connotes the ideal of physiological balance (e.g. Hipp. *Aer.* 12). By the mid-fourth century when this speech was delivered the term *melankholē* seems to have become common in a non-technical sense meaning "crazy."[34] Here it is less a precise diagnosis than a medical metaphor. As such, it translates into psychosomatic terms the thematics of the contract: against the contract's *isomoiria*, *melankholē* symbolizes internal contradiction, imbalance, *anōmalia*.

The metaphor is ethical as well as medical: Olympiodorus is melancholic specifically in his *prohairesis tou biou*. While Callistratus' decisions are bound by the consistency and legitimacy of the contract, Olympiodorus' are inconsistent, irrational, illegitimate. Breach of contract, then, is a variety of ethical madness: "is he not mad who believes he need not do any of the things he agreed and voluntarily contracted and swore to do?" (54). It is a diseased relation to others and to oneself: "How is he not manifestly mad and out of his mind who makes such decisions about himself?" (55). The decision to abide by the contract is now the defining feature not only of the good man (the *kalos kai dikaios*) but of the sane man. Legality is rationality. Olympiodorus has contracted a disease of anti-contractualism. No longer in fair and *isomoiros* partnership with himself, he is out of his right mind, and his violation of the contract proves it. The metaphor has quite literally become a symptom.

[32] Hipp. *Nat. Hom.* 3–7; cf. *Aer.* 10; *Aph.* 3.14; *Morb.* 1.3, 30; *Aff.* 36. On *melankholē* see further Flashar 1966; Pigeaud 1981: 122–38, 1988; Padel 1995: 48–57; Toohey 2004: 27–33.

[33] Cf. 955a29–31: "In sum melancholics are *anōmaloi* because the force of black bile is *anōmalon*." Cf. Arist. *NE* 1152a18; Pigeaud 1988: 21–25: "La bile noire est un mélange parfaitement instable" (21).

[34] E.g. Ar. *Aves* 14, *Ecc.* 251, *Pl.* 12. See Flashar 1966: 37–38; Dunbar 1998: 111–12 *ad* Ar. *Aves* 14.

If rationality is a contract, irrationality is a whore. Late in the speech we hear the etiology of Olympiodorus' sickness. Despite his reluctance to speak about such shameful things (52), Callistratus explains: "Gentlemen of the jury, Olympiodorus never married a citizen woman according to your laws; he does not have and never has had children. Instead, he bought a courtesan (*hetairan*) and keeps her at home. She is the one who has ruined us all and made him even more mad" (*peraiterō mainesthai*, 53). The scandalous life choice (*prohairesis tou biou*) Olympiodorus has made is his decision to live with a *hetaira*. Named as the reason why he has broken the contract, this *hetaira* is both means and metaphor of his *anōmalos* madness.

It is a common theme in Greek ethical thought that a man's domestic condition reflects his mental state. On the one hand, there is the propriety of a legitimate marriage; this orderly existence and well-balanced home economics is the *prohairesis* of a man who is orderly in himself and in his relations to others. Marriage is a contract, both in the literal sense (it is a legally binding pledge between two men) and in the symbolic sense operative in this speech, the life choice of a good man and solid citizen.[35] A *hetaira* in the house, on the other hand, could imply a bad domestic and psychic economy. While it wasn't uncommon or illegal for a wealthy man to keep a mistress in addition to or even instead of a wife (Pericles is one famous example), the normative value placed on legitimate marriage made this decision vulnerable to criticism on the grounds that money and reproductive energy that should be spent building a reputable *oikos* and producing citizen sons were being expended instead on showy luxuries and unnecessary desires. The choice of a *hetaira* instead of a wife might be frowned on, as it clearly is here, as the choice of an irresponsible and immoderate man, a profligate, a bad citizen.[36] Callistratus reinforces the negative implications by lingering on this *hetaira*'s gold and jewels – finery bought, he says, with wealth that was rightfully his (55) – and by denigrating her status by first insinuating that Olympiodorus bought his mistress from a brothel (53) and later flat-out calling her a whore (*gunaiki pornēi*, 56).

When Callistratus accuses Olympiodorus of choosing to keep a mistress instead of marrying a wife (an accusation, we should remember, that may well be baseless, despite Callistratus' claim that it is common knowledge),

[35] The locus classicus is Xen. *Oec.* 1–10. See also Plut. *Coniug. Praec.*, where a happy marriage is the product of philosophical *prohairesis* (139d4). Foucault 1985: 143–84, 1986: 145–85; Murnaghan 1988; Wohl 1997.

[36] Here the key text is Dem. 59 *Against Neaira*. See also Dem. 36.45; Foucault 1985: 143–51; D. Cohen 1991a: 98–171; Ogden 1996: 100–06; Davidson 1997: 109–36; Kurke 1997; Cox 1998: 170–89; Lape 2004: 81–83, 137–70; Roisman 2005: 38–41; Glazebrook 2006: 126–30; Gilhuly 2008: 29–57.

he reiterates in a domestic and sexual register the same ethical charges he is making against Olympiodorus in regard to the contract. Olympiodorus is not a man of his word. His *prohairesis biou* is illegitimate and sick. He refuses to abide by the unwritten contracts of social life and to govern his behavior in accordance with their norms. The metaphoric register in this speech – as befits a world of contract – is extremely consistent: legal, medical, and sexual signs all point in the same direction. Thus in Callistratus' inflammatory description, Olympiodorus' *hetaira* echoes the thematics of the broken contract. Appearing in finery "beyond all propriety" (*peraiterō tou kalōs ekhontos*, 55) and making Olympiodorus "more mad" (*peraiterō mainesthai*, 53) she is an excess that unbalances the equality of the partnership: her robes and gold are bought with money Olympiodorus stole from Callistratus and thus her ostentatious public appearances (*exodous lampras*, 55) are a visual display of their violated agreement. Drawing on Solon's inheritance law, Callistratus builds around her a case for a madness that is not just embarrassing but legally invalidating. "Solon decreed that everything be invalid that is done under the influence of a woman, especially a woman like this one" (56). Choosing a *hetaira* over a wife, Olympiodorus becomes legally *non compos mentis*. The contract is no longer valid. It has been replaced by this whore.

It is not coincidental that Callistratus refers frequently to his own wife and child, Olympiodorus' sister and niece. They, he claims, "are wronged no less than I but even more" by Olympiodorus' scandalous home-life (54). He stages the difference between his own legitimate marriage and Olympiodorus' domestic impropriety as a tense encounter between the two women, his wife and Olympiodorus' mistress:

> Are my wife and daughter not wronged and don't they suffer terribly when they see this man's *hetaira* dressed in fine robes and lots of gold beyond all propriety, going out in splendor and arrogantly flaunting (*hubrizousan*) luxuries bought with our property, while they themselves are too poor for such finery? Are they not wronged even more than I? (55)

The bad faith and mistrust between Olympiodorus and Callistratus extends to their women. The wife and daughter gaze at the *hetaira* with the legitimate outrage of legitimacy outraged; their jealous glance transforms her finery into a metaphor of *hubris*, both hers against them and Olympiodorus' against Callistratus. Their embarrassed sense of inferiority encapsulates Olympiodorus' violation of the contract's *isomoiria*. Moreover, Callistratus' wife expresses uxorial indignation not only for her husband's *oikos* but also for her brother's. Her disapproving look makes Olympiodorus' failure to marry a breach of his marriage contract before the fact: he has been unfaithful to his future wife by preferring a courtesan. It is also a breach of the marriage contract that binds the two brothers-in-law, as if Olympiodorus were an unfaithful husband and Callistratus the outraged brother. Olympiodorus has broken his troth to Callistratus not once but twice.

Callistratus looks through the eyes of his wife with righteous shame and invites the jurors to do the same. They are urged to watch the wife watching the *hetaira* and to redress the wrong she has suffered:

> I beg you – and not only I but also my wife, Olympiodorus' sister, and my daughter, Olympiodorus' niece. We pray and beseech you, jurors, all of us – for you must imagine that they are here in court. Persuade (*peisai*) Olympiodorus not to wrong us, or if he won't be persuaded, remember everything I have said and vote as you think best and most just. Doing so, you will reach a just verdict and one that benefits all of us, not least Olympiodorus himself. (57–58)

The speech closes with this appeal on behalf of the wife and daughter. Like the contract, the women are both present and absent in court, physically absent (as legally they must be) but imaginatively present. The jurors do not hear the text of the contract, but in its place Callistratus conjures up the words of the women who represent that other violated contract, marriage. He asks the jurors to see through their eyes the meretricious excess of Olympiodorus' life and the melancholic *prohairesis* that guides it. Olympiodorus has broken the contract "persuaded by a whore" (*gunaiki peithomenos pornēi*, 56). The jurors must reverse this baleful influence and persuade (*peisai*) him to end his criminality. Against the irrational suasion of the *hetaira* they must exert the beneficent pressure of a wife and cure his madness with the balm of a just verdict against him. In this way they will restore the contractual bond between the two men (putting the "law" back in brother-in-law, as it were) and reconcile feuding kinsmen, as Callistratus requests at the opening of the speech (3). At the same time they will uphold their own contractual obligation, their oath to decide the case as seems most just.

Callistratus thus uses the two metaphors, the contract and the courtesan, to construct two diametrically opposed subjects in two opposed relations to the law. Through these metaphors he tries to transform actions into *ēthos* and in this way to seal both himself and his opponent immutably in his respective identity. Metaphor is deployed in the speech like a contract, fixing the subject as only and always what he is: a keeper of contracts or a keeper of mistresses, *dikaios* or mad. But the two metaphors are perhaps harder to hold apart than Callistratus pretends. A contract, after all, has two partners, and while Callistratus calls Olympiodorus diseased and deranged, it is clear that Olympiodorus is saying much the same about him. In fact, the bad faith the contract is ostensibly designed to prevent was built into it from the start: even if the contract does not represent Callistratus' attempt to defraud Olympiodorus of an inheritance that is rightfully all his (as is quite possible), it does represent the two men's concerted attempt to preempt the potentially legitimate claims of other relatives. Adherence to the contract involves the two in further questionable dealings, including possible prevarication to delay judicial proceedings (23–25) and conspiracy to commit perjury (45). A record of dishonesty and an inducement to impropriety, the contract comes to look far less like a symbol of legitimacy and far more like a courtesan.

If there is, in fact, a whiff of hetairic illegitimacy about the contract, then is there a madness to the document as well, a melancholy not only in its breach but written into its very text? If we pursue Lacan's suggestion that metaphors function like symptoms, what latent pathology does this metaphor symbolize? Read symptomatically, the contract is the record of a frustrated – we might even say melancholic – desire. What each litigant really wanted was the whole estate all for himself, as Callistratus more or less admits at the beginning (5, 6). The contract is thus by nature a compromise, in which each renounces his selfish wish for the whole in return for guarantee of the half: it is a sort of concession of the pleasure principle (the urge to maximize enjoyment) to the reality principle. This *prohairesis* of security over satisfaction is documented in the contract. But signing that document does not eradicate the original desire for the whole. Instead that desire persists throughout the case – indeed, in the very fact that we have this case, which is just the latest of numerous attempts on the part of each man to get the other's half. But the symbolic equity of the contract and its wan contentment with propriety, legitimacy, and sanity makes it impossible to admit this deeper desire, or even to acknowledge its renunciation. There is no legitimate symbolic space left for it, and it can figure in the speech only as a species of madness. In psychoanalytic theory the technical name given to such unacknowledged loss is melancholia.[37]

The melancholic longing beneath the contract – the repressed desire for the whole – resurfaces at the end of the speech, however, and precisely at the moment when it comes face-to-face with the law itself in the person of Solon:

[37] Freud 1957 [1917]; cf. Butler 1997a: 132–98.

Such a man is Olympiodorus. Not only is he unjust, but all our relatives and acquaintances believe he is melancholic in his choice of a way of life and, as the lawmaker Solon says, he is crazy (*paraphronōn*) as no other man has ever been crazy (*parephronēsen*), under the influence of a whore's persuasion (*gunaiki peithomenos pornēi*). Solon decreed that everything be invalid that is done under the influence of a woman, especially a woman like this one. (56)

Callistratus speaks in the voice of the censorious nomothete in order to declare the man mad and the woman a whore. Solon is often called on to play such a role in Attic oratory and despite some obvious prejudicial interpolations, the provision Callistratus cites is reasonably close to the apparently genuine Solonic law stipulating that a man without legitimate male heirs could dispose of his property as he wished "unless he is mentally impaired (*maniōn*) due to old age or drugs or disease, or unless he is under the influence of a woman (*gunaiki peithomenos*), and is not thinking straight (*paranoōn*) because of one of these things, or is under compulsion or restrained in prison."[38]

Strictly speaking, though, this law is irrelevant to Callistratus' situation, as Louis Gernet notes, since Solon's law applies only to inheritance cases.[39] Now, it is true that Attic orators tend to be somewhat "capricious" (Gernet's word) in the way they cite the law.[40] But just because a citation is capricious doesn't mean it is insignificant; indeed, in the language of metaphors and symptoms the irrelevant detail is often the most telling. Callistratus' loose citation of Solon's law assimilates the contract to a will and the greedy brother-in-law to a senile testator. This assimilation extends the force of the contract – which already covers property, marriage, sanity, and subjectivity – to life and death: breaking his oath, Olympiodorus is not merely deranged but deceased.

When the contract becomes a will, moreover, this case returns – repetition being the modality of the symptom – to the original dispute over Comon's estate. By declaring Olympiodorus *non compos mentis*, Callistratus retroactively reopens the question of the inheritance and, by virtue of the owner's mental incompetence, lays claim to the whole estate. In this momentary conflation of the will with the contract and Olympiodorus with Comon, Callistratus imaginatively grasps for the whole while litigating for the half. On the one hand he renounces his desire for all and

38 Dem. 46.14. Cf. Is. 2.19. This law is discussed further in Chapter 6.

39 Gernet 1957: 246 *ad* Dem. 48.56: "La citation est empruntée à la loi testamentaire . . . qui n'a rien à faire ici." Todd, however, notes that there was no clear distinction between wills and contracts in Athenian law (1993: 224, 267).

40 Gernet 1957: 246 *ad* Dem. 48.56: "la vérité est que les textes, chez les orateurs, sont très capricieusement invoqués." Cf. Carey 1996; Johnstone 1999: 21–25, 62–69.

basks in the legitimizing glow of the contract, its sane and proper subject. On the other hand he still dreams, if only in the symptomatic form of this legal fantasy, of the promiscuous pleasure of having it all, the pleasure the contract curtails. He gets to enforce the contract even as he has Solon declare it invalid. He gets to have the *hetaira* and marry her too.

This misapplication of Solon's law reveals behind the proprieties of the contract an unacknowledged desire not only outside of the agreement but in breach of its grounding logic. Callistratus may represent himself as sane to the extent that his *prohairesis* and pleasure are fully circumscribed by the contract, but he too has his melancholic anomalies. At one point in their ongoing legal negotiations, after other family members (including Callistratus' brother Callippus) had filed claims to Comon's property, Callistratus and Olympiodorus decided that Olympiodorus should sue for the whole of the estate and Callistratus for half (since his brother would claim the other half). That is, they would go to court against one another, but agreed that whoever won would share his award with the other "well and justly (*kalōs kai dikaiōs*) as we swore to one another and contracted" (30). Olympiodorus then swore in court that both houses were his and Callistratus was merely renting one from him, and that the money Callistratus had from the estate was just a loan (44). Callistratus allowed Olympiodorus to present witnesses to that claim and raised no objection: "I didn't contradict them. No one heard a thing from me, not a peep or a shout, when he was arguing this case, but I agreed to the truth of anything he wanted to say, for I was suing in common with you, as it seemed best to you and me" (44). The brothers-in-law colluded to deceive the jury and cheat the other claimants. (As it turns out, of course, the strategy backfires on Callistratus: Olympiodorus wins the whole estate but then refuses to share with Callistratus – hence this present case.) Callistratus, however, offers this tale of past deception as proof of his present honest dealings: "for if I am not telling the truth now, why would I have kept quiet then, and not come down hard on the witnesses for testifying as they did?" (45).[41]

Earlier in the speech Callistratus contrasted his own *tekmēria alēthina* to the mad lies and pretexts of Olympiodorus (39), but here he turns his own truth claims against themselves: the proof that he tells the truth (*alēthē*) now is that he falsely agreed that Olympiodorus spoke the truth

[41] Humphreys 1983: 6 notes "a point which frequently appears, that where kin make an illegal compromise in order to avoid open enmity, the illegality of the agreement often provides an excuse for a later piece of double-crossing." Roisman 2006: 19–31 studies the rhetoric of conspiracy in inheritance disputes; he notes that this speech is unique in that the speaker represents himself as a victim not of a conspiracy but of a fellow conspirator (28–31).

(*alēthē*) in the last case "since I was working with you, as seemed best to you and me" (44). In this echo of the language of their oath, the contract not only becomes a conspiracy and induction to perjury. It also entails Callistratus in a self-contradiction that, in the case of his opponent, he labeled madness. In his melancholy, Olympiodorus had been "proven to be lying and speaking against himself and making imaginary claims" (45). But these same charges could just as easily be laid against Callistratus. Contracting against his own desire, Callistratus, too, becomes *anōmalos*. Keeping the contract with Olympiodorus means breaking a contract with himself, the very contract that supported his claims to veracity, integrity, and sanity. That contract breached, his whole speech becomes not the enactment of a lawful *prohairesis* but instead a mere *prophasis*, a false pretext; and Callistratus himself, split between his contractual rhetoric of equity and his inadmissible desire for the whole, is shown to be suffering from the same anti-contractual *melankholē* that he diagnoses in Olympiodorus.

The subjective metaphors in Demosthenes 48 simultaneously consolidate and destabilize the self they describe. Defining by condensing dispersed meanings (rhetorical, legal, and psychic), metaphors stabilize identity by replacing it with something that is not itself. In this double movement, they work both with and against the immutable self-consistency of the contract. In some ways, in fact, metaphors are rather meretricious: transgressing linguistic boundaries and wantonly joining separate terms, dressing up a plain idea in borrowed jewels, they are seductive and improper figures. Simultaneously contract and courtesan, the metaphor creates an *anōmalia* within the contractual text of the forensic speech and uncovers a latent *melankholē* in the legal subject it constructs. In the process it suggests that the law's attempt to define a rational, coherent, unchanging subject and to bind it within the terms of its own discursive contract will always fail, for if that contract is ever unsealed and read, a rhetoric of madness may be found inside.

IMPOSSIBLE METONYMIES (LYSIAS 24 *VIA* DEMOSTHENES 21)

Among every speaker's goals is to forge an identification with the jurors and to show that, despite any apparent differences of wealth or upbringing, he is one of them. The crime against me is a crime against each of you, he says; my plight is your plight, my interests your interests. Such claims, ubiquitous and loud throughout forensic oratory, rely on a metonymic logic. Whereas metaphors define through vertical substitution, metonyms work through contiguous association. The former condense disparate meanings around a single, universalizing term; the latter displace meanings laterally along chains of related terms. While metaphors posit a fixed one-to-one relationship, metonomies operate within provisional networks of associated parts and take their sense from the whole network. These rhetorical figures do not name fixed ontological categories, of course, but instead designate different relations of substitution or association. They also carry different political implications. Ernesto Laclau suggests that metonymy is the basic trope of politics, which forges contingent alliances and articulates different sets of interests.[42] Michael Ryan aligns metaphor, with its vertical orientation of meaning, with conservative politics and metonymy, with its web of lateral associations, with progressive politics.[43] We might even go further and say that while monarchy is metaphoric ("*l'état c'est moi*") democracy – especially a direct democracy like Athens' – is structurally metonymic.

If that is true, then a forensic speaker's attempt to solicit the jurors' identification appeals to the fundamental logical structure of Athenian democracy: through that identification, the speaker becomes a metonymic embodiment of the demos and the polis. This has obvious advantages for the litigant, who weaves around himself a web of symbolic associations in which his own strategic interests become inseparable from the ideals of the polis. I suggested in Chapter 1 that this subjective strategy also has advantages for legal discourse, situating it at and as the suture between the democratic city and the individual citizen. In the metonymic strategies of its subjects the law thus tells a *logos* about itself and its own life within the democracy. And yet, because metonymy is a trope of displacement (in contrast to metaphor's condensation), that *logos* lacks finality, and its subjects emerge not as sites of symbolic fixity but as incarnations of a perpetual and never-realized civic and jurisprudential desire. Far from an empty formal exercise, then, tracing the metonymies of forensic oratory reveals the basic logical architecture of both the political and the legal discourse of democratic Athens.

To see how metonymy works to construct a juridical self, we can look briefly at one paradigmatic and highly self-conscious example,

42 Butler, Laclau, and Žižek 2000: 78–79. Cf. Laclau and Mouffe 1985: 141: "hegemony is basically metonymical: its effects always emerge from a surplus of meaning which results from an operation of displacement."

43 Ryan 1989: 111–33. See also Gilmore 1994: 65–86 for an illuminating discussion of the politics of metonymy as an autobiographical strategy. On metonymy see further Burke 1945: 503–17; Jakobson 1956: 90–96; H. White 1973: 35–36; Silverman 1983: 109–22.

Demosthenes 21 *Against Meidias*.[44] Metonymy is the central rhetorical strategy and the key legal argument of this speech. Demosthenes charges that Meidias punched him when he was serving as *khorēgos* (chorus producer) at the dramatic festival. The jurors may be inclined to take this as an essentially private affair between two elite enemies, but Demosthenes is anxious to prove that the punch is in fact a matter of national security (8). For in striking him Meidias has insulted not just an individual but a civic official and thus the city itself:

> It was not just me, Demosthenes, whom he insulted that day, but your chorus . . . If on any other day Meidias had committed any of these crimes against me as a private citizen it would be right for him to be punished in a private suit. But if it is shown that he committed all these crimes of *hubris* against me when I was your *khorēgos*, during a holy day, he deserves public anger and retribution. For a *khorēgos* was insulted at the same time as Demosthenes. (31, 33–34)

Demosthenes is more than just Demosthenes. The one name signifies two entities, the public *khorēgos* and the private individual. The homonymy that occasioned panic in Demosthenes 39 is here a deliberate tactic.

Demosthenes develops this nominal conflation through an analogy. None of the individuals who serves in the office of thesmothete has the name Thesmothete, but "whatever name each man has" (32). If someone insults a thesmothete as an individual, he will be tried and fined, but if he insults him as a thesmothete he risks disenfranchisement "because the man who does this is also insulting the laws and your common crown and the name of the city. For Thesmothete is not the name of any man but the city's name" (32). His point is obvious, but the analogy is devious, because it implies that, just as the name Thesmothete signifies an individual as well as an office, the name Demosthenes signifies the *khorēgia* as well as the man. "Demosthenes" becomes an official title, "the city's name." In a literal *metonymy*, Demosthenes' name becomes interchangeable with Athens'. That exchange is in turn one node in a larger network of metonymic connections that ultimately encompasses the entire universe. In his crime against me, Demosthenes insists, Meidias committed a crime not only against the chorus but also "against the tribe, which is a tenth of you. The *hubris* he plotted and committed against me was also against the laws, which keep each of you safe, and against the god, to whom I was appointed as *khorēgos* and against the revered and holy divinity, whatever that may be" (*to tēs hosias, hotidēpot' estin, to semnon kai to daimonion*, 126). "Demosthenes"

[44] This speech has received excellent analysis. See especially MacDowell 1990; P. Wilson 1991, 2000: 156–68; D. Cohen 1991a, 1995a: 90–101; Ober 1994.

names the center point of a centrifugal web of associations that spreads so far its edges disappear in the theological mists. The cosmos reels when Demosthenes is punched in the mouth.

The brilliance of this strategy is the way it threads the warp of personal identification into the weft of Athens' democratic ideology to create a fabric so tightly woven that a rip in any part threatens to unravel the whole. Like every litigant, Demosthenes works hard to forge a bond of empathy with the jurors. "I request of you all, jurors: as you listen to everything you are about to hear, ask yourselves what one of you would have done if he had suffered this violence and what attitude he would have held on his own behalf toward the man who inflicted it" (108). This primary metonymy both rests upon and itself supports other, more far-reaching associations. Demosthenes asks each juror to imagine himself hurrying home after the trial, glancing nervously over his shoulder in fear of the kind of assault from his enemies that Demosthenes has suffered from Meidias (221). In painting this vivid picture, he not only plays on personal fear but also implicitly invokes one of the basic tenets of Athenian democratic ideology, the personal sanctity of the citizen. David Halperin has shown how the political sovereignty of the Athenian demos was instantiated in the corporeal inviolability of each individual citizen.[45] This analogy between part and whole, between citizen microcosm and civic macrocosm, is played out in this speech as a metonymic identity among all the parts of the whole: the attack on Demosthenes' body is a potential assault on every citizen's body and by extension on the entire Athenian citizen body. Demosthenes offers his own body as a metonym for the corporeal sanctity of the individual citizen and the political sovereignty of the demos as a whole. In so doing he also metonymically links the individual members of the jury to the fantasy of a sovereign body politic. That the jury is the demos is one of the primary fictions of Athenian forensic oratory. Demosthenes makes that fictional identity depend upon the jurors' identification with himself.[46]

[45] Halperin 1990: 88–112; cf. Winkler 1990a. See also the discussion of Ariston's violated body in Dem. 54 (above, Chapter 2).

[46] See, for instance, 140 where Demosthenes reminds the jurors that although they may be weaker individually than Meidias and his ilk, they are stronger collectively. By defending him they are defending one another and their own collective power; cf. 142, 219–21. On the jury as the demos, see Ober 1989a: 147, 1989b: 329–33; P. Wilson 1991: 164; Blanshard 2004. Ober (1989a: 147) characterizes this relation as synecdochic. While synecdoche is a useful trope for understanding political relations, it is too imprecise for this discussion, since it can be understood either as a metaphor (a microcosm that condenses the essence of the macrocosm) or as a metonym (a part of a whole made up of its parts).

At the same time, Demosthenes' connection with the jurors also links him, via a different set of associations, to the rule of law. The jurors' oath to "vote in accordance with the laws and the decrees of the demos" made each individual *dikastēs* an agent of *dikē*. Thus by insulting him, Meidias has also insulted the laws (7), which Demosthenes asks the jury to picture standing by his side pleading on his behalf, just as Meidias' sobbing children do on his (186–88). Demosthenes prosecutes not only for his own sake but, as he repeatedly tells the jurors, "on behalf of myself and you and the laws" (20, 40, 213, 222; cf. 127). How could he do otherwise, since he has shown these three – Demosthenes, jurors, laws – to be just three different names, *metonyma*, for the same democratic ideals.

Finally, he weaves the whole web of metonymies together in one of the speech's most famous passages. Why is it, he asks, that the individual members of the jury don't fear the sort of attack that he himself has suffered? Because as jurors they are "strong and sovereign over everything in the polis" (223). This, he continues, isn't because they are armed or younger or physically stronger than the other citizens "but because your strength lies in the laws."

> And what is the strength of the laws? If one of you is attacked and cries out, will they come running to help? No, they are just written texts and they couldn't do that. What is their power, then? You – if you secure them and make them valid for anyone who asks. The strength of the laws lies in you and your strength lies in the laws. (223–24)

The jurors are the laws' strength; the laws are the jurors': popular sovereignty and rule of law – never far apart in forensic oratory – are here one and the same. Through this rhetorical synthesis, individuals are endowed with the authority of a city in which law is the only king and its monarchy secures the sovereignty of each citizen. At the same time, the laws, no longer mere written documents, are infused with the living spirit of justice and the will of the people.[47]

At the center of this symbolic union stands Demosthenes. He situates himself at the precise intersection between Athens' political and jurisprudential ideals and the living body of its citizens: the two seem to meet in – and thanks to – him. The entire symbolic structure of the democracy is at stake in the jurors' verdict. By defending him (he implies) they will be

[47] This passage and the relation between popular sovereignty and rule of law are discussed further in Chapter 1. Cf. 21.225: you must defend the laws as you would yourselves and see that wrongs against the laws are wrongs against everyone, no matter who brings them to trial. Christ (in press b) examines the language of "helping" in these passages.

defending not only the laws but the sovereignty they themselves derive from the laws, not only themselves but the vitality the laws borrow from them. If they fail to convict, on the other hand, then the laws are just lifeless carvings and they themselves just a bunch of feeble old men. The strength of Demosthenes' argument is that it both draws on metonymic connections already deeply embedded in Athenian communal thought and at the same time seems to be the sole thing holding those vital connections together, the single thread without which the whole precious ideological fabric would unravel.

Of course, Demosthenes can weave himself so seamlessly into the pattern of the democracy only by erasing the significant economic and social differences dividing the powerful orator from a jury of average Athenians. Peter Wilson has shown the way the speech's overtly egalitarian ideology – which posits that the bodies of all citizens are equally inviolable – glosses over the real social differences that, as he says, made some bodies more equal than others.[48] We can see the role of metonymy in this social misrecognition when, for instance, Demosthenes claims that the assault on him is also an assault on "the laws and your common crown and the name of the city" (32). "Your common crown" explicitly associates the jury (you) with the sovereign demos, but also, more insidiously, conflates popular sovereignty with the crown that symbolized individual, and generally elite, excellence. Demosthenes would later receive a crown of his own, a reward for his service to the city and the object of another famous speech. When his body becomes the citizen body, he and the demos share a common crown. But what are the politics of this metonymic collapsing of elite prerogative and popular authority and whose interests are erased in the process? Rhetorical figures conceal as much as they reveal, and one thing they may conceal is their own politics.

Demosthenes discourages us from pursuing this question by smoothing over any rough edges created by the artificial equation between himself and the mass jury. He does this, first, by projecting all difference onto Meidias, who is presented as a monster of elite *hubris* and antidemocratic individuality (e.g. 142, 195, 197). At the same time, he empties his own person of any particularity and turns himself into an abstraction, a symbol. To that end he even occludes the central event of the case, the punch. In the drama of *hubris* Demosthenes so vividly recreates, the punch is the

[48] P. Wilson 1991: 173–74, 2000: 177–78. See esp. 21.111–12, where Demosthenes first admits that he is not entirely "friendless and destitute," then discusses the way the law treats the rich as opposed to "the rest of us." Cf. 123–25. See also, more generally, Todd 1990c on the class dynamics of the relation between speaker and jurors.

one thing never actually narrated. In fact, Demosthenes says, it cannot be narrated:

> A man who throws a punch can do many things, jurors, some of which the victim could not report to anyone else – with his posture, his look, his tone of voice, acting arrogant, acting like an enemy, punching, striking in the face. These things shake a man up; they make him beside himself if he's unused to being insulted. No one reporting these things, jurors, could make listeners experience their terror as clearly as the *hubris* appears to the victim and spectators during the actual moment of the event. (72)

The punch is described as indescribable, and Demosthenes' wounded body is rendered invisible. It is obliterated not only as the object of violent assault but even as subjective witness to that assault: the scene is staged as a disembodied hypothetical and any real pain or anger is placed beyond the descriptive language of the speech. Instead, Demosthenes leaves the jurors to imagine the scene for themselves: the look of the attacker, the sound of his voice, their own distraught rage. The jurors are invited to substitute themselves into a picture from which Demosthenes has disappeared.

By emptying himself of any particularity – as an elite and an individual – Demosthenes transforms his body into a repository of political and legal meaning, the invisible center of the web of associations that he himself has woven. At this moment, metonymy reaches toward metaphor, as Demosthenes makes himself a transcendent symbol of inviolable citizenship. Douglas MacDowell expresses the reaction Demosthenes no doubt hoped for: "As he approaches the conclusion of his speech," MacDowell writes, "Demosthenes rises above the details of his dispute with Meidias, and is telling a universal truth with both pathos and power."[49] His particular, private, elite body becomes an abstraction, a metaphor that consolidates politics precisely by affecting to transcend them. Personal grudges, a private feud over honor, social and economic differences are all made to disappear. All we see is the universal truth of the sovereign law and sovereign demos, embodied in the idealized person of the individual orator.[50]

[49] MacDowell 1990: 37. He continues: "His defense of legal justice is as valid today as when he wrote it. Elsewhere we can analyse his cleverness and skill at arguing; at the close we can simply admire a masterpiece of eloquence."

[50] Cf. P. Wilson 1991: 187 on Dem. 21.7: "In this scenario all other difference is elided so that Demosthenes' body can stand for that of each and any citizen." On law's abstraction of the body, see A. Hyde 1997: 151–64, 244–51. In Isocrates 20 a poor man has been struck by the wealthy Lochites. He tells the jurors that by avenging him "each of you will vote as if he were voting on his own behalf" (21), since "those who dare to transgress the law that protects your bodies are committing a crime against all of you" (21). Democracy is defined by its protection of the bodies of all citizens, and Lochites' violence against the speaker is analogized to the *hubris* of the oligarchs against the demos in the civil war (10–14). The speaker offers his body simultaneously as a metonym for the jurors and as a metaphor for the democracy.

Demosthenes thus forges a metonymic network connecting jurors, demos, law, and polis, and attempts to consolidate this rhetorical structure in the metaphor of his own universal body. This strategy of self-abstraction would no doubt have been facilitated if, as some believe, the speech was not actually delivered in court.[51] Freed from the specific context of the trial, the speech's "I" would have been disembodied from the start and thus more easily elevated into a civic symbol. But in the end it doesn't matter whether the speech was delivered or not, because its metonymic strategies appear in some form in every forensic oration. Every litigant hopes to weave himself into the fabric of Athenian civic ideology, to make it impossible to disentangle his private legal interests from the communal ideals of the polis or to sustain the latter without supporting the former. Demosthenes deploys this strategy so skillfully that he conceals its artifice: his metonymies seem natural and inevitable, and the civic and jurisprudential desires they engage are obscured.

In order to see those desires more clearly, we can turn to a harder case, perhaps even an impossible one. Lysias 24 is titled *Huper tou Adunatou*, *For the Disabled Man.* The speaker is *adunatos*, disabled, impoverished, powerless. His multiple incapacity blocks idealizing identification of the sort Demosthenes establishes: how could his crippled body symbolize the Athenian citizen body? The speech *Huper tou Adunatou* is both about an *adunatos*, a disabled man, and about an *adunaton*, an impossible metonymy that exposes the incapacities and impossibilities within the metonymic structures of juridical discourse.[52] Putting this impossible body on the stand, the case exposes what is at stake for the speaker, the polis, and the law in the metonymic strategy of self-presentation.

Lysias 24 is a *dokimasia* case: the disabled man is presenting his case in the Boule for continuation of his disability pension of one obol. This minimal dole – barely enough to live on – was available to Athenian citizens who owned less than three mna worth of property and were physically unable

[51] Aeschines insinuates that Demosthenes let himself be bought off before the case went to trial (3.51–52) and some conclude based on internal evidence that the text we have is unfinished. Aeschines' slander of his enemy seems a weak foundation for any argument about the status of the text, though, and internal repetitions may have been eliminated in delivery. On the issue of delivery see Dover 1968: 172; Harris 1989; MacDowell 1990: 23–28; Ober 1994: 91–92; Fredal 2001: 255–56, and the interesting comments of P. Wilson 1991: 187 about the non-transparency of the text and its author.

[52] See Harding 1994: 203 on the ambiguities of the title. A. Hyde 1997 analyzes the many contradictory ways in which modern legal discourse constructs the human body; see esp. 205–66 on the law's role in expelling abjected bodies from the purified body politic.

to work.[53] His opponent has apparently charged that the speaker is able to work and has enough income to disqualify him from the pension (4). The speech is not a response to the specific charges which, in fact, he addresses only glancingly and with a suspect vagueness. Instead, the speaker frames it as an autobiography, a defense of his life and character. "I am almost grateful to my accuser that he has brought this suit against me, councillors, for before I did not have an opportunity to give an account of my life (*tou biou logon*), but now thanks to him I have one" (1). In announcing this speech as a *biou logos*, the *adunatos* is perhaps parodying a familiar trope of *dokimasia* cases, where the usually elite litigant proclaims his eagerness to give an account of his invariably admirable life (cf. Lys. 16.9; Dem. 18.8; [And.] 4.37). This case, though, is the accounting of a life worth a single obol.

Many readers identify a tone of parody in this opening gambit, "a claim that is appropriate for a proud and ambitious aristocrat like Mantitheus at his *dokimasia* [in Lysias 16] but is faintly ridiculous in the present context."[54] This tone pervades the cripple's *logos biou*. Indeed, it is so marked that some scholars believe the text is a rhetorical exercise, not intended for delivery.[55] But the sardonic tone is not a stylistic experiment, but the central legal strategy of the speaker, who is both its beneficiary and its victim. The cripple claims his opponent is not serious in his charges "but playing around (*paizōn*), not wishing to persuade you that I am what he says, but wishing to make a joke of me (*kōmōidein*), as if he were saying something clever" (18). In fact, it is he who makes a joke of himself: his is a derisible *bios* narrated in the form of a derisive *logos*.

53 [Arist.] *Ath. Pol.* 49.4. By Aristotle's day, the amount had apparently been raised to two obols a day. As Garland comments, "the pension was at all times barely sufficient to support the disabled at the poverty line" (1995: 36). In the fourth century, it seems that an obol was the price charged by the cheapest of street-walkers (Philemon fr. 4; Halperin 1990: 107). Public laborers (like the builders working on the Erechtheum at the end of the fifth century) earned at least a drachma (six obols) a day (Halperin 1990: 107). Jury pay at this period was three obols. On the purpose and pragmatics of the dole, see Rhodes 1981: 570; Garland 1995: 35–58; Dillon 1995. On the understanding of poverty in classical Athens see Hands 1968: 62–76; Dover 1974: 109–12; de Ste Croix 1981: 179–204; Markle 1985; Sinclair 1988: 121–22; Todd 1990c; Rosivach 1991; Christ (in press a).

54 Todd 2000a: 253; cf. Bonner 1922: 100–01; Edwards and Usher 1985: 263; Carey 1990: 49; Harding 1994: 203. Scholars note too the incongruity between the speech's lofty, poetic style and the speaker's lowly status (Usher 1965: 112; Edwards and Usher 1985: 263–64; Harding 1994: 203). Most commentators believe that the purpose of the humor is to distract the jury's attention from a weak case: Edwards and Usher 1985: 263; Carey 1990: 45–47. But see also Garland 1995: 73–86 on ancient ridicule of the disabled. Biraud 1991 notes how uncommon it is for speakers to discuss their own bodies.

55 Roussel 1966; cf. Lavency 2007: 22–23. Most commentators, however, defend its authenticity: see, e.g., Dover 1968: 189.

Throughout the speech, the cripple savagely mocks himself. He suggests that the prosecutor is harassing him out of envy (*phthonos*, a word connoting class resentment) because he is the better citizen, despite his disability (2–3). To his opponent's accusation that he is wealthy enough to ride a horse, he answers sarcastically that he rides a horse because he is unable to walk and by that logic it might also be held against him that he walks with two walking-sticks instead of one as most Athenian men did (12). Alluding to the practice of *antidosis* (which allowed an Athenian chosen for a liturgy to challenge another citizen to assume the liturgy or else accept an exchange of property) he speculates that if he were selected as tragic *khorēgos*, his opponent would take the liturgy ten times over rather than submit to the exchange of property (9). The cripple is no Demosthenes: for him the idea of being *khorēgos* is just a sad joke.

The butt of his grim humor and the primary exhibit in his case is his own impotence, physical and social. In this *logos* of a miserable *bios*, all accounts add up to the same thing: disability. His body is offered as an indisputable sign of his incapacity, but there are others. Old age, disease, and "all the evils that follow from them" have doubled his initial misfortune (8), as if multiplying the privation of the alpha-privative (*a-dunatos*). Further signs: he walks with two sticks and rides a horse. His opponent offers these details as evidence that he is not as poor as he claims, but he reinterprets them as manifest proof of his poverty (the horse is borrowed and if he were rich enough to own a horse he would instead buy a comfortably saddled mule, 11–12) and of his disability (he needs the horse and the two sticks only because he cannot get around without them, 12). Even such small comforts as he enjoys, feeble inventions for the mitigation of his suffering (10), are tallied in the column "*adunatos*."

His *logos biou* is not just an account of his life but an accounting (*logos*) of his livelihood (*bios*): "The alleged luxury from my trade and the rest of my livelihood (*bios*), such as it happens to be, are, I believe, well known to all of you" (5). That trade, too, is credited to the account of his disability. This *tekhnē* (which he never specifies) is "able to help little" (*brakhea dunamenēn ōphelein*), and he performs it only with difficulty and is "not yet able" (*oupō dunamai*) to pay an assistant (6). His *tekhnē* is merely another word for his incapacity: like him it is *adunatos*. All the accounts tally in this *logos biou*, and they all add up to one obol.[56]

[56] He associates his trade verbally with the one-obol dole. If you deprive me (*aphelēsthe*) of the meager income from this trade, he says, I will likely meet with the most desperate fate (*duskherestatēi . . . tukhēi*, 6). *Aphairein* (to deprive) is used throughout of the revocation of the pension, and the miserable fate he anticipates from the loss of his trade echoes that he suffers from his disability (*sōmatos dustukhēmata*, 3).

Of course, the mere existence of this *logos*, the product of one of the most capable logographers of the day, might seem to skew the account and suggest that the speaker cannot be as resourceless as he claims. This is another reason some scholars have judged the speech an exercise, not a real forensic oration (although others have suggested that the cripple had a wealthy patron, or that Lysias worked *pro bono*). But the speaker deflects the suspicion of deceit by making his crippled body speak for itself. My opponent is so shameless that he is trying to persuade you that I am not *adunatos*, he says. But he's obviously insane. "For he has come to dispute over my misfortune as if it were a wealthy heiress (*epiklērou*) and he tries to persuade you that I am not such a man as you all see. But you must trust more in your own eyes than in his words; this is the task of sensible men" (14). His disability, he claims, is displayed unambiguously on his body: the councillors have only to look at him to know it. Seeing is believing. The striking simile to the *epiklēros* – the wealthy heiress who was the object of frequent legal wrangling – figures the speaker as passive and effeminate, and also ridicules his opponents for squabbling over such a miserable legacy.[57] At the same time, it suggests that while the opponent reads his body metaphorically or rhetorically – as something it is not – he and the jury see it for what it literally and manifestly is. In this way he denies his own role in constructing his body as crippled, even though that is the primary project of the speech. The body seems to be beyond rhetorical manipulation, a clear and unequivocal proof.

What sort of metonymies can be forged around such an impossible body? If, as I have suggested, metonymy is a seminal strategy of forensic self-presentation, where does that leave the *adunatos*? The speaker's bitter humor turns the very possibility of metonymic identification into a veiled threat. Imagine me as an exemplary citizen and target of other citizens' envy, he challenges the jury (3). Imagine me as a *khorēgos*, a member of the liturgy class, rubbing shoulders with the wealthiest men in town (9). Imagine me as an archon (13). And the corollary: imagine yourselves as cripples. "My opponent so surpasses all other mortals in shamelessness that he is trying to persuade you . . . that I am not *adunatos*. But if he can convince you of this, councillors, what is to stop me from being chosen as one of the nine archons? What is to prevent you from taking away my obol on the grounds that I am healthy and awarding it to him on the grounds that he is impaired?" (13). He sarcastically invites the jurors to identify with him, to see him as one of them, or, worse, to look at him and see

[57] On the effeminizing effects of poverty, see Halperin 1990: 99. The simile also suggests a contrast between his own visible body and the invisible body of the *epiklēros*, who was the object of legal conflict but never physically present in court.

themselves. My opponent says I am not *adunatos*, that I am no different from him or from you. But if he insists on that identification, what's to say that the basis of similarity is my capacity and not your incapacity. Maybe he is *adunatos* like me; maybe you all are *adunatoi* like me. But the very thought is absurd, he scoffs. Just look at me.

Through these sardonic hypotheticals, the cripple metonymizes himself as a social *adunaton*, the unthinkable embodiment of a crippled citizenry. His body is a potential threat to the councillors' faith in their own bodily integrity and in the wholeness and health of the body politic. But he offers them a deal. They can be *dunatoi* if they look on him as *adunatos* and give him his obol. If they are to see themselves as they wish to imagine themselves, they must see him as he wishes to be seen. It is a cruel and humiliating spectacle, one that actively solicits cruelty and humiliation. His bitterly self-denigrating humor forces the councillors to laugh at him as *adunatos* and *adunaton*, to buy the promise of their own *dunamis* by mocking the very possibility of this cripple as a *khorēgos* or archon or member of the Boule. Thus in contrast to Demosthenes' strategy of metonymic identification, this speaker employs a strategy of dis-identification, an anxious metonymy in which symbolic contiguity works like physical contamination, spreading the disease of disability to the councillors' bodies, the citizen body, and the body of the law.[58]

But perhaps the cripple's metonymic strategy is less different from Demosthenes' than it first appears. For if he invites the jurors to mock his crippled body, he himself joins in the mockery, and the identification that is impossible at the level of the body is forged at the level of the soul. In a passage that seems to run against the generally pathetic tone of the speech, the cripple speaks philosophically about his fate. His opponent is jealous, he says, because he is the better citizen. "For I think it is necessary, councillors, to heal (*iasthai*) the sufferings of the body by the practices of the soul. If I hold an attitude and lead a life that is equal to my misfortune, how will I be any different from him?" (3). The speaker draws on a familiar Athenian ethics in which the good man is master over himself, carefully regulating the desires and appetites of his body with the disciplined practices of his soul.[59] He is, as the metaphor here implies, a "doctor of himself." Building on the dichotomy between body and soul, the speaker identifies

[58] A remarkably similar strategy can be witnessed in the modern French street signs marking handicapped parking: "Si vous prenez ma place, prenez mon handicap." This sign claims a right for the disabled by forcing the viewer to imagine him or herself as disabled and to recoil from the parking space as if from the handicap.

[59] Foucault 1985: 97–108, 1986: 99–144.

himself with the latter against the former: he is an autonomous ethical agent, master and doctor of himself, a philosopher. All who have suffered some misfortune, he later says, must devote their thought (*philosophein*) to how they can best bear the suffering that has befallen them (10). In this way the speaker distances himself from his body, which becomes base and unfortunate matter, the mind's slave.

As philosophical mind and body's doctor he aligns himself with the eye of the capable councillors ("trust in your own eyes," he said, "for this is the task of sensible men," 14). From that perspective he sees his body as an object not only of ethical mastery but of social derision. He and the jurors bond over the spectacle of his body, sharing a good laugh over its obvious disability. Only a fool could fail to see it and to recognize the impossibility of taking it seriously. Thus the speaker does forge a sort of identification with the councillors, but only by looking at himself in the same way that he has forced them to look at him: with a nervous laugh and philosophical contempt.

Irony, pervasive throughout the speech, is a particularly apt device here. Irony results when a speaker's words seem to imply more than he literally intends: it is a joke at one's own expense, a sort of collusion with the audience against oneself.[60] The life story of the *adunatos* is ironic in this sense. Narrated in the mode of irony, it establishes an ironic, divided relation between its subject and its object: the speaker and his own crippled body. Lysias writes a *logos biou* that solicits the councillors' identification not with the *bios* but with the *logos*, the ironic telling of that sorry life. To his client he offers a cruelly effective strategy of self-naming. For if the speaker wins his case, he will be legally *adunatos* and will have the obol to prove it; if he loses his case, he loses the obol and thus becomes (if we can believe his claims) truly *adunatos*. Either way the humor is performative: it turns him into what he claims (manifestly) to be. And either way, the joke is on him.

Jacques Lacan suggests that metonymy is a dynamic of desire: because desire is always a desire for "something else," it can never be satisfied by any object but instead moves laterally from one thing to another, seeking what it "really" wants.[61] What civic and legal desires are invested in this speech's metonymies and in the single obol that itself moves metonymically between the speaker and the city? For the cripple, this paltry sum symbolizes his entire relation to the polis and his entire being as a citizen. This pension

[60] Freud 1960 [1905]: 173–75; Burke 1945: 111–17; H. White 1973: 37, 1978: 73–74.
[61] Lacan 1977a, 1993: 214–30.

was given to him by the vote of the polis; it is his civic allotment and to rob him of it, he asserts, would be to deprive him of "the only share fate has given me in my fatherland" (*hou monou metalabein edōken hē tukhē moi tōn en tēi patridi*, 22). This is the language of political belonging. Aristotle defines a citizen as one who has a share in the decisions and offices of the state (*Pol.* 1275a22–23). This trial's verdict is the speaker's only share in the city's decisions; it is a *dokimasia* for the only office he can hold, the office of pensioner (26). The obol, then, is not merely his livelihood but his *bios* as a citizen. It stands metonymically for the cripple's desire for a metonymic connection to the city, his wounded attachment to the civic fantasy of a whole and healthy body politic.[62]

This desire is not only the cripple's but also the city's. Demosthenes offers the jurors a fantasy of a perfect citizen body. The threat to that body in his speech is the lawless *hubris* of a violent elite. The cripple embodies a threat to that same democratic body from the opposite direction: poverty. Solon's prohibition on debt-slavery guaranteed a free citizenry as one of the cornerstones of democracy, but Athenians recognized that extreme poverty could render that civic freedom meaningless. The speaker in Demosthenes 57, for instance, complains that his citizenship was revoked at a deme meeting merely because he was impoverished and sold ribbons in the agora for a living. The plaintiff in Isocrates 20, suing a certain Lochites for punching him, argues that though he doesn't own any property he – like all citizens – owns his own body and if the polis fails to secure that minimal right it will spell the end of democracy. These speakers feel they must prove that a poor citizen is still a citizen and that the city has an interest in protecting his civic autonomy. That interest was also recognized institutionally in things like the subsidy for civic offices and, of course, the dole at issue in Lysias 24. The dole guaranteed that although a citizen might get down, he was never totally out: he was, minimally, still free and master of himself.

Such sovereignty may have been more symbolic than real, but it is precisely the symbol that is at stake in this speech. The cripple claims to need the dole for his survival, but implies that the city needs it too, for that single obol symbolizes Athens' democratic commitment to protect its most vulnerable members. Indeed, this commitment was one theoretical

[62] On "wounded attachments" see Brown 1995a: 52–76. She uses this phrase to designate the dynamic by which politically marginalized identity becomes invested in its own exclusion and incapable of critiquing the social conditions that produce it. See also Brown 1995b, 2001: 45–61.

justification of the egalitarian polis, as Leslie Kurke has shown.[63] As Solon tells the tyrant Croesus in Herodotus, since life is uncertain and no man self-sufficient, the safest and happiest existence is provided by the egalitarian city (Hdt. 1.30–32). The *adunatos* evokes this political theory. "Since the divinity deprived me of the greatest things in life the polis voted me this money with the idea that everyone shares equally in good and bad fortune. Would I not be most miserable if my misfortune robbed me of the greatest goods and then the prosecutor robbed me of what the polis gave me out of consideration for those in my condition?" (22–23). If the one obol represents his wounded attachment to the city, it also symbolizes the city's self-grounding at the site of the individual's vulnerability: its promise to protect the citizen and its claim to be just and equitable by virtue of that promise. It is perhaps no coincidence that one obol was also the daily stipend for attendance at the Ecclesia during this period ([Arist.] *Ath. Pol.* 41.3): it is the minimal cost of the democratic ideal of full participation. The polis is no less invested in this fantasy of civic wholeness than the cripple himself.

The law, too, is invested in that obol. If defending the vulnerable against misfortune is a theoretical foundation of the egalitarian city, defending the weak from the strong is the origin of *dikaiosunē* (justice). In his genealogy of justice in Book 2 of the *Republic*, Glaukon offers what he says is the common view of the genesis and nature of *dikaiosunē*. To commit wrong is naturally good; to be wronged is naturally bad, but the evil of the latter outweighs the good of the former. So when men have tried both, "those who are unable (*mē dunamenois*) to do wrong or to escape suffering it decide it is advantageous to contract with one another neither to do wrong nor to be wronged." So they establish laws and "call the law's command right and just" (*Rep.* 358e2–359a4). Justice, then, is "a compromise between the best situation, committing wrong without punishment, and the worst, suffering wrong and being unable (*adunatos*) to get revenge" (*Rep.* 359a5–b1). In this proto-Nietzschean genealogy of morals, *dikaiosunē* is a virtue of the *adunatoi*, and civic life begins with a community of cripples who manage to turn their weakness into strength. Aristotle puts the same idea in more neutral terms when he predicates political justice and the just polis on "proportionate reciprocity" (*to antipoiein analogon*), the ability of equals

[63] Kurke 1999: 148–50. She cites Hdt. 1.32.8–9; Arist. *Pol.* 1252b27–1253a1, 1253a25–29; and Simonides fr. 37/542 *PMG*. See also Dem. 10.35–45; Dillon 1995: 36.

to repay good with good and evil with evil.[64] For both philosophers, the law's aspiration to justice begins with its protection of the *adunatoi.*

Our philosophical *adunatos* alludes in a backhanded way to this argument. His opponent has accused him of *hubris*, violence, and extravagance. He laughs these charges off with a traditional *eikos* argument: it is not likely for the poor, old, and powerless to commit *hubris* but for the young, rich, and strong (15–16). "The powerful can commit *hubris* against whomever they want and suffer nothing themselves, but the weak can neither defend themselves against *hubris* nor if they want to commit it can they prevail over those they would harm" (18). The speaker does not call upon the law to remedy this social injustice, to secure him "proportionate reciprocity" or to protect him from the depredations of the *dunatoi.* The cripple does not demand full rights for the disabled or a redistribution of wealth. He is no revolutionary; all he asks is that the law recognize his disability and grant him his obol.[65]

And yet by gesturing, however ironically, to the utopian principles of equity and social justice, the speaker marks a gap – a failed metonymy – between law and justice and between the polis and its egalitarian ideals. He savagely ironizes the fiction that the citizen body is inviolable. He threatens to expose as *adunaton* the law's claim to protect the weak from injustice and the city's claim to secure the sovereignty and equality of all its members. The cripple's *logos biou* thus tells the story of an incapacity within the city and its legal system and hints at the impossibility of both the city's and the law's own aspirations to justice, equality, and a perfect civic body. Viewed in this light, the cripple's black comedy is a political and jurisprudential tragedy, and he himself – ironically – is the tragic *khorēgos.*

The cripple offers the Athenians a cheap way out: they can avert this civic tragedy for a single obol. But if the price is cheap, the symbolic logic of this deal is rich: it is the minimum social contract of the democratic state, its

64 "The city depends upon proportionate reciprocity" (*NE* 1132b33–34); cf. *Pol.* 1318b4–5: "the weaker always seek justice and equality, while the stronger ignore them;" Pl. *Gorg.* 483b4–6. Compare the similar idea implicit at Dem. 21.112, 123, 201, and cf. Nietzsche 1967 [1887]: 57–96. The provision for voluntary prosecution on behalf of those who had been wronged and could not avenge themselves, an innovation attributed to Solon and listed by the author of the *Ath. Pol.* as one of his most democratic (*dēmotikōtata*), institutionalizes this notion of justice as a defense of the weak ([Arist.] *Ath. Pol.* 9.1). Dillon 1995 argues that protection of *adunatoi* strengthened the democratic city by avoiding the possibility of direct aristocratic patronage of the needy. For the courts as defense against the rich or powerful, see further Lys. 1.2; Eur. *Suppl.* 433–37; de Romilly 1971: 142–46; Mossé 1987: 165–76; Ober 1989a: 217–19.

65 As in Nietzsche's genealogy of morals, a virtue derived from a slave mentality remains committed to slavery. Nietzsche 1967 [1887]: 44–56. See also Brown 1995a: 66–76 on *ressentiment,* and Wallace 1996 on the question of individual rights in Athens.

investment in the least of its citizens. The cripple's painful *logos* thus exposes the political and juridical desires invested in the *bios* of the individual citizen. The civic ideals that Demosthenes promised to consolidate with his own idealized body are shown in Lysias 24 to be not essential qualities of the democratic polis but at best objects metonymically contiguous to it, objects reached for but never finally and fully reached.

In the life stories of Demosthenes and the *adunatos*, as in those of Callistratus and Olympiodorus and of Mantitheus and his homonymic half-brother, we can see a fundamental tension at work in the law's rhetoric of subjectivity. Legal discourse works to stabilize meaning at the site of the subject. In his singular name it attempts to establish itself as a coherent symbolic order. With the contractual metaphor it hopes to seal his consistent and unchanging *prohairesis* and banish irrationality. Through metonymy it situates itself as the suture between the individual citizen and the ideal of the just city. But in all these cases, the subject marks precisely the failure of those attempts at fixity. The name always signifies ambiguously; metaphors are unstable and displace the identities they define; metonymies reveal the impossibilities within the very political and jurisprudential relations they forge. Composed in the ambiguous and homonymic tropes of forensic rhetoric, the legal subject is always double and divided, even where the logographer hopes to make him unitary and unified. His *logos biou* is always a complicated text: it tells a complex story about a complex life. The language in which the law narrates that story and by which it hopes to establish its own vital existence as a discourse – its *bios logou* – slides away beneath it, changing names and transferring meanings. The subject of law embodies that tropological slide.

PART III

Time, Memory, Reproduction: Law's Past and Future

CHAPTER 5

Civic amnesia and legal memory: to remember and forget in the lawcourts

> There is a temporality particular to each type of rhetoric: to deliberative oratory the future, since it gives advice, pro or con, concerning what will happen; to forensic oratory the past, since both prosecution and defense always speak about events that have happened; and to epideictic oratory the present, since all speakers issue praise or blame according to existing conditions, though they often also recall the past and anticipate the future.
>
> Aristotle *Rhetoric* 1358b13–20

> What if banning memory had no other consequences than to accentuate a hyperbolized, though fixed, memory?
>
> Loraux 2002: 261[1]

ATHENS' AMNESTY AND LAW'S *ALĒTHEIA*

Forensic oratory, as Aristotle notes, is oriented toward the past. The law can try only events that have already happened. The speaker of Isocrates 20 bemoans this limitation. It would be best, he says, if criminals bore some mark (*sēmeion*) that enabled us to punish them before they committed their crime, "inasmuch as it is better to find a means of averting future problems than to punish those that have already occurred" (12). As it is, one should consider it a windfall when a criminal does come before the court, and punish him before he does something worse (12–14). Inherently retrospective, *dikē* is associated in Greek thought with memory. Zeus "does not overlook (or "forget," *lēthei*) that sort of justice that a city holds in it," says Hesiod (*Erga* 268–69). The avenging spirit of the murder victim, a demonic agent of justice, is called the *alastōr*, literally the "unforgetting

[1] My thinking on amnesty and civic memory has been influenced by Loraux 2002. The subtitle of this chapter acknowledges my debt in its allusion to the first chapter of that work, "To forget in the city."

one."[2] Punishment may take time – sometimes generations – but the wrong is not forgotten and justice comes in the end. Thus the trial, as Danielle Allen argues, engages and enacts social memory.[3] Its truth is a not-forgetting (*a-lētheia*) of unavenged wrongs.[4] The past to be remembered is never uncontroversial, though. There are, at a minimum, two opposing views of what happened. In order for the law to remember the past event the trial must reconstruct it, examining eye-witnesses, analyzing documents, and subjecting claims to logical scrutiny. In this sense, the trial becomes a vehicle for an agonistic historiography with high stakes not only for the litigants but for the community as a whole.[5]

The law reconstructs the past not merely for its own sake, however, but for the sake of the future. The fantasy in Isocrates 20 of punishing criminals before the crime projects a lawful future in which criminality will have been preempted before the fact: by punishing the defendant, says that speaker, "you will judge rightly in the present case and make the other citizens more law-abiding and make your own lives more secure" (18). It is a sentiment echoed in virtually every courtroom speech: justice toward the past – remembering and punishing crimes – is the key to a just future.[6] From the urgent present of the trial (completed in one day with the water-clock running) the jurors' verdict extends into the future by extending into the past. The law is thus structured by the ideal of temporal unity: its claim to truth (*alētheia*) is based on a strong theoretical link between the past crime, the present trial, and future justice. In this taut temporality it resembles the fifth-century democratic polis itself, which looked back on its glorious past and forward to a promising future from the seemingly boundless moment of its present power.[7]

[2] On the *alastōr*, see Loraux 2002: 162–64. Memory and *dikē* are also linked at Hes. *Erga* 711–12; Pind. *Ol.* 1.64; Soph. *Ajax* 1390; trag. adesp. 487. See also Gernet 1981b: 235; R. Thomas 1996: 19–25; Gagarin 2008: 117–19 on the *mnamōn*, a legal magistrate mentioned in the Gortyn Code.

[3] Allen 2000a: 65–68, 168–79, 202–05. Goodrich 1990a: 32–52 considers the law in general as a form of memory, although the English common law on which he focuses, with its "time immemorial" of precedent, differs in significant ways from Athenian law; cf. Goodrich and Hachamovitch 1991.

[4] On truth as not-forgetting in Greek thought, see duBois 1991: 75–91; Detienne 1996; and on *lēthē* and *alētheia*, Heidegger 1996 [1953]: 28–30, 201–05.

[5] Cousins 1987: 131–34 analyzes the similarities between law and history. I return below to the question of whether law makes for good history.

[6] Cf. e.g. Lys. 1.47, 14.12, 15.9, 30.23–24, 31.30; Dem. 21.37; Lyc. 1.10. As Rubinstein 2007: 366 points out, this topos crosses the line between the dikastic and the symbouleutic, as Aristotle defines them.

[7] On the "democratic temporality" of fifth-century Athens see Loraux 1986: 118–31; Csapo and Miller 1998: 100–04; Dunn 2007: 12–36. Gernet 1981b traces the evolution of this legal temporality: originally, he argues, the judge operated entirely in the present, but as legal thought in Greece developed, he "created the conditions for a control that signified the mastery of time," both past and future (236).

This ideal temporal chain was abruptly broken for both Athenian politics and jurisprudence by the historical crisis at the end of the fifth century. Following its devastating defeat by the Spartans in the Spring of 404 BCE, a group of thirty oligarchs took control of Athens. For eight months the Thirty governed by violence, seizing property, exiling or executing citizens without trial, suspending the apparatus of democracy. In all they may have caused the deaths of 1,500 Athenians, some 5 percent of the citizen body.[8] Civil war erupted between the supporters of the oligarchy (often referred to as the "men of the city" because they stayed in Athens during this period) and the democratic exiles (known as the "men of the Piraeus") and further blood was shed before (with the help of Sparta) the Thirty were deposed and democracy restored in the autumn of 403/2.[9]

This traumatic episode constituted a violent breach in the historical continuity of the polis. It disrupted the Athenians' relation to their own political past and their sense of their present as the extension of a single democratic moment beginning with the murder of the tyrant Hipparchus a century earlier. It also constituted a break in the continuity of law. Athenian law has no formal system of precedent, but it is innately conservative, tracing its origins and prestige back to the founding lawmaker, Solon. The Thirty disrupted that lineage. On the pretext of restoring the ancestral constitution they tore down the ancient laws of Ephialtes and Archestratus from in front of the court of the Areopagus and abolished any laws of Solon they deemed "ambiguous." They may also have erased some of the laws that were inscribed for public consultation near the Stoa Basileios.[10] "On the grounds that they were correcting the constitution and making it unambiguous," ps.-Aristotle reports, "they dissolved the sovereignty of the juries" (*Ath. Pol.* 35.2). Legal proceedings were moved from the *dikastēria* to the Boule, where the Thirty personally supervised the voting (Lys. 13.37–38). Even after the democracy was restored and the traditional "Solonic" laws reaffirmed, the radical disruption of these years would still have been clearly visible to anyone who consulted the code inscribed near the Stoa Basileios in the agora: the part inscribed before 403 was written in Attic script and the part after 403 in Ionic.[11]

[8] [Arist.] *Ath. Pol.* 35.4; Wolpert 2002a: 22 and n. 67.

[9] See Xen. *Hell.* 2.3–4; [Arist.] *Ath. Pol.* 34–38; D.S. 14. For clear synopses of the complicated events of this period, see Krentz 1982; Ostwald 1986: 460–524; Strauss 1986: 89–120; Munn 2000: 218–91; Wolpert 2002a: 3–28. The most detailed analysis is still Cloché 1915.

[10] Fingarette 1971: 333; Krentz 1982: 61–62; Wolpert 2002a: 23. On the legal reforms of the Thirty see [Arist.] *Ath. Pol.* 35.2 and Rhodes 1981: 441–42 ad loc.; Krentz 1982: 60–61; Ostwald 1986: 475–80; Bauman 1990: 78–79; Christ 1998a: 72–73, 80–81; Wolpert 2002a: 20, 23.

[11] Dow 1961 describes the fragmentary remains; cf. Fingarette 1971: 334; Sickinger 1999: 103–04. I return to the revision of the legal code in the final chapter; further references can be found there.

The break caused by the reign of the Thirty was formalized in the reconciliation agreement that ended the civil war. As part of this agreement, every Athenian citizen swore, "I will not hold a grudge [*mnēsikakēsō*, literally "remember evils"] against any of the citizens except the Thirty and the Eleven [the magistrates in charge of arrests and executions], nor even against any of these if he is willing to give an account (*euthunas*) of his magistracy" (And. 1.90).[12] This amnesty, as Nicole Loraux has argued, attempted to impose a sort of civic amnesia – an *a-mnēsteia* – upon the political traumas of this period. By forgetting the "evils" of these years it hoped to heal political differences, to repair democratic unity in the present and continuity with the past "as if nothing had happened."[13]

The oath required citizens to forget before they forgave, and to forget that there was anything even to forgive. But the amnesty was a ban not on memory in general but on prosecutorial memory in particular. As Loraux points out, the form of the oath as Andocides records it (*mē mnēsikakēsō tōn politōn oudeni*) imagines memory as a weapon of revenge.[14] The amnesty agreement seems to have been designed to prevent citizens not from remembering what they had suffered (as if that were possible) but from bringing legal prosecutions for crimes committed during this period. This design was strengthened soon after by the institution of the *paragraphē*, a legal procedure that allowed defendants to prevent a case from being brought on the grounds that it contravened the amnesty.[15] Andocides implies that jurors repeated the amnesty's *mē mnēsikakein* as part of their dikastic oath (1.91). The amnesty agreement was thus a ban specifically on legal memory. By placing the crimes of this period under erasure it aimed to restore the unity of the fractured citizen body. But in the process it exacerbated a fracture within the law itself, erecting a barrier of *lēthē* between the present of the trial and the unprosecutable crimes of the recent past. In order to help the city forget, the law itself is banned

[12] Cf. [Arist.] *Ath. Pol.* 39.6. In ps.-Aristotle's version the Ten and the governors of the Piraeus are also exempted: see MacDowell 1962: 130–31 *ad* And. 1.90; Rhodes 1981: 469–70 *ad* [Arist.] *Ath. Pol.* 39.6; Loening 1987: 24–25, 41–46 on the discrepancy. On the reconciliation agreement see further Cloché 1915: 251–77; Dorjahn 1946; Ostwald 1986: 509–24; Loening 1987; Allen 2000a: 237–42; Wolpert 2002a: 30–35. I disagree with Carawan, who argues that the oath *mē mnēsikakein* was intended to prevent not legal prosecution but extralegal vendettas (1998: 128–33; cf. 2002: 4–10).

[13] Loraux 2002, esp. 145–69; the quotation is on p. 150. Compare Isoc. 18.46: "After we came together and exchanged pledges with one another we governed so well and unanimously that it seemed like the crisis [i.e. the civil war] had never happened to us." Loraux notes that the word *amnēsteia* does not occur in the sense of amnesty until the second century BCE (2002: 299 n. 3; cf. LSJ s.v.).

[14] Loraux 2002: 149.

[15] Isoc. 18.1–2; Harrison 1971: 106–24; Isager and Hansen 1975: 123–31; Loening 1987: 102; Todd 1993: 135–38.

from remembering. What does the amnesty's mandate to forget do to the law's need to remember? If the law cannot prosecute past crimes, how can it ensure a just future? How does law maintain its desire for *alētheia* in the face of a willful civic *amnēsteia*?

Perhaps forensic oblivion was never a real risk, though. The amnesty did not prevent the court cases of the early fourth century from returning with obsessive regularity to the past and trying both the "forgotten" crimes and the crime of not forgetting them. Not only were the provisions of the amnesty vague enough to leave logographers many ways to argue around it, but the very principle of the amnesty required the law's support. Isocrates 18, for instance, a *paragraphē* case, is in large part a defense speech for the amnesty. By casting their verdict for him, says the speaker, the jurors will come to the aid of the amnesty which alone saved Athens and restored the city to its former glory (27–32): for me the case is about a private charge; for you it is about the sanctity of your agreements and the safety of the city (33–34). Almost every case of this period is a more or less explicit memorial to the amnesty.[16]

Civic amnesia required legal memory both of the agreement to forget and of its forgotten evils. Thus, as Loraux suggests, the ban on memory had the paradoxical effect of fixing memory under negation.[17] The site of this fixation was the courts. The legal system becomes the organ of memory for a city that wills itself to forget the past. But again we must ask what this means for the law: do the evils repressed in the political sphere return in the juridical and does the "forgotten" violence of the oligarchy live on in the vengeful memory of the democratic courts? If the mandate to forget ruptured the law's temporal unity, the inability to forget paralyzes its temporal progression. It threatens to trap the law in a traumatic recursivity in which the legal present is an endless reliving of the violent past, with no possibility of a just future. As it remembers past evils for an oblivious city, does the law's *alētheia* become a repetition compulsion, a pathological symptom of civic repression?

[16] The speaker in Isocrates 18 suggests that the Athenians felt the need to prove through their verdicts that they signed the amnesty willingly, not under compulsion (2); that they didn't regret having signed it (21); and that whatever doubts they may initially have had, they now saw the benefit of the amnesty and the need to abide by it (25). Wolpert 2002b analyzes this speech's treatment of the amnesty. Other cases dealing with the amnesty include And. 1, 3; Lys. 6, 12, 13, 16, 18, 25, 26, 30, 31, 34; Isoc. 16, 18, 20, 21. Cf. Quillin 2002: 73 n. 6; Wolpert 2002a: 57: "Far from preventing antagonisms from erupting, the amnesty was itself a source of contention. It did not end hostilities; rather, it redirected, rechanneled, and reconfigured them." Of course, law was not the only contemporary discourse to react to the challenge of the civil war and amnesty: for other responses, see the essays in Osborne 2007.

[17] Loraux 2002: 146, 261.

This chapter looks at how the law forgets and remembers the traumatic events of 404–403. Andrew Wolpert (2002a, 2002b) has recently shown how the court cases of the early fourth century allowed the Athenians to work through these events, constructing an official history of the period and deploying a rhetoric of reconciliation to smooth over past differences in the interest of future harmony. It was through the rhetoric of these speeches, he argues, that the amnesty achieved the political effect of reunification. Thus like Loraux, Wolpert shows how legal memory helped the Athenians to forget the recent trauma of political conflict and to restore the fiction of a timeless democratic unanimity.

While I draw on the work of Wolpert and Loraux in examining the speeches of the post-amnesty period, my focus in this chapter is less on what the law's remembering does for the city than on what the city's forgetting does to the law. The civil war and amnesty, I suggest, posed a crisis for the temporality of law. Forgetting – obeying the amnesty – threatened to rupture the law's temporal unity between past crime and present trial and thus to foreclose the possibility of future justice. Remembering – despite the amnesty – posed a complementary danger of repeating past violence in the course of punishing it. This chapter analyzes how three speeches of this period (Andocides 1, Lysias 12, and Lysias 13) negotiate these twin temporal problems of breach and recursivity and attempt to reforge the crucial links between past crime, present trial, and future justice in the face of the amnesty's amnesia. In their anxious attempt to figure out how to punish without remembering and how to remember without repeating, these cases work through the legal symptoms of civic forgetting; indeed they become the symptoms of that forgetting. Moreover, at the same time as they repair the law's temporal unity these cases also seek to restore the temporal unity of the polis, linking the uncertain present to the glorious past, and predicating that historical continuity upon a hard-won legal continuity. In this way, these cases establish juridical discourse as the historical memory of Athens, the chief archive of past conflict and monument to future harmony, and establish the law's unbroken temporality as the unfolding of the city's timeless democratic present.

LITIGATING ACROSS *LĒTHĒ* (ANDOCIDES 1)

Andocides 1 is a speech about returning. Andocides has returned to Athens from exile, but in order to return to his full civic status he must return juridically to the time of his initial crime. These returns are complicated by the temporal gap caused by the oligarchy, civil war, and amnesty. How does one litigate over this breach in Athens' history and the amnesty's mandated *lēthē*? Andocides' speech uses law as a bridge over this historical gulf and as a means both of his own return to Athens and of Athens' return to its glorious past. In this way he helps to repair what Loraux calls the eternality of the city, the temporality that made the present a direct continuation and perpetual renewal of the democratic past.[18] This eternal democratic moment – ruptured by the events of 404–403 – is mended in this speech, reconstructed on the basis not of Athens' democratic institutions but of a progressive legal history of which Andocides' restoration to his full ancestral rights is the clearest exemplum.[19]

The problem of historical and legal breach is especially complicated in this case because the crime itself spans fifteen particularly tumultuous years. In 415 Andocides was implicated in a religious scandal that shook Athens: a number of citizens were accused of profaning the Eleusinian Mysteries (probably by parodying the sacred rites in private households) and of defacing the Herms, statues sacred to Hermes that stood around the city. The Athenians took these acts of impiety seriously: at best they seemed an inauspicious omen for the naval expedition about to depart for Sicily; at worst, evidence of an oligarchic conspiracy to overthrow the democracy. The perpetrators were energetically sought and many prominent Athenians were charged. Among these was Andocides, who probably confessed to participating in one or both impieties and also lay information against others, including his own father.[20] The decree of Isotimides, passed in around 415, banned from the agora and temples anyone who had admitted to impiety (*asebeia*). This decree effectively barred Andocides from a public life in Athens, and soon after he went into voluntary exile. After the amnesty, Andocides returned to Athens. In 400 he attended the Eleusinian Mysteries and was promptly charged with impiety for violating the decree

[18] Loraux 1986: 118–31, 132–71; 2002: 255.

[19] This was not Andocides' first attempt to return to Athens. Andocides 2 (*On his Return*) tells of Andocides' attempt in 411 to reingratiate himself with the Athenians by procuring timber for the fleet. His timing was bad: he returned to Athens to reap the rewards of his patriotic act at the precise moment when the oligarchy of Four Hundred seized control of the city; he was imprisoned and later fled Athens. In that speech, delivered after the fall of the Four Hundred (some time between 410 and 405) he tried to gain delayed recognition for his good deed but apparently failed and returned to exile. See Missiou 1992: 25–49.

[20] See Thuc. 6.60.2–4, where the unnamed suspect may well be Andocides. MacDowell (1962: 167–76) believes that Andocides probably did participate in the profanation of the Mysteries and did inform against his father in order to secure immunity for himself, but that he was not involved in the mutilation of the Herms. Furley 1996: 49–69, by contrast, argues that Andocides was involved in the mutilation (even if only passively) but not the Mysteries; cf. Marr 1971. On the accusation and Andocides' defense see further MacDowell 1962: 11–18; Seager 1978; Bauman 1990: 109–10, 115–16; Roisman 2005: 60–63, 2006: 69–72.

of Isotimides; this is the charge against which he defends himself in this speech.

This trial is thus not about Andocides' behavior during the oligarchy and civil war. Instead it is about the hole this period creates in the legal account of Andocides' crime and its prosecution. The immediate crime in this case post-dates the amnesty but it only constitutes a crime due to actions taken in 415. Andocides commits a crime by illegally returning to the scene of his original crime, the Eleusinian Mysteries, a ritual which itself deals with cyclical return.[21] In defending himself against the recent accusation, Andocides defends himself against the original accusation but also asserts that neither action requires a defense. On the one hand, he reopens the case of 415, claiming (despite his apparent confession at the time) that he didn't in fact commit impiety in the first place. On the other hand, he argues that the decree of Isotimides no longer applies in 400 and that his previous acts are protected by the amnesty and other legal revisions.[22] These two arguments are, strictly speaking, logically contradictory, for if the decree really was invalid it wouldn't matter what he had done in the past, and if he really were innocent of past crimes it wouldn't matter if the decree were valid. Thus he takes up contradictory relations to the past, returning to it even as he declares it no longer relevant to the present.

Where to begin his defense? he asks. Should he start from the recent and illegal prosecution, from the decree of Isotimides, from the laws and oaths (i.e. the legal revisions and amnesty), or should he recount what happened from the beginning? "I'll tell you what causes me the most uncertainty (*aporein*): perhaps not all of you are equally outraged by all the charges and each of you has something different he would like me to address first in my defense. But I can't speak about everything at the same time" (8). How to narrate the past and make a defense that spans the temporal divide of

21 The Eleusinian Mysteries celebrated the return of Persephone to her mother Demeter and the annual rebirth of nature. The Mysteries provide a leitmotif throughout the speech: Andocides calls upon the jurors in the name of the two goddesses, Demeter and Persephone, to acquit him (32). He sarcastically calls his opponent Callias (who belonged to the Kerykes, one of the families that traditionally administered the Mysteries) "priest of the Mother and Daughter," a reference to his affair with his wife's mother (124). The case as a whole becomes a divine judgment in which the gods themselves cast a verdict (113, 137–39). The religious aspects of the trial are emphasized in Lysias 6, which may be one of the prosecution speeches from this case. On the authenticity of the Lysianic speech see Dorjahn 1946: 47; MacDowell 1962: 14; Dover 1968: 78–83; Furley 1996: 104; Todd 2000a: 63–64, 2007: 403–08. On the religious argument in Lysias 6, see Furley 1996: 103–18.

22 See MacDowell 1962: 200–03 and Loening 1987: 140–46 on this defense. This double defense is quite common in amnesty cases. Compare, for example, Mantitheus in Lysias 16, who argues that he was not a member of the cavalry under the Thirty and even if he were he would be protected by the amnesty. Wolpert 2002a: 114–15 notes that no defendant who claims immunity under the amnesty actually admits to the crime.

these difficult years? The jurors' various desires – perhaps a veiled allusion to the division of the civil war – create diegetic aporia and fragment the narrative of the past into a series of discrete temporal moments: 400, 403, 415. This opening aporia anticipates the temporal challenges of the speech as a whole as it attempts to weave a continuous narrative thread between now and then.

In the face of this temporal uncertainty, Andocides promises a full and complete history: "It seems best to me to teach (*didaskein*) you everything that happened from the beginning and to omit nothing" (8). He begins in 415 and brings that past vividly into the present through, for example, his detailed account of the jailhouse scene of 415, complete with the minute representation of his conversations and thoughts from that time (48–53). He supplements personal memory with both written evidence (a list of names of the condemned, 13) and the living memory of the investigator, who under direct examination attests to his present knowledge of those past denunciations (14). He further challenges anyone denounced by him fifteen years ago in the case of the Mysteries to come forward now and accuse him; he will cede his time to allow them to speak and pauses to see if anyone gets up (25–26). In this way Andocides turns the trial of 400 into a belated retrial of 415 and his defense against recent *asebeia* into a defense against past *asebeia*.

Identification with the jury, a key strategy in virtually all forensic speeches, likewise spans the gap between 400 and 415. "Come then, jurors: you must approach the issue with human empathy (*anthrōpinōs*) as if you yourself were in the situation. What would each of you have done?" (57). The situation into which he asks the jurors to imaginatively retroject themselves is the jailhouse of 415, where Andocides pondered whether to inform against those he knew to be involved in the impieties. Thinking "humanly" they are urged to think now as he did then, an identification across time that he facilitates by representing his own thinking at the time as itself dikastic: he was motivated in his decision (he says) not by self-interest or fear but by justice, the desire to see the guilty justly punished and to prevent the innocent from unjust execution (51–53). His denunciations were an attempt to prosecute a crime and right a wrong against himself and the city (60). By presenting his own past motivations in juridical terms, he turns his past self into a proto-juror in his own future trial.

The present jurors are encouraged to identify not only with his past self but with their own. Throughout the speech, Andocides figures them as a point of continuity in his fragmented narrative. In his account of the profanation of the Mysteries the jurors of 400 become members of the Ecclesia and Boule of 415: "you sentenced them [those denounced] to death" (13); "you handed Diokleides over to the courts to be put to death" (66).[23] Their collective memory becomes the suture between the pre-war past and the post-war present. Introducing the testimony on the mutilation of the Herms, he urges the jurors to pay close attention and "recall (*anamimnēiskesthai*) whether I am telling the truth and teach (*didaskein*) one another, for the arguments were made in front of you and you were witnesses to them" (37). "Those of you who were present remember (*anamimnēiskesthe*) and teach (*didaskete*) the others" (46). "Recall (*anamimnēiskesthe*) if I am telling the truth, jurors, and those who saw it teach (*didaskete*) the others" (69). Andocides' own pedagogical history of the past – "it seems best to me to teach (*didaskein*) you everything that happened from the beginning" (8) – is handed over to the jurors, who are urged to themselves remember and pass down that memory as part of a communal tradition. The eternal present of the city would seem to be repaired in the abstract person of the demos, whose memory spans 415 and 400.[24]

But the jurors will remember 415 only by forgetting all the years in between. Judging justly means remembering to forget. When Andocides urges the jurors to "vote according to the oath, for this alone holds the city together, despite the wishes of those who don't want it to do so" (9), he conflates the dikastic oath sworn by each juror that morning in 400 with the amnesty oath of 403. He alone of our sources suggests that the amnesty was included in the dikastic oath: "with what oath do you sit as jurors (*ti omosantes dikazete*)? 'And I will not remember evils (*mnēsikakēsō*) nor be persuaded by someone else to do so, but I will vote according to the laws'" (91).[25] Strictly speaking, the amnesty is irrelevant to Andocides' case, since it covered neither the events of 415 nor the immediate crime of 400.[26] But its logic of *lēthē* governs the speech's narrative of the *alētheia* of the past. Andocides promised a full and complete narrative of events "from

23 Likewise, Andocides equates the dikastic oath of 400 with the oaths the individual jurors took when each was initiated into the Eleusinian Mysteries (as all the jurors in this case were) and calls upon the Eleusinian goddesses to remind them of the impiety of falsely convicting an innocent man (31–32). The jurors' oath thus links 415 and 400 in the atemporality of religious ritual.

24 The jurors are also asked to remember the good reputation of Andocides' ancestors before the war (141, 142, 146, 148) and the bad reputation of his opponent Callias (130). Lysias 6 asks speakers to remember 415 and condemn Andocides for his actions then. "Let your mind seem to see what he did then" (50), says the speaker, and he recreates in vivid detail the profanation of the Mysteries as he imagines it.

25 Contrast Dem. 24.149–51. For this rhetorical conflation of the dikastic and amnesty oaths, cf. Isoc. 18.34.

26 MacDowell 1962: 201–02; Loening 1987: 140–46.

the beginning," but while the events of 415 are narrated in full (9–70) and the jurors repeatedly encouraged, as we have seen, to remember them, the fifteen years that follow are wrapped in the amnesia of amnesty:

> After you made peace with the Spartans and tore down the Long Walls, and you welcomed back the exiles, and the Thirty were established, and then Phyle was taken and they took Munychia – what happened to you after that I need not recall nor remind you of the troubles that befell you (*ouden deomai memnēsthai oud' anamimnēiskein humas tōn gegenēmenōn kakōn*). But when you returned from the Piraeus, you could have taken revenge but you decided to let it go. You put the safety of the city ahead of private retribution and decided not to bear a grudge (*mē mnēsikakein*) against one another for what had happened. (80–81)

The events of 404–403, from the final defeat of Athens to the amnesty, are skimmed over rapidly only to be banished with a repudiation of memory that closely echoes the amnesty (*anamimnēiskein . . . kakōn*). The communal memory that Andocides calls upon to pass down the true history of 415 is here banned, and the remembering of a troubling past drawn under the more circumscribed negation of the amnesty's *mē mnēsikakein*, as if every memory were a memory of evils and therefore prohibited. But this not-reminding also reiterates the paradoxes of the amnesty's not-remembering: the reason Andocides does not need to remind the demos of these "troubles" is presumably that they already remember. This irony reveals precisely the labor of Andocides' historical reconstruction: he must make the Athenians remember a past they do not remember by discreetly not reminding them of what they do remember.

Thus Andocides' continuous history "forgets" the political traumas of 404–403: the humiliating surrender to Sparta, the oligarchy, the civil war. But his narrative – which promised to tell everything from the beginning and omit nothing – does not leave those years blank. It fills the gap with law. "You have heard all about what happened then [i.e. in 415] . . . Now I will teach (*didaxō*) you about the laws" (70). In the place left by his non-recalling of the events of 404–403, Andocides inserts a lengthy exegesis on the legal reforms of these years: the decree of Patrocleides of 405 which restored citizen rights to those who had previously been deprived of them, the amnesty of 403, the decree of Teisamenes on the revision of the laws under the restored democracy, a law against unwritten laws, a law giving laws priority over decrees, a law banning *ad hominem* legislation, a law validating all laws passed after the archonship of Eucleides in 403/2 (71–91). These legal revisions are recounted in great detail, with the decrees of Patrocleides and Teisamenes read in full and their provisions carefully analyzed. This amplitude is especially remarkable given that these legal provisions are, as D. M. MacDowell shows, almost completely irrelevant to Andocides' case.[27] It is as if the detailed memory of this legal history replaces the forgotten history of conflict these laws and decrees were designed to address; indeed, the former is elaborately remembered precisely so the latter can be forgotten. Law fills the gap in the complete and continuous narrative Andocides promised and provides a bridge by which he can return to the Athens of 415 without recalling the traumatic events in between.

All of these legal revisions are in Andocides' telling designed expressly for the purpose of reconciliation: to reenfranchise the disenfranchised (73), to allow the return of exiles (80), to reestablish the traditional laws of Solon (83). This is a legislative narrative of return, a return to a democratic and harmonious Athens, a return to the lawful past. The amnesty proper emerges out of this progressive history of legislative retrogression: deep in the text of Patrocleides' decree (read aloud to the jurors by the court clerk) lies a provision against *mnēsikakein*. The verb occurs again as the motive for the revision of the lawcode (81), and a related prohibition on prosecution (86) is the goal of the laws against unwritten and *ad hominem* laws. Finally, Andocides' legal history culminates in a reciting of the oath of reconciliation and the dikastic oath (90–91). This conflation of the two oaths completes a process at work throughout this section, transforming the amnesty's *mē mnēsikakein* from a tenuous political negation into a positive legal achievement, associated with the justness of the jury system itself. Detached from a political history slated for forgetting ("I need not recall nor remind you . . . "), the amnesty's oblivion instead becomes the proud telos of a triumphalist narrative of Athenian law. The obliteration of legal memory becomes what is most worth remembering about law. In this way, the gap left in Athens' history by Andocides' not-remembering of 404–403 is bridged by a legal history of amnesty: memory of amnesty displaces and replaces the forgotten history it was designed to forget.

Athens' history is thus repaired in the form of a legal history, and a narrative of legislative returns allows the Athenians to return to and remember an Athens past. At §§106–09 Andocides recounts in brief the glorious history of fifth-century Athens. This is a hackneyed account,

[27] MacDowell 1962: 200–03; cf. Loening 1987: 140–44. The decree of Patrocleides seems not to have restored rights to those guilty of impiety of the sort Andocides committed; the crime for which he was charged fell after the time covered by the amnesty; an unwritten decree (which the decree of Isotimides presumably was) was probably not included in the law against passing *agraphoi nomoi*. This legal account is also, as Robertson 1990 and Todd 1996: 126–27 show, highly tendentious and misleading. See also Carawan 2002.

familiar from the annual Athenian oration for the war-dead, and it hits all the usual high-points: the demise of the Pisistratid tyranny, the battle of Marathon, the rebuilding of Athens after the Persian Wars, the growth of the Athenian Empire.[28] But what is remarkable about Andocides' account is that it turns Athens' heroic history into a history of amnesties. The defeat of the tyrants and victory over the Persians illustrate the wisdom of recalling exiles (106–07) and of not bearing a grudge (*mnēsikakēsai*, 108). Imperial hegemony is the result of unanimity (*homonoein*, 108). Even the final years of the Peloponnesian War provide an uplifting example of return and reenfranchisement.[29]

The historical details may not be wholly accurate but the moral is unambiguous: "What share of your ancestors' excellence remains for you? Not to bear a grudge (*mē mnēsikakēsai*), jurors, knowing that in time past this city, starting from a much smaller beginning, became great and prosperous and it can do so again now, if we citizens are willing to restrain ourselves and live in harmony (*homonoein*) with one another" (109). Amnesty is no longer a negation added to the troubles of the recent past, a desperate decision not to recall what cannot be forgotten ("I need not recall nor remind you . . . "). Instead it is transformed into a positive principle (*mē mnēsikakein* = *homonoein*) under which all of Athenian history – from the founding of the democracy to the present moment – is unified. Freed from historical amnesia, amnesty becomes the one thing worth remembering about the Athenian past. The alchemical agent of this transformation in Andocides' account is law: the legislative history that bridged the gap of 404–403 replaced the barely forgotten political crises of those years with a jurisprudential narrative of amnesty triumphant. Legal memory rewrites Athenian history as a glorious legacy of forgetting. Not only does it bridge the historical gulf left by the amnesty's *lēthē*; it makes *lēthē* – remembering amnesty – the only true path to the past.

In Andocides' account, amnesty becomes not only a positive historical principle but an innate national characteristic:

[28] Loraux 1986: 132–71. On the great victories of the fifth century as rhetorical exempla, see Nouhaud 1982: 147–64. Shrimpton 1997: 91–94 notes that heroizing history can serve as a way of forgetting a traumatic event.

[29] On these earlier amnesties, see Dorjahn 1946: 1–5. The historical inaccuracies are documented by MacDowell 1962: 140–41; Missiou 1992: 51–52. Compare Isoc. 18.31: many cities have waged war gloriously but none has resolved its civil disputes better than ours. Therefore "it is worth remembering that, of the many noble deeds of our ancestors, the city has won not the least of its glory from its reconciliations." Cf. 18.46: during the war "everyone thought us stupid and wretched, but now we seem to be the wisest and most blessed of all the Greeks." On *homonoia* in the orators see Ober 1989a: 297, and on the amnesty as a positive rhetorical exemplum, Nouhaud 1982: 313–16.

> Furthermore, you should bear in mind, jurors, that all Greeks now consider you the best and most sagacious of men (*andres aristoi kai euboulotatoi*) since you have not turned toward vengeance for what has happened but toward the salvation of the city and unity (*homonoian*) of the citizens. Catastrophes no less serious than ours have befallen many others as well before now. But to handle our differences with each other well, this rightly seems the task of good and temperate men (*andrōn agathōn kai sōphronōn*). Therefore, since everyone, friend or foe, agrees that this is a quality of yours (*tauth' humin huparkhei*), do not change your mind and voluntarily deprive the city of this reputation nor make it seem that you have passed your votes by chance rather than by decision. (140)

Homonoia – the positive incarnation of *mē mnēsikakein* – becomes the essence of the Athenian character, an excellence (*aretē*) inherited from their noble forefathers. The Athenian ancestors, *hoi pateres hoi humeteroi* (106), were good men who handed down their *aretē* to their sons (109); by reconciling with the exiles the current generation of Athenians, "good men born from good fathers, have displayed their innate excellence" (*agathoi ex agathōn ontes apedote tēn huparkhousan aretēn*, 109). The genealogical narrative of hereditary excellence projects the legal present into the historical past: a historically contingent and politically controversial act is retrojected as an innate quality that is then passed down as a natural legacy. Past and present are unified in the timelessness of Athenian *aretē*, and Andocides' legislative history is naturalized as a patrilineal succession.

The jurors can maintain that idealized national lineage, however, only by securing another more concrete bloodline, Andocides' own. Andocides offers the jury his own ancient and aristocratic genealogy as a model for historical continuity. This patriline had been threatened in 415: one of the original accusations against Andocides was that he denounced his father in the affair of the Mysteries. Andocides denies the charge but also imagines the Oedipal implications. Were the prosecution's accusations true, he asks the jury, do you think my father would have stayed in Athens and faced a trial in which either I would be the cause of his death, if I were found to be telling the truth, or he would be the cause of mine if I were proved to be lying (20)? The historical crisis of 415 is represented as a war between the generations in which either the father must kill the son or the son the father. Andocides' family again faces destruction, the elimination of its last remaining member, in the current trial at the hands of an opponent whose own *oikos*, incidentally, is perverted by scandal and depravity. Callias (Andocides charges) was living with both his wife and her mother and had a son by the latter. "What name should one give his son? Oedipus or Aegisthus or what else should one call him?" (129). Now this "priest of the

Mother and Daughter" (124) also wants the grand-daughter, who happens to be the orphaned daughter (*epiklēros*) of Andocides' kinsman. In fact, Andocides asserts, that was his real motive for bringing this malicious suit, to get Andocides to drop his own claim to the girl (117–31).[30]

By voting in his favor, the jurors will save not only Andocides himself but his entire lineage and, through his, their own. The peroration is a paean to genealogical and national succession. When the jurors' collective *pateres* defeated the tyrants, Andocides' own actual great-grandfather was one of the generals (106). The metaphor of hereditary national excellence is literalized in the bloodline of this elite family. "I ask you, then, to hold the same opinion (*tēn autēn gnōmēn*) about me that you did about my ancestors so that I might be able to imitate (*mimēsasthai*) them, remembering that they were equal to those responsible for the most and greatest benefits to the city" (141). The contemporary demos is collapsed with its fifth-century ancestor, with whom it is called to share one mind (*tēn autēn gnōmēn*) and one body ("you") in its attitude toward the successive generations of Andocides' family. The continuous mimetic excellence of that family is both the support for the continuous sameness of the demos and its desired consequence. That is to say, if the demos hopes to claim continuity with its noble fifth-century ancestors it must vouchsafe the continuity of Andocides with his. Past and present are now linked not by a tenuous chain of legislation but by blood, both Andocides' and Athens'. Linear history becomes a cyclical genealogy as each generation of Athenians imitates the eternal excellence of its – and Andocides' own – ancestors.[31]

Andocides' salvation will be Athens' salvation and vice versa: "It is reasonable for you to remember my ancestors, since the excellence of your own ancestors (*hai tōn humeterōn progonōn aretai*) was so valuable to the city" (142). The Spartans spared the defeated Athenians "because of the excellence of those men who established freedom for all of Greece;" likewise, "since Athens was saved by the *aretē* of your ancestors, I should also be saved by the *aretē* of my ancestors" (143). Moreover, just as Andocides' ancestors

[30] It is hard to see what the real issues in this quarrel were. The *epiklēros* was not wealthy and Andocides represents his own claim to the girl as fulfilling an obligation to his relative. Callias seems to be claiming the girl for his son (although Andocides insinuates that he wants her for himself). See MacDowell 1962: 145–50. Andocides and Callias were apparently related by marriage: see Missiou 1992: 15–20 on Andocides' family. This trial is analyzed as a family feud by Cox 1989 (esp. 41–46), 1996; Furley 1996: 49; and Strauss 1993, who shows how Andocides' defense exploits the symbolic connection between *patēr* (father) and *patris* (fatherland).

[31] Contrast Lys. 14.18–19, where the private genos of Alcibiades is set against the civic genealogy of the Athenian demos. Ober 1989a: 251–70 discusses how aristocratic litigants represented their high birth in court. On the oligarchic sentiments in Andocides' speeches, see Missiou 1992: 25–54; Furley 1996: 59–61, 68–69.

helped save Athens, Athens must return the favor and save Andocides; indeed, he suggests that his ancestors did so much good for the city not only out of patriotism but also "so that if they or their descendants should suffer some set-back they would be saved by obtaining your forgiveness" (141). Not only does each generation imitate the last, but each anticipates the next.

This elaborate interweaving of the past generation and the present and of Andocides' lineage and the demos' culminates with Andocides calling his own dead ancestors and unborn descendants to the witness stand:

> Do not forget (*epilathēsthe*) what they did because they themselves are dead but remember (*anamnēsthentes*) their deeds and imagine that you see them in the flesh begging you to save me. For whom can I put on the stand to plead on my behalf? My father? He is dead. My brothers? I don't have any. My children? They are not yet born. You, then, take the place of my father and brothers and children. I take refuge with you and beseech and supplicate you. You must beseech yourselves and save me. (148–49)

The demos who have pledged to forget their own past sufferings are urged to remember instead the past glories of Andocides' ancestry and, by analogy, their own. That selective memory will make the glorious past present in court. The genealogical link that has been broken by the historical traumas of the past decade – here embodied in this noble family reduced to one sole survivor – must be repaired by the jurors who themselves become both its ancestors and descendants, Andocides' fathers, brothers, and sons. The elite house of the defendant and the glorious history of the city, which Andocides has been at pains to equate throughout this peroration, here become one, as the jurors themselves join the family. Their grateful memory will save this aristocratic patriline for its glorious past and secure it in the face of its uncertain future. And in the process, the jurors will repair their genealogical link to their own dead fathers, the *aristoi pateres* of the fifth century, and the civic ancestry that guarantees the prosperity of their unborn future generations.

Thus Andocides returns to the Athens of the past and to the home of his ancestors. His case selectively forgets the past and sutures over the resulting holes in its historical narrative by elaborately remembering the details of recent legal history, including the legal agreement to forgive and forget. That legal forgetting then becomes a positive memory of *homonoia* around which is articulated a new narrative of the city's past and a new hereditary connection to it: amnesty is passed down in the blood. The Athenians are urged to remember that lineage by remembering Andocides' own, calling both his and their own noble ancestors into court in order to secure the hopes of the future. In this way Andocides naturalizes the historical continuity he has so laboriously forged as the foundation for his own return, rooting it in the memory and the blood of the jurors.

Apparently this strategy worked, for we know that Andocides won the case. The orator returns to his family home and through his own return also promises to return the Athenians to their ancestral legacy, an inherited excellence that remembers the past by imitating its most salient and saving quality: the national genius for forgetting.

TIME ON TRIAL (LYSIAS 13)

Lysias 13 also returns to the past, but not to the glorious past of the fifth century. Instead it returns obsessively to the traumatic history of the civil war. In the process it shows both the way legal discourse attempts to heal political and historical rupture and the limits of its ability to do so. Whereas Andocides used law to rebuild Athens' historical continuity, in this case it is the law's own continuity that needs repair, its fundamental connection between past crime, present trial, and future punishment. Lysias 13 offers this legal temporality as a model for the polis in its own relation to time but also raises the possibility that law's temporality may be structured by different needs from those of the city and its remembering and forgetting driven by different desires.

The case prosecutes a man named Agoratus, who it claims was an informant for the Thirty. In the tense months after the Athenian naval defeat at Aegospotami, as the prosecutor tells it, two factions emerged, one resisting surrender to Sparta because they feared it meant the end of the democracy, the other for accepting Sparta's terms and simultaneously scheming to overthrow the democracy and establish an oligarchy. The oligarchs persuaded Agoratus to give information against the democratic faction and the citizens he denounced to the Boule were put to death after the Thirty came to power. This case was brought in around 399 or 398 BCE by the brother and brother-in-law of Dionysodorus, one of those put to death on Agoratus' information.[32] Technically the case is an *apagōgē*, a procedure allowing the summary arrest of a felon caught in the course of committing the crime.[33] In this case the crime was presumably murder, and

[32] On the date see Todd 1996: 118–20, 2000a: 138–39; Carawan 1998: 355 n. 73.

[33] On the *apagōgē* see Gernet and Bizos 1955: 187–89; MacDowell 1963: 130–40; Harrison 1971: 222–29; Hansen 1976, esp. 99–108; Loening 1987: 72–73; Todd 1993: 117–18; Harris 1994b; Carawan 1998: 370–71; Wolpert 2002a: 60–61.

the Eleven, the magistrates in charge of arrests, required that the phrase *ep' autophōrōi* ("caught in the act") be added to the arrest warrant (30, 85–87). The speaker's burden in the case, then, is to prove that Agoratus was "caught in the act" of murdering Dionysodorus and the other democrats whom he denounced in 405/4.

The charge implies a temporal proximity between crime and punishment, but this trial comes at least five years after Agoratus' denunciations, and between the two lie the rise and fall of the Thirty, the civil war, and the amnesty. The speaker thus faces the problem of prosecuting around this temporal and legal disruption. While Agoratus will defend himself by emphasizing the lag between crime and punishment, the speaker must attempt to create a sense of temporal continuity, even immediacy, between the two. At stake in this temporal strategy is not only civic memory and the Athenians' forgetting of the crimes of the civil war, but also the temporal continuity of the law itself. If law's claim to justice is based on its ability to remember and prosecute past crimes, then the amnesty's *amnēsteia* poses a serious problem for law's *alētheia*. This speech attempts to repair the law's temporal unity by creating a tight bond – a connection both instantaneous and eternal – between the past crime and the present trial, and in this way attempts to preserve the law's promise of future justice. This temporal ideal is anticipated in the opening passage of the speech. "It is proper (*prosēkei*) for you all, gentlemen of the jury, to exact punishment on behalf of the men who died . . . " (1). The first line, with its initial impersonal verb, sets the case within the timeless deontic present of justice. Within that temporal framework, the past deed is followed by present hatred and prospective vengeance: "He committed such crimes through which now he is understandably hated by me and, if the god is willing, will be justly punished by you" (1). This sentence moves from past to present to future tense, laying out synoptically the temporality of justice that the civil war and the amnesty have so disrupted and that this speech aims to restore.

The speaker anticipates that Agoratus will seek to magnify the temporal disruptions: "evidently he considers these things stumbling blocks: the oaths and agreements; time; the fact that he was not 'caught in the act,' (*ē horkous ē sunthēkas ē khronon ē to ep' autophōrōi*). But he does not trust enough in the facts to defend himself on that basis" (88). The speaker addresses each of these defenses in turn and in doing so seeks to close the temporal gap between past crime and present prosecution. Agoratus will object to this case being brought after such a long delay (*hoti pollōi khronōi husteron timōroumetha*, 83), the speaker predicts. "But there is no statute of limitations upon such crimes, but in my opinion, regardless of whether they are punished immediately or after some time, he must show that he did not do the things he is charged with" (83). Indeed, he continues, Agoratus should count himself lucky that he is being prosecuted long after he should have been, since he has lived that many years longer, while the men he killed have been no less dead that whole time (84). Against the backdrop of death's timelessness, the speaker argues that there is no time limit on justice. He thus reaffirms law's temporal unity by removing the element of time and transposing the human legal system to the atemporality of divine Dikē, which will inexorably avenge a murder, no matter how long it takes.[34]

The theme of pollution that runs throughout the speech is part of the same strategy of detemporalization. In Greek religious thought, as we saw in Chapter 3, murder polluted the murderer with a moral stain that persisted until the crime was expiated. The speaker evokes this theory of pollution when he calls Agoratus *miaros* (defiled, 77) and *alitērios* (a religious offender, 79). A pariah wherever he goes, Agoratus was universally shunned as a murderer at Phyle (79), the speaker claims: he was driven out of the celebratory procession after the return of the democrats and told to "go to hell" (*es korakas*, 81). By his mere presence he has "polluted" the demos (*humas elumaineto*, 64). Pollution converts a single crime into durable criminality in the form of an indelible stain. Time becomes irrelevant: the gods will ensure that the crime is punished in the end.

The delay in prosecution is no defense, then. Nor, the speaker asserts, does the amnesty impose a barrier to the past. The speaker claims that the amnesty does not apply in this case because the agreement was between those in the Piraeus and those in the city, not between those in the Piraeus and those in the Piraeus, as Agoratus and the speaker were (89–90).[35] This weak claim belies the extent to which the spirit if not the letter of the amnesty does govern the legal argument and temporal structure of the case. It seems that direct murder (*autokheir*) was exempted from the amnesty, but those who denounced or informed were protected.[36] This means that in order to get around the amnesty, the speaker must transform murder

[34] Cf. Lys. 6.20: "The god does not punish immediately: that is human *dikē*. I can offer testimony from all over, having seen other men who have committed *asebeia* pay the penalty in time, and their children, too, through the crimes of their ancestors." (The criminal in question is Andocides.) There was no statute of limitations on murder; Loening 1987: 76 therefore suggests that Agoratus raised this defense in regard to some lesser crime, perhaps planning (*bouleusis*).

[35] On this fallacious argument see Cloché 1915: 336–38; Bateman 1958: 281, 1962: 169–70; Loening 1987: 100; Carawan 1998: 369.

[36] [Arist.] *Ath. Pol.* 39.5; Isoc. 18.20. These exemptions are discussed by Loening 1987: 39–40, 69–84; Carawan 1998: 125–28; Wolpert 2002a: 32–33.

by denunciation into murder by Agoratus' own hand (the root meaning of *autokheir*). The Eleven may have added *ep'autophōrōi* to the charge specifically to force the speaker to prove this argument, perhaps as a way of ensuring that the case didn't violate the amnesty.[37] Thus although the speaker claims the amnesty doesn't apply to this case, it shapes his argument by forcing him to draw a probative connection between Agoratus' intention and the effects of his act and between his act and its legal detection.

The amnesty, in other words, forces the speaker to "catch Agoratus in the act" of a past murder within the present time of the case. The phrase *ep' autophōrōi*, which started as a procedural technicality, becomes a central rhetorical strategy in the speech, used to suture intent to action and past to present. Indeed, the speaker argues paradoxically that the Eleven insisted on this phrase precisely to make it easier to convict Agoratus:

> For how could he not have been "caught in the act" when he denounced some men first in front of five hundred [in the Boule] and then in front of all the Athenians [in the Ecclesia] and thereby killed them and was responsible for their death? Surely you don't believe that a man can only be "caught in the act" if he strikes down another with a club or a knife? By your argument, it will appear that no one killed the men whom you denounced, since no one struck them or slit their throats, but they died under the compulsion of your denunciation. Isn't the man responsible for the death the one "caught in the act"? And who is responsible other than you who denounced them? Therefore how are you not "caught in the act," you who killed them? (86–87)

Link by link the speaker forges the logical chain from Agoratus' information to the men's deaths and from the crime to its public detection. This rhetorical chain obscures the legal and theoretical difference between planning a murder (*bouleusis*) and executing it (*autokheir*). Even if one believes the speaker's assertion that Agoratus named names voluntarily and not under compulsion by the Thirty (18, 31, 52), the argument strains the limits of legal responsibility. It also obscures the temporal and political difference between the democratic Boule of 405/4 to whom Agoratus denounced the men and the kangaroo court of the Thirty that sentenced them to death (20).[38] Through these temporal and legal conflations, the complex factional

[37] On the meaning of the phrase and its use here, see MacDowell 1963: 132–33; Hansen 1976: 48–53; Loening 1987: 77–78; Todd 1993: 80, 117; Harris 1994b, 2006: 373–90; Carawan 1998: 362–70; Gagarin 2008: 211–12. See also Gernet 1981b: 221 on the temporal logic of "flagrancy" and the ideal unity of criminal law: "the sanction is absolutely and intimately united with the criminal deed. Everything belongs to the present . . ."

[38] Carawan 1998: 360: "The rise of the oligarchs and the changes that they brought about, particularly the change of venue that brought the officers to trial before a partisan council, constitute an outright break in the causal chain connecting Agoratus to judicial murder."

intrigues of the civil war are transformed into a brutally straightforward murder committed in view of the whole Athenian demos.

The logical maneuvers of this section are mirrored in the tactics of the speech as a whole, which by vividly representing the act in progress and detecting Agoratus in the process of committing it makes the entire Athenian citizenry (now in its role as jury not Assembly) eye-witness to it. The shift between past and present tense in the narrative of the crime, a common rhetorical ploy in Attic forensic oratory, collapses act and detection and gives a sense that the jurors are uncovering the crime as it unfolds. That sense is reinforced by the calling of eye-witnesses, the direct cross-examination of the defendant, and the reading of the death-warrants in which Agoratus is listed as informant. The speaker calls upon all the technical resources of the law in order to create a sense of immediacy between crime and punishment. The speech's rhetoric thus heals the rupture in the law created by the turmoil of the civil war; it leaps over the barrier of the amnesty back to the moment of the original crime. The case for the prosecution itself, as the speaker says, will catch Agoratus in the act (*ep' autophōrōi egō auton exelenxō*, 30).

By collapsing the discrete moments of the denunciation, the execution, and the present prosecution, this speech presents itself as an immediate trial not just of Agoratus' crimes but of the Thirty's. Temporal condensation allows the speaker (via a spurious *post hoc ergo propter hoc* argument) to hold Agoratus "responsible for all the evils that befell the city" (33).[39] Because he denounced the men who opposed peace with Sparta, "Lysander sailed into your harbors, your ships were handed over to the Spartans, the walls were demolished, the Thirty were installed, and every other manner of suffering befell the city" (34). Agoratus is thus held accountable both for Athens' military defeat and for all the crimes of the Thirty (cf. 43, 48).

By making Agoratus responsible for the rise of the Thirty, the speaker promises the jurors that by condemning Agoratus they will also obtain justice for all the oligarchs' crimes. Thus he presents this case as a retrial of the Thirty's trumped-up trial and execution of Agoratus' victims. "If they had been judged in the courts, they would easily have been saved; for you all already knew what a crisis the city was in, a crisis in which you were no longer able to help" (36). This case allows the jurors to redeem their former juridical impotence by overturning the unjust verdict of the Thirty: "You should vote the opposite way from the Thirty. Those whom

[39] Gernet and Bizos 1955: 189; Todd 2000a: 146 n. 22, 148 n. 26. See Wolpert 2002a: 121–29 on the conflation of surrender to Sparta and the overthrow of the democracy, esp. 126 on Lys. 13. Roisman 2006: 72–83 shows how Lysias' anachronisms play into a rhetoric of conspiracy.

they condemned to death, you acquit and those whom they acquitted, you condemn" (96). The decisions of history are reversed on appeal. "Now, men of Athens, since you were not able to help those men at the time when they were killed, now when you are able, avenge their murder" (93). The case offers a means for the democratic jurors to try the past and – merely by voting to condemn – both to obtain vengeance for the sufferings of those years and to absolve themselves retroactively of any responsibility for them. Through the speech's temporal synopticism the jurors can undo the effects of time; years after the fact they can "catch the Thirty in the act" and bring them to a just and (at last) immediate punishment.

Like Andocides, Lysias works to naturalize the temporal schema he constructs. He does so, first, through an appeal to *ēthos*. Like most forensic speeches, this one locates intent not in the contingent decisions and circumstantial pressures of a specific historical moment but in a man's innate character. Agoratus is both an audacious criminal and a cowardly tool of the Thirty, who did not even trust him to join their conspiracy but only to serve as an informer (18). He is not merely a murderer but a known sykophant (65), a father-beater (91), an adulterer and corrupter of free women (66). This emphasis on character turns a temporally punctual crime into a durable criminal disposition. The crime of 405/4 persists into the present in the form of Agoratus' despicable character, and by voting against the latter the jury can punish the former. Moreover, Agoratus' criminal *ēthos* is the legacy of his criminal *genos*. A "slave born of slaves" (18, 64), Agoratus is the scion of a family of scoundrels: his three brothers were put to death for treason, kidnapping, and burglary (67–68). Criminality is in his bloodline. He is guilty not only by his actions, but in his very *phusis*, and there is no statute of limitations on that.

Agoratus' bad bloodline is part of a larger genealogical metaphor through which Lysias narrates the regime of the Thirty and civil war. Like Andocides, Lysias imagines Athenian history as a patriline and in this way seeks both to conceptualize historical rupture and to naturalize historical continuity. The speaker interrupts his attack on Agoratus to praise the men killed by his denunciation (62). In its language and themes this section resembles the Athenian funeral oration and resonates closely with the patriotic historical narrative at the end of Andocides 1. With its collective praise, its emphasis on service to the state, and the public laudation of those who survived as *agathoi andres*, this section assimilates these men to war heroes and also to the heroic ancestors who made Athens great: "serving as generals many times, they handed the city down to their successors greater than they received it" (62).[40] If the dead men are imagined as Athens' glorious fathers, then Agoratus is a parricide:

In every possible respect he seems to me to deserve multiple deaths, since he claims to have been adopted (*pepoiēsthai*) by the demos but then shows himself abusing the very demos which he claims is his father by betraying those who made it greater and stronger. And the same man who beat his own birth father and refused to provide for his daily needs also robbed his adoptive father of the blessings that belonged to him. For this he surely deserves the death penalty according to the law on abuse of parents. (91)

Agoratus is not just a literal father-beater but – even worse – a metaphoric one. He has killed the civic ancestors and abused the demos that "adopted" him by granting him, "a slave born of slaves," citizenship (a grant the speaker also disputes, 70–76). The trope of paternal abuse figures in genealogical terms the breach Agoratus' crime has caused in the city's history: the peaceful succession from one generation to the next – good men handing down the city greater than they received it – has been violently disrupted by his crime against the dead "fathers" and the demos as a whole.

Against Agoratus the treacherous son the speech calls upon the jurors to prove themselves good sons by avenging their fathers' murder. In a pathetic scene, the speaker describes the men denounced by Agoratus as they await execution in their jail cells. They call to them their wives, mothers, and sisters to say their last farewells. Dionysodorus summons his pregnant wife, the speaker's sister, and charges her to tell their child that Agoratus killed his father and bid him to avenge his murder; he also enjoins the speaker, his brother, and his friends to seek vengeance against Agoratus (41–42). This emotional scene stands in both synecdochic and causal relation to all the crimes that followed, the speaker asserts, upon the death of these democratic leaders. These crimes against the city – all of which are Agoratus' fault (43) – are also crimes against the Athenian family. The speaker echoes the dying plea of Dionysodorus and calls for vengeance against the man who caused them:

Remember (*memnēsthe*) too those here in Athens who were led to prison through personal enmities. Men who had done the city no harm were forced to die the most shameful and inglorious death. Some left behind elderly parents, who had

[40] For this epitaphic rhetoric, see Loraux 1986, esp. 77–131. The praise for both living and dead in this passage makes Agoratus responsible for murdering even those who survived: "those who survived and were saved, whom he killed all the same and whose death sentence was passed, chance and the divinity protected" (63). Compare the explicit invocation of the funeral oration at Lyc. 1.46–51: "the eulogy for good citizens (*agathōn andrōn*) is clear proof against those who behave the opposite way" (46). Wolpert 2002a: 130–33 discusses the praise of the democratic resistance as *andres agathoi.*

expected their children to care for them in their old age and bury them when they died; some left unmarried sisters, or young children in need of care. What opinion do you think these men would have of Agoratus, jurors, and what vote do you think they would cast, if they were able to, deprived as they have been of all that is sweetest to them thanks to him? (44–46)

The vote of the jury will fulfill the deathbed request of the condemned men. The jurors themselves, made vividly present at the prison-house scene through the force of Lysias' description, act as and for the unborn child of Dionysodorus, carrying out his paternal injunction. Remembering (*memnēsthe*) the crimes against their collective fathers, they must become avenging sons of the democratic dead. All of you must avenge these men, the speaker tells the jurors, as must each and every one of us. "For as they died, they commanded us and all their friends to take vengeance on Agoratus as their murderer and to do him whatever harm each of us could" (92). If those men benefited the city, he continues, they must be considered friends and intimates (*philous kai epitēdeious*), "and thus the injunction falls no more upon us than upon each one of you" (92). The "we" of the family and the "you" of the city join forces under the paternal demand for vengeance.

Through this genealogical trope Lysias, like Andocides, seeks to repair the historical continuity ruptured by the oligarchy and civil war and to reunite the Athenian jury with their civic forefathers. Genealogy also repairs legal continuity between past crime and present trial and naturalizes that juridical unity: in a lawful city, punishment follows crime as son follows father. Analogized to *phusis*, *nomos* becomes a natural and inevitable succession. And yet the genealogical model of justice solves one legal problem only to raise another, for in shifting the linear progression of history into the cyclical time of natural reproduction it raises the possibility that the present, instead of repairing and redeeming the past, will simply repeat it. In Greek mythology, succession myths are often dramas of violent repetition, as the crimes of each generation are reiterated and compounded in the next. In the paradigmatic case of Orestes, whose trial for killing his mother in order to avenge the murder of his father was famously dramatized in Aeschylus' *Oresteia*, the recursive violence of familial justice is imagined as the prehistory of Athenian law: the blood-guilt passed down over generations is erased in a democratic court of law under the beneficent eye of Athena herself. Lysias 13 threatens to reverse this mythic progression, turning law into an instrument of rather than a solution to the generational repetition of blood-guilt. By imagining the jurors as vengeful sons of the dead it risks engendering a cycle of familial violence in which sons become murderers in the process of avenging their father's murder.

In this speech's juridical succession myth, natural reproduction veers toward nightmarish repetition. Acquitting Agoratus, the speaker tells the jurors, would be "the most wretched deed of all" (93), an "unholy and unlawful" act (93). For if you fail to condemn,

> you will also by the same vote pass a death sentence against those men [Agoratus' victims] whom you agree were loyal to you. By acquitting the man guilty of their death your vote will mean nothing other than that he killed them justly. These men would suffer the most awful fate if those they enjoined as friends to avenge them, themselves will cast against those men the same vote (*homopsēphoi*) as the Thirty. By the Olympian gods, jurors, do not in any way by any means condemn to death these men who died at the hands of Agoratus and the Thirty just because they benefited you. (93–95)

The wrong vote will turn the democratic jurors into the Thirty: they will "share a vote" (*homopsēphoi*) with the tyrants whose vote epitomized lawlessness (cf. 97).[41] Time contracts. The jurors of 398 become the corrupt council of 404; present action becomes violently retroactive as the jurors kill men already dead. The present disappears beneath the shadow of the past, and the democratic jurors – by the very symbol of their democratic legitimacy, their dikastic vote – become belated agents of the Thirty, perpetuating their violent and unjust regime.

In this speech, the threat of juridical recursivity is pointedly not associated with violent vengeance. This is presumably a risk Agoratus himself emphasized. Its catastrophic civic and legal implications are also imagined in Lysias 12, as we will see. But this speaker refuses to view Agoratus' condemnation as another murder, a continuation of the Thirty's ruthless elimination of its enemies or of the civil war's *stasis*. Instead, he associates the danger of repetition not with vengeance but with the failure to avenge, not with excessive prosecutorial zeal but with judicial leniency. That is to say, he associates repetition with forgetting not remembering. He implies that the amnesty's forgiveness is a continuation of the violence of the oligarchy and civil war, not its cure and guarantee against its future recurrence. The only way to avoid repeating the crimes of the past and becoming *homopsēphoi* with the Thirty is to remember: "By the Olympian gods, jurors, do not in any way by any means condemn to death these men who died at the hands of Agoratus and the Thirty just because they benefited you. Remembering

[41] This compound is rare in classical Greek: Hdt. 6.109, 7.149; And. 2.28. On this rhetorical strategy see Quillin 2002: 91–97.

(*anamnēsthentes*), then, everything you suffered after these men died, both collectively as a city and individually, punish the man responsible" (95, cf. 48). Memory of evils thus becomes an act of filial piety and civic justice. Remember (*memnēsthe*) the men dragged off to prison, the old parents abandoned and children left orphaned (44–45). Vengeful memory, a legacy passed down from father to son, becomes the basis for the law's *alētheia*. The amnesty is forgotten. *Mnēsikakein* is the only route to future justice.

Between the law's injunction to remember and the city's injunction to forget, this speech pins its hopes on the law's *alētheia* and not on civic amnesia. It seeks to repair the law's temporal unity by remembering the past, closing the gap of forgetfulness between Agoratus' crime and his trial and "catching in the act" all the historical traumas the amnesty aimed to place beyond the reach of legal memory. In healing the law's temporal unity, though, the speech threatens to rupture the city's precarious political unity, reopening civic wounds in the course of avenging remembered evils. The law's temporal crisis is overcome in this speech at the expense of the city. We do not know whether the Athenian jurors accepted this bargain, whether they were willing to forget the amnesty in order to secure law's *alētheia*. But whatever their verdict, the speech's tension between the law's relation to the past and the city's goes against the amnesty's predication of civic reparation on legal forgetting. Truth and reconciliation can go hand in hand, but this speech suggests that the law's desire for an unforgetting truth can also stand in conflict with the city's need for a forgetful reconciliation. In exposing this disjunction between the law and the city, Lysias 13 reveals that the law, too, has a stake in the amnesty's determination to forget, and that that stake may not be identical to the city's. This speech's temporal strategies show that law has a time of its own, distinct from although entangled with the time of the city, and its own distinct need to remember and forget.

TRAUMATIC MEMORY AND LEGAL HISTORIOGRAPHY (LYSIAS 12)

Lysias 12 begins at the rhetorical pitch at which Lysias 13 ends, with an angry call to memory. Like Lysias 13, it offers *mnēsikakein* as a path to justice, but it also acknowledges much more explicitly than 13 the dangers of this route: the traumas of the past are not just remembered in this speech but violently replayed, and replayed whether the jury votes to acquit or to condemn. Memory becomes a form of paralysis, and the present an endless reenactment of personal and civic trauma. If the past is problematically distant in Lysias 13 and Andocides 1 and the speakers' burden there is to bridge the gap of amnesty, in this speech – delivered perhaps as soon as three months after the reconciliation – the past presses too close, overwhelming the present. The question then becomes how to forget differently, in a way that doesn't merely repress the past but allows some working through of its traumas. Alongside the visceral immediacy of memory Lysias limns another approach to the past, through a critical historiography. The law turns out to be a blunt instrument of historical analysis, and Lysias' history of the civil war risks merely reproducing the fatal divisions that, despite the amnesty, the case cannot forget. Yet despite its failure to find a way out of its own aporetic memory, the speech does perhaps pry enough critical space between the past and the present to allow for the imagination of a different juridical future.

This case is extraordinary in a number of ways. First, it is the only case we have that Lysias pleads in his own voice. The sufferings of the city are inseparable in this account from the personal suffering of Lysias during these years: his harassment by the Thirty and flight from Athens, the confiscation of his property and loss of much of his family wealth, and the arrest and execution of his brother Polemarchus, which is the specific crime on trial.[42] The memories in this case are thus particularly immediate, without the usual intervention of the logographer between the speaker and his reported experiences. Second, the fact that Lysias spoke at all is extraordinary. Lysias was not an Athenian citizen but a metic (resident alien), and would normally have been excluded from speaking in the *dikastēria*. This has led some scholars to believe that Lysias 12 was in fact circulated as a pamphlet and never actually delivered in court.[43] Metics were granted full citizen rights, however, in 403/2 by a decree of Thrasybulus that was revoked several months later by Archinus. It is possible that Lysias delivered this speech during that brief window, perhaps in December 403.[44] If this is true, it lends a further urgency to the speech. The decree of Thrasybulus may have provided the fleeting opportunity for Lysias, a non-citizen, to remember aloud and in public all the memories the amnesty bound citizens to forget.

The case is also exceptional in another way: it is the only extant speech prosecuting one of the Thirty. The amnesty oath exempts any member of

42 On the life of Lysias, see Bizos 1967: 1–10; Edwards 1999: 1–3; Todd 2007: 5–17.

43 Carawan 1998: 376–77. Many commentators suppose that Lysias lost the case, but there is no way of knowing that. Quillin 2002 argues that despite widespread hostility toward oligarchic sympathizers successful prosecutions were rare, in part because the negative consequences of a wrong verdict in the prosecution's favor seemed more severe than those of a verdict for the defense.

44 [Arist.] *Ath. Pol.* 40.2. There is much debate on the decree of Thrasybulus and its implications for the date and delivery of this speech; see Whitehead 1977: 154–59; Loening 1981: 282, 289–91; Edwards and Usher 1985: 235; T. M. Murphy 1989: 40 n. 1; Edwards 1999: 86–87; Munn 2000: 256–58; Todd 2000a: 114, 2007: 13–14. See also Whitehead 1977: 89–97, Patterson 2000 on the legal rights and status of metics.

the Thirty from the ban on *mnēsikakein* unless "he is willing to give an account (*euthunas*) of his magistracy" (And. 1.90). This case was probably such a *euthunē*, and thus it operates in a gray area within the amnesty itself, an area where forgetting admits the possibility of remembering and forgiving even those presumed to be most guilty.[45] Again this extraordinary speech seems to escape from a crack in the armature of forgetting. An exception to the amnesty from within the terms of the amnesty, a non-citizen's call to remember civic suffering, this speech in a sense should not exist. If, as Loraux says (quoting Lacan), the unconscious is in man "the memory of what he forgets," does Lysias' speech represent a momentary eruption of the Athenian unconscious from beneath the self-censorship of oblivious repression?[46]

The speech opens in aporia: "I am not at a loss (*aporon*) as to how to begin my prosecution, jurors, but rather how to stop speaking" (1). If this case is a *euthunē*, setting the account straight will be difficult. "Such is the plenitude and magnitude of his crimes that I could neither accuse him of worse than he has done if I lied nor, if I wanted to tell the truth, could I speak them all, but either the prosecutor must necessarily fail (*anankē . . . apeipein*) or the time of the trial be insufficient (*epilipein*)" (1). This is a forensic commonplace: the deeds of the defendant exceed the bounds of legal speech, the legal speech proclaims; they surpass the abilities of an individual prosecutor and the limits of legal time. With crimes so excessive, failure (*apeipein, epilipein*) is a necessity (*anankē*), and the prospect of his own inadequacy in the face of Eratosthenes' deeds fills Lysias with despair (*athumian*, 3).[47] In his attempt to match words to deeds, a prosecutor might talk forever: "I am not at a loss as to how to begin my prosecution, jurors, but rather how to stop speaking." The roads (*poroi*) of prosecution open in all directions before him, and there is nothing to block them or stop him: this is his aporia, an infinity of paths that lead only in circles. The litotes of the opening sentence – the speaker's lack of a lack of means (*ouk . . . aporon*) to stop speaking – reiterates the double-negative logic of the amnesty, which

[45] Gernet and Bizos 1955: 157; cf. Dorjahn 1946: 42–43; Carawan 1998: 376–77 and 2006 (arguing that the exemption clause was a later addition to the amnesty); And. 1.90; [Arist.] *Ath. Pol.* 39.6 for the *euthunē* clause of the amnesty oath. Loening argues that the case was exempt as a *dikē phonou* (1981, 1987: 67–71). Lysias does not explicitly accuse Eratosthenes of murder *autokheir* in this speech, but he does go to great lengths to make Eratosthenes directly responsible for the crime. This could be an argument a fortiori, however, not a matter of speaking to a specific charge.

[46] Loraux 2002: 264, quoting Lacan 1992: 231–32.

[47] Cf. 99. The opening section (1–3) is replete with privatives (*a-*). Lysias feels *athumia* (despair) at his *apeiria* (inexperience) lest he prosecute the case *anaxiōs kai adunatōs* (unworthily and incapably); against this, there is an *aphthonia* (abundance) and no *aporia* (lack) of things to be angry about.

would seem to be designed as precisely the aporia Lysias is missing: it should function as a roadblock for the paths of memory that lead always back to the traumatic past. Lysias' despondency (*athumia*) results from a lack of negation upon memory and speech: he dreads he will never stop remembering and speaking. The speech thus starts from a negation of the amnesty's negation of *mnēsikakein* and details the psychic burden of this failure to forget.

Lacking a way not to remember, the present case is obsessed with the past. Like Lysias 13, it narrates the events of the past vividly, often in the present tense. The narrative opens with a detailed account of the night of Lysias' arrest, complete with reported conversations and reconstructed thoughts and motives, his own (9, 15) and others' (14). As in Lysias 13, the past also speaks in the present trial in the form of a cross-examination of the defendant (25), a procedure for which these two cases are virtually our only examples.[48] Likewise, Eratosthenes' shameless and audacious defense is not merely a continuation of his past crimes, but their culmination. "I believe he would dare anything who now has come to make his defense before the very witnesses of his criminality, for the jurors are none other than his victims" (84, cf. 22). The present jurors are the victims both of his past criminal acts and of his current criminal self-defense. The present is less a judgment of the past than a judgment *in* the past, one executed not with the retrospection that Aristotle attributes to forensic oratory but in the very moment, the past moment that lives in the present in the memory of the jurors who were/are also witnesses and victims. Thus the verdict is imagined as having effect not only in the future (discouraging or encouraging future oligarchs, 35) but also, paradoxically, in the past. The dead are watching this vote, Lysias concludes. "I believe they are listening to you and will know you as you cast your vote, realizing that those of you who vote to acquit will be condemning them to death and those of you who vote to condemn will be taking vengeance on their behalf" (100). The past is alive in this case's present, as the dead haunt the courtroom to judge the judges.

This speech offers the same promise of redeeming the past as Lysias 13 and poses the same risk of repeating it:

> You must show what attitude you take toward the matter. If you condemn Eratosthenes, you will make it clear that you are angry at what happened; if you acquit, on the other hand, you will show that you desired (*epithumētai*) the same deeds

[48] The only other instances are at Lys. 22.5 and Pl. *Ap*. 24c–28a. On the procedure see Carawan 1983; Krentz 1984: 25–28; Sommerstein 1984; Edwards 1999: 97.

as the defendant and you will not have the excuse that you were following the Thirty's orders. For now there is no one forcing (*anankazei*) you to vote against your own judgment. So I advise you (*sumbouleuō*) not to condemn yourselves by acquitting him. And do not think that this vote will be hidden: you will make your opinion manifest to the whole city. (90–91)

This is a trial not only of the Thirty but of the demos themselves and their own role in the events of 404–403. This passage recalls the Assembly in which the Thirty came to power, described earlier in the speech (73–75). Theramenes advocated entrusting the city to thirty individuals. The demos, although demoralized, shouted their dissent, "for you knew that on that day the Assembly was deciding a matter of slavery or freedom" (73). But the Spartan king Lysander joined Theramenes in insisting, "and those among the Assembly who were good men (*andres agathoi*) recognized the compulsion and the conspiracy (*paraskeuēn kai anankēn*). Some stayed and kept quiet while others left, telling themselves that at least they had not voted for anything that would harm the city" (75). In this present trial, with Lysias replacing Theramenes as their advisor, the demos can now redeem themselves as jurors for their past passivity and silence as Assemblymen. By condemning Eratosthenes they will declare their independence from the compulsion (*anankē*) of the Thirty and at the same time will prove that their former vote in fact reflected that compulsion (*anankē*) not their own desire (*epithumia*). They will acquit themselves by condemning Eratosthenes. If, on the other hand, they vote in Eratosthenes' favor, they will condemn themselves not only for silence and passivity but for active complicity in the rise of the Thirty, and show that they acted not under compulsion but through a desire they share in common with the Thirty.

Thus Lysias presents the jurors with the same choice as in speech 13. There the jurors were urged to redeem their former impotence by condemning Agoratus: "Now, men of Athens, since you were not able to help those men at the time when they were killed, now when you are able, avenge their murder" (13.93). If they voted to acquit, however, they would reveal that they were *homopsēphoi* with the Thirty and would repeat the violence of the past in their own verdict. Here, too, the jurors, by voting against Eratosthenes will punish the crimes of the Thirty and absolve themselves of any responsibility for those crimes; an acquittal, on the other hand, would repeat those crimes and perpetuate the lawless desires of the tyrants, both symbolically in the jurors' vote and literally in the survival of Eratosthenes, who would be free to destroy the city again (12.88).

But whereas Lysias 13 associates recursivity only with acquittal and refuses to imagine any adverse consequence of condemnation, in Lysias 12 either vote seems to lead aporetically back to the same violent past. This is not the moment (*kairos*) for pity or forgiveness, Lysias tells the jurors, but for *dikē*. "Don't be mightier than your military enemies (*polemiōn*) when you are fighting but inferior to your personal enemies (*ekhthrōn*) when voting" (79). The civil war, which turned countrymen into enemies (*polemioi*, cf. 56, 92), continues in the courtroom, where the demos will reap the fruits of their victory over the oligarchs. The *dikē* of this urgent present moment (*kairos*) is merely a perpetuation of the past conflict, suspended between the defendant's false promises for the future and the demos' anger at his actions of the past (80).

Moreover, just as Lysias himself lacks a way to stop speaking about the past, the Athenians may lack a way to stop prosecuting it and in their vengeful anger may become worse tyrants than those they seek to punish. The opening passage's anxiety about commensurability – the impossibility of finding adequate words or punishment to match Eratosthenes' crimes – is reiterated throughout the speech. I believe I have said enough when I have shown that his acts deserve death, says Lysias, since that is the most extreme penalty we can exact. "So I don't see the point in a detailed prosecution against men who not even if they died twice for every one of their crimes would be able to pay an adequate penalty" (37). No punishment will be enough. But alongside the fear that the punishment will fail to equal the crime is the danger that it might exceed the crime. "They killed the innocent without a trial; you think it right to judge those who destroyed the city according to the law. Not even if you wanted to prosecute them illegally (*paranomōs boulomenoi dikēn lambanein*) could you impose a judgment equal to the wrongs they did the city" (82). *Paranomia* has been associated in the speech with Eratosthenes (23, 48). Lysias contrasts this judicial hearing and its lawful punishment to the lawless violence of the Thirty who killed the innocent without a trial. But does the counterfactual in this sentence concede more than it appears to? Does Lysias, in his desire to make the penalty match the exorbitant crime, in fact desire to punish Eratosthenes *paranomōs,* beyond the crime and beyond the law? And if they are persuaded by his argument, do the jurors share this desire? If no legal penalty is adequate, must the jury go – or at least want to go – beyond the law, *para-nomos*? Will their desire for vengeance turn the demos, too, into lawless tyrants?

Eratosthenes can be killed only once, but one can dream of more and want (despite the counterfactual) a vengeance beyond the law itself:

Not even if you wanted to prosecute them illegally (*paranomōs*) could you impose a judgement equal (*dikēn . . . axian*) to the wrongs they did the city. For what would they have to suffer to pay a penalty equal (*dikēn tēn axian*) to their deeds? If you killed them and their children would it be a sufficient punishment (*hikanēn . . . dikēn*) for us, whose fathers and sons and brothers they killed without a trial? If you confiscated all their money would it be good either for the city, from which they stole so much, or the individuals whose houses they demolished? Since even if you did everything you would be unable to exact a sufficient punishment (*hikanēn dikēn*), isn't it shameful if you fail to impose any punishment whatsoever that anyone wants to inflict? (82–84)

Since no punishment is enough, none can be too much. Killing them is not enough; killing their children is not enough. The genealogical metaphor, the just cry for vengeance handed down in the blood that we saw in Lysias 13, here points to a future of endless violence. Many citizens and foreigners have come to hear the verdict of this case, Lysias warns, and to take from it a lesson for their future behavior (35). The future is at stake in this judgment of the past, but given the criminality of that past "is it not necessary to punish both them and their children with the most extreme punishments?" (36).[49] The future reproduces only death, with no aporia to stop the march toward retribution. By acquitting the jurors will show they share the desire of the Thirty. But even in condemning they show that same tyrannical desire: a desire to punish their enemies, without law and without end.

Unable to stop talking about the past Lysias is unable to stop punishing it. And so he urges the demos: "Remember!" (*anamnēsas*, 92; *anamnēsthentes*, 94; *anamnēsthēte*, 95; *anamnēsthēte*, 96). The speech climaxes in a mnemotic fugue: remember the murder and violence; remember the crimes of the Thirty and the horrors of the civil war. In a strategy unique in the oratory of this period, Lysias appeals separately to the men of the city and the men of the Piraeus in an attempt to unite them in a shared memory of their past suffering and a shared hatred of the one man who caused it.[50] The men of the city he urges to remember the compulsion and enslavement they suffered under the Thirty (92–94); the men of the Piraeus to recall the

[49] The prosecutorial claim that even multiple deaths are insufficient is a common trope, as Allen 2000a: 63–65 shows, and is parodied at Ar. *Plut.* 482–85. In this section, Lysias offers as a comparandum the collective conviction of the generals after the battle of Arginusae: since you imposed a death sentence on them, you should impose even heavier punishment on Eratosthenes, whose crimes were so much worse (36). The decision after Arginusae was considered unjust even at the time (Pl. *Ap.* 32b5–e1; Xen. *Hell.* 1.7.35; [Arist.] *Ath. Pol.* 34; D.S. 13.101), and the argument a fortiori here underlines the excessive nature of Lysias' call for punishment: he is urging the demos to be harsher now than they were even at their harshest moment in the past.

[50] Wolpert 2002a: 91. Cf. Edwards and Usher 1985: 251 *ad* 92: "Lysias refers to the oligarchic remnants and the democrats (respectively) as if they were not yet reconciled."

arrests and executions and miserable exile, the men dragged away from the altars to their deaths or ripped away from wives and children and parents, the people (like Polemarchus) forced to drink hemlock and then deprived of proper burial (95–97). But the *mnēsikakein* (*anamnēsthēte de kai tōn allōn kakōn,* 96) that Lysias hopes will unite both sides in anger at Eratosthenes risks reproducing the fatal division of the civil war as each side remembers its own suffering. Moreover, the details of the experiences of the exiled democrats – details that resonate closely with Lysias' own experience – remind us that the orator is not a neutral arbitrator in this new war of memories and that even if the rest of the demos can forget and forgive, he cannot. Unable to block the visceral memory of the past, unable to punish it enough or to stop wanting to punish it too much, the speech repeats the very violence it cannot forget: the lawless retribution of the Thirty, the division of the civil war. All roads lead back to that traumatic past. Memory of evils will be the jurors' paradigm (*paradeigma*, 92) as they cast their verdict, and that verdict will thus merely enact *mnēsikakein*: "You have heard. You have seen. You have suffered. You have him. Cast your verdict!" (100). Lysias can finally stop speaking (*pausomai katēgorōn*, 100) only when he has ensured that the jurors will never stop remembering.[51]

This case cannot escape the endless *poros* of memory: it cannot find aporia in amnesia or amnesty. And yet if Lysias cannot forget the past perhaps he can offer a different way to remember its evils. Alongside its visceral and immediate representation of the past, this speech does perhaps find a path – one Lysias himself cannot yet travel, but a future *poros* – toward a different relation to the past in the form of historical analysis. Historian Pierre Nora draws a contrast between memory and history. Memory, he writes,

> is life, borne by living societies founded in its name. It remains in permanent evolution, open to the dialectic of remembering and forgetting, unconscious of its successive deformations, vulnerable to manipulation and appropriation, susceptible to being long dormant and periodically revived. History, on the other hand, is the reconstruction, always problematic and incomplete, of what is no longer. Memory is a perpetually actual phenomenon, a bond tying us to the eternal present; history is a representation of the past.[52]

[51] Felman 2002: 5: "while the law strives to contain the trauma, it often is in fact the trauma that takes over and whose surreptitious logic in the end reclaims the trial." Felman analyzes the way law reenacts historical trauma and thus itself becomes traumatic; her discussion resonates closely with the dynamics of memory in Lysias 12. See esp. 54–105.

[52] Nora 1989: 8. Cf. LaCapra 1994: 175: "historiography involves work on memory that inquires into its operations, attempts to retrieve what it has repressed or ignored, and supplements it in ways that

Memory experiences the past as still alive and active in the present; history, by contrast, takes a critical and mediated stance toward the past and thus figures it as truly past. The latter is not necessarily more accurate or impartial – or less troubled – but it does imply a theoretical distance between the past event and its analysis in the present.

Lysias' *euthunē* of Eratosthenes, in the course of setting the record straight on the past, subjects it to critical scrutiny and thus engages in a sort of forensic historiography. Trying the past, Lysias insists, requires remembering the evils of the past. But that memory itself requires a historical investigation. "I will try to recall" (*anamnēsai*) everything that happened after the Thirty came to power, he says (5), starting with their "purification" of the city. Theognis and Peison, two of the Thirty, proposed arresting the metics on the grounds that they were hostile to the new regime. "This made a superb pretext (*kallistēn prophasin*) for seeming to take vengeance on them, while really (*tōi d'ergōi*) making some money: the city was in extreme poverty and the regime needed funds" (6). The space between words and deeds, between pretexts and true motives is the terrain of historiography, which attempts to uncover, in Thucydides' words, the "truest motive" (*alēthestatē prophasis*) behind events.[53] Here that historiographical critique is necessitated by the duplicity of the Thirty, who themselves are made cynically to advertise the schism between the ostensible and real motives behind their deeds. Their deceit means that the jurors must differentiate carefully between words and deeds, weighing the one against the other. Eratosthenes' deeds have shown clearly that he did what he did willingly (*hēdomenou*, 32):

> Therefore the jurors must cast their verdict based more on your deeds (*ek tōn ergōn*) than your words (*ek tōn logōn*), and take the actions which they know to have been committed as evidence (*tekmēria*) for the words said at the time (*tōn tote legomenōn*). It is impossible to provide witnesses for the latter, since not only were we not able to be in their presence, but we were not even able to be present in our own homes (*par' hautois*). As a result, men who have committed all evils against the city can say all good things about themselves. (33)

That jurors should attend to a defendant's deeds, not his words, is a commonplace in forensic oratory: deeds, not words, are on trial. But

may provide a measure of critical distance on experience and a basis of responsible action." The distinction I am drawing here between memory and historiography is similar to that LaCapra draws between historical "acting out" and "working through" (205–23). The distinction is useful, I think, even if we accept the claim of Shrimpton 1997: 26–29 that ancient historiography was primarily intended to record collective memory.

[53] Thuc 1.20–23: *alēthestatēn prophasin* occurs at 1.23.6. Thucydides' emphasis on *aitia* and *tekmēria* and his preference for eye-witnesses but recourse to *eikos* (*ta deonta*, 1.22.1) in their absence resonate with Lysias' juridical historiography; cf. the judicial metaphor at Thuc. 1.20.1: *abasanistōs*.

words, as this passage suggests, are key to reconstructing motive and intent and hence the true nature of the deed. In this case, the word is the deed, for one of the questions at issue is whether Eratosthenes spoke against the arrest of the metics and consequently whether he acted voluntarily or at the command of the Thirty. His words, however, pose a historiographical problem. Eratosthenes claims under cross-examination to have opposed the others (25); but in light of his subsequent acts, can the jurors believe his present words about his past words? There were no witnesses to the private conversations or closed-door sessions of the Thirty; thus the words of the past (*tōn tote legomenōn*) must be inferred from later deeds. The jurors must become historians, weighing the evidence (*tekmēria*) of *logoi* against *erga* and of one *logos* against another in order to uncover the *alēthestatē prophasis* behind Eratosthenes' and the Thirty's *kallistē prophasis.*

The past, then, must be interpreted and reconstructed in order to be tried. The evidentiary problems that surround all crimes are compounded here by temporal and spatial distance. The jurors were not present themselves at the scene of the crime or the discussions leading up to it. They were not even in the city at the time, "present in their own homes" (*par' hautois*). Exile separated the demos from their own political history: they were not present as witnesses to all the crimes against them. Thus their relation to their own political past is necessarily mediated and they must approach it critically. They will hear the intricate history of the civil war second-hand, as Lysias brings on witnesses to the Spartan intervention in the Athenian conflict. "You yourselves know these things," he says, "and I don't know that I need to offer witnesses. I will nonetheless, though, since I need a rest from speaking and some of you find it more pleasant (*hēdion*) to hear the same words from as many sources as possible" (61). The jurors, he says, already know the facts but prefer to hear them from others. Lysias contrasts the mediated account of the witness testimony to the visceral memory that exhausts him: his admission that he needs a rest reminds us of the anxiety about his own adequacy to the labor of remembering with which he begins the speech. Remembering induces despair (*athumia*, 3); hearing about the past from others is "more pleasant" (*hēdion*).

The absence of exile is part of the memory of past suffering, and the Athenians' inability to themselves remember all the crimes against them is one of the crimes against them. But Lysias' speech turns their exile from the facts into a critical distance. Moreover, into that epistemological gap he inserts not only witness testimony ("as many sources as possible") but his own historical narrative. His speech reconstructs for the Athenians both what they didn't themselves experience (conversations between the

Thirty, his arrest, things that happened after their exile) and what they did (the meetings of the Ecclesia, the violence of the Thirty). In this way, it presents the Athenian jurors with their own memories in alienated form, in the voice of another and an other, a non-Athenian. By mediating their memory and forcing them to subject it to logical and evidentiary critique, Lysias transforms the jurors from witnesses and victims into historians of their own past.

This is a specifically legal historiography, though. Thucydides' history, for instance, claims to serve a prognostic purpose: when similar circumstances arose in the future (as Thucydides predicted they would, human nature being what it is) readers would at least know what to expect (1.22). Lysias' history, by contrast, is prosecutorial: it aims less to explain causes (*aitia*) than to lay blame (*aitia*). In this sense it is a form of *mnēsikakein*, remembering the past in order to hold it against (*epi-*) someone. It also follows the amnesty's polarizing logic which consigns all evils to oblivion except those perpetrated by the Thirty and Eleven. Eratosthenes apparently conceded in his defense speech that he did kill Polemarchus, but not with his own hand or by his own volition: he was compelled by the other members of the Thirty and was just following orders. Although post-Eichmann audiences recognize the banal evil at work in such a defense, the argument does not present a totally unnuanced notion of historical causality. In acknowledging that agents sometimes act under compulsion and differentiating between various degrees of wrongdoing, it allows for a relatively complex understanding of the historical situation. Lysias, on the other hand, attempts to eliminate any extenuating circumstances or complicating factors. His view of history, even a history as murky as the recent civil war, is polar and absolute: the Thirty are guilty, all other Athenians are innocent.[54] The amnesty's exception clause that allowed *euthunē* even for the Thirty and Eleven (and was probably the basis for this case) is ignored: for Lysias there are no exceptions, and the only relevant question is which group Eratosthenes belonged to, the innocent demos or the guilty oligarchs. For, as he says, the demos can blame the Thirty, but the Thirty cannot blame themselves (29).

For Lysias, history is a lawsuit. On the one side stand the plaintiffs, the demos; on the other, the defendants, the Thirty. In discussing the actions

[54] Wolpert (2002a: 100–18) shows how this polarity, which operates throughout speeches of this period, serves to exonerate and unify the demos even while limiting blame for the civil war to thirty (or at most forty-four) individuals. See also Quillin 2002: 86–87. Nouhaud 1982 excludes this speech from his analysis of the Greek orators' use of history, arguing that Lysias treats the events of 404–402 as current affairs not history (301, 307, 369–76). He judges a properly historical sensibility rare in forensic oratory (55–81).

of the Ten who replaced the Thirty, Lysias delineates this case clearly. The Ten "made war against both sides, the Thirty who had committed all the crimes and you who had suffered all the crimes (*tois te triakonta panta kaka eirgasmenois kai humin panta kaka peponthosi*). And yet it was clear to all that if the Thirty had been justly exiled, you had been so unjustly, and if you had been justly, then they had been unjustly" (57). The Thirty and the demos ("you") are polar and mutually exclusive entities, their polarity articulated in the juridical terms of victim/perpetrator and just/unjust. In this case of Demos v. Thirty there can be no middle ground. As Stephen Usher notes, "Lysias' argument in 57 is rhetorically neat in its antithesis of the two parties, but politically simplistic."[55] This antithesis – more juridical in its structure than political or historical – organizes Lysias' entire historical narrative. Thus even as the case turns the law into a form of historiography, it also turns historiography into a form of legal prosecution.

The complex and overdetermined history of the civil war – the long-standing alienation of the elite within the democracy, the fall-out of the Peloponnesian Wars and Athens' loss of its empire, the intervention of Sparta – is thus reduced to a simple contrast between two sides, which themselves are further reduced to ideological slogans: tyranny vs. democracy. Throughout the speech Lysias paints the Thirty as tyrants, motivated solely by greed (e.g. 14, 20) and driven by "insatiability and shameful love of gain" to commit acts of *hubris* against innocent citizens (19).[56] Eratosthenes is tarred with the same brush: "He killed my brother not because he had been wronged by him personally or had seen him wronging the city, but from eager servitude to his own lawlessness" (23). And so, Lysias concludes, citizens watching this case will see either, if Eratosthenes is condemned, that they will be punished for crimes they commit or, if he is acquitted, that "accomplishing whatever they desire they will become tyrants (*turannoi*) over the city, and if they fail they will still be your equals" (35).

By painting Eratosthenes and the Thirty as tyrants, Lysias 12 preempts serious political analysis. It excludes consideration of the many factors that allowed the Thirty to come to power, any real political program (negative or positive) they sought to implement, and most importantly for this case, the differences among them. The Thirty act as one. The label "tyrant" leaves

[55] Edwards and Usher 1985: 246 *ad* 58.

[56] On tyrannical *hubris*, greed, and insatiability, see Pl. *Rep*. 573a–575d; Xen. *Hieron* 8.10; [Arist.] *Ath. Pol.* 6.3, Arist. *Pol.* 1311a5–6; Balot 2001: 53–55; Wohl 2002: 219–21, 236–49. Even the seemingly anticlimactic finale to the litany of the Thirty's crimes contributes to their depiction as tyrants: "they prevented the marriages of many daughters who were about to be given away" (21), either by impoverishing their fathers or by raping the girls. Corruption of free women and interference in the citizen's domestic autonomy figure prominently in Aristotle's discussion of tyrants.

no room for more moderate oligarchs, who may have tried to temper the excesses of the regime or complied under compulsion.[57] In this way Lysias tries to pull the rug out from under Eratosthenes' defense: Eratosthenes was a member of the Thirty; the Thirty were tyrants; case closed. At the same time, by condemning the Thirty as monolithically tyrannical Lysias can simultaneously exculpate all the other Athenians as wholly and uniformly democratic. In eliminating the possibility of moderate oligarchs the speech also eliminates the possibility of moderate democrats, those who failed to join the democratic resistance or actively fight the Thirty. Those "good men" who withdrew in silence from the Ecclesia rather than vote for the Thirty (75), citizens whose valor consisted in silence and inaction, are redeemed as democratic heroes in the epic struggle between democratic good and tyrannical evil. The complex history of civic division is obliterated by a polarizing legal historiography that paints over the chiaroscuro of remembered evils in the simple black and white of a court case.

This strategy of historical simplification and forensic polarization may explain why Theramenes is such a problem for Lysias. Sections 62–78, nearly 20 percent of the whole speech, are devoted to an assault upon Theramenes, one of the more moderate members of the Thirty put to death by Critias for his opposition to the regime.[58] These sections constitute a trial within the trial (*katēgorō*, 62; *katēgorēmena*, 79). Theramenes is condemned as principally responsible (*aitiōtatos*) for bringing the oligarchic Four Hundred to power in 411 (65) and later cynically betraying them to the democrats (67), for negotiating unfavorable terms of surrender with the Spartans in 405 in order to undermine the democracy (70–71), and for proposing the appointment of the Thirty (73). This long harangue is ostensibly a preemptive answer to a line of defense Eratosthenes plans to take, that he was a friend and follower of Theramenes (62), but its length and vehemence are out of all proportion to that purpose. More generally, the attack on Theramenes eliminates the middle ground on which Eratosthenes

[57] Cf. T. M. Murphy 1989: 46: "Lysias is concerned with political extremes: he simply ignores all the degrees of partisanship – or individuality – that lie between." On the representation of the Thirty in post-amnesty forensic speeches, see further Nouhaud 1982: 301–16; Wolpert 2002a: 120–29. Krentz 1982: 57–68 attempts to reconstruct the positive program of the oligarchs and to identify the political differences among them.

[58] On the purpose and tenor of this digression, see Gernet and Bizos 1955: 157–58; Bizos 1967: 84; Edwards and Usher 1985: 236; T. M. Murphy 1989: 44–45; Edwards 1999: 86; Munn 2000: 303. See also the attack on Theramenes at Lys. 13.9–17. This prosecution of the dead Theramenes is both the democratic trial Theramenes was denied under the Thirty and, since he is unable to defend himself, a repetition of his unjust condemnation by Critias (12.77).

seeks to position himself as a moderate oligarch. It works to maintain the simple juristic dichotomy between a guilty tyranny and an innocent demos by removing the figure who negotiated most prominently between the two. Thus it is little surprise that the digression on Theramenes culminates with the inflammatory rhetoric of tyranny: "Twice he enslaved you, despising what was at hand, desiring what was absent, using the most noble name [i.e. aristocracy] to set himself up as the instructor of most terrible deeds" (78).[59]

A contrast with other historical accounts of Theramenes' career shows precisely how prejudicial Lysias' version is. Xenophon depicts Theramenes as a moderate oligarch who opposed the violent extremism of Critias, including the execution of innocent democrats (*Hell.* 2.3.15–16) and the arrest of the metics (2.3.21–22), and pushed for expansion of the franchise (2.3.17–19). Theramenes emerges as a hero in Xenophon's account (sympathetic as it is to oligarchic principles), an advocate of a just and lawful oligarchic government whose conflict with Critias is the central drama of the narrative (2.3.23–56) and whose unlawful death-sentence represents a tragic turning point in the oligarchic regime: after eliminating this obstacle the Thirty felt they could rule with impunity like tyrants (*hōs exon ēdē autois turannein adeōs*, 2.4.1). Likewise, the fragmentary "Theramenes Papyrus" (*P. Mich.* 5982), in which Theramenes himself defends his peace negotiations with Sparta, may be part of a historical treatise or political pamphlet written to rebut Lysias' negative depiction of the politician.[60]

What in Xenophon (and perhaps the Theramenes Papyrus) is staged as a principled but ultimately unsuccessful political career is depicted in Lysias' history as deliberate malice against the state. Theramenes' failure to broker the favorable peace with Sparta that he had promised, for example, Lysias attributes to his desire to weaken the city: pulling down the Long Walls was his own suggestion, Lysias says, and not a condition demanded by the Spartans (70). Since these negotiations were secret (as Lysias points out, with sinister insinuations that the Theramenes Papyrus tries to refute) there is no way of knowing whether Theramenes betrayed the Athenians or merely took the best terms he could get for the suffering city. But

59 The insatiable desire for what is absent, the reduction of free citizens to slaves, and the disingenuous pretext of aristocracy are all part of the Athenian discourse of tyranny: see Wohl 2002: 184–88, 215–69.

60 There is much debate on the nature and purpose of this text. Andrewes 1970 argues that it is a fourth-century political pamphlet; Merkelbach and Youtie 1968; Henrichs 1968 and Sealey 1975 that it is a historiographical treatise. Peseley 1989 believes it was a later rhetorical study. Other treatments of Theramenes are at [Arist.] *Ath. Pol.* 28.5, 36–37; D.S. 14.3–4, and (for the earlier part of his career) Thuc. 8.89–94. On the debate surrounding Theramenes, see also Usher 1968, Harding 1974.

in Lysias' account complicated political contingencies – decisions made under constrained circumstances with no certainty of their outcome – are transformed into *mens rea*, the criminal intent of a calculating agent. This is historiography in the "paranoid style" and also in a juridical mode, reducing complex situations to the intentional and actionable crimes of individuals.

Through his "damnatio memoriae" of Theramenes,[61] Lysias seeks to damn the memory of any middle ground between the guilty Thirty and the innocent demos. In this speech law writes a reductive and polarizing history, one that seeks to prosecute the past not to explain it, and aims not for nuance and comprehensiveness but clarity and closure. The closure it offers as a result is false, both for the Athenians, who are encouraged to accept comforting simplifications of their political past in place of the more complex understanding that might help them to prevent its recurrence, and for Lysias himself, for whom historiography, far from providing a critical perspective on the past becomes a tool of its repetitive, vindictive remembering. Law would seem to make for bad history and bad therapy for collective trauma, offering not a way of working through the horrific memories of the past but merely another mode of *mnēsikakein*.[62]

And yet if Lysias' polarizing, prosecutorial historiography cannot break free of the horrific memory of past suffering, if it is not yet a vehicle for nuanced understanding of the past, it does perhaps suggest a future path toward a different way of remembering. Merely by subjecting the past to analysis – gathering multiple sources and witnesses, searching for the deeper motives behind ostensible pretexts, and subjecting words to the testimony of deeds – it opens the past to critical debate and in this way eventually to different interpretations. This debate is perhaps anticipated already by the Theramenes Papyrus, if indeed it is an apologetic rebuttal of Lysias 12: not just a raw cry of remembering, Lysias' speech has already become part of a collective discussion and evaluation of the civic past. By prying open a critical space between past and present, Lysias' legal historiography may, for all its own historical distortions, allow the Athenians to work through a past they cannot simply decide to forget.

[61] Edwards and Usher 1985: 250 *ad* 79.

[62] Cook 2004: 431: "law is poorly equipped for historical accounting." Douglas 2004 (cf. 2001: 257–61) discusses the possibilities and limitations of law as a mode of historiography. The debate as to whether a trial can serve the purposes of history and of justice at the same time has focused in particular on the Holocaust trials, following Hannah Arendt's famous assertion, apropos of the Eichmann trial, that "the purpose of a trial is to render justice, and nothing else" (Arendt 1963: 253). See Douglas 2001: 97–182; Felman 2002: 106–66.

Indeed, historiographical reflection may enable the Athenians not only to remember differently but even, eventually, to forget and forgive. In light of its juridical historiography, the speech's closing calls to remember begin to feel like a defensive gesture against a forgetting that, if it hasn't already begun, seems inevitable in the future. In this light, Lysias' *aporia* and *athumia* (3) could be seen as anxiety not about unending recollection but about premature forgetting, as if the reason he must keep speaking about the civil war is that he fears the Athenians will stop speaking about it.[63] His closing imperative – remember evils – thus may be motivated by an imagined future in which *mē mnēsikakein* has already become a psychic reality. From this perspective, memory is an attempt to close a distance from the past that historiography has already created and to reopen a wound historiography promises eventually to heal. Ironically, then, the speech's call to memory evokes not only the traumatic past but also, prospectively, a future in which that past will have finally been forgotten.

Between the double threat of violent repetition and historical rupture, these speeches seek, with varying degrees of success, a way to remember without merely repeating and to forgive without forgetting. From the urgent *kairos* of the trial, they rebuild the law's temporal unity, linking the memory of past crimes to the imagination of a just future via the jurors' present judgment. In this way they repair the temporality not only of the law but also of the polis. Through the amnesty, juridical discourse helped the city work through its recent political crisis by itself becoming the *lieu de mémoire*, in Nora's phrase, for everything the city wanted to forget.[64] It offered the city, as we have seen, a new ground upon which to build a continuous history of civic virtue (in Andocides 1) and a means of gaining some critical distance from the traumatic past (in Lysias 12). Even when the law's need to remember conflicted with the city's need to forget (as was the case in Lysias 13), juridical discourse provided a model for naturalizing the succession of past, present, and future. Civic time became legal time, and legal time biological time. By helping Athens both to remember and to forget the painful past, the law's *alētheia* became the foundation for the city's renewed present and prospective memory of its peaceful future.

The future these cases project is not only the city's, however. It is also the future of juridical discourse itself. For in helping the city write its own history, the forensic speeches of the early fourth century also claimed

63 This would be in keeping with the proposal of Caruth (1996: 64) that the true experience of trauma is not the encounter with death but the fact of survival.

64 Nora 1989: 19. He defines *lieux de mémoire* by the presence not solely of memory but of a will to remember.

a new place for the law in that history. The amnesty is often seen as a key moment of transition in Athenian political history from fifth-century "popular sovereignty" to fourth-century "rule of law."[65] After the political upheaval of the Thirty and the civil war, the polis regrounded itself upon a new foundation of law: the lawcode was revised, the ancestral laws of Solon restored and inscribed on the Stoa Basileios in the democratic center of the city, as if to "show that law was to be supreme in the new democracy."[66] In this historiographical narrative, an exhausted demos reaches out to the law as a life-preserver that will save it from the tumult of its own politics. This chapter has shown how legal discourse itself actively contributes to this flattering narrative by offering itself as the city's salvation. Even as the Athenians were inscribing the written laws in the physical heart of the city, juridical discourse inscribed itself in its psyche, presenting the courts as the new organ of civic memory and seat of political hope for the restored democracy. In the speeches of the early fourth century, law supplements civic history, creating continuity across the civil war's breach; law also supplants civic history, as the memory of legal amnesty replaces the forgotten trauma of civic conflict. That political trauma is subsumed within legal discourse as its own historical past, gone if not entirely forgotten. The future promised is a timeless expanse of justice and *homonoia*. And the democratic present of the polis – an eternal moment from which past and future radiate unbroken – is refounded upon the temporality of the law, laboriously forged between the *amnēsteia* and *alētheia* of legal discourse itself.

[65] See Ostwald 1986: 497–524, especially 509: "it is no exaggeration to say that the reconciliation agreement, including the amnesty, represents a triumph of *nomos*..."

[66] Ostwald 1986: 522. On the placement of the laws and on changes to the agora in response to the oligarchy and civil war see Shear 2007.

CHAPTER 6

Family/law: legal genealogies

> Genealogy does not pretend to go back in time to restore an unbroken continuity that operates beyond the dispersion of forgotten things . . . On the contrary, to follow the complex course of descent is to maintain passing events in their proper dispersion; it is to identify the accidents, the minute deviations – or conversely, the complete reversals – the errors, the false appraisals, and the faulty calculations that gave birth to those things that continue to exist and have value for us; it is to discover that truth or being do not lie at the root of what we know and what we are, but the exteriority of accidents.
>
> Foucault 1977b: 146

> His father, Theopompus, has died, but the laws have not died, nor justice, nor the jurors who cast the vote.
>
> Dem. 43.60

NARRATIVE OF A FAMILY TREE

If in the amnesty cases juridical discourse masters civic time through legal memory, in inheritance cases it controls biological time via familial succession. Through the contested movement of property, inheritance law links the present generation to its dead ancestors and future heirs. In these cases, the law constructs and reproduces a normative family structure. In the process it also reproduces itself, projecting itself into both the past and the future. Inheritance cases are thus about genealogy in two different senses: they record the legitimate reproduction of the *genos* and at the same time write a history of the law.

The extant inheritance speeches (eleven speeches of Isaeus, one of Isocrates, and several by Demosthenes) are a soap opera of family squabbles. Secret mistresses, squandered dowries, estates ruined through neglect, bastards raised as legitimate sons, scheming in-laws, manipulative mothers, suppositious wills – these cases narrate every variety of familial back-biting and in-fighting. In the course of staging these family romances they not only arbitrate property disputes between kin, but define the meaning and limits of kinship and thus both produce and reproduce the Athenian family. One characteristic of inheritance cases is that the *diēgēsis*, the part of the speech that in other cases is devoted to describing the crime and narrating the events leading up to it, in these cases is a description of family relations. The family itself is the legal event (the "crime"?) that the forensic speech must explicate.

Like the crime, the family does not preexist the speech but is its rhetorical product. The Loeb edition of Isaeus' speeches provides a convenient family tree in front of each case. These static snapshots of family relations necessarily simplify the convoluted narratives from which they are derived.[1] They also belie juridical discourse's commitment to such narratives. Sositheus, the speaker in Demosthenes 43 and member of a particularly intricate genealogy, comments on the issue:

> At first I thought I would write out all the relatives of Hagnias on a board, and in this way explain them to you one by one. But since not all the jurors would have an equally good view, and those sitting in the back would be at a disadvantage, it is perhaps necessary to instruct you in a speech (*logōi*), since this is accessible to all. I will try, then, to explain as succinctly as I can the *genos* of Hagnias. (Dem. 43.18)

This speaker can conceptualize his genealogy in schematic form, but he prefers to present it as a narrative (*logōi*). He explains this by oblique reference to the democratic principle of equal access for all the jurors to the facts of the case. But the narrative form also has tactical advantages for him, as it allows him to construct the family as he wants the jury to see it. A family chart might reveal things he does not want to show, like the superior claim of kinsmen he wholly omits from his speech. It would also exclude factors that he presents as crucial to the question of the bequest, like his own superlative behavior and the shamelessness of his opponents. In forensic oratory, family relations are not fixed and static as in a family tree but, as David Cohen puts it, "ambiguous, manipulable, and hence open to interpretation and construction."[2] The *genos* is the product of juridical *logoi*.

[1] On the family tree and its distortion of practice, see Bourdieu 1990: 35. He is skeptical of the objectifying category of "genealogy" (162–99) and stresses the inadequacy of a legalistic understanding of kinship (150–51, 162–63), which he explains instead as a set of strategic practices; cf. R. Thomas 1989: 175–80.

[2] D. Cohen 1995a: 163–80; the quotation is on p. 169. *Genos* in the inheritance cases seems to indicate not a formal "clan" but a loose kinship group, the boundaries and internal relations of which were

These *logoi* are extremely complicated. Bilateral descent and equal partition among sons make for multiple possible claims on any given estate. Endogamy and internal adoption graft the family tree back onto itself; any two individuals can be related in numerous ways. Premature deaths collapse generations unevenly. Affection and other intangibles bring closer individuals who are genealogically further. Gender, too, can warp distances, as the male line inherits before the female. Moreover, each birth, marriage, and death shifts the entire web of relations. So Sositheus, claiming Hagnias' estate for his son, remarks that he had accepted the award of the estate to his opponent's father until he himself had a son whose adoption by the testator's first cousin gave him, he argues, a stronger claim. "When this boy was born it seemed to be a moment of opportunity (*kairos*)" (Dem. 43.11). All claims are provisional and competitive: one man's claim is only as strong, and strong for as long, as another's is weak, and each birth or death changes everything. Inheritance cases are thus part of an ongoing and contested negotiation of the shape and extent of the family tree.

Of course, not every transmission of property ended up in court, and in the normal course of things most families probably got along fine without the intervention of the law. Many successions must have been unproblematic, either because the testator left natural-born legitimate sons or because he clearly indicated his wishes and his family honored them. There was a strong sense (expressed often in the speeches as a rebuke to the opponent) that family quarrels should be resolved within the family, and it appears that this pressure led to extensive use of arbitration as a means of avoiding the embarrassment of a feud in the public courts.[3] No doubt the speeches we have represent extreme cases, where arbitration or other informal modes of negotiation had failed. But presumably the sorts of argument one would use before a family arbitrator would be similar in kind (if perhaps different in pitch) to those one used in court. If so, then arbitration marks not the limit of the law's influence over the family, but precisely its extent, as the family tries itself and reaches its own verdict in a proto-juridical proceeding.[4] Moreover, the very decision to claim or not to claim an estate was a juridical decision, based on viewing family relations through the lens of inheritance law. In a sense, then, once inheritance claims could be argued in court they always were, figuratively, argued in

under constant negotiation. See Bourriot 1976: 199–235, 1367–81; Lambert 1993: 59–74; Patterson 1998: 78.

[3] See, e.g., Is. 1.5–7; Humphreys 1983: 6–7; Hunter 1994: 55–67; Scafuro 1997: 117–41; Christ 1998a: 168–73.

[4] Scafuro 1997: 25–67, 279–326.

court and every succession – even those in which relatives chose not to litigate – reproduced the family as a legal entity, a structure that always could be (and on occasion had to be) presented in the form of a forensic *logos*.[5]

The leitmotif of the forensic family narrative is legitimacy: the legitimacy of marriages and of children, and hence of legal relations to the *oikos* and legal claims on the estate. Like the family itself, "legitimacy" is produced in the course of these speeches; it is not a pre-defined external standard that they merely apply. Indeed, legitimacy is a surprisingly slippery legal category. First, the Athenians kept virtually no official documents relating to the family. There were no birth certificates. Fathers took an oath in their phratry attesting that their newborn son (and perhaps daughter) was *gnēsios*, natural-born of legal wedlock (*enguē*). The child was probably then entered into the phratry register, on the basis of which he would at eighteen become eligible (after a public hearing) for admission into a deme and full-fledged citizenship.[6] But it is not clear that it was legally required for all legitimate children to be registered at the phratry level, and the phratry lists are never introduced in these cases as hard evidence for or against legitimacy. In fact, their existence is barely even acknowledged in the many instances where accusations of fraudulent registration are lodged or denied.[7] For forensic purposes, a written registry may as well not exist. Instead litigants rely upon witnesses (relatives or phratry members) whose testimony is rarely impartial and can usually be countered by equal testimony on the other side.[8]

One reason phratry membership was contestable is that it rested on a prior uncertainty, the legitimate marriage of the child's parents. This

[5] For this reason I make no attempt to measure forensic representations of the family against the realities of social practice in contemporary Athens. Even if we could reconstruct practice independent of the legal evidence and use it to identify the distortions of that evidence, my point is that family relations are always shaped by the law even when they don't end up in court. As we shall see, the extra-juridical ("natural") family is itself a juridical construct.

[6] W. K. Lacey 1968: 97; Lambert 1993: 35–40, 161–89; Ogden 1996: 110–15. But even this minimal form of certification is contested; so Scafuro 1994: 156: "It is a well-known phenomenon of Attic life that no central or local archive preserved a written record of the births of polis inhabitants." The phratry oath is cited at *IG* II^2 1237.109–11 (on which see Lambert 1993: 285–93); Is. 7.16, 8.19; Dem. 57.54. On the lengthy process by which a father legally recognized his son, see Rudhardt 1962: 56–60; W. K. Lacey 1968: 111–12; Scafuro 1994: 158–65; Ogden 1996: 83–135. That deme registers were similarly problematic is suggested by the mid-fourth century proposal to reexamine all the citizen rolls: see D. Cohen 2003: 82.

[7] See especially Dem. 39, 59; Is. 6. The only explicit references to a written phratry registry I have found are at Is. 7.13, 17, 43 and involve an adopted son.

[8] Witnesses to enrollment in the phratry are called at Is. 2.14–17, 3.75–76, 7.17, 8.9. See Scafuro 1994, 1997: 42–50; D. Cohen 1995a: 166, 170, 174; 2003, and on the role of witnesses in Athenian courts more generally, Humphreys 1985b.

was, if anything, even harder to verify. A legal marriage in Athens was marked by an *enguē*, an agreement between the husband and the bride's guardian (usually her father or brother), and was generally accompanied by a dowry.[9] There was no marriage certificate; instead, speakers had to rely on witnesses who were present at the *enguē* or at the various rituals normally performed by newly married couples. But these rituals too, while customary, were not mandatory; nor was a dowry. Even if reliable witnesses to a ceremony might support the claim for a legitimate marriage, the lack of witnesses or the non-performance of the rituals did not prove that there was no marriage (although this is frequently asserted). In the absence of records, litigants must often resort to gossip about unions that took place (or didn't) decades earlier. Virtually no marriage, and hence no child, was impervious to malicious imputations.[10]

Not only are legitimate unions and children hard to document in Athens, but the very laws governing legitimacy are ambiguous and contradictory, as we will see. The law of succession, for instance, is frequently referred to in Athenian inheritance cases, but its relatively detailed prescriptions apparently did little to prevent legal squabbling over who was next of kin or the comparative priority of linear and collateral descendants. Even Pericles' Citizenship Law (passed in 451/0 and reinstated in 403/2), the single most important law concerning citizenship, specifies that citizens must be born of two citizen parents but fails to state whether those parents must be legally married. As a result, scholars are divided on some of the most fundamental questions of Athenian family structure: whether the child of two unmarried Athenian parents was a citizen, for instance, or even what counts as a bastard.[11]

The author of the *Athenaion Politeia* believes that Solon made his laws deliberately unclear so that judgments would have to be referred to the demos, and he offers the laws on inheritance and heiresses as an example (*Ath. Pol.* 9). Presumably the Athenians could have kept archives of births

9 On the practice of *enguē*, see Wyse 1904: 289–93; Wolff 1944: 51–53; Harrison 1968: 3–9; W. K. Lacey 1968: 105–06; Sealey 1984a: 120–22, 1990: 25–36; Just 1989: 40–75; Vernant 1990: 55–56; Todd 1993: 211–14; Lape 2002–03: 120–22.

10 On the means and difficulty of verifying the legitimacy of a marriage, see Harrison 1968: 17–21; Just 1989: 47–50; Cox 1989: 43–44, 1998: 178–89; Vernant 1990: 55–59; Scafuro 1994: 162–64; Ogden 1996: 84–88; Patterson 1998: 108–12; Lape 2004: 149. I return to this problem at length below. On the importance of gossip and its relation to the law see Hunter 1990, 1994: 96–119; Wolpert 2001.

11 Wolff 1944: 75–85; Harrison 1968: 61–68; Humphreys 1974; Rhodes 1978; Just 1989: 55–62; Sealey 1990: 12–19; Patterson 1990, 2005: 278–89; Mossé 1991: 274–77; Ogden 1996: 37–44, 59–69, 151–65; Lape 2004: 6 (and n. 18) believe that children of two unmarried Athenian parents were not citizens; MacDowell 1976a, 1978: 68 and Sealey 1984a, 1990: 33–36 that they were. See further Ar. *Aves* 1656–70; Dem. 43.51; Just 1989: 50–55; Boegehold 1994; Kapparis 1999: 10–13.

and marriages had they wished (as they did, for instance, lists of magistrates) or at least made greater use in court of the documents they did have: registry lists could presumably have been read out to the jurors, as laws often were. Legislation could have been composed so as to eliminate ambiguity: Pericles' Citizenship Law could have explicitly stipulated birth from the legitimate marriage of citizen parents (as phratry oaths did). Although it is hard to say why the Athenians chose to leave such vital issues so ill defined, one effect is that, as the *Ath. Pol.* suggests, questions not clarified in the statutes were decided in the courts. In the absence of an undisputed living male head (*kurios*), the democratic jury became sovereign (*kurios*) over the private household, legally empowered to dispose of the property of these elite families as it thought best (Dem. 43.81, 44.43; Is. 2.47, 5.37, 6.4). The *oikos*, always a matter of public interest, was brought under the control of the democratic polis as the demos settled the questions of genealogical legitimacy that in turn determined the legitimacy of the Athenian body politic, which was itself imagined as the aggregate of its *oikoi*.[12]

But the demos and the city are not the only beneficiaries of vague inheritance laws. Juridical discourse itself benefits, flourishing in the cracks of illegitimacy opened by the law's ambiguities. The inheritance cases conceive of the family as a natural structure at constant risk of failure. They operate against a backdrop of potential familial catastrophe in which fathers fail to have sons, bastards insinuate themselves into the bosom of the family, wills are forged, and the *oikos* is ultimately obliterated, with no one left to carry on its name or perform its rituals. The only way to avoid these dire eventualities, the speakers suggest, is to take the matter to court: what legislation failed to prevent litigation will rectify after the fact. In this way legal discourse justifies its own incursion into the *genos* and extends its reach to matters not only of property but of life and death. It constitutes itself as something like a bio-power, a power "situated and exercised at the level of life, the species, the race, and the large-scale phenomena of population."[13]

[12] Inheritance law thus conforms to the broader social dynamic that Josiah Ober identifies in Athenian law, by which the elite were brought under the ideological control of the demos (1989a, esp. 248–70, 293–339). Speakers often defend their familial claim by pointing to their civic virtues, referring to their past record as liturgists and promising that, if they are awarded the estate, they will spend it on the city (while their opponent will squander it). See, e.g., Is. 5.34–47, 7.34–42; Hardcastle 1980: 19–22. Although citizenship per se is rarely directly at stake in these cases (but see, e.g., Is. 8.43–44), it is often a possible implication of the verdict. On the imbrication of kinship and citizen status, see Is. 12; Dem. 57, 59; Davies 1977–78; Patterson 1990: 54–63, 1994, 2005: 281–83; Lape 2002–03, 2004: 68–109.

[13] Foucault 1978: 137.

This chapter examines how the inheritance speeches produce and reproduce the family as a structure always in potential crisis and requiring juridical *krisis*, a jury verdict. The crisis is particularly intense at two stress points of genealogical reproduction: the will and the woman. These are two crucial means of transmitting legitimacy from one generation to the next, but each also introduces the possibility of illegitimacy. The will insures continuity between past and present. But wills can be forged. When a will is contested (as it often is), legal discourse itself becomes the source of that continuity, as speakers reject the written letter of the testament in favor of the living intent behind it, an intent that only the jurors can reanimate. If the will grants legal discourse a hold over the past and the dead, the woman extends its reach into the future. As wife and mother, the woman's legitimacy is key to many of these cases, but her status is extremely hard to determine. Is she a wife, a mistress, or something even worse? Individual litigants need decisive answers to this question and provide them in the form of vivid fictions. Juridical discourse as a whole, however, leaves the question of the woman open precisely so that it can be answered in court: it requires a woman's status to be indeterminate and perpetuates itself by simultaneously producing and resolving indeterminacy around the character of the female. But this institutionalized indeterminacy also means that the female resists discursive overdetermination: an object of juridical inscription, she is also a potential site of alternate fictions, narratives that blur the polarity between legitimacy and illegitimacy and the genealogies, familial and juridical, built upon it.

The questions this chapter asks about the family are thus not primarily anthropological or sociological.[14] These texts are, to be sure, a treasure trove of information concerning social and familial norms in Athens and the logic of the practices of Athenian kinship. But these cases also show legal discourse going about the business of its own reproduction: discourse, too, has a practical logic and its own reproductive strategies. Narrating a family romance in which genealogical legitimacy is always open to contest, legal discourse inserts itself into the reproduction of the *genos*. It referees conflicts in which it is itself hardly neutral – conflicts between *nomos* and *phusis*, wife and mistress, heir and bastard – and tells a story in which it itself is a character. In the process it writes its own genealogy, a history of its institutional power as the living will of the past and perpetual hope for the future. This history lacks the clear origin and linear directionality

[14] There is, of course, a vast body of anthropological work on genealogy and inheritance. See, for instance, Goody 1962: 273–357, 1969: 120–46, 1976, and for the Athenian context Humphreys 1986; Cox 1998.

of a succession myth; it does not start with a first ancestor and proceed naturally from father to son. Instead, it produces family trees twisted with graftings and tangled overgrowth. Legal discourse does not aim to prune these genealogies but to promote their chaotic fertility and in this way to constitute itself as the essential nutrient without which they would die. Thus the legal genealogy written in the inheritance cases serves to reproduce law's power not by consolidating it at the start but by dispersing it over myriad impromptu interventions, provisional responses to the constant local breakdowns of a family structure defined – or rather ill defined – so as to require such intervention. The result is an institutional power less unitary but no less effective, as the law insinuates itself into the very lifeline of the polis.[15]

LAW'S FULL HOUSE

Every unhappy family, as Tolstoy said, is unhappy in its own way. The inheritance cases tell of particularly unhappy families and of the family in general as an infelicitous structure. Ideally, the *oikos* passes from the father to his natural-born legitimate (*gnēsios*) son in a smooth and endless succession.[16] These cases exist because that succession has failed. In practice, such failure may have been a rare misfortune, the exception that proved the rule. But within forensic oratory, it is the rule. There failure is not an unhappy contingency but a structural feature of kinship. Luckily, law is on the scene, ready to lend a hand.

Succession of father by son is represented in inheritance speeches as natural and incontestable, a relationship exterior and prior to the law. Men who had *gnēsioi* sons were barred by law from adopting another heir or bequeathing substantial property to anyone else. Indeed, in this situation the estate did not even come to trial; it was termed *anepidikos*, not adjudicable.[17] Rhetorically, as well as legally, father–son transmission was granted special priority. The speaker of Isaeus 3 refers to the legal sanctity

[15] Contrast Goodrich 1990a: 108–10, who sees legal genealogy (in early English law) as the theocratic reaffirmation of an authorizing origin. On genealogical history, see Foucault 1977b (including the epigram to this chapter) and Foucault 1994 for a genealogy of juridical forms and their productive relation to power and truth. Legendre 1974, 1985 and Goodrich 1995 are stimulating genealogical histories of law with emphasis on its strategies of institutional reproduction: see Goodrich 1990a: 281–93, 1995: 22–30 for exposition of the methodology.

[16] On the meaning of *gnēsios*, see Patterson 1990: 41–42; Ogden 1996: 17–18. This word, like all familial vocabulary, is imprecise, indicating both legitimacy (as opposed to *notheia*) and natural birth (as opposed to adoption).

[17] Harrison 1968: 156–58; Todd 1993: 220–21.

of the *anepidikos* inheritance of natural-born children (*gnēsioi paides*); concerning these, he comments, "no argument need be made" (*oudena logon lekhthēnai dei*, 3.59). In these cases' elaborate rhetorical construction of *genos* the automatic inheritance of a natural son is represented as unconstructed by and, in fact, alien to juridical *logos*. The speaker of Isaeus 8 presents this notion as universally accepted (*homologoumena*): "for all of you inherited the estates of your father and your grandfather and those still further back, receiving them by birth through the incontestable (*anepidikon*) right of familial succession" (8.34). Ideally, son replaces father in a straight and endless line of natural reproduction.

This natural succession is the structural core of the *oikos*, which in turn is the core of each inheritance speech. The *oikos* – the household, headed by the male *kurios* and including his legitimate wife, their children, slaves, and whatever extended family happen to live with them – is represented in the inheritance speeches as the physical and emotional focus of family life.[18] It is a symbolic center-point from which kinship radiates in concentric circles to the outer edges of *genos* (where outliers are said to be "outside of kinship," *exō tēs sungeneias*, Is. 11.3). The speeches describe the competing forces of centrifugality and centripedality that buffet the *oikos*: its dispersion with married daughters and the division of property among brothers, its reconsolidation through endogamous marriages and adoptions. Amidst this ebb and flow, the *oikos* persists through the succession of father by son. This lineage prevents the *oikos* from becoming extinct or, in the Athenian idiom, "empty" (*exerēmōthēnai*).[19] It is the law's job to keep the house full.

Emptiness menaces the family. Freud, in his juridical origin myth, postulated that law was first instituted to compensate for the death of the father, murdered by his sons in an Oedipal rage.[20] But in Athenian inheritance cases it is the death or lack not of the father but of a son that demands legal intervention. In the absence of a *gnēsios* son, the estate became adjudicable and the family became an object of law. At that point, there were two main legal claims to an estate: *kata genos* (on the basis of birth or kinship), supported by the law of *ankhisteia*, succession by next of kin; and *kata dosin* (on the basis of "gift," meaning a bequest or adoption), supported by testamentary law. Although in practice these two legal arguments could be combined (as testators tended to bequeath property to their next of kin),

[18] On the *oikos* in Athenian law see W. K. Lacey 1968: 15–32; Foxhall 1989; Todd 1993: 204–10; Patterson 1994; Cox 1998: 130–67; Roy 1999; and MacDowell 1989, who believes that the *oikos* was not legally significant, despite its rhetorical importance in family court cases.

[19] E.g. Is. 1.44; 2.15, 35, 43; 7.30, 31, 43, 44. See further MacDowell 1989: 15–17.

[20] Freud 1955 [1913]: 140–61.

rhetorically the speeches present them as alternatives. The formulation at Isaeus 1.3 is typical: "my opponents rely upon the will . . . but we rely on *genos*." The cases thus often play out as a legal *agōn* between birth and gift, *genos* and *dosis*. This is not a fair fight, though, for even as the speeches seem to prioritize *genos* and the claims of blood, they show that the *oikos* requires the gift of life that only law can give. In the speeches' contest of *nomos* and *phusis*, it is *nomos* that ultimately holds the full house, as legal discourse deals itself a winning hand.

Litigation *kata genos* was based on the law of *ankhisteia*, which stipulated that the property of a man who died intestate without legitimate sons went first to the father's brothers, his sons, and descendants on the father's side as far as the children of cousins, then to the mother's side in the same order.[21] This law is often cited as though it were obvious and incontrovertible.[22] The speaker in Isaeus 4, for instance, develops an extended contrast between wills and *ankhisteia*: with the former it is hard to verify whether the testator left a will and whether he was of sound mind when he did so. "You see, then, what a task it is to perceive if those claiming *kata dosin* are telling the truth" (15). Those claiming *kata genos*, by contrast, don't need witnesses – "for it is universally accepted (*para pantōn gar hōmologētai*) that the property of the dead goes to his closest kin" (15) – nor do they need to prove that the testator was of sound mind in order to claim the estate (16). Speakers also seek to support the claims of *genos* by equating it with the natural succession from father to son, which (unlike *genos*) really was "universally accepted." So the speaker who in Isaeus 8 reminded the jurors that "all of you inherited the estates of your father and your grandfather and those still further back" evokes this timeless patrilineal succession in order to support the "incontestable right of familial succession" (*tēn ankhisteian anepidikon*, 34), as if *ankhisteia* made an estate *anepidikon* in the same way that a direct heir did. Legally this is not true, but rhetorically it has the effect (or so speakers hope) of assigning all blood relations, however remote, to the category of *phusis* and granting them the privileged status of the father–son blood bond.

But despite these litigants' self-interested attempt to represent *ankhisteia* as natural and indisputable, it like everything else was open to rhetorical manipulation. The case of the estate of Hagnias (Dem. 43 and Is. 11), the only one in which we hear from both sides (in successive generations),

[21] Dem. 43.51; cf. Is. 7.20–22 and Wyse 1904: 564–69 ad loc.

[22] [Arist.] *Prob.* 950b5–8: "Why in some lawcourts will the jurors vote in favor of kinship (*tois genesi*) rather than the will (*tais diathēkais*)? Because it is impossible to lie about family relations, but the truth is revealed. But many wills have also been proven to be false."

offers a clear illustration. Sositheus in Demosthenes 43 quotes the law of *ankhisteia* and concludes that it expressly (*diarrhēdēn*) gives Hagnias' estate to his son: "This is what the law says and this is what is just" (Dem. 43.52). Theopompus, the father of Sositheus' opponent, appealed to the same principle and cited the same law in laying his own claim to Hagnias' estate (Is. 11.1–3). He, too, claimed that the law is obvious and "reveals the intent of the lawmaker" (11.3). Theopompus' whole case in fact depends on a tendentious reading of the law of *ankhisteia*: the law stipulates the order of succession down to the children of first cousins but he argues that this means the first cousin of the deceased's father, which would include himself (11.10–13).[23] Speakers may attempt to naturalize *genos* as an extension of linear succession and to grant it the status of *phusis*. But this case shows that *genos*, based as it is on the law of *ankhisteia*, is a thoroughly legal category, the "natural" definition of which must be hashed out in court.[24]

Moreover, despite speakers' attempts to equate *ankhisteia* with the linear succession of the *oikos*, the two in fact represent quite different and often competing interests. Without a rule of primogeniture, a kin group could contain a number of separate *oikoi*, as the estate of Hagnias illustrates: there the five sons of the progenitor Buselus become *kurioi* of five different *oikoi*, of which the members of one (Theopompus and Macartatus) sue for the property of another (Hagnias). "Do not allow this *oikos* to be left empty by these foul beasts," cries the speaker in Demosthenes 43, "who belonged to the house of Stratius and were never part of the house of Hagnias" (83). A first cousin might be related by blood, but could he be counted on to tend to the interests and rituals of the testator's *oikos* and neglect his own? The speaker in Isaeus 2, an adopted son, argues that while he always acted like a natural-born son (*hōsper gonōi onta*, 18) to the testator, nursing him when he was sick and burying him with all due rituals when he died, his opponent, the testator's own brother, robbed him during his life and now that he is dead tries to deprive him of his heir, his name, and the posthumous honor of his ancestral cults (37, 46). By challenging the speaker's adoption, he is trying to "empty" his brother's *oikos* to the benefit

[23] It is appropriate, then, that Theopompus speaks of "being-next-of-kin" (*ankhisteuein*, 11.11): for him *ankhisteia* is a verb. This complicated family is examined by Davies 1971: 77–89; Thompson 1976; Cox 1998: 3–10. On the law of *ankhisteia*, see further Wyse 1904: 680; Harrison 1968: 130–49; Thompson 1970; Just 1989: 85–89; Hunter 1993: 101–2; Todd 1993: 217–18; D. Cohen 1995a: 175–79. Wyse's comment on the law's ambiguous phrasing is apt: "What is the use of a limit that is in perpetual motion?" (1904: 566).

[24] So the speaker in Isaeus 4 argues that while claims *kata dosin* are impossible to verify, claims *kata genos* are self-evident because the jurors can rely on their own experience (*di' humōn autōn*, 17). That experience, it turns out, is not belonging to a *genos*, though, but writing laws: "for kinsmen litigate on the basis of laws that you wrote" (17).

of his own (15, 35). Such charges apparently often hit their mark: those claiming an estate *kata genos* go out of their way to prove that they will use the estate to protect the interests of the testator's *oikos* (e.g. Is. 9.27–33). In this way, they acknowledge that kinship in itself does not guarantee preservation of the *oikos*. Blood may be thick but it is not in itself thick enough to keep the *oikos* "full."

Claims *kata dosin* are presented as a remedy to precisely this problem: the law, they promise, will secure what *genos* alone cannot. *Dosis* indicated inheritance by will or adoption, the two being virtually interchangeable. Solon's testamentary law, which allowed any man "to dispose of his own property however he wishes, unless he has *gnēsioi* sons" (Dem. 46.14), is the legal basis for adoption, and Louis Gernet argues that it was in fact the purpose of the law to enable a man without natural-born sons to adopt an heir.[25] Adoption repaired the linear succession by "making" a son (*eispoiein* is the verb) where nature failed to provide one.[26] An adoptive son was "made" (*poiētos*) not born, but frequently was made from genetically related material: often the adoptee was a collateral relative, in which case adoption reverses the centrifugal pull of *ankhisteia* by turning a cousin or nephew into a son to fill the empty patriline. Like the law of *ankhisteia*, the testamentary law is frequently cited in the inheritance speeches and it, too, is treated as universally authoritative. "All men, Greeks and barbarians alike, approve this law of adoption and therefore all make use of it" (Is. 2.24). "The law that supports wills is approved by all Greeks; this is proven by the fact that although they disagree on many other things, they concur on this" (Isoc. 19.50–51). But despite the claims of speakers, this legal principle, too, like *ankhisteia*, was open to interpretation: by one reckoning eleven of the seventeen adoptions recorded in extant oratory are contested.[27]

Another way in which Athenian inheritance law attempted to preserve the *oikos* against the centrifugal pull of *ankhisteia* was through the peculiar institution of the epiclerate. The law of *ankhisteia* specifies that rules of succession come into effect if a man dies intestate leaving no female children, for if he has daughters the property goes "with them" (*sun tautēisin*,

[25] Gernet 1955: 121–49; cf. Thompson 1981; Todd 1993: 222. All adoptees were legitimate: a man was not allowed to adopt his bastard sons. On the practice and law of adoption see further Is. 2.13 and Wyse 1904: 248–49 *ad* Is. 2.13, 341 *ad* Is. 3.60; Plut. *Solon* 21.3–4; Harrison 1968: 82–96; W. K. Lacey 1968: 88–90, 131–37; Todd 1993: 221–25; Cox 1998: 125–28, 148–51, and especially Rubinstein 1993, who includes a catalogue of all attested fourth-century adoptions.

[26] *Poiēsis* is contrasted to *phusis* at Is. 2.11, 6.28, 7.16. Rudhardt 1962: 53–65 discusses the term *poiēsis*, which he takes to refer to paternal recognition, not solely adoption; Greek generally uses *eispoiein* to specify adoption.

[27] Hunter 1993: 106.

Dem. 43.51). A woman in this position, the legitimate daughter of a man who died intestate without sons, was called an *epiklēros*. This is often translated as "heiress," but that is something of a misnomer, for the father did not leave his property to her (women did not inherit directly) but instead through her to the posthumous grandsons he hoped she would bear him. The property was held in suspension by an imagined lineal succession from grandfather to hoped-for grandson.[28] The law stipulated that the *epiklēros* was to marry her nearest agnatic relative (according to the same order of *ankhisteia*) and that whoever was awarded the estate must also either dower or himself marry an *epiklēros* attached to it, even if that meant he had to divorce his wife and she her husband. In this way the epiclerate, like adoption, worked to shore up the *oikos* and its ideal of natural lineal succession by choosing one of the collateral kin in effect to father a grandson for the dead father. In practice an *epiklēros* was often claimed by her father's adopted heir, who worked like a legal stent in the broken bloodline, standing in for the father long enough to produce the natural-born heir he himself had died before having.[29]

The "gift" at issue in claims *kata dosin* is thus both the testator's to his (immediate or eventual) heirs and the law's gift of life to an *oikos* facing the risk of extinction. The testator in Isaeus 7, Apollodorus, had a beloved natural son whom he always expected to succeed him. When the son died Apollodorus, in despair (*athumēsas*), adopted the speaker (14). All men, the speaker says, take precautions to prevent their houses from becoming empty (*exerēmōntai*) and to ensure that there will be someone to perform the rituals for them after death. This is the reason they adopt heirs. "And not only do they make this decision for their own private interest, but the commonwealth of the polis makes the same decision in the public interest. For by law (*nomōi*) it commands the magistrates see to it that *oikoi* not become empty" (30). Apollodorus knew, the speaker says, that if he left his estate to his first cousins, the other litigants in this suit, they "would make his house empty" (31) and this is why he adopted the speaker, even

28 A law that the husband must have intercourse with an *epiklēros* three times a month was presumably intended to secure this succession: see Plut. *Solon* 20.2–3. Plutarch further comments that if the husband was unable to have sex with her, she could have recourse to his next of kin in order to obtain sons, but we know of no instance in which this actually occurred.

29 On the epiclerate, see Is. 10.12–13; Gernet 1921; Harrison 1968: 132–38; W. K. Lacey 1968: 24, 89–90, 139–45; Schaps 1975, 1979: 25–47; Lane Fox 1985: 225–27; Just 1989: 95–98; Katz 1992a; Rubinstein 1993: 88–104; Todd 1993: 228–31; Scafuro 1997: 281–305; Cox 1998: 94–99; Patterson 1998: 91–106. Katz 1992a: 698: "it makes sense to regard the epiclerate as an extraordinary remedy for the threatened extinction of an *oikos*." She notes the strong endogamous impulse at work in the institution, as well as an incestuous logic that requires the daughter to provide an heir for her dead father.

though he was more distant by *ankhisteia*. The polis perpetuates the *oikos* when the *genos* fails to, this speaker asserts, and it does so through the law of adoption.[30]

Isaeus 2 makes a similar argument in favor of *dosis*. Menecles was childless. In order that he might have someone to care for him in old age, bury him when he died, and perform the customary rituals after his death, he adopted a son (10). This son, the speaker, cites Solon's testamentary law in support of his adoption:

> I want now to show you that the adoption was lawful (*kata tous nomous*). Read for me the law that allows a man to dispose of his own property however he wishes, if he does not have natural-born legitimate sons. Jurors, the lawmaker established this law in this way because he saw that this was the only refuge against desolation (*kataphugēn . . . tēs erēmias*) and only comfort in life (*parapsukhēn tou biou*) for people without children, to be able to adopt whomever they want. (2.13)

The speaker waxes poetic in his attempt to elicit from the jurors the same sympathy for the plight of the childless that he claims the lawmaker himself felt. Adoption in this case is not only the city's remedy but the law's charity, the *dosis* of a son in place of the child longed-for but never born. It is the lawmaker's paternal empathy for the desolation (*erēmias*, literally "emptiness") of old age – an empathy, he notes bitterly, that his opponent obviously does not share (23–26). The speaker of Isocrates 19 puts the same idea succinctly: support the law that enables men to adopt, he tells the jurors, "bearing in mind that this is what we who are childless [literally, 'empty'] have in place of children" (*tois erēmois tōn anthrōpōn anti paidōn houtos estin*, 19.49). The law not only provides a substitute for natural children; it is itself that substitute. *Nomos*, not *phusis*, keeps the *oikos* full.

Legal discourse thus stages a contest between *genos* and *dosis* but the deck is always loaded. First, although speakers try to align kinship with *phusis*, it is as much a product of *nomos* as is adoption. Not only is the category of *ankhisteia* sustained by law, as we have seen, but so too is the sanctified relation between father and son. Juridical discourse represents this relation as beyond the reach of law (*anepidikon*) but *anepidikon* itself is, of course, a legal status, defined and protected by law: the non-adjudicable status of an estate must be adjudicated by the court (e.g. Is. 6.4). Likewise, although "natural-born legitimate children" inherit without legal interference, they

[30] Rubinstein 1993: 104–12 argues against taking these claims at face value: she shows that the polis did not intervene to prevent the extinction of an *oikos* and that "adoption was seen as a purely individual concern and not as the concern of the entire community" (115).

are often forced to define and defend that status in court.[31] *Phusis* itself is a matter of *nomos*.

Further, even as they set the two in opposition, the inheritance speeches suggest that "natural" reproduction is always in need of legal support. Fathers fail to produce sons; the next of kin fail to guarantee the future of the *oikos*. Law must "make" an heir to refill an *oikos* at constant risk of emptiness. Thus claimants *kata dosin* and *kata genos* alike ultimately appeal to the jurors to save the *oikos* from extinction. "Support the laws and take care for the dead, that their house may not become empty" (Dem. 43.84). "After you have cast your vote, adopt a son for the dead man from among us, his nearest kin, so that the house will not be empty" (Dem. 44.43). By their correct decision, the jurors will preserve the lineage that the patriarch himself failed to perpetuate and apply the remedy of law to the hazards of natural reproduction. If juridical discourse gives *phusis* priority, then, it is partly in order to let it fail so that *nomos* can intervene.

My opponent complains that he is being forced to defend his claim because his father has died, says the speaker in Demosthenes 43. But he forgets that his father was a mortal man. "His father, Theopompus, has died, but the laws have not died, nor justice, nor the jurors who cast the vote" (60). Mortality is the condition of familial reproduction: fathers die, leaving contested property; sons die, leaving the *oikos* empty. The laws, however, are immortal and with their help the *oikos*, too, can live forever. Thus whoever wins the estate in any given case – adopted heir or next of kin – the real winner is always legal discourse itself, which reproduces itself as the surest means of reproducing the full and living *oikos*.

LIVING WILL (ISAEUS 1)

Inheritance proceedings belong to the living but they are haunted by the ghostly presence of the dead. What did the testator intend? What would he want? Whose claim would he support? These are among the questions raised but not clearly answered by the will. The will (*diathēkē, diathēkai*) is a mode of communication between living and dead, but it is recognized to be problematic, difficult to read, much less to trust. An opaque record of the wishes and motives of the dead man, the will demands imaginative interpretation in order to be legible in the present. Speakers call upon the

[31] See, e.g., Is. 6.28. Likewise, the same speaker who claimed that "concerning natural-born children (*gnēsioi paides*) no argument need be made" (Is. 3.59) is arguing a case in which precisely the definition of both *gnēsioi* and *paides* is contested. What reads like a statement of universal principle may in fact be an attempt to muddy the legal waters.

jurors to supply that interpretation, reaching back over the barrier of death to recover the true intent of the testator, the will behind the will. In the process, these cases not only repair a patriline broken by death and fill a bereft *oikos* with the reanimated presence of the deceased patriarch. They also make the law the embodiment of that presence, its posthumous body and living will. In this way, legal discourse secures the genealogy of both the family and the law itself, extending their lifespan into the future by extending it into the past.

Inheritance cases are often represented as posthumous legal actions, the dead man overseeing his interests from beyond the grave. The dead are imagined to want essentially two things: to ensure that the proper rituals (*ta nomizomena*) are performed for them after their death and to guarantee the perpetuation of their *oikos*.[32] The speaker in Isaeus 7 generalizes: "everyone who is about to die makes provision (*pronoian*) for his property so that his house won't be left empty and there will be someone to sacrifice and perform all the customary rites for him" (7.30). In the absence of an undisputed heir, the law becomes the instrument for fulfilling the dead man's *pronoia* and posthumously securing his wishes. Many of the speeches revolve around the question of which litigant would be the better executor, but it is ultimately the jury, the speakers suggest, who must complete the dead man's intended action and "ratify the intent" of the dead (*epikurōsēte tēn gnōmēn*, Is. 7.42). So the speaker of Isaeus 2 ends his appeal by begging the jurors not to invalidate the wishes of the dead man: "since the matter has come before you and you have the authority (*kurioi gegonate*), help me and the dead man in Hades, and do not allow him – I pray you by the gods and spirits – to be insulted by my opponents!" (2.47). The authority of the dead *kurios* is executed and perpetuated in the authoritative (*kurios*) vote of the jurors.

Calling upon the jurors to enact the will of the dead, the speakers also cast the case as a retroactive action upon the dead. Speakers who are adopted sons of the dead claim that their opponents are trying to make the dead man retroactively childless, to undo his careful planning, and to make the *oikos* empty. This is the central argument of the speaker in Isaeus 2: the testator's brother, who opposes the speaker's claim to his adoptive father's estate, is "trying in every way possible to make his own dead brother childless" (2.1). It is his job, he avers, to help his adoptive father and, incidentally, himself (2.1). Other speakers accuse their opponents of trying retroactively to strip the dead man of his authority or even to render him insane. So the speaker

[32] On an heir's ritual obligations to the dead, see W. K. Lacey 1968: 147–50; Rubinstein 1993: 68–76.

of Isaeus 9 argues, if you vote for my opponent you will be adopting for the dead man a son he would never have adopted while alive and declaring him mad for having adopted an enemy into his family (9.37). The judgment of the estate is a retroactive judgment upon the testator (*katēgorein*, 1.9, 34, 49–50). It is little surprise, then, that the dead man is thought to take an active interest in the case. The speaker of Isocrates 19 imagines both the dead man and the dead man's dead father watching the trial from the underworld – "if the dead perceive what is happening here" – and casting a verdict in his favor (43–44).

In these cases, then, the border between living and dead is permeable. Communication across it is not easy, however. A man's best way of conveying his wishes to the next generation is through a natural-born son; failing that, he can leave a will.[33] But the will is a tenuous document, without the clear legal force it has today. Speakers whose case depends on doing so are happy to detail the problems. The speaker in Isaeus 4, for instance, notes that in other types of suit you can prosecute witnesses if they give false evidence because the person they bear witness against is "alive and present;" "but with a will, how can one know if witnesses are not speaking the truth . . . since the person they bear witness against is dead, and the relatives don't know the facts and there are no clear means of examination" (4.12). Witnesses are frequently called to testify to the veracity of a will, but as this speaker points out, they usually don't know its actual contents or whether the document produced in court is the same one they saw sealed (4.13). If those who were present when the will was made can't determine its authenticity, how can the jurors? (4.14). "Consider, then, what a job it is to perceive if those claiming the inheritance on the basis of a will are speaking the truth," the speaker concludes (4.15), and award Nicostratus' estate instead to his next of kin, who happens to be the speaker himself.[34]

[33] Gernet 1981a: 184–87 examines the will as a form of communication with the dead man, and attributes the document's efficacy to a magico-religious mode of thought that precedes the emergence of law per se. His readings often identify anomalous or striking moments within juridical discourse, even if we reject (as I believe we should) his insistence that all such moments mark the residue of primitive "prelaw."

[34] Cf. 6.53–54: how can my opponent know that the testator did not leave a will if he was not present? "Jurors, it is just as if he were saying that he knows what each of you is doing when he is not present." In Isaeus 4, the inaccessibility of the will is correlated with the difficulty of knowing about events that happened in a foreign land, as did the death of the testator Nicostratus. "With events that happen overseas it is not possible to find witnesses nor is it easy to refute one's opponents . . ." (4.1). Cf. 4.21–22: many have claimed the property of those who died abroad though they did not even know the dead man, since attempts to refute their statements are "examinations of the unknown" (*elenkhoi peri aphanōn*, 22). On the insecurity of the will, see further Is. 1.41; Dem. 46.28; Wyse 1904: 382, 386–87; MacDowell 1978: 99–101; Thompson 1981; Lane Fox 1985: 209; Maffi 1988: 202–03; Christ 1998a: 222–23; D. Cohen 2003: 90–92; Gagarin 2008: 200–01.

Of course, this speaker and others in his position have a vested interest in discrediting the will. But written documents in general were weak evidence in Athenian courts. As we saw in the case of the contract in Demosthenes 48, even where the contractors were alive and a copy of the contract was present in the courtroom its actual terms remained opaque.[35] Likewise, wills are ubiquitous in inheritance speeches, but in only two cases are their contents actually read out to the jurors.[36] Wills compound the secrecy of contracts with the inaccessibility of death. Apollodorus in Demosthenes 46 asserts that no one ever makes a copy of a will as he would of a contract, "for this is the very reason men leave wills, so no one will know how they are disposing of their property" (46.28). Case after case contrasts the publicly witnessed acts of living men to the private writing of the dead. While the former are easy to verify, with the latter it is difficult to determine not only if the document is "true" (in the Athenian idiom) but whether it exists at all. The speaker of Isaeus 9 sets out to prove that the testator Astyphilus "did not bequeath his property and did not leave a will" (9.1). His opponent, having no legal claim to the estate, has "contrived a false will" (*diathēkas pseudeis kateskeuasan*, 9.2). The falsity of the extant will and the non-existence of the true will are mutually supporting, but neither can be proved by independent means. Thus the speaker resorts to arguments from probability – if Astyphilus really wanted to preserve his *oikos* he wouldn't have drawn up a will but would have gathered his relatives and informed them personally of his wishes (9.8) – and calls witnesses to attest to their non-knowledge of the non-will and non-presence at its non-sealing (9.9–10). The obvious weakness of these arguments highlights how tenuous a legal object a will was thought to be. Since a will can be forged, all wills are potential forgeries. A secret document, written and sealed by a man who can no longer attest to its accuracy and notarized by witnesses who never knew its contents to begin with, the will is a dead letter; it cannot speak for itself or explain what its author really intended.

One way a testator could try to circumvent this problem was by adopting the heir named in the will: adoptions and wills, as we saw, were virtually interchangeable. The adopted son functioned as a sort of living will, a

[35] Cf. Chapter 4. There is debate over whether the Athenians conceived of wills as contracts: see Todd 1993: 224.

[36] At Isoc. 19.12 and Is. 6.7, where the will is not central to the speaker's argument. It is possible that the will was read and its contents agreed to during pre-trial arbitration. But even where written documents are read, the text does not stand for itself but must be backed up by witness testimony: Humphreys 1985b: 324–25.

speaking, breathing embodiment of the testator's *pronoia* (2.10, 46; 7.30). In fact, the only extant speeches defending wills are delivered by adopted sons and, moreover, by sons who were (or claim to have been) adopted during the testator's lifetime, not in the will itself.[37] The claims of the former, as Stephen Todd shows, were in general much stronger than those of the latter.[38] So the speaker in Isaeus 2 cites in support of his claim to the estate the fact that he was adopted not in *logos* but in *ergon*. "And he adopted me, jurors, not writing it in a will when he was about to die, as some other citizens have, nor when he was failing, but while he was healthy and of sound mind" by introducing me publicly into his phratry (2.14; cf. 2.44, 7.13). The *diathēkē* is associated with death and debility, writing and secrecy. The speaker in Isaeus 7 makes the same distinction and explains further: in a living adoption the testator makes his wishes manifest (*phaneras*) and validates (*epikurōsas*) the whole matter in accordance with the law; by contrast, "the man who has sealed up his wishes in a will makes them invisible (*adēlous*), with the result that many will claim the will is a forgery and dispute the estate with the adopted child" (7.2). Thus adoption, even while supporting the will in principle, reiterates the suspicion surrounding the document itself and reaffirms the hierarchy of presence in which a living son trumps a dead document and the intent of the living father supersedes his written word. This privileging of presence may explain why, as noted in the previous section, so many adoptions were contested. Adopted sons may represent (or represent themselves as) their adoptive fathers' living will, but instead of their vital presence validating the will, the questions surrounding the authenticity of the will draw their own authenticity into question.

In the end, therefore, arguments about the testament always become arguments about the intentions of the dead man. This is one of the objections the speaker of Isaeus 4 levels against the will as legal evidence. "The law makes a will valid, jurors, not only if someone wrote it but if he wrote it while of sound mind (*eu phronōn*). So you must examine first if he left a will and second if he was not deranged (*paranoōn*) when he did so" (4.14). The will's validity ultimately depends on the testator's mental state. Indeed,

[37] One exception is Isaeus 6: the litigant there bases his claim on testamentary adoption, but the speech focuses on discrediting his opponents, not on his own status. Rubinstein 1993: 76–86 shows that one motive for testamentary adoption could be to disrupt the natural order of intestate inheritance through *ankhisteia*. In such instances the parallel between adoption and a will is especially clear.

[38] Sons adopted *inter vivos* had the same legal rights as a natural son (i.e. they inherited the estate automatically); sons adopted by will had to sue for the estate (Todd 1993: 222–24; Rubinstein 1993: 38–55). But even a son adopted *inter vivos* could not dispose of the estate by will: unless he himself had natural sons, the estate was opened for adjudication on his death. Cf. Gernet 1955: 122–23.

this is written into Solon's testamentary law, which holds wills valid unless the testator is "mentally unfit (*maniōn*) due to old age, drugs, or disease, or is under the influence of a woman, and is *non compos mentis* (*paranoōn*) due to one of these factors, or is under compulsion or is imprisoned" (Dem. 46.14). These vague mental exemptions turn the question of the will into a question of the will behind the will. Does the document reflect the sane intent of the living testator? Litigants are eager to help the jurors settle this question, yes or no. In the process, they project themselves back across the divide of death and reconstruct the living mind behind the legal document, the *dianoia* (intent) behind the *diathēkē* (testament). The will's opacity as legal evidence thus entails not only a project of judicial hermeneutics (what does the testament mean?) but also a labor of posthumous psychoanalysis (what does the testator want?).

Isaeus 1 deals at length with the problem of the will behind the will. The speaker is the nephew of the testator, Cleonymus, who died without sons but with a testament that bequeathed his entire estate to the speaker's opponents. The speaker does not contest the authenticity of the will, the fact that there really is a will and that it was truly written by Cleonymus; nor does he argue with much conviction against the principle of inheritance by will in general. Instead, his argument is that the written will does not accurately represent the desires and intent of the testator and is therefore invalid.

The speaker's claim rests on *genos*, he says, while his opponents' relies on the *diathēkē*:

> Consider what each of us puts our trust in when coming before you. They rely on the will (*houtoi men diathēkais*), which Cleonymus drew up not because he had some complaint against us but because he was angry with one of our kinsmen, and he annulled it before he died, sending Poseidippus for the magistrate. We, on the other hand, rely on the fact that we are nearest in kinship (*hēmeis de genei*), that we were most intimate (*oikeiotata*) with him of anyone, and that the laws have given the estate to us by succession of next of kin (*ankhisteian*), as did Cleonymus himself through the fondness (*philian*) that existed between us. Even Polyarchus, Cleonymus' father and our grandfather, commanded that if Cleonymus should die childless he bequeath his property to us. (1.3–4)

This passage, which presents *in nuce* many arguments that will be developed over the course of the speech, establishes a clear but unequal dichotomy between *genos* and *diathēkē*. On the one side is the will, which does not even reflect the intent of the testator when he died. On the other side is *genos*, which the speaker aligns with the law of *ankhisteia* but also with intimacy and fondness (*oikeiotēs*, *philia)*. For good measure he even throws in the grandfather's injunction, a mysterious and seemingly gratuitous detail that is never mentioned again.

With this opening the speaker would seem to set a clear agenda: as he himself says, the speech should end once he has shown himself closer in *genos* to the dead (17). He characterizes the arguments about the will as *periergon* (17), superfluous, a needless labor, and implies that *genos* is the true *ergon* of the speech. But *ergon* and *periergon*, *genos* and *diathēkē*, are harder than we might expect to keep separate in this speech. Despite the firm distinction the speaker draws between his own position and his opponents', it seems that they, too, will claim the estate based on *genos* (36); they, too, will speak ("shamelessly") about their intimacy and kinship (*tēn oikeiotēta kai tēn ankhisteian*, 47). Likewise, he reasons (rather sophistically) that his opponents, who base their claim on the will, are actually trying to contest the will, for if they really think Cleonymus would cut his beloved nephews out of his bequest, then they must believe he was out of his right mind and therefore must consider the will invalid (33–35). "If they intended to prosecute both the will and the testator, I don't know what more they could say to you" (34).

Meanwhile, the speaker's case relies not on *genos*, as he pretends (he spends very little of the speech supporting his superior claim by kinship, so little, in fact, that he never specifies his opponents' relation to himself or to the dead man), but almost entirely on the will – not the written will, which he vigorously repudiates, but the intent of his dead uncle. In arguing for the validity of the will, "my opponents are trying to persuade you to cast your vote against the laws, justice, and the intent (*gnōmēi*) of the dead" (26). "I will show that the will is against the law, justice, and the intent (*dianoian*) of the dead" (35). That intent is filled out with affection, *oikeiotēs* and *philia*.[39] Throughout the speaker pairs *genos* with these terms of affection, implying that his uncle's fondness for him was a natural concomitant of his familial relation: his emotional intimacy to his uncle's *oikos* makes him (he suggests) biologically *oikeiotatos*. Yoked in this way to *genos*, *oikeiotēs* becomes the content of a will more true than the written testament and the former logically invalidates the latter. My uncle loved me, claims the speaker, so he could not have intended to cut me out of the *diathēkē*.

39 *Oikeiotēs* can denote a family relation or a close bond of friendship; in this case its link to *sungeneia* (42) and to *ankhisteia* (47) shows how we are supposed to understand it. Forms of *oikeios* and *philos* appear more often here than in any other inheritance speech, with twenty occurrences of the former and nine of the latter. *Philia* also plays a prominent role in Isocrates 19 and Isaeus 7. See Hardcastle 1980: 18–19 on *philia* as a moral argument in forensic oratory; cf. Christ 1998a: 167–91; Sternberg 2006: 21–41. For a stimulating discussion of obligation and the will in eighteenth-century British law, see Macpherson 2003.

Despite the obvious logical weakness of this argument (both its premise, which is never proven, and its conclusion, which does not follow), it plays a vital role in the speaker's brief. *Oikeiotēs* allows the speaker to by-pass the written will as obviously flawed and to recover behind it the dead man's true will, a will now in alignment not in conflict with the claims of kinship.

Implicit in this argument is an eschatological theory in which death changes nothing. The speaker's fundamental (and often repeated) rhetorical tactic is to assert that his uncle loved him while he was alive and still feels the same in death. He took me and my brothers in when we were children; he educated us and cared for our affairs as if they were his own. How could he want to harm us now? (12–13). Who would he rather have inherit his property than those for whose benefit he used that property when he was alive? (27; cf. 34). This assumption that Cleonymus' feelings and desires have remained constant even across the divide of death grounds the arguments from probability that comprise the bulk of the speech. *Eikos* arguments are ubiquitous in forensic oratory, as we saw in Chapter 3. This speaker uses *eikos* to extrapolate not just between intent and action or between possible and actual but also between life and death. Suppose Cleonymus were alive, he posits. If I were to die childless he would be my heir, so *mutatis mutandis* my brothers and I should be his heirs (45). "For we would never when we were alive have entrusted our property to him such that his wishes (*dianoian*) became more authoritative than our own, but then when we were dead have wanted someone else to inherit instead of the man who was closest (*oikeiotaton*) to us of anyone" (46). In this convoluted analogy, the speaker trades places with his uncle and imagines himself dead. He discovers that his own feelings have not changed. The hypothetical constancy of his own feelings after this contrafactual death is then used to prove by analogy the actual constancy of his uncle, who really is dead. This imaginative metempsychosis is enabled by *oikeiotēs* (46; cf. 45 and three occurrences in §47) and is described in terms that reaffirm the case's testamentary logic: the posthumous desire that the speaker imagines still feeling when dead validates the posthumous *dianoia* of his dead uncle, which the speaker asks the jurors to ratify with their vote (43). Death has changed nothing of his uncle's enduring intent, no more than it would his own. That persistent purpose (*dia-noia*) should, in theory, be recorded in the *diathēkē*, a document composed (*tithenai*) to persist (*dia*), even across the barrier of death.

Death changes nothing. But in another sense it changes everything, as the speech's opening sentence acknowledges. "The death of Cleonymus has brought great change (*metabolē*) for me, jurors. For when he was alive he left me his property, but by dying he has put me at risk of losing it" (1). The will, like the dead, should be frozen and static. But life is dynamic. The living change their minds: they quarrel with their relatives, for instance, and later make up. The will is at best a snapshot of a moving image, but is it a record of fixity or of change? *Metabolē* troubles the speech's theory of testamentary consistency. Cleonymus, the speaker argues, had written his will years ago while he was feuding with the speaker's guardian Deinias and wanted to make sure Deinias didn't get hold of his property. But Deinias was now long dead and Cleonymus wanted to change the will to reflect the affection he had always felt for his nephew. He sent for the magistrate and the document, but died unexpectedly in the night before he could carry out his plan. Death comes suddenly (14), interrupting the transposition of *dianoia* into *diathēkē*.

This deathbed *metanoia* (change of mind), although incomplete, would seem in principle to suture the document to the intent behind it: but for the untimely interruption of death, the will would accurately reflect Cleonymus' true intent. But, of course, there is no way of knowing why Cleonymus called for the will, whether he wanted to annul it, add a codicil, or "confirm" it (an idea the speaker scornfully attributes to his opponents). This uncompleted emendation, the codicil that was never added, drives a wedge between the testament and the testator's intent. If the will is a snapshot of a life in motion it just misses what it aimed to capture. Instead of a fixed and centered image, we get a blur of indistinct movement. The *diathēkē*, in other words, becomes a testament not to the dead man's continuously affectionate *dianoia*, but to an obscure and shifting *metanoia*.

But even before this last minute *metabolē*, the will was a poor guide to the testator's purpose. Cleonymus wrote the will in anger when he was not in his right mind (*orgizomenos ekeinōi kai ouk orthōs bouleuomenos*, 11); he annulled it when he returned to sanity (*eu phronōn*, 43). This speaker has no inherent objection to wills in general, only to this will: because it was written in anger, it does not reflect the dead man's true desires. *Orgē*, anger, functions in the speech as a mental aberration, a sort of temporary insanity. The speaker associates it with *paranoia* and *mania* (19, 20). A man under its influence is not in his right mind (*eu phronōn, orthōs bouleuomenos*, 11, 20, 43) but is mad (*paraphronōn*, 21). He also associates it with change: "Other men who have wronged their kin under the influence of anger later regret it" (*metamelei*, 19; cf. 48). The will, he claims, is the product of just such an aberrant and erratic mentality. Indeed, in proposing that it represents Cleonymus' true state of mind his opponents are actually accusing the dead man of madness for having left his property to his enemies (19–20; cf. 34).

Although he accuses them of making Cleonymus out to be mad in drawing up such a will, this is in fact his own imputation. The opponents presumably made a similar argument to the speaker's: that Cleonymus was fond of them all along and wanted them to have his estate. For them the will represents that sentiment directly and unproblematically. Thus their Cleonymus is consistent and sane. It is the speaker's Cleonymus, with his crazed anger, his *mania* and changes of heart, who is mad – and the will is a transcript of that madness. In order to maintain the consistency of his uncle's *philia* toward himself, he must posit an inconsistency, a passing *paranoia*, that was accidentally recorded in the will. This opens the door for numerous other queries, which his opponents no doubt raised in their counter-speech: if he was merely angry at Deinias, why didn't he change the will after Deinias died years earlier? If his anger was an aberration, when did he recover? How can the speaker know or the jury decide whether the will represents the *dianoia*, *metanoia*, or *paranoia* of its author?

Paranoia (19) is a loaded term. In Solon's testamentary law it indicates the state of incapacity that legally invalidates a will. By using this term, the speaker hopes to catch his opponents (and the jurors) in a logical double bind. If they think that Cleonymus, despite his obvious love for his nephews, cut them out of his will, then they are clearly accusing him of *paranoia*, in which case the will is invalid. If, on the other hand, he intended to change the will but died before he could do so, then Cleonymus was sane but the will is inaccurate and therefore invalid (21). This sophistical reasoning sets up an antinomy between the legal document and the intent it should, in theory, document. If the one is right, the other is wrong. Cleonymus' *dianoia*, sane or insane, is freed from its terrestrial body; fluttering away from its *diathēkē*, it assumes a ghostly independence.

The jurors' decision then becomes less a reading of the document than a diagnosis of the desires behind it. Who in his right mind would wish to leave the nephews whom he loved without a share in his estate? By advancing this argument, the speaker concludes, his opponents "have made it easy for you to reach a *diagnōsis* about them" (21). *Diagnōsis* is common for a juridical verdict. It is also the term for a medical diagnosis.[40] Thus this case will become a retroactive judgment on the sanity of both the opponents and the testator. The jurors must adjudicate, the speaker says, not only between the claims of *genos* and the *diathēkē*, but also between enduring sanity and temporary insanity: "it would be most terrible if you make his

[40] Juridical (mostly in the related verbal form): Is. 1.21, 10.2; Ant. 6.18, Isoc. 1.34, 10.42, 15.51; Lys. 7.22; Dem. 18.7, 128; 28.10. Medical: Hipp. *VC* 10; Gal. 8.766. The same notion of the verdict as a posthumous diagnosis of the testator's sanity occurs at Is. 9.36.

orgē more valid (*kuriōteran*) than his *dianoia*" (43). *Kurios* is the adjective used throughout for a valid will, but here the jury are being asked to validate not the *diathēkē* but the *dianoia* of the dead man. The written document is set aside: it becomes a record of anger, derangement, *paranoia*. The jurors must reach back beyond the written will to validate the true and enduring wishes of the dead man, his undying *philia* for his nephew.

How are they to perform this posthumous diagnosis? The speaker appeals to a familiar hierarchy of presence: Cleonymus' state of mind must be reconstructed not from the dead document but from his living actions. He stages a scene in which Cleonymus proclaims "in front of all the citizens" that he was angry not at his nephews but at their guardian and thus testifies "that he made the will when he was not of sound mind" (*orthōs bouleuomenos*, 11). The "greatest proof" (*megiston tekmērion*, 12) of his true feelings is his behavior, taking his nephews in after Deinias' death and raising them in his house. From here the speaker builds to a statement of general principle:

> And yet one must examine (*theōrein*) his mentality (*ennoian*) from his deeds (*ergōn*) rather than from the will (*diathēkōn*) and take as proof (*tekmēriois*) not what he did through anger – through which all men by nature err – but the subsequent acts through which he made his intention (*dianoian*) manifest (*phaneran*). (13)

This passage, with its uncharacteristically abstract tenor, brings together two antitheses developed throughout the speech, that between document and deed and that between angry *paranoia* and consistent *dianoia*. The will, a product of anger, is a record of human folly; it provides poor proof either for theoretical reflection (*theōrein*) or for legal judgment (*tekmēriois*). Instead, the *ennoia* of the dead man, his inner mind, is to be found in the manifest acts of his life. The circularity of the logic – the *ennoia* is to be seen in the *erga* that make manifest the *dianoia* – is in fact the point: a man's intent resides in the living, breathing individual himself and not in anything he might have left behind. But that living intent becomes manifest (*phaneran*) only in the jurors' eyes. Their forensic *theōria* transmutes hidden, internal *ennoia* into a visible and lasting *dianoia*.

By looking through the dead document to the living *erga*, the jurors resurrect the dead man's purpose, purified now of the errors of human nature recorded in the will. You must cast your verdict based on *genos* and the "truth of the matter," the speaker tells them, not on the *diathēkē*:

> For you all know the intimacy of kinship (*tou genous oikeiotēta*) and it is not possible to deceive you on this score. But many have produced false wills, wills that don't exist at all or that were not composed in sound mind. You all know the

kinship (*sungeneian*) and intimacy (*oikeiotēta*) on which I base my case, but none of you knows whether the will, which they have used to trump up this case, is valid. (41–42)

"You all know the intimacy of kinship." *Oikeiotēs*, along with *philia*, is the force that binds uncle and nephew throughout the speech. It is the consistent affection that makes Cleonymus' *dianoia* show clearly in his actions and that consequently allows the nephew to know the true intent of his dead uncle, despite the false testimony of his will. That intimate knowledge now also becomes the basis for a legal verdict: the jury, too, know the "intimacy of kinship," both their own and the speaker's. By gazing into Cleonymus' inner mind (*ennoia*), they enter the intimate circle of his *oikos* and this *oikeiotēs* allows them, like the speaker, to imagine what he would have wanted when alive and will still want now he's dead. Then they will discard the false will – the ossified product of a momentary madness – in favor of the true, unwritten will, the *dianoia* of the dead. Their proper verdict: the will is dead but the dead man's will is alive.

By rejecting the will, then, the speaker resurrects the will behind it, the living purpose of the testator. In the speech's contrast between *diathēkē* and *dianoia*, law, justice, and juridical truth are all arrayed with the latter, and so must be the jurors (26, 35). It may seem paradoxical that the jurors, as agents of the law, are asked to disregard the legal document. Indeed, by pressing the superior claim of *genos* against the *diathēkē*, the case might seem to privilege blood descent and thus to limit the law's role in the transmission of family property and negotiation of intergenerational relations. But in fact, as we have seen, the speech rejects the letter of the will only to revive its spirit. If the testator's will lives on, it is not in a dead document that misrepresents his true wishes. Nor is it in the living heir, whose right to carry out his uncle's purpose is precisely what this case contests. Instead, the dead patriarch's will is reanimated through the intimate knowledge and validating verdict of the jurors. The trial becomes a ritual of juridical necromancy, as the law itself becomes the dead man's living will and truest heir, enacting his constant *dianoia* through its just *diagnōsis*.

FEMININE FICTIONS AND THE GENEALOGY OF LAW (ISAEUS 3 AND 6)

If the will is testament to law's mastery over death and the past, the woman represents its power over birth and the future, both the family's future and its own. Women were not legal agents in Athens. They could not speak in court or bring cases in their own name. They did not serve as witnesses nor did they sit on juries; hence the common practice of addressing the jurors simply as "gentlemen" (*andres*).[41] This is not to say that they could not exercise considerable *de facto* power behind the scenes, especially in family matters, as Lin Foxhall and Virginia Hunter have both stressed.[42] They were no doubt active in the less formal forum of arbitrations (see, e.g., Lys. 32.11–18), and even in the *dikastēria* it is often clear that although a man brings the case, a woman is behind it. The language of female agency is not uncommon in the inheritance speeches ("my mother disputed the claim," Is. 3.3; "this boy's mother defeated in court all those disputing her claim," Dem. 43.6), although it always functions as shorthand, conflating women's unofficial and extrajudicial agency with the legal actions of their official male representatives.

Whatever their practical influence behind the scenes, within the discourse of family law women's primary role is structural: they serve as pillars – load-bearing but also fragile – in the edifice of kinship. Respectable women, as David Schaps has shown, were almost never referred to by name in forensic oratory; instead, they are named by their position within the *genos*: daughter of X, wife of Y.[43] But that position was surprisingly hard to determine. Pericles' Citizenship Law made the woman's legitimate birth and her legitimate union to her husband a prerequisite for the legitimacy of her children.[44] The integrity of the individual *oikos* and, ultimately, of the polis itself depended on the possibility of distinguishing between a legitimately married wife (*gunē enguētē*), given by formal agreement by her *kurios* to her husband, and a mistress (*hetaira* or *pallakē*), whose children were neither citizens nor usually heirs.[45] But in the absence of marriage certificates or other official archives such distinctions could be extremely difficult to draw. Indeed, a certain indeterminacy is built into the linguistics of femininity: *gunē*, the standard Greek word for woman, also means

41 On the restrictions, see Gagarin 1998.

42 Foxhall 1989, esp. 37–39, 1996; Hunter 1994: 9–42. Women are even listed on the curse tablets that anxious litigants composed against their opponents and asked the gods to execute (Faraone 1991: 16; Eidinow 2007: 63–64). For further discussion of the role of women in forensic oratory, see W. K. Lacey 1968: 151–53; Schaps 1977; Just 1989: 26–39; Patterson 1994; Cox 1998: 69–77; Gagarin 1998, 2001; Johnstone 1998; Wolpert 2001; Omitowoju 2002: 13–133; Glazebrook 2006.

43 Schaps 1977. See also Thuc. 2.45; Just 1989: 28; Glazebrook 2005: 166–68.

44 Osborne 1997 shows that the citizenship law increased the importance of women in Athenian marital ideology. See also Lape 2004: 68–72.

45 The cases examined here show that the practical realities of marital relations in Athens were muddier than this sharp ideological distinction between wife and mistress suggests. See also the case of Antiphon 1 (discussed in Chapter 2 above) where the speaker may be the son of a *pallakē*.

"wife."[46] But not every *gunē* was a *gunē*, as we shall see, and the gap between the two posed both problems and opportunities for forensic orators.

Sometimes the woman herself risked disappearing into that gap, for when her status as a wife was challenged, her very existence as a woman could fall into doubt. In Isaeus 8, the speaker claims to be the son of the daughter of Ciron, the testator; but his opponents charge, as he puts it, "that I am not the child of Ciron's daughter and indeed that he never even had a daughter at all" (*oude genomenēs autōi pōpote to parapan*, 8.1). For the speaker's purposes, his mother's legitimacy and her existence are interchangeable, since if she was not Ciron's legitimate daughter her existence is irrelevant to his brief. But since he claims she was, he must prove not only that she was legitimate but that she existed to begin with. The best evidence of this, he says, would come from the household slaves. They could testify whether his mother had grown up in Ciron's house, whether he gave her a marriage feast and provided a dowry. But his opponents have refused a *basanos* (8.9–14, 17; cf. Is. 6.16). The woman falls into the evidentiary black hole of the *basanos* examined in Chapter 2: her identity and legitimacy, indeed her very being, are represented in the same counterfactual mood as the slave's inaccessible truth. Playing throughout on a trope of visibility, the speaker represents the interior of the *oikos* as invisible and the woman within as unknowable, in contrast to the transparent world of male activities, the public sacrifices and phratry rituals in which he participated with his father and grandfather (8.15, 19). He further correlates this binarism with juridical verity, linking the woman's invisibility to forensic oratory's own strategies of clarity and opaqueness. His opponents hope "to make the rights of the laws disappear (*aphanizein*) by their words" (8.1); by contrast, his own speech is as manifest (*phanera*, 8.6; cf. 30) as the facts of his case (*tēi periphaneiai tou pragmatos*, 8.20).

The woman thus functions much like the will: she is another cipher that demands juridical interpretation. But if the will is an obscure text that the law must read (and by reading which extends its power over the family's genealogical past), the woman is an obscure text that the law must write, a blank page where forensic speakers compose competing narratives of legitimacy and illegitimacy.[47] These feminine fictions serve the specific purposes of individual litigants like Ciron's supposed grandson. They also serve juridical discourse as a whole, which by defining the woman claims

[46] Just 1989: 43–44 notes that this is true in most modern European languages as well.

[47] Gagarin 2001: 162 compares the female characters of oratory to those in Attic tragedy; he shows how on those rare occasions when women's speech is reported in forensic oratory it sounds suspiciously like the larger argument in which it is embedded.

the power to define the legitimate family and reproduce it in the next generation. Thus what juridical discourse inscribes in the empty space of the female – a space emptied precisely in order to bear such inscription – is an account of its own discursive productivity and power of legitimation; in writing the woman, it writes an institutional genealogy not only of the family but of the law itself.

And yet precisely because the woman is figured as a lacuna within the family and its structures of legitimacy, she is open to errant interpolation, alternate inscriptions that legal discourse inadvertently fosters but does not fully control. Forensic orators tell one story about the *gunē*, a binary narrative of legitimacy or illegitimacy, wife or mistress. But alongside that juridical narrative others sometimes emerge, counter-genealogies that disrupt the family histories the woman is supposed to secure. In these stories, legitimacy and illegitimacy share a house, as patriarchs embrace their bastard sons, lovelorn young men mistake mistresses for wives, and brothers give away their inconvenient sisters on a phony handshake. These narratives are not composed by the women themselves: they have as little discursive agency within the world of Athenian law as they do practical. Instead, these counter-genealogies proliferate in the empty space legal discourse clears around them, a genetic mutation of its own discursive fecundity.[48]

Isaeus 6 *On the Estate of Philoctemon* tells two competing narratives built around two competing female characters. One narrative is about a father and his legitimate sons, good citizens all. The other is about a senile old man, a scheming prostitute, and her illegitimate children. In the courts' agonistic format these two should be easy to keep apart, as the jury is asked to find for one or the other. But in this case it is impossible to separate the two families and their two narratives. Illegitimacy enters the *oikos* in the person of a prostitute, but it is invited in by the patriarch himself and asked to stay by his legitimate heir. The law's own interest in this case

[48] I borrow the idea of the woman as the site of counter-genealogies from Goodrich 1995 (esp. 16–40, 144–80). Katerina Ladianou (in an unpublished seminar paper) also discusses feminine counter-histories in Isaeus 3 and 6. I am grateful to her for sharing her ideas with me. The paradigm case for the construction of women in forensic oratory is Dem. 59 *Against Neaira*. That speech creates and deploys vivid female characters in order to prosecute its case against its actual opponent, Neaira's "husband" Stephanus. Many of the issues I discuss in Isaeus 3 and 6 are also at work in Dem. 59: the ambiguity of the woman's status and the difficulty of distinguishing a wife from a *hetaira*; the problem of legitimacy, familial and civic; the threat posed by a disreputable woman to the ritual, genealogical, and political purity of the city. I will make reference to Dem. 59 where it provides a relevant parallel, but since it is not an inheritance case I will not treat it directly. The speech has been much and well studied: see especially Carey 1992; Patterson 1994; Kapparis 1999; Hamel 2003; Miner 2003; Glazebrook 2005; Gilhuly 2008: 29–57. Glazebrook 2005: 173–81 notes the close parallels in the representation of women in Dem. 59 and Is. 3 and 6 (as well as in Dem. 39 and 48, discussed in Chapter 4 above).

is vital: in the face of the family's apparent indifference to maintaining a pure genealogy, will the law reimpose order on this chaotic clan or will it perpetuate the confusion?

The case centers on the legitimacy of the two young claimants to the estate of Euctemon. The speaker is a friend of the young Chaerestratus, the nephew and adopted son of Euctemon's son Philoctemon, who predeceased his father. Chaerestratus is now suing for the estate of his adoptive father's father. The case is weak on the face of it. Adopted in Philoctemon's will, Chaerestratus had a claim on Philoctemon's estate but not on his father's, which, since he was still alive at the time, Philoctemon had no right to bequeath (if in fact he did: the opponents dispute the will). The speech thus focuses largely on challenging the legitimacy of the two opponents (minors, like Chaerestratus, who are represented by their relative Androcles), who claim to be Euctemon's natural and legitimate sons by a second marriage. The identity of their mother is the crux of the case.

The speaker denies that there was such a marriage and sets out to prove the non-existence of his opponents' purported mother. Everyone knows of Euctemon's first marriage to the daughter of Meixiades, which produced Philoctemon. But no one has ever heard of Euctemon having married a second wife (11; cf. 15–17). His opponents, he asserts, were not even able to give her name when asked during the preliminary hearings. When pressed, to buy time they said she was a Lemnian: Athenians who had settled in the colony at Lemnos retained Athenian citizenship but were unlikely to be well known in Athens. Finally, they produced a name: Callippe, daughter of Pistoxenus (13). But that is insufficient, the speaker complains. It is not enough for his opponent merely to mention a woman's name. He must prove that she existed: he must supply witnesses to the marriage and specify where she is buried and who has ever seen Euctemon or his sons performing the rituals at her grave (64). In the absence of such proofs, he insinuates, they could simply be making her up, "fabricating an exceedingly shameless story that never really happened" (*pragma plattontes anaideiai huperballon kai oude genomenon*, 13).

Against his opponents' fictive mother the speaker fabricates one of his own and traces from this dubious origin a genealogy and legal narrative to counter those derived from the putative Callippe. His own "exceedingly shameless story that (quite possibly) never really happened" is a morality tale and, the speaker apologizes, a particularly unpleasant one (*aēdes*, 17), a parable about good sense corrupted and a fine family destroyed. Euctemon lived to ninety-six years and for most of that time was happy and prosperous (18). The anticipated reversal follows fast: "but in old age he suffered no small disaster" (*sumphora*, 18), which ruined his wealth and his household. This *sumphora* comes in the form of a woman. Euctemon owned an apartment building that was used as a brothel. One of the prostitutes there was a freed slave named Alce, "whom I believe many of you know" (19). Euctemon set this Alce up as manager of another apartment building, where she lived with her two sons. Euctemon would visit to pick up the rent; his visits got more frequent and eventually he was virtually living with her. Somehow she persuaded Euctemon to introduce her older son into his phratry under his name, as his own child. That child, the speaker asserts, the son of a former slave and prostitute, is his opponent (18–21).

Alce is a strong character in the narrative – her name means "strength" or "force" (*alkē*) – and, indeed, one of the most vivid female characters in forensic oratory. Yet the speaker never supplies external witnesses either to her existence (since "many of you know her") or to the many criminal actions he ascribes to her. Her social position places her outside the courts' usual circle of the rich and famous and allows the speaker considerable creative latitude. He claims his opponents have invented Callippe; for all we know, he may himself have invented Alce, if not entirely then in all details pertinent to this case. The speech is structured, then, as an *agōn* between these two feminine fictions: the second wife no one knows and the ex-prostitute everyone knows.

Around Alce the speaker constructs for his opponents an illegitimate genealogy to set against Chaerestratus' legitimate lineage. But the two lines immediately converge. After setting Alce up as apartment manager, the speaker says, Euctemon would visit frequently to collect the rent and "he spent a lot of time in the apartment building (*sunoikiai*), and sometimes he would eat with the woman, abandoning his wife and children and the house (*oikian*) where he lived. His wife and sons were upset about this but couldn't stop it. Finally he was spending all his time there (*pantelōs diēitato ekei*)" (21). Euctemon sets up a shadow *oikos* with Alce. This illegitimate household may stand at a vast ideological distance from his proper marital household, but lexically it is just around the corner. *Sunoikia* is the standard word in Attic for an apartment building. But the verbal form *sunoikein* generally denotes married cohabitation.[49] When Euctemon visits Alce and her children in her *sunoikia*, is he merely "spending time" (*diaitein*) with her or is he "living with" her (*sunoikein*)? The *sunoikia*, like the *oikia*,

[49] Dem. 59.122: "this is what it means to cohabit (*sunoikein*): when one has children and introduces his sons into the phratry and deme and marries off his daughters as legitimately his own." Cf. Wolff 1944: 65–68; W. K. Lacey 1968: 110–11; Just 1989: 43, 62–64; Carey 1992: 92 *ad* Dem. 59.16, 147–48 *ad* 59.122; Cox 1998: 182–83.

is a place of familial reproduction but, as we might expect, it rears an illegitimate brood. Alce was herself raised in a house where "prostitutes were kept" (*paidiskas etrephe*, 19): the addition of a diminutive suffix turns the rearing of children (*paidas trephein*) into the keeping of prostitutes (*paidiskas trephein*).[50] She in turn raises illegitimate children, the sons (so she says) of Dio, a fellow freedman with whom she was living in the brothel.

The speaker goes to some lengths to keep these two households separate: his case depends on a sharp line between the marital *oikos* and the sordid *sunoikia*, between *paides* and *paidiskai*. Alce was never Euctemon's *gunē* (the speaker refers to her throughout as *hē anthrōpē*, "the female," to avoid that confusion[51]) and the children, he claims, are not Euctemon's own. Euctemon himself appears less certain about that, however, and regardless of their biological paternity, they become legally his once he enters Alce's son into his phratry under his own name. Parallel genealogies, the legitimate and the illegitimate, then converge and become entangled; *oikos* and *sunoikia* merge. Illegitimacy enters the house and, shockingly, it was the patriarch himself who opened the door.

The ramifications for the *oikos* are dramatized in the scene of Euctemon's death. Alce and her gang broke into his house and carted off the valuables before the body was even cold. They shut out his real family, first locking up the slaves so Euctemon's wife and relatives would not learn he was dead and, when they did find out, refusing to let them in, saying "it was not proper for them to bury Euctemon" (*ou prosēkein autais thaptein Euktēmona*, 40). The proprieties (*ta prosēkonta*) that define family relations (*hoi prosēkontes*) are brutally violated, along with the family property (*ta prosēkonta*). Meanwhile, Euctemon's body lies there for two days, the burial rituals left undone. That scandalous impiety is now about to be repeated unless the jurors intervene: they must decide whether Alce's son will be allowed to offer libations and sacrifices at the family tomb (51).

Once inside the house, Alce's corrupting influence spreads. The introduction of her son is not merely – although this is bad enough – the fault of Euctemon, who might be excused by the old age and *anoia* to which the speaker frequently refers (21, 29, 35). His relatives are also in on it. When Euctemon first proposes registering the child Philoctemon, his oldest natural son, naturally objects. Euctemon then proceeds to blackmail him. He

50 Cf. Dem. 59.18–19, where the brothel-keeper makes extra profit by fostering the ambiguity between *paidiskai* and *paides*. *Paidiskē* is not uncommon for prostitutes, but it also occurs in the masculine (*paidiskos*) as an affectionate diminutive of "son." Cf. E. Cohen 2006: 107–08 on a parallel use of *paidion*.

51 On this deprecatory term, see Sosin 1997; Glazebrook 2005: 168–69, 177. The word is often used of female slaves.

engages to marry the sister of Democrates, intending to introduce her children into his *oikos* if Philoctemon will not let him introduce Alce's child (22). This scheme reenacts a legitimate version of Alce's plan. It threatens to introduce new children into the house and new claimants to the estate. Having *gnēsioi* sons, Euctemon could not legally adopt these new children (and his relatives have no fear of him bearing more natural children at his age), but the danger is that once they "appear in some manner" (23) they will have a legal stake in the estate. If he cannot introduce an illegitimate son, Euctemon threatens, he will introduce a legitimate stepson.

The blackmail works. On the advice of his relatives and "ashamed by his father's foolishness and at a loss as to what to do in this crisis," Philoctemon allows his father to register Alce's son on condition that he only be given a single farm (24). By this deal, the rightful heir agrees to compromise the reputation of his family and purity of his bloodline for guaranteed inheritance of the property. William Wyse puts the situation in a clear light:

> The veil of euphemistic verbiage does not conceal the ugly features of the accusation. In plain English father and son were alike guilty, if the tale is true, of the gravest offence against the constitution of Athenian society. Euctemon smuggled into the cherished privileges of citizenship the offspring of a freedman and a prostitute of servile birth. Philoctemon, the patriot of §9, connived at the crime, when menaced with curtailment of his inheritance.[52]

The *kurios*, his kinsmen, and his legitimate heir voluntarily bastardize their own *genos* and genealogy. They plant a family tree in which any future limb may be rotten and there is no way to tell which is sound. They simultaneously threaten to spread that blight to another elite *oikos*, the house of Democrates, which traced its lineage all the way back to Harmodius and Aristogeiton.

This taint of illegitimacy threatens not just the *oikos*, moreover, but also the polis, for once introduced into Euctemon's phratry Alce's son – the bastard child of two former slaves – stands to become an Athenian citizen.[53]

[52] Wyse 1904: 503–04. Cf. Dem. 59.55–61, where Phrastor's adoption of his son by Phano, despite his knowledge that she was the daughter of a foreign *hetaira*, is represented as the desperate act of a sick man facing an heirless death.

[53] It is their servile, not their foreign birth that is at issue, although slaves in Athens generally were foreign-born. The speaker doesn't explicitly say Alce and Dio are non-Athenian, but the fact that when Dio gets into some unspecified legal trouble he flees to Sicyon may suggest his civic status is tenuous. Alce is presumed to be a metic based on her occupation, but citizen prostitutes (though rare) were not unheard of in Athens: see below, note 64. Foreignness is the central issue in Dem. 59, which is technically a *graphē xenias* against Neaira, charging her with claiming the rights of a citizen although she was a foreigner.

Alce's crime against the family is thus also an act of *hubris* against a polity that imagined itself as a pure and unified *genos*.[54] "She committed such *hubris* that she shows her contempt not only for Euctemon's family but for the whole city" (48). That *hubris* is epitomized by Alce's sacrilegious participation in the Thesmophoria, a festival of Demeter open only to citizen women. "The mother of these children, an admitted slave who lived disgracefully her entire life, who should never have entered the temple nor seen what is inside, had the gall to march in the procession during the sacrifices to these goddesses [Demeter and Persephone] and to enter the temple and to see what she was not permitted to see" (50). By entering the temple, Alce arrogated to herself the exclusive prerogatives of an Athenian citizen, just as she had done for her son by persuading Euctemon to register him in his phratry, and her presence tainted the purity of the festival just as her progeny threaten to taint the purity of the citizen body and the sacred lineage of the Athenian demos.[55]

For this civic and domestic catastrophe, the speaker lays the blame solely on Alce. Becoming involved with her, the speaker says, was the beginning of his woes (*kakōn ērxen*, 21). She "destroyed Euctemon's sense" (48) and persuaded him to bring ruin on his family. After living with Alce for some time, the speaker says, Euctemon "was in such a state, either from drugs or from disease or from something else that he was persuaded by her to introduce her older son into the phratry under his own name" (21). The irrelevant reference to drugs and disease is a clear allusion to Solon's testamentary law, which, as we have seen, invalidated wills written if a man "is mentally impaired (*maniōn*) due to old age or drugs or disease, or under the influence of a woman (*gunaiki peithomenos*), and is not thinking straight (*paranoōn*) because of one of these things" (Dem. 46.14).[56] This citation, coupled with the emphasis throughout on his senile *anoia*, is meant to suggest that Euctemon was *non compos mentis* during the whole vile affair. The wording of the citation at §21 is odd, however. The woman's influence is mentioned not as one of the legally invalidating conditions (as

54 On the imaginary genealogy of the Athenian demos, see Loraux 1993, esp. 37–143.

55 Cf. Is. 3.80, 8.19. On the requirement of sexual purity at the Thesmophoria, see recently Goff 2004: 125–38, 152–59; and on the gendering of ritual purity in Greek thought more generally, S. G. Cole 2004: 92–145. In Dem. 59, Phano is accused of a similar crime against civic religion. This daughter of a foreign-born prostitute was married under false pretenses to the Archon Basileus and, acting as his wife, performed secret sacrifices on behalf of the city (72–87). The speaker elaborates on this charge in detail, reminding the jurors of the antiquity and piety of this venerable ritual and the scandalous sacrilege of its being performed by "this sort of a woman, who has performed these sorts of act" (73). See Patterson 1994: 208–09; Goff 2004: 171–74; Glazebrook 2005: 180–81; Gilhuly 2008: 46–49.

56 On the "persuaded by a woman" clause of the testamentary law, see Sundahl 2005.

it seems to have been in the text of Solon's law) but as a result of those conditions.[57] As it is phrased, Alce does not cause Euctemon's *paranoia* so much as exploit his mental incapacity for her own purposes. Is Alce really the *arkhē kakōn*, then, the cause of all problems for father and son? Or is she rather a force (*alkē*) fabricated to name the preexisting *anoia* of these men? If the speaker is telling the truth, Euctemon and Philoctemon display a *mania* in bastardizing their own *genos* that no drugs or feminine persuasion can excuse.

Through senility or avarice, in this speech the *kurioi* themselves willfully corrupt the purity of their own household, creating a genealogical chaos in which legitimacy and illegitimacy are indistinguishable, with dire consequences for both the *oikos* and the polis. With this trial, the law would seem to step in to remedy their failures and to restore the purity of Euctemon's *oikos* through clear contrast to his shadowy *sunoikia* with Alce. But even as it purports to resolve the family's crisis of legitimacy, this speech in fact perpetuates it. For if (as seems entirely possible) the speaker is lying and his opponents actually are the legitimate sons of Euctemon and Callippe,[58] then the speech itself does rhetorically precisely what it accuses Euctemon of doing in actuality: creating illegitimate children and attaching them to the family name. While Euctemon (he claims) tried to pass off bastards as legitimate sons in his phratry, the speaker tries to pass off legitimate sons (if such they are) as bastards in the courtroom. And even if he is not lying, like Philoctemon the speaker places profit before the family's honor, publicly recounting the "unpleasant" scandal of Alce in the hopes of winning Chaerestratus the estate. Thus Alce's bastard bloodline reproduces at the level of forensic rhetoric the genealogical *anoia* her character is introduced (or invented) to explain at the level of domestic reality: the fiction created to help the jurors distinguish legitimate heirs from bastards has made that distinction more impossible than ever.

This case is often treated as anomalous in its apparent disregard for Athens' ideology of familial legitimacy and civic purity. But the *anoia* of this

57 A similar phrasing occurs earlier in the speech where the speaker is defending the will by which Philoctemon adopted Chaerestratus. Wills are valid, he says, "unless the testator is deranged by old age or is not of sound mind because of one of the other things mentioned in the law" (9). The influence of a woman is again ellipsed in this (admittedly casual) citation of the law. Perhaps, as Wyse (1904: 495) proposes, the speaker is trying to preempt the counter-argument that Chaerestratus' mother persuaded Philoctemon to adopt her son.

58 Wyse 1904: 485. While illegitimate children did, on occasion, slip past scrutiny in the phratry (as the periodic cleansing of the lists suggests), the public nature of life in Athens made it difficult to get away with. The phratry would have asked all the questions this speaker is asking – who was their mother? who was her father? who will bear witness to the marriage? – and apparently they, at any rate, believed the answers they received.

case is in fact the subtext of all inheritance cases inasmuch as they routinely construct fictions of kinship, legitimate and illegitimate, in order to defraud potentially rightful heirs. Claimants who don't make Philoctemon's choice don't take their claims to court. Those who do expose their *oikos* to the same scandals of illegitimacy as this case both depicts and performs. The domestic chaos attributed in this speech to a woman's persuasion is in fact the result of legal discourse's own persuasive maneuvers. Alce both names and displaces this rhetorical *alkē*.

Individual litigants like the speaker of Isaeus 6 want the case of the woman to be closed: legitimate or illegitimate, wife or mistress, they want a decisive verdict. Likewise, the *oikos* and the polis. But juridical discourse requires her case to remain perpetually open so that it can decide it in each new iteration. This means, however, that the woman remains a point of openness within juridical discourse and that the indeterminacy the discourse generates around her may undermine the finality of its own determinations about her and everything else. Such is the case in Isaeus 3 *On the Estate of Pyrrhus*. This trial revolves around the question of Pyrrhus' nameless *gunē*: competing answers produce competing genealogies and legal claims. The case is complicated, one in a series of ongoing disputes over Pyrrhus' troubled bequest. Pyrrhus adopted Endius, his sister's son, and left his substantial estate to him by will. On Endius' death, the estate was claimed by Xenocles on behalf of his wife Phile, who he asserted was the legitimate daughter of Pyrrhus. His claim is opposed by Endius' mother, who is Pyrrhus' sister and next of kin. This speech is delivered by her son (Endius' brother), technically as a charge of false-witnessing against Nicodemus, the brother of Phile's mother, for testifying in a previous action that his sister was legitimately married to Pyrrhus. Phile was deemed illegitimate in that previous trial, but the case of these women, Pyrrhus' wife and daughter, is still open.

The central question of the speech is whether Phile's mother was Pyrrhus' *gunē enguētē*, his legitimate wife given in *enguē* by her brother Nicodemus, or a courtesan (*hetaira*) he took to live with him. It is crucial to the speaker's case that the two categories be mutually exclusive: Phile's mother was either one or the other, a point he makes by slyly collapsing the two. Nicodemus claims he gave his sister to Pyrrhus as a *gunē enguētē*, but in that case, the speaker says, I'd like to know if anyone beside Pyrrhus also had his sister as a wedded wife, either someone who knew her before she met Pyrrhus or one of the many who "approached" (*eplēsiazon*) her with his knowledge or after his death. "For it's obvious that her brother had betrothed her in the same way to all those who approached her" (*plēsiazousin*, 10). *Plēsiazein*, which literally means "to draw near," often bears a sexual meaning in Greek.[59] This woman, the speaker insinuates, was the wife of many men, both before she met her "husband" and after. And yet, he says, explaining the joke, "when they themselves have agreed that the woman (*gunaika*) was common property of anyone who wanted, how can the same woman reasonably be considered a legally wedded wife (*gunē enguētē*)?" (11).

The speaker supports this slander not by calling the other men to testify – although he says he could – but by cross-referencing it with her other behavior. He mentions "the quarrels and drunken serenades and lewdness that surrounded her when she was living with Pyrrhus" (13). "And yet I dare say no one would have the nerve to serenade a married woman, nor do married women come to dinner with their husbands or think it right to dine with strange men, much less with anyone who happens along" (14). Proper wives do not dine with strange men. They do not party or quarrel in public. And they certainly do not sleep around.[60]

The woman's status is determined by her own actions but even more so by the men's. Witnesses are called to testify to the non-performance of various expected rituals. "For it is obvious that if Pyrrhus had been persuaded to marry her he would also have been persuaded to hold a wedding feast (*gamēlian*) for her in his phratry and to introduce her daughter as his legitimate child" (79–80). But since such rituals were not mandatory, the speaker uses their non-performance less as proof in itself than as evidence for the arguments from probability that dominate the speech. In trying to prove that there was no *enguē* between Pyrrhus and Nicodemus, for example, the speaker floats two contradictory probabilities. On the one hand, he argues, it is unlikely that Nicodemus would have brought only one witness for such an important transaction; since he did there could not have been an *enguē*. On the other hand, Pyrrhus brought his uncles as witnesses, whereas it is much more likely that he would have wanted to keep such a shameful arrangement secret from them. The uncles, therefore, must be lying (18–27).

With this same impeccable logic the speaker analyzes the probable behavior of every kinsman who had any stake in this woman: Nicodemus her brother, Xenocles her husband, the dead Pyrrhus, Pyrrhus' heir Endius (also long dead), Pyrrhus' uncles. Surveying their actual and potential actions,

59 Cf. Dem. 59.19, 20, 37, 41.

60 A similar picture is painted of the *hetaira* Neaira at Dem. 59.33–34: not only did she go to parties and get drunk with her then-partner Phrynion, but she even had sex there with other men, including slaves, while he was passed out. Cf. 48: "she ate and drank with [the men] like a *hetaira*" (*hōs hetaira ousa*).

the decisions made and alternatives rejected, the speaker concludes that neither Endius, Nicodemus, nor the uncles treated Phile "like an *epiklēros*," a legitimate, property-bearing daughter. If they had considered her an *epiklēros*, then the uncles would have tried to marry her, Endius would never have given her away to a poor husband, Nicodemus would have claimed the estate immediately upon Pyrrhus' death instead of waiting (49–50, 64–71). Instead, they treat her "like the daughter of a *hetaira*" (*hōs ex hetairas*, 47–54, 70). These *eikos* arguments define the woman, but do so in a way that renders her inherently fictional: what is the status, marital or ontological, of a woman who is what various men probably considered her? The logical (or often illogical) apodosis of a hypothetical protasis, the tendentious "then" to the speaker's posited "if," she is the unreal product of law's rhetoric of probability.

Amidst all these hypotheticals, the dowry might seem to offer the solidity of hard, cold cash. The existence of a dowry was one marker of a legitimate union, and (since dowries were returned to the natal family if the marriage was dissolved without children) the movement of the dowry was a way of tracking the history of a relationship.[61] The speaker in Isaeus 3, as we might expect, makes much of this issue. What dowry did Nicodemus give with his sister? Did he get it back when the marriage ended? If not, why did he not sue to recover it? (8–9). But there was no formal legal requirement that all marriages include a dowry and one can imagine scenarios (and indeed we shall soon see one) in which a dowry might not be given.[62] Moreover, the existence of a dowry was proved in the same way as the existence of a wife – through witnesses and probabilities – and thus it operates within the same logical economy as the dubious marriage. Would Nicodemus have given his sister without a dowry, especially knowing that the dowry would revert to him if she died childless, the speaker asks? "Does any of you really think that Nicodemus is so unconcerned about money as to overlook these considerations? I don't think so" (37, cf. 39).

This rationale is later spelled out explicitly. Do you think that if Phile were Pyrrhus' legitimate daughter, Pyrrhus' uncles would have allowed her to be given to a husband from outside the family, instead of one of them taking her (and the estate) himself? "Don't believe it, jurors. For

[61] The nature of the dowry in Attic law and practice is much discussed: Wolff 1944: 53–65; Harrison 1968: 45–60; W. K. Lacey 1968: 109–10; Schaps 1979: 74–88, 99–107; Foxhall 1989, esp. 32–39; Hunter 1989: 295–96; Sealey 1990: 26–28; Todd 1993: 215–16; Cox 1998: 75–77, 116–20; Omitowoju 2002: 117–19.

[62] Wyse 1904: 308: "The truth is that, if the speaker's description of Nicodemus' sister is true, she was just the sort of person to be married without a dowry." Cf. Just 1989: 48; Foxhall 1989: 33–34.

no man hates profit or puts another's advantage before his own" (*oudeis gar anthrōpōn misei to lusiteloun, oude peri pleionos tous allotrious heautou poieitai*, 66). This generalization is the latent premise behind all the speech's probabilities and governs the hypothetical economy within which it imagines women to circulate. In this economy, any behavior that does not seek to maximize profit is logically suspect and improbable. "No man hates profit" thus functions as the epigram of a master-narrative about normative matrimonial strategies, about rational actions and reasonable motives, legitimate unions and contractual exchanges of property. This normative tale is twice told in the speech: in the positive version the opponents are expected to give as they defend the legitimacy of the marriage, and in the negative version given by the speaker as he asserts its impropriety. These two narratives, the opponents' implicit morality tale and the speaker's explicit immorality tale, are two sides of the same coin: they reinforce the same norms and obey the same logic of practice, a logic predicated on the simple principle that no man hates profit.

But alongside these twin narratives the speaker also, almost inadvertently, tells another, a story in which the profit motive does not operate, norms are irrelevant, and the difference between wife and *hetaira* doesn't matter. In short, he tells a love story:

> Let's consider how a person might surmise that there was a legal union (*enguē*) to such a woman, supposing such a thing actually happened to my uncle. Some young men, desiring (*epithumēsantes*) such women and having no self-control, have in the past been persuaded by their own foolishness (*anoias*) to commit such a crime against themselves (*eis hautous toiouton ti exhamartein*). (16–17)

From the speech's dominant economy of legitimate (and profitable) alliances we shift momentarily to an alternate social world, vaguely conjured through imagined surmise and provisional supposition. In this indistinct world "some young men" have already "in the past" fallen in love with *hetairai* and it seems (although the speaker can't quite bring himself to say it) even married them. Perhaps this is an allusion to the world of contemporary comedy where, as Susan Lape has shown, love often appears to conquer economic differences and status distinctions.[63] Foolish young men in love with *hetairai* are a staple of the comic stage; they occasionally even marry them. A window is tentatively opened onto this world only

[63] She argues that although comic marriages are ostensibly motivated by love, they invariably conform in the end to the civic norms of marital legitimacy (as the *hetairai* are ultimately revealed to have been legitimate Athenian girls all along), thereby naturalizing those norms. See Lape 2004: 96–109, and on the way middle comedy challenges the distinction between wife and *hetaira*, 159–67, 244–48.

to be immediately closed by the moralizing language that subjects akratic desire to self-mastery and makes the seduction of foolish love into a crime against oneself (*exhamartein*; cf. *hamartēma*, 27). But even veiled by censorious morality, this glimpse aside suggests a counter-narrative that challenges the terms of the speech's probable universe. The grudging admission that "some young men" might actually marry "such women" undermines the hard distinction between *gunē enguētē* and *hetaira*: a courtesan might become a wife; a wife might once have been a courtesan. Akratic desire skews the speech's economy of matrimony, undoing the dichotomies on which it is grounded and the proprieties and probabilities it governs. Who knows what a man would do in the grip of such a foolish passion?

Money should clarify the confusions of desire: some foolish young men may have married *hetairai*, but no man hates profit. Everyone knows that love matches rarely last, says the speaker (29). If my uncle did marry that kind of woman under the influence of desire (*di' epithumian*) then obviously her brother would have made all the more certain to reach a dowry agreement so that Pyrrhus could not "easily get rid of the woman whenever he wished" (28). The dowry is an anchor against the vagaries of desire, a public and enforceable contract between two men. But if, as the speaker implies, a dowry might have legitimated a foolish and improper love match, then the dowry too is set adrift. Not only does the absence of a dowry not prove the absence of a marriage, but the presence of a dowry would not – according to the speaker's own argument – necessarily prove that the *gunē* had not once been a *hetaira*.

The dowry, supposed seal of legitimacy, cannot fully cover the embarrassments of *epithumia*. Indeed, it comes to look rather embarrassing itself, for what the speaker offers as a hedge against fickle passion is in fact a phony financial agreement. If Pyrrhus did marry Nicodemus' sister for love, "then obviously the man giving her away would have made all the more effort to make the other agree that he received money with the woman" (28). The speaker seems to be insinuating that the two would conspire to produce a fictitious dowry, Pyrrhus in order to lend an air of legitimacy to his lust, Nicodemus in order to rid himself with minimal scandal of a promiscuous sister. The details of this "agreement about a dowry" (*homologias proikos*, 29) are naturally left vague. But we get a general sense of the deal later in the speech. Nicodemus would never have given his sister to Pyrrhus without a dowry, speculates the speaker, especially knowing the impermanence of such unions and that the dowry would revert to him if she died without issue. "Do you think that Nicodemus was so unconcerned with money that, if the matter were true, he would not calculate his own advantage quite precisely? By Zeus, I think he would, since even those who give their own women as concubines (*pallakai*) first reach agreements about what will be given to the concubine" (39).[64] Nicodemus, the speaker implies, has pimped his sister to Pyrrhus, offering her as a mistress upon agreement to a fictitious dowry. If a dowry is the sign of legitimate genealogy, legitimate relations between men, and the legitimate status of a woman, then what does a phony dowry signify?

The fictional dowry turns the principle of rational self-interest ("no man hates profit") into another variety of akratic desire. As Pyrrhus may have desired a *hetaira*, Nicodemus desires money (*epithumōn*, 39), and like Pyrrhus, he will transgress social proprieties to satisfy his desire, even perjure himself in court and prostitute his sister (39). The two desires, erotic and financial, are in fact entangled from the start. Foolish men sometimes do marry *hetairai*, but if there were a marriage in this case Pyrrhus logically should have called no relatives to witness the shameful "crime" (27) and Nicodemus, guarding his financial interests, should have had many friends present. For only when events are "sudden and unforeseen" do men get random witnesses (19). As it is, the speaker notes, Pyrrhus called his uncles to attend the "wedding" and Nicodemus had only one witness who later recanted his testimony (17–27). Thus it is Nicodemus, not Pyrrhus, who treats the affair as something shameful and scandalous, "sudden and unforeseen." His is the secretive and erratic behavior of a man committing a crime against himself. The profit motive that drives the speech is just another foolish passion, as impermanent and unpredictable as love itself. The dowry has been counterfeited, as have the relations between the men who exchange it. Is the woman (*gunē*) transferred with such a dowry a wife (*gunē*)? Desire, whether for a woman or for money, has made the question unanswerable.

The fundamental indeterminacy that surrounds the women in this speech is encapsulated in the question of the girl's name:

I am extremely irritated at this, that her husband when he filed this suit for the paternal estate on behalf of his wife listed the woman's name as Phile, while Pyrrhus' uncles, who claim they were present at her ten-day celebration, testified that her father gave her the name Cleitarete, after her grandmother. I am surprised if the man who has been living with her for more than eight years did not yet

[64] A *pallakē* was a long-term live-in *hetaira* (see Wyse 1904: 318; Wolff 1944: 73–74; Just 1989: 52–53). This passage has led many scholars to believe that there was a class of citizen *hetairai* in Athens: Harrison 1968: 13–15; MacDowell 1978: 90; Sealey 1984a, 1990: 31–32; Just 1989: 54; Mossé 1991; Patterson 1991; and (most forcefully) E. Cohen 2000: 167–91 (and n. 66) and 2006. *Contra*, see Ogden 1996: 158–63; Kapparis 1999: 9–10.

know the name of his own wife. Was he unable to find it out from one of his witnesses? Did the woman's mother never mention her daughter's name to him in all that time, nor her uncle Nicodemus? But instead of her grandmother's name (if anyone knew that her father gave her this name), her husband put down the name Phile – and this when he was filing a claim to the ancestral inheritance! (30–32)

Heir to two competing genealogies, Pyrrhus' daughter has two names. One, Phile ("Love" or "Dear"), is the name of a *hetaira*'s daughter; it denominates the scandalous affair from which the speaker claims she was born and is part of the maternal legacy passed down from an improper mother to an "improperly born daughter" (12).[65] The other is the name of Pyrrhus' mother and inserts the girl into a legitimate, public family lineage: it is, the speaker says, her paternal inheritance (32). The two names – and the maternal and paternal genealogies they symbolize – are presented as mutually exclusive: she must bear one or the other, but which is the true one? Both her husband (the speaker improbably claims) and the law are confused. The girl's double name bespeaks an irreducible indeterminacy: wife or *hetaira*, legitimate or illegitimate, Cleitarete or Phile? The speech attempts to resolve that indeterminacy, but in the process opens the way to a counter-narrative that reproduces it, a narrative in which love (*philia*) becomes indistinguishable from matrimonial virtue (*aretē*). For if a young man married a *hetaira* – as some young men have apparently done – what more appropriate name could he give the child of that unnameable union than "Phile or/and Cleitarete"?

What if "Phile" were the name not only of her father's desire but also of the law's desire? Phile's mother, the speaker claims, was available to "anyone who wanted" (*ho boulomenos*), and that availability is partly how the speaker identifies her as a *hetaira* not a *gunē*: "when they themselves have agreed that the woman was the common property of anyone who wanted (*koinēn . . . tou boulomenou tēn gunaika*) how can the same woman reasonably be considered a legally wedded wife (*gunē enguētē*)?" (11). The same phrase, *ho boulomenos*, denotes the voluntary prosecutor and (as I argued in Chapter 3) the idealized subject of Athenian law.[66] Inheritance

[65] Name changes or pet names may be characteristic of *hetairai*: Cox 1998: 176–77; cf. Carey and Reid 1985: 175 *ad* Dem. 39.9. Neaira's daughter ("whom they used to call Strubele but now call Phano," Dem. 59.50) is a close parallel. On Phile's name, see Ogden 1996: 96, and on the theoretical ramifications of naming for women, Butler 1993: 153: "Expropriation is thus the condition of identity for women. Identity is secured precisely in and through the transfer of the name, the name as a site of transfer or substitution, the name, then, as precisely what is always impermanent, different from itself, more than itself, the non-self-identical."

[66] I owe this connection to Gilhuly 2008, who stresses the democratic connotations of the phrase. She comments on its use in reference to Neaira's sexual availability in Dem. 59 (19, 20, 23):

cases were *dikai*, not *graphai*, and therefore in theory restricted to interested parties, but even here the ideal of volition is strong: the speaker in Isaeus 6, for instance, says that in the absence of a natural, legitimate son "it is possible for any Athenian who wants (*Athēnaiōn tōi boulomenōi*) to dispute the inheritance and come before you in a direct trial and, if he seems to speak more justly, to gain the estate" (6.3). The speaker in Isaeus 3 makes a similar argument: if his opponents really believed Phile was Pyrrhus' daughter, they could have just taken the property without recourse to a legal adjudication, since the claims of legitimate children (*gnēsioi paides*) are indisputable (59).[67] This argument suggests that if Phile really were legitimate the law would have no right to intervene in this inheritance. That is to say, it is because her mother was sexually available to *ho boulomenos* that the estate is legally available to *ho boulomenos*. Legal discourse thus wants (*boulesthai*), indeed needs, the woman to be ambiguous: her double name invites its discursive "approach" (*plēsiazein*) to the *oikos* and her always potential illegitimacy – is she a *gunē* or a *gunē*? – opens a point of voluntary intervention into the reproduction of the family and the future of the city.

By simultaneously resolving and producing indeterminacy around the person of the *gunē*, legal discourse writes its own genealogy, but that genealogy bears traces of its ambiguous feminine legacy. The juridical woman oscillates uncertainly between wife and mistress, legitimate and illegitimate, an oscillation the discourse fosters in order to impose its own certainties. The case of the *gunē* is thus never closed. Even as juridical discourse uses women to secure its own institutional reproduction and discursive legitimacy, these feminine fictions remain a locus of possible variation or mutation within the discourse and institution of the law. This is not because they are feminine: to be sure, woman as such is unrepresentable within the Athenian judicial symbolic, but in that she is not unique, for as I have argued in previous chapters, that symbolic order defines itself through myriad such exclusions. Instead, they remain open because they are fictions, paradigmatic products of the fertile but

"Apollodoros' displacement of this term [*ho boulomenos*] onto the trade of Neaira denigrates her through the uneasy assimilation of the accessibility of her services to participation in the Athenian democracy. The analogy makes Neaira's body into a parody of democracy, one that is available for hire" (41).

[67] Cf. 3.46: if he really thought Phile was Pyrrhus' legitimate daughter, Nicodemus could have sued Endius for mistreatment of an *epiklēros* (for marrying her off with such a paltry dowry), "since it is open to anyone who wants (*tōi boulomenōi*) to come to the aid of an *epiklēros*" (46). Cases involving *epiklēroi* were *graphai* and therefore actually could be prosecuted by "anyone who wanted."

unsystematic creativity that generates the entire discursive cosmos of Athenian law.

The institutional genealogy predicated on these fictions is, as a result, truly a genealogy in Foucault's sense of the word: continuously disrupted by "the singular randomness" of forged wills and spurious dowries, bastard children and erratic, unprofitable desires, this genealogy of law resists the closed self-identity and "monotonous finality" of an eternally self-replicating patriline.[68] Legal discourse perpetuates itself through its perpetuation of the family, but does so, I have suggested, not only by resolving family crises but also by creating them: by generating ambiguity in the structures of kinship, illegitimacy in the bloodline, opacity in the written testament, and indeterminacy in the status of the woman. It claims control over the definition of legitimacy (both familial and civic) and the continuity of succession not by simplifying the family tree and clarifying its outlines with definitive edicts in advance, but by fostering the countless uncertainties that will drive its members repeatedly back into court, generation after generation, for trials in which *nomos* itself is the ultimate victor. But if legal discourse reproduces itself by way of such familial uncertainty, its own succession is no more unitary or secure than that of the families it creates, and its domestic sagas contain narrative mutations and genetic variations – counter-genealogies of the family and the law – that prevent the hermetic closure of perfect discursive self-replication. Producing illegitimacy even as it disowns it, juridical discourse can never finally vouch for its own legitimacy, as its promise of genealogical continuity – the family's, the city's, and the law's – comes with the guarantee that no generation will be fully identical to the last.

[68] Foucault 1977b: 139, 154–55, and see the epigram at the head of this chapter.

Conclusion: the paradigmatic law

> Androcles of Pitthus, prosecuting a proposed law, was shouted at when he said "The laws need a law to set them right. Fish need salt, although it is neither probable nor plausible that they should since they grow up in salt water. Likewise, olive cakes need olive oil, although it is hard to believe that something that produces oil would need oil."
>
> Aristotle *Rhetoric* 1400a9–14

> Were one forced to offer a conclusion as to the significance of the legal tradition, it would be in terms of a system of transmission, of messages and so of texts, specialised writing systems or structures of notation. Were one to build a critique of that tradition of transmission, then it would have to start with the question of texts and of the linguistics of legal texts.
>
> Goodrich 1990a: 110

> Being taught with many examples (*paradeigmata*) makes your verdict easy.
>
> Lycurgus *Against Leocrates* 124

LAW, CODE

Modern jurisprudence is characterized by an ideal of systematicity: it aims at (even if it necessarily fails to achieve) completeness, unity, consistency, and stability. Since the compilation of the Justinian *Corpus Iuris Civilis* in sixth-century CE Rome, these goals have been attached to the idea of a written code, and a written code has in turn been seen as the essence of the law. The commitment to codification has been particularly strong in the civil law tradition that traces its origins to the *Corpus Iuris Civilis*, but common law, too, is predicated on the notion of a legal code, though one that takes the form not of a single authoritative text but of a historical accretion of decisions in individual cases. Both traditions are governed by a principle of law's coherence and comprehensiveness as a system, by the idea of the code as "a complete source of law . . . a closed system of binding rules," a law of law, as it were.[1]

Athenian law, by contrast, not only lacked a written code but was resistant to the very idea of codification. Indeed, from a modern perspective one of the most striking features of Athenian law is precisely its asystematicity: the "open texture" that enabled plaintiffs to choose among a variety of procedures; the amateurism that left individual litigants responsible for identifying and locating the laws pertinent to their case; the loose (if not outright misleading) citation of statutes in court. Adriaan Lanni suggests that this asystematicity was the result of a conscious choice: in the popular courts, she argues, the Athenians adopted a discretionary, ad hoc approach to legal decision-making and were willing to sacrifice consistency and predictability to pursue a highly individualized notion of justice.[2] This resistance to codification was due in part, as Lanni and others have stressed, to the Athenians' commitment to the democratic principle of popular sovereignty. As a source of legal authority beyond and above that vested in the judgment of the democratic jury, a codified law might have seemed to many Athenians inherently antidemocratic, and it is perhaps no coincidence that the most rigorous theoretical attempt at codification was undertaken by Plato, no friend of the demos.[3]

That said, Athenian law does show some impulses toward systematization. The frequent appeals to the laws of Draco and Solon – appeals more to the idea of a lawcode than to an actually existing collection – are one instance. The Athenians gathered dispersed statutes under the name of the original lawmaker, whose beneficent intent and traditional authority granted the laws attributed to him legitimacy, consistency and permanence.[4] References to the "unwritten laws," rare in forensic oratory but well documented in other Athenian literature, likewise imagine a

[1] Goodrich 1986: 99, and see further 21–60 on the place of codification in civil and common law.

[2] Lanni 2006. See further Ruschenbusch 1957; Osborne 1985; Harris 2000; and Carey 2004: 132: "The Athenians never pursued structural neatness for its own sake, either in the law code or in the democratic constitution. It would be unwise to impose on them a degree of systematisation in the approach to law which they never attempted."

[3] Ober 1989a: 302; Allen 2000a: 179–90; Lanni 2006: 110–11, 175–79. Ostwald's (1986) progression "from popular sovereignty to the sovereignty of law" both assumes and argues that a written lawcode functioned as a (salutary) check on popular sovereignty: see esp. 409–11, 509–24. Nightingale 1999 emphasizes the distance between Plato's lawcode, in which the written laws achieve the status of a sacred text, and the role of the written laws in contemporary Athenian legal theory and practice; see also Gagarin 2000.

[4] Johnstone 1999: 25–33 analyzes the lawgiver as "an Athenian form of legal reasoning" (26) by which the law was imagined as coherent in purpose and logic. By contrast, R. Thomas 1994 posits a tension between the democratic appeal to written law and the anti-democratic notion of a single legislator. I don't find the two concepts as antithetical as she suggests.

timeless, coherent body of moral law.[5] While these divinely sanctioned laws were imagined as all the more authoritative for being unwritten, writing seems to have been central to the conceptualization of Greek law from the late seventh century on. Michael Gagarin has argued that during the archaic period writing in fact served to define "the law" as an authoritative institution by standardizing legal rules and setting them apart from general norms and customs. "Writing thus created the sense of a self-contained set of legal regulations that fixed substantive standards of conduct in many areas as well as standards and rules for judicial procedure. As a single cohesive set, existing at a specific time and place, written law also conveyed the sense of a fixed, stable institution – the Law."[6] The move toward written inscription of law was particularly marked in classical Athens, no doubt as a way of making the laws more accessible and democratic. A ban against unwritten laws seems to have been part of the legal reforms undertaken at the end of the fifth century.[7]

These reforms themselves show the clearest indication of an impulse within Athenian jurisprudence toward codification. Undertaken partly in response to the oligarchic coups of 411 and 404 and the civil war of 403, these reforms aimed to clarify and regularize the traditional "laws of Solon." Statutes previously written on stone stelai scattered throughout the city were now to be collected and inscribed collectively on the wall of the Stoa Basileios; conflicting laws were to be reconciled or removed; boards of *nomothetai* were established to oversee the introduction of new laws.[8] While

[5] Aristotle recommends appeal to the unwritten laws for those whose case is not supported by written laws (*Rhet.* 1375a–b), but such appeals are found in forensic oratory (to my knowledge) only at Lys. 6.10–11 and Dem. 18.275, 23.70. Outside oratory references occur at Soph. *Ant.* 454–55; Ar. *Ach.* 532; Thuc. 2.37; Pl. *Laws* 793a; Arist. *Pol.* 1287b; *Rhet.* 1368b, 1373b; Xen. *Mem.* 4.4.19–20. See further de Romilly 1971: 25–49; Ostwald 1973; Carey 1996: 40; R. Thomas 1996: 16–19, 2005: 52–53.

[6] Gagarin 2003b: 67–72; the quotation is on p. 72; cf. now Gagarin 2008: 6, 92. See also C. Thomas 1977; Maffi 1988; R. Thomas 1989: 34–83, 1996, 2005; Hölkeskamp 1992; Svenbro 1993: 109–22; Robb 1994: 125–56; Gehrke 2000; Mirhady 2000a: 183; Sickinger 2002; Gagarin 2004. Even when law was written, forensic procedure probably remained predominantly oral: see D. Cohen 2003; Gagarin 2003b, 2004: 25, 2005: 37–38, 2008: 195–97, 206–09.

[7] And. 1.85–87. On the democratic nature of written laws see, e.g., Eur. *Suppl.* 433–44: "When the laws are written down, the weak and the rich have equal justice." Cf. Pl. *Laws* 680a and the balanced discussion in R. Thomas 1992: 128–57, 1996, 2005: 42–43. Others have noted the potentially anti-democratic force of written law; e.g. Hedrick 1994: "It is precisely the fixity and disengagement of the written word and the law from the living mind of the people which make them at the same time potentially an egalitarian standard and an unresponsive instrument of authority" (168). Cf. Steiner 1994: 127–85 on the association of writing with Eastern tyranny.

[8] The key ancient sources are *IG* I^3 104, Lys. 30, And. 1.81–89. The exact nature and effect of these reforms is one of the most debated topics in Athenian legal history. See Harrison 1955; Fingarette 1971; MacDowell 1978: 46–49; Sealey 1982: 293–96, 1994: 44–50; Ostwald 1986: 509–24; Hansen 1990; Robertson 1990; Rhodes 1991; Todd 1993: 57–58, 1996: 120–31; R. Thomas 1994: 120; Sickinger 1999: 93–105, 2004; Munn 2000: 261–72; Volonaki 2001; Carawan 2002: 12–23; Sundahl 2003; Lanni 2006: 142–48; Gagarin 2008: 183–88.

the details of these revisions are highly uncertain, their general rationale seems clear enough: an authoritative written text is the surest protection of legality in times of civic turmoil. By collecting, scrutinizing, and inscribing the various existing laws, the revisions seem to aim to secure the law as a complete and permanent code. In terms of jurisprudential logic, at least, they are the distant ancestor of the code of Justinian and modern civil law.

In practice, however, it is uncertain whether these revisions were completed or the comprehensive code they envisioned actually ever established.[9] Stephen Todd observes that, apart from the confusing and tendentious account in Andocides, we never hear of this supposedly authoritative code again – "presumably because of the sheer physical awkwardness of keeping up to date such a single inscribed stone text" – and that when fourth-century orators cite the laws, they never give the inscription at the Stoa Basileios as their source.[10] On the contrary, he notes, the laws governing *nomothesia* underwent repeated emendation throughout the first half of the fourth century, of which "the general effect seems to have been to make it progressively easier to change the law; and an increasing readiness to do this would be a public admission that codification had frozen the law in an artificial and unacceptable way."[11] Todd argues that the codification that had seemed like such a good idea in 403 proved to have two serious flaws: first, it made legal innovation difficult (for "unlike a word-processed typescript, an epigraphic text does not automatically re-format itself"); second, it made it obvious, challenging the antiquity of the supposedly traditional laws. "When it came to the crunch," he concludes, "we might suspect that the Athenians collectively preferred chaos and a sense of continuity to coherence at the price of admitting change."[12]

While the pragmatics of epigraphy and the politics of democracy provide compelling explanations of the Athenians' historical equivocation toward a written legal code, they do not fully explain the pervasive ambivalence

[9] Robertson 1990 is the most skeptical. He doubts that a permanent code was in fact published and remarks, "It is clear that the talk of a 'law-code' revised and published in the years 410–399 comes mainly from the preoccupations of modern scholars and from their preference for tidiness and thoroughness" (45). Even if the revisions were completed, they may not have amounted to a real "code of law" in the modern sense, as Sealey 1994: 55 notes: "A Greek 'code' was no more than a list of *leges*," and never developed into a *ius*, a concept of the law as "a continuum, embracing all relations between persons." Cf. Westbrook 2000; Sundahl 2003: 153–54; Gagarin 2008: 74–75.

[10] Todd 1993: 58; cf. 1996: 129. He is building on the observations of Hansen 1990: 70–71; cf. Robertson 1990; Hansen 1991: 164.

[11] Todd 1996: 129. On the fourth-century theory and practice of *nomothesia*, see further Harrison 1955; Hansen 1971–80, 1985, 1991: 161–77; MacDowell 1975; Sealey 1982: 289–93; Rhodes 1985.

[12] Todd 1996: 130. De Romilly 1971: 203–25 traces the tension between desire for stability and love of progress in Athenian jurisprudential thought; cf. Boegehold 1996, arguing for the stability of Athenian law.

toward legal systematization within forensic oratory. Athenian forensic orators, as we have seen in the preceding chapters, were exceptionally skilled at squaring the circle, at aligning competing ideologies and harmonizing even manifestly discordant principles. When contradictions remain, then, as they do surrounding the notion of legal codification, they ask to be explained not in terms of external factors – the demands of politics or pragmatism – but in terms of tensions internal to Athenian jurisprudential thought.

This concluding chapter argues that the orators' equivocation about the idea of a legal code reflects a fundamental ambivalence toward the very discourse that they themselves created and within which they operated. Juridical discourse was, of course, itself a sort of noetic code, governed (as the preceding chapters have documented) by its own ambitions toward consistency, comprehensiveness, and permanence. While the code is by no means a simple stand-in for the discourse, this chapter proposes that in its competing desire for and wariness of codification, forensic oratory reflects on the systematicity – the limits and logic, coherence and stability – of juridical discourse itself.

More specifically, I suggest that the ambivalence toward a legal code reflects forensic oratory's simultaneous desire for and antipathy toward discursive closure. We have seen throughout the preceding chapters the way these speeches strive for autopoietic closure. In Demosthenes 25 (Chapter 1) the speaker aimed to build a juridical cosmos and seal off *nomos* with an iron chain from everything that might threaten it (including the hateful Aristogeiton, but also *phusis* and its errant desires). Not just closed, law's imagined cosmos is also internally consistent (as Antiphon's *Tetralogies*, with their alignment of psychology and metaphysics, illustrate) and eternal, projecting itself into the past and replicating itself in the future (as the last chapter argued). But if forensic oratory longs to construct a fixed and permanent juridical world, it also displays some anxiety about the hermeticism this project might entail, a fear that the law will become closed in on itself and divorced from both reality and justice. Thus, for example, in Chapter 2 we saw that the law's discursive boundaries are haunted by its excluded objects, like those victims of judicial violence whose suffering was judged legally irrelevant and yet still echoed within the rhetoric of the speeches. Even in Antiphon's hermetic judicial scenario, a litigant will occasionally up and run away.[13]

[13] On the problem of closure in modern jurisprudential thought, see especially Stewart 1987; Fish 1991; Cornell 1992a: 116–54, 1995a; Goodrich 1993; N. Lacey 1993. Much of the discussion has been in

Forensic oratory's ambivalence to the notion of a legal code reflects this tension. This chapter examines this seminal ambivalence and in so doing recapitulates many of the themes of the previous chapters. It offers a conclusion to this book as a whole by way of brief readings of two speeches that approach the law as a system (Demosthenes 24) or a text (Lysias 10). Both cases dream of a law that is internally consistent, completely lucid, fixed, and eternal. Demosthenes 24, a case prosecuting an illegal law, puts on trial the legality of the legal system as a whole. It constructs a pure legal code and attempts to defend it against the defilement of illegality only to find that the walls it guards are already breached and that the law it defends cannot easily be segregated from the illegal law against which it defends. While Demosthenes 24 fears the failure of codification, Lysias 10 fears its success. In that speech, the code is imagined as all too well secured: fixed to the point of immobility, its spirit trapped in an unchanging text, the law risks petrification. In their simultaneous desire for a fixed legal code and their fear of its vulnerability or static rigidity, these speeches situate the law in an uncertain space between codification and asystematicity. But that uncertainty is figured not as a failure but as a victory. In Demosthenes 24 the code's ambivalence is transmuted into the fantasy of a paradigmatic law. This single law encapsulates with paradigmatic clarity the ideal of Athenian legal discourse: a jurisprudence that is simultaneously fixed and flexible, closed and open, inscribed and alive.

THE LAW OF LAW (DEMOSTHENES 24)

Demosthenes 24 *Against Timocrates* prosecutes an illegal law; in the process it defends a vision of law as a rational, fixed, and coherent whole. The case is a *graphē nomon mē epitēdeion theinai*, literally "a public suit for proposing an improper (*mē epitēdeion*) law," an action closely related to the *graphē paranomōn*, a suit prosecuting an illegal (*paranomon*) decree.[14] These procedures judged whether a proposed law or decree was consistent with existing laws; they read the new law or decree side-by-side against the existing laws and in effect cast a verdict in favor of one or the other. The

critical response to the work of Niklas Luhmann and Hans Kelsen: see, e.g., Kelsen 1967; Luhmann 1988, 1992; and the articles in Teubner 1988. The *Cardozo Law Review* Vol. XIII, Issue 5 (1992) is devoted to discussion of Luhmann's theories.

[14] The target of the two procedures is different (a law vs. a decree) but their underlying logic is the same; the latter are far better attested (and hence more studied), likely due to the preponderance of decrees over laws. On the distinction between the procedures, see Wolff 1970: 37–44; Hansen 1974: 44–48. The classic work on these procedures is Wolff 1970; see also Hansen 1974: 28–65, 1991: 205–12.

graphē nomon mē epitēdeion theinai and *graphē paranomōn* imagine the law as a bounded system, but also presuppose the vulnerability of that system: the law needs a law to protect it. Demosthenes 24 elaborates the implicit logic of the procedure. Its mission is to guard the boundaries of the law, but it fears that this effort may already have failed – may in fact be failing even as the speech is being delivered.

Timocrates has proposed a law that grants bail to state debtors. Diodorus, the speaker, brings the suit on the ground that the law is, as he says, "neither appropriate nor just, but against all the laws" (*para pantas tous nomous nomon . . . out' epitēdeion oute dikaion*, 1). The case has an intricate back-story of personal enmity and political in-fighting: the debtors for whose sake Timocrates proposed this law (Diodorus claims) were his political allies, as well as known criminals.[15] Like most *paranomōn* cases – and, indeed, like most *graphai* in general – this brief blends political and legal arguments: Timocrates' proposed law is an assault simultaneously upon the laws and upon the democracy that established those laws and is protected by them.[16]

The laws Diodorus defends are not just individual statutes but an entire system of jurisprudence.[17] If Timocrates' law is valid, says Diodorus, "the other laws which you [the demos] have written against those who harm the polis will be invalid" (5). Were he to list every one, he says, it would consume all his allotted time (51, 61): suffice it to say that Timocrates' law contravenes not only all the laws he has mentioned but "I would practically say all the laws there are in the city" (66; cf. 38). Despite the immensity of the project, Diodorus does cite a good number of specific laws

[15] Roisman 2006: 103–14. A high percentage of extant *graphai paranomōn* deal with decrees proposing civic honors for individuals (Aesch. 3 and Dem. 18 are the most famous examples, indicting and defending, respectively, a decree to crown Demosthenes). This has led some scholars to argue that the primary thrust of the procedure was political, not legal: see especially Hansen 1974: 63–65. This distinction between the political and legal is difficult to maintain, however, and I am convinced by the argument of Yunis 1988 that the *graphē paranomōn* played a double role as political and legal review. See also Sundahl 2003.

[16] In the hyperbolic doom-mongering typical of public suits, Diodorus continually reminds the jurors that the laws are responsible "for everything that is good in the city and the fact that it is democratic and free" (5), and that if Timocrates' law is passed, it will undermine the democracy and destroy the city (e.g. 5, 31, 91, 98–99, 153–54, 216–17). The speech also makes frequent reference to the Thirty (57–58, 90, 154, 163–64). Timocrates' proposed law is compared to the sort of legislation they passed and the speaker's brief represented as the sole bulwark against another oligarchy. Fifty years after the coup these allusions may seem tenuous, but they do have some historical basis. The Thirty came to power by persuading the Ecclesia to vote itself out of existence (Thuc. 8.67; [Arist.] *Ath. Pol.* 29–33; cf. Dem. 24.154); the only law it needed to abolish in order to do so was the *graphē paranomōn*. See Hansen 1974: 55–61.

[17] Ostwald 1986: 125–29, 135–36. The very name of the procedure implies a coherent legal whole into which the new law does not "fit," a primary meaning of *epitēdeios*.

Timocrates has transgressed, both procedural rules governing ratification of new legislation (17–38) and substantive rules concerning the punishment of debtors (39–67). As he goes through them one by one, calling for the clerk to "read the next law" (*anagignōske ton hexēs nomon*, 49), he rhetorically weaves discrete provisions into a single continuous text, as if "the next law" were next within that text and not within the order of his own argument. By reading the laws he writes a unitary book of law.

The law's unity is predicated on its internal consistency. Among the countless laws Timocrates has transgressed is one stating that no law can be introduced in contradiction to another law (33). "Of all the excellent laws in the city, none was composed in a more praiseworthy manner than this one," opines Diodorus, for without it the laws would contradict one another. Then two rival litigants could each rightly claim the support of the law and the jurors would be forced to break their oath to judge according to the law, since voting for one litigant would mean contravening the law that supports his opponent (34). "The laws," although plural, constitute a coherent unity, and it is the mandate of the *graphē nomon mē epitēdeion theinai* to protect that unity. Diodorus carries out that mandate by reading Timocrates' law clause by clause – "from the first syllable to the last" (70; cf. 110) – and explaining how each and every one contradicts a commendable existing law.[18]

At the same time as it guarantees internal consistency, this supremely praiseworthy law also promises continuity between the text of the statute and the verdict through which it is enacted. Conflicting statutes would create practical chaos, forcing the jurors to vote against the law and against their oath to uphold it. Timocrates' law would thus set the jurors against the law. It would also set the law against the prior verdict of the jurors who sentenced debtors to prison, as well as those who, in the Ecclesia, voted to ratify the "established laws." "Timocrates thinks your opinion and the vote of the court and the rest of the laws should be invalid (*akurous*) and himself and his law valid (*kurion*)" (117).[19] Behind this warning lies an ideal in which the written *nomoi* and the jurors' vote are perfectly harmonized and mutually supporting. We saw in Chapter 1 how orators use this carefully forged convergence to authorize their own discourse. Here the same rhetorical strategy also works to authorize a vision of the law

[18] Timocrates' proposed law even contradicts a law he himself proposed in the past (62–64): "Timocrates prosecutes Timocrates" (64; cf. 87). On the laws' consistency, see further Aesch. 3.37–40; Dem. 20.90–91.

[19] Cf. 78: "Does anyone think it beneficial to the city for such a law to be more authoritative (*kuriōteros*) than the verdict of the court?" Cf. 2, 9, 47–48, 73, 87, 152.

that seamlessly integrates jurisprudential principle and forensic practice. The law is not just a code of written statutes but also its enactment in the vote of a jury. But there is no discontinuity between the two.[20] In fact, ideally, the two would be collapsed entirely. At §68 Diodorus imagines a law to set against Timocrates' proposed law, a law that is "proper and will benefit the demos." This law would be immediately intelligible and its meaning incontrovertible: "first it must be written straightforwardly so that everyone can understand it and it can't be interpreted one way by one person and another way by another." In contrast to the chaos imagined as the result of contradictory laws, this law eliminates potential conflict between the verdict of the jurors and the text of the law since it contains the jury's correct verdict within its own perspicuous text.[21]

Consistent and unified, the laws are also permanent. Timocrates' proposed law would obliterate (*ēphanisen*, *exēleipsen*, 38) "the established laws." The *graphē nomon mē epitēdeion theinai* by its very nature acknowledges that laws have a temporal origin: even the established laws once had to be established (*theinai*). But Diodorus' speech, in repulsing the intrusion of the new, pays deference to the old. The authority of tradition, here as in so many speeches, is embodied in the august person of Solon, whose laws – including many laws that have nothing to do with the subject of Timocrates' proposal – are held up as models of well-written legislation. "What different sorts of legislator are Solon and Timocrates," remarks Diodorus (106): Solon imprisoned criminals while Timocrates grants them immunity (103); Solon deterred crime while Timocrates rewards it (113). For each, "the law that he has dared to establish reveals his character" (138).[22] This sort of pointed juridico-ethical comparison is ubiquitous in forensic oratory, but what is more unusual here is the temporal idiom in which it is expressed. Solon's laws improve citizens in the present and future, while Timocrates' provides immunity for criminals past, present, and future (106). This chimes with a tune Diodorus sings throughout the speech: the illegal retroactivity of Timocrates' law. By granting bail to debtors already sentenced to prison, it overturns the past verdict of the jury

[20] *Pace* Allen 2000a: 180, who believes the speech "betrays a tension between the idea that laws are the authority in or masters of the city and the idea that jurors and their judgment are."

[21] Compare Dem. 23, a *graphē paranomōn*. There one of the primary objections to the proposed decree is that its phraseology treats the accused criminal as though his guilt were already established, thereby ellipsing the trial (22–36, 63–64). The verdict of the jurors should be written into the very language of the statute. In that speech, too, the illegal proposal transgresses the ideal of a legal system that unites written statutes, the protocols and practices of the courts, and the venerable institutions of jurisprudence. See also Dem. 20.2–5, 93.

[22] De Brauw 2001–02 shows how legal arguments mutate into ethical arguments in this speech. Cf. Papillon 1998: 43–76 for a similar dynamic in Dem. 23.

and draws within its criminal purview "the boundless time of the past" (*aoriston gar hapanta ton parelēluthota . . . khronon*, 44). That retroactivity, which Diodorus labels "the most terrible and most illegitimate (*paranomos*) of all the shameful and terrible provisions in this law" (194; cf. 72), will confuse past, present, and future, and use a new law to dissolve valid existing laws (72–74; cf. 116). In its retroactive force, Timocrates' law is like those passed under the Thirty, "for under oligarchies, each man is licensed to undo past deeds and to arrange future deeds however he wants, while [in a democracy] the laws tell us what must happen in regard to future deeds by convincing people that they will benefit those who use them" (76). Good laws legislate for the future not for the past (116). By insisting on the laws' prospective force the speech secures the permanence of the existing laws: established in the past and enduring endlessly into the future, they become eternal.

Finally, the legal system this speech imagines is self-regulating and self-bounding. The laws Timocrates' law transgresses are not just substantive laws concerning debtors and their punishment, but even more importantly, the procedural laws of *nomothesia*. In this often technical speech, secondary laws (the laws that govern the working of substantive law) are granted the same status as primary laws. Indeed, in places secondary laws become primary.[23] "Among the existing and valid laws, it has been clearly and precisely determined what must be done regarding the establishment of proposed laws," says Diodorus (17). He goes through the clear and orderly procedure for *nomothesia* – posting of the new law for public scrutiny, revocation of contrary laws – and has read aloud the statutes that lay out these provisions. These legal procedures, he concludes, are themselves venerable laws that have proven so beneficial (*sumpherontes*) that "no one has ever denied their excellence" (24; cf. 25, 43). Likewise, the secondary law that forbids a proposed law to contradict an existing statute is described as "just and democratic" and among the most praiseworthy of all the well-established laws (34). Procedural rules are thus described in the same terms as the city's most cherished substantive laws: indeed, in their just and democratic spirit, they attain a substance of their own.[24]

This, of course, is the logic of the *graphē nomon mē epitēdeion theinai* in a nutshell: the law that guards the sanctity of the law is the most sacred

[23] Fish 1989: 509–15 neatly deconstructs the distinction between primary and secondary rules and between precedent ("established laws") and the laws supposedly based on it. On the distinction within Athenian law see Carey 1998, esp. 106–07 on the "constitutional" laws cited in this speech.

[24] Cf. 59, 78, 79, 90. Contrast Dem. 23.86–87, where the speaker cites secondary laws transgressed by the proposed *paranomos* decree, but differentiates clearly between substantive and procedural statutes.

law of all. This elevation of procedural rules to the same status as the rules they govern constructs the law as a self-regulating system. The law judges and defends its own legality. The hermetic circularity of this vision of law is illustrated in §§36–38. Diodorus has just praised the law forbidding contradictory laws on the grounds that it prevents the jurors from voting against their oath. "Guarding against (*phulattomenos*) this eventuality on your behalf, the lawmaker proclaimed this law," Diodorus tells the jurors, "and also because he wished to establish you as guardians (*phulakas*) over the law" (36).[25] The jurors' power to protect the laws is protected by the very laws that they protect. If, as Diodorus concludes, the jury is "the only just and secure guardian (*phulakē*) of the laws" (37) that is because a phalanx of secondary laws secures them as such. The circularity of the metaphor in this passage marks the closure of the system: the law guards the law that guards the law.[26]

This speech thus imagines the law as a closed and complete system: unitary, consistent, eternal, and self-regulating. But the integrity of this system is in jeopardy from Timocrates, whose illegal *nomos* would "defile" its purity (*lumainesthai*, 1, 92, 95, 107, 210). The speech ends with a telling anecdote. They say that Solon once prosecuted someone for establishing an improper law. In his speech, Solon reminded the jurors that virtually every city has a law prescribing the death penalty if someone corrupts the city's currency (*nomisma*). Silver is the currency of private transactions, but the laws are the currency of the entire polis (*tous de nomous nomisma tēs poleōs einai*, 213). Therefore if someone should corrupt the city's common currency and make it counterfeit (*parasēmon*), he deserves all the more punishment; for cities have survived having their currency adulterated, Diodorus warns, but not if their laws have become corrupted (212–14).

Solon is brought back from the dead to deliver a model *graphē nomon mē epitēdeion theinai* speech, one that proleptically convicts Timocrates and justifies not only the case's procedure but also its jurisprudential vision.[27] Law (*nomos*) is a currency (*nomisma*), a bounded system of fixed and agreed-upon values. But law, like any coin, can become corrupted. Timocrates has introduced a counterfeit law and, as Solon warned, the effect has been to

[25] The lawmaker is not specified as the subject of the verb in this sentence, and the previous sentences might suggest that the law more naturally be supplied as subject. But the volitional nature of *boulomenos* and, especially, *eidei* in the following sentence make the lawmaker more likely.

[26] Cf. 118: "It is our laws being authoritative that makes the jurors authoritative over everything."

[27] It is a particularly brazen anachronism, as the *graphē nomon mē epitēdeion theinai* and *graphē paranomōn* weren't introduced until the late fifth century. Dem. 20.90–93 seems to credit Solon with establishing the *graphē paranomōn* (as well as the other procedures of *nomothesia*), all in the interests of legal consistency and accessibility to the average citizen.

devalue the entire currency of legality. How is it right to call Timocrates' *nomos* a *nomos* and not *anomia*? Diodorus asks (152). Searching around for a way to undermine the established laws without getting caught, he lit upon an ingenious solution: "to subvert the laws by means of a law (*nomōi tous nomous katalusai*) so that his crimes might go by the name of salvation, since laws are what save the city and what he proposed, although it is nothing like them, is also called a law. Thus he took advantage of the positive associations of the word (*tou onomatos philanthrōpian*) . . . and put the name *nomos* on his own crimes" (*nomon etheto onoma tois hautou kakourgēmasin*, 156–57). Timocrates' *paranomos nomos* (194) has called into question the very meaning of the word *nomos*. If a law can be illegal, then what is law? What guarantees its authenticity and fixes its value? What is to ensure that "law" will not end up meaning "crimes"?

This speech and the procedure of the *graphē nomon mē epitēdeion theinai* are designed to forestall that threat of counterfeiting, to preserve the legality of the law. But its very attempt to preserve this legal system reveals its fragility. We have seen the way this speech encircles the law with a phalanx of *phulakes*, as the laws protect the jurors who protect the laws. Within this charmed circle, the law would seem to be safe from the attack of illegitimacy. But its very circularity renders this boundary permeable, for the laws that protect the laws are themselves laws that need protecting. The speech simultaneously deploys the *graphē nomon mē epitēdeion theinai* as a procedure and defends it as a law. This *graphē* is both within the borders of law and what protects those borders. In that double position it is the positive inverse to Timocrates' counterfeit law, which in spirit stands against the law but in name stands within it. The ambiguous position of both these laws, the law against improper laws and Timocrates' improper law, suggests that the line between inside and outside the law, a line the speech works so hard to define and defend, may be essentially indefinite and indefensible.

Once that line becomes perforated, moreover, the *graphē nomon mē epitēdeion theinai* starts to look uncomfortably like the *nomos mē epitēdeios* it prosecutes. In the same section that boasts of the laws' various safeguards, the speaker acknowledges that all of those safeguards can fail. The lawmaker made the jurors the *phulakes* of the law, Diodorus posits, because "he knew that the other safeguards (*phulakas*) which he had written could frequently be circumvented" (36). These "other safeguards" are the written laws governing *nomothesia*, and Diodorus details the ways in which these may become corrupted. Advocates are elected to defend statutes whose repeal was under consideration, but these men can be "persuaded to keep quiet." Proposed laws are displayed for public inspection, but a bad clause may escape attention. Anyone can bring a *graphē nomon mē epitēdeion theinai*, but "if someone gets rid of (*apallaxēi*) the proposer, the city is led astray" (37). The procedural laws that protect the laws, the very procedures that are themselves lauded as unimpeachably excellent laws, are liable to circumvention, misuse, neglect. The *graphē nomon mē epitēdeion theinai* itself can be adulterated. In this admission, the speech verges on corrupting its entire project: the guards can be bought off and the barriers fail to hold. Apparently no one "got rid of" Diodorus but the vague language allows for other possibilities: what's to say that this very speech is not some sort of counterfeit? Diodorus sidesteps this possibility by a rousing appeal to the jurors – "What, then, is the only just and secure *phulakē* of the laws? You, the demos!" (37) – but we have already seen that this guardianship is secured by the very safeguards that have just been declared insufficient.

What if the law that protects the law is itself *anomia* masquerading as *nomos*? That possibility seems to be circulating like a bad coin long before Timocrates' *nomos paranomos* was even introduced. The law needs laws to protect it but those laws, simultaneously inside and outside the boundary of legality, are potentially corrupt. The jurors operate within the same unstable economy, as the laws that grant them authority over *nomothesia* pay them in potentially illegal tender. The very hermeticism by which the speech seeks to secure the law would seem to be its undoing: in this legal phalanx, every piece is connected and they all go down together.

The only solution the speech offers is to kill Timocrates. Like many orators, Diodorus insists that Timocrates deserves the death sentence for a crime that is technically punishable only by a fine (171, 203, 207; cf. 119, 153, 177). This rhetorical excess functions as an argument a fortiori, but it also transforms the legislative contest into a matter of life or death. Timocrates would release all the criminals Solon condemned to jail, warns Diodorus. "Therefore it seems to me – and I will speak undeterred, even if what I am going to say will seem somewhat crude – he deserves the death penalty on these very grounds, so that he might establish this law for the sinners in Hades and allow us, the living, to use these holy and just laws [that is, Solon's laws] for the future" (104). The retroactive effect of Timocrates' law, which gives it authority over "the boundless time of the past" (47), is reconfigured as the return to a past already dead and buried: the criminals for whose benefit he legislates are not just in prison but in Hades. Meanwhile, Solon is brought back to life, reanimated in the courtroom through and as the living spirit of his laws: the passage continues, "Read those laws . . . "

The established laws of the venerable nomothete live on, their immortality assured by the same gesture that banishes Timocrates to Hades along with his *nomos* and his *nomothesia.* This gesture is not just a matter of expelling a bad penny. To be sure, Timocrates is represented as a particularly insidious nomothete. But the speech's zeal to protect the laws suggests that any innovation poses a mortal danger for the lawcode. The differences between the new law – always potentially counterfeit – and the established laws is as stark as that between Timocrates and Solon, or between death and life. But in order to secure that ontological difference, Timocrates must be killed. As in the counterfeiting analogy of Solon's own *graphē nomon mē epitēdeion theinai*, only the threat of death can secure the precarious line between coin and counterfeit, *nomos* and *anomia*. Death is necessary, moreover, to guarantee the law's fixity and permanence: Timocrates is killed so that the laws of Solon can endure in their unchanging purity, alive for "us, the living." This sacrifice hints at a certain morbidity within the legal code, an idea that the speech expresses (in a paradigmatic episode to which we will return in the final section of this chapter) in a fantasy of men proposing new laws with their necks literally in the noose.

Finally, the extremity of this eschatological rhetoric (awkwardly acknowledged in the apology for the crudity of the image) alerts us to the orator's own investment in the legal system he describes and defends. It is the speech, after all, that closes the circle around the law. The speech enacts that most praiseworthy law against contradictory statutes and those venerable and democratic laws of *nomothesia.* It enforces the law that makes the jurors guardians over the laws and ensures that they, in turn, will uphold those laws with their correct verdict. The speech itself is the capstone in the wall it builds around the legal code, and if that code is corrupted – if Timocrates' *nomos mē epitēdeios* sneaks in – it is the speech's failure as well as the law's. Furthermore, if the *graphē nomon mē epitēdeion theinai* is itself always potentially corrupted, if someone can "get rid of" its prosecutor, then the speech is protecting its own purity and legality even as it is defending that of the laws. It is worth remembering that there was an opposing speech in which Timocrates would have claimed that Diodorus is the counterfeit and that his own law was perfectly legal. From that perspective, this law against illegitimate laws is itself illegitimate. Illegality is not only potentially within law's walls; it potentially *is* its walls, and the same forensic rhetoric that would defend it renders it indefensible.

THE LETTER OF THE LAW AND ITS SPIRIT (LYSIAS 10)

Demosthenes 24, I have argued, constructs the law as a coherent and self-sealing system: it makes defending that system a matter of life or death and fears the consequences if it fails. Lysias 10 *Against Theomnestus* offers a similar imagination of law as a code, in this case a written text. It fears not that the code will fail, though, but that it will succeed. What if the law were actually as well guarded as Diodorus wants? In this speech the threat to the law lies not in corrupting innovation but in stagnation, a legal system that seals its boundaries so tightly that it suffocates itself.

The case, part of an ongoing and complicated legal dispute, prosecutes Theomnestus for slander (*dikē kakēgorias*). The speaker was a witness against Theomnestus in a previous suit, where he was on trial for addressing the Assembly after having thrown away his weapons in battle, an act of cowardice that disbarred a citizen from public speech.[28] Theomnestus was apparently acquitted of that charge (and went on to sue two other witnesses for false testimony), but the speaker claims that in the course of his defense Theomnestus had accused him of killing his father. In saying this, he asserts, Theomnestus spoke one of the "forbidden words" (*aporrhēta*) that it is illegal to say of another, a category that included calling someone a murderer (*androphonos*), accusing him of abusing a parent or throwing away his weapons, and speaking ill of the dead. It is for this slander that the speaker is prosecuting Theomnestus in the present case.[29]

This speech deals with the linguistic force of law. The law against "forbidden words" protects the law's right of efficacious naming. Law reserves for itself the exclusive power to pronounce a man a murderer and, by its verdict, to transform him legally into one. By speaking one of the *aporrhēta*, Theomnestus has appropriated that performative power for himself: he has by-passed the verdict of a jury and claimed for himself the law's right to name a man an *androphonos*.[30] Theomnestus has thus robbed the law of its words.

He has also robbed its words of their meaning. He has done this, ironically, by insisting upon both the word and its meaning. Much of the speech is a proleptic response to the argument Theomnestus is expected to

[28] On the ideology and realities of hoplite cowardice see Christ 2006: 88–142, and esp. 118–24 on possible legal responses. Todd 2007: 627–31 lays out the history of litigation behind this case.

[29] On the *aporrhēta* see MacDowell 1978: 126–30; Hillgruber 1988: 4–8; Todd 1993: 259–62; Wallace 1994: 115–24; Montiglio 2000: 134–37; Todd 2007: 634–35.

[30] Cf. Dem. 23.26: the trial converts the *onomata* of accusation ("if someone kills or robs or betrays") into the *adikēmata* of conviction ("a murderer," "a traitor").

make, an argument that the speaker characterizes as "fighting over words (*onomasin*) and not paying attention to the facts (*ergois*) for the sake of which everyone uses words" (10). His opponent, he claims, has conceded the facts (23). His defense will therefore fall back on mere semantics:

> Perhaps, jurors, Theomnestus will make no defense against these arguments [concerning the excellence of the speaker's father and his lack of motive for parricide] but will say to you what he dared to say in arbitration: that it is not one of the *aporrhēta* to say that someone "killed his father" (*ton patera apektonenai*), since the law doesn't forbid this but doesn't allow one to say "man-slayer" (*androphonon*). But in my opinion, jurors, you must dispute not about the words (*peri tōn onomatōn*) but about their meaning (*tēs toutōn dianoias*). I think you all know that those who have killed someone are also man-slayers and those who are man-slayers have also killed someone. It would have been a tremendous labor for the nomothete to write (*graphein*) every word that holds the same force (*dunamin*), so by speaking about one he elucidated all of them (*peri henos eipōn peri pantōn edēlōsen*). (6–7)

Theomnestus will insist on the letter of the law: the forbidden word is *androphonos*; he said *ton patera apektonenai*; therefore he cannot be prosecuted under the law. The law, in Theomnestus' argument, is the text of the law, narrowly written and literally read.[31]

The speaker counters this anticipated argument with a series of *reductiones ad absurdum*. Without allowance for synonyms, legal procedure would be thrown into chaos: the Eleven would refuse to prosecute a thief because someone had arrested him "for stripping off his cloak" and had not technically "named him a clothes stealer" (10). The Areopagus would have to acquit a man who confessed to being a murderer (*androphonos*) because the prosecutor charged under oath not that he was a murderer but that "he killed" (*ekteine*, 12). Criminals will be let free and justice perverted. Theomnestus would even contradict himself, since he counter-sued the plaintiff of the earlier case for saying he "threw away" (*rhipsai*) his shield, when the law prohibits saying someone "cast off his shield" (*apobeblēkenai*, 12).

[31] Todd 2000a: 103: "We may wonder how far Theomnestus could have expected the jury to sympathize with such a sophistic argument, but it is notable that the speaker feels the need to meet the defense head on, with a detailed and in places equally technical rebuttal;" cf. Todd 2007: 635–37; Edwards and Usher 1985: 229: "Theomnestus' defense appears to be weak . . . [He] has taken forlorn refuge in the form of words." As Christ 1998a: 193–224 points out, arguments that stood on the letter of the law were always dangerous, given the Athenians' suspicion of legal expertise. But *contra*, see Hillgruber 1988: 11–21, who argues that Theomnestus' position is not as weak as the speaker makes out.

In Demosthenes 39 *On the Name* (discussed in Chapter 4), Mantitheus claims that a legal language in which two men bear the same name would create social and jurisprudential chaos: law's language would lose its denotive power and when the law said "Mantitheus son of Mantias" no one would be able to tell who it meant. In that speech, the law's intelligibility was predicated on a positivist language in which each word has one clear and single meaning. A similar theory of legal semiotics is attributed to Theomnestus in this case, only to be laughed out of court as evidence of either his stupidity (*skaion*, 15; *anoētōs*, 14; *ēlithion*, 16) or his cynical cleverness (*deinos*, 9, 13). But the dire effects of Theomnestus' semiotics are imagined at length. Read literally, the speaker claims, legal language becomes divorced from conventional human language. Law's words (*onomata*) lose any connection to the actual facts (*pragmata*) they name: thus the excellent son of an excellent father can be named "parricide."[32]

If Theomnestus' literalist reading prevails, the law cannot accurately reflect the world. It cannot even say what it means. "You must dispute not about *onomata* (words, names) but about their *dianoia* (meaning, spirit, intent)," the speaker tells the jury in the passage quoted above (7). The word cramps and confuses the law's intent. That intent in itself is expansive and true. The lawmaker (introduced here as a personification of the law's *dianoia*) comprehends the single force expressed in myriad ways by myriad words. He can conceive of all meanings. He just cannot name them all. More precisely, he cannot write them all (*graphein*). The written word constricts the lawmaker's totalizing vision; taken at face value, as it is by Theomnestus, it distorts that vision. The lawmaker tries to overcome that failure with a single synoptic utterance; he tries to elucidate everything by speaking about one thing (*peri henos eipōn peri pantōn edēlōsen*, 7). But as Theomnestus' brief shows, that synoptic gesture merely introduced into legal language an ambiguity that belies the claim to clarity and opens a space for illegitimate readings of the legal text.

At stake in Theomnestus' purported theory of legal language is the relation not only between words and their meaning but also between law and justice. The inability of the lawmaker to write all the words with the same meaning repeats in a linguistic register the gap Aristotle identifies between law and justice (*NE* 1137b10–1138a3; *Rhet.* 1374a18–b1).

[32] I disagree with J. B. White, who reads this speech as "an argument that the law should be regarded as creating a distinct discourse of its own, in which words are given their meanings by reference to the purposes and contexts of the law, not to the shifting usages of ordinary speech" (1990: 240). His comments on the politics of "plain meaning" in the Olmstead opinions (141–59) seem to hit closer to the mark of Lysias 10.

"The law is by nature general, and it is impossible to speak accurately about specific cases in a generalization" (*NE* 1137b13–14). But justice lies not in the general but in the specificity of individual situations. The lawmaker's whole life would not be long enough to anticipate every possible situation (*Rhet.* 1374a26–33), and so he writes his laws in general terms and, like the nomothete in Lysias 10, by proclaiming one law tries to clarify as many situations as possible. Since he can never enumerate them all, however, the law will always fall short of justice in certain specific cases. Aristotle bridges this gap between the generality of law and the particularity of justice with the concept of equity (*to epieikes*), a "rectification of legal justice" (*NE* 1137b12–13) and an extension of the lawmaker's general intent to the unique situation ("what the lawmaker himself would have said were he present and the law he would have written had he known the case," *NE* 1137b22–24). In Lysias 10, the equation is reversed: the law is too specific and justice (the speaker argues) requires generalizing. But the gap between them is just as problematic. The lawmaker himself tried to close this gap with his single clarifying word – a particular word with general application – but Theomnestus' failure to see the general in the particular reopens the space between them and prevents the law from doing justice in this specific case.

A literal reading of its letter renders the law unjust and unintelligible, then: its *onomata*, no longer linked to either true *pragmata* or the lawmaker's *dianoia*, become meaningless, and the law's just intent is lost. Codified so rigidly, the laws become literally obsolete. You all know, says the speaker, that different words can mean the same thing: to kill a man is to be a murderer, to throw away your shield is to lose your shield. He then reiterates this argument about synonyms in a diachronic mode: the ancient laws of Solon are still in effect even if their language is archaic. He has the laws read one by one and translates each into modern vernacular. For instance:

> The law: "Let his feet be bound for ten days in the foot-binder (*podokakkēi*) unless the courts add a further penalty."
>
> The foot-binder (*podokakkē*) is what today we call being bound in the stocks (*en tōi xulōi*). If after his release the prisoner should come forward at the audit of the Eleven and charge them with binding him not in the foot-binder but in the stocks wouldn't you think he was a fool (*ēlithion*)? (16)

Language is a living thing that evolves over time. But the written text of the law does not evolve, and the result is a danger that the law's meaning will become as obscure as its outdated language, that the ancient laws (*nomous tous palaious*, 15) will become obsolete laws (*nomous tous palaious*).[33] Inscribed in stone, the text that fixes the law's meaning and grants it permanence also risks petrifying it. The written letter kills the law's spirit, and the stele on which it is carved becomes its tombstone. And if Theomnestus insists on the letter, he is as calcified as it is: "unless he is made of iron (*sidērous*), I think he is aware that the facts (*pragmata*) are the same now as in the past, but in some cases we don't use the same words (*onomata*) now as they did then" (20).

As in Demosthenes 24, so here legal codification becomes a matter of life or death, but it is the life or death not of the opponent but of the law itself. Whereas in Demosthenes 24 codification keeps the laws of Solon perpetually alive, here the written text consigns the law's spirit to obsolescence. The death of the law's *dianoia* is closely correlated in this speech with the death of the speaker's father. The father's noble life and patriotic death at the hands of the Thirty are the true facts that disprove Theomnestus' false words, since it is inconceivable that such a father could have been killed by his son (2, 26–28).[34] Denying the speaker's father his patriotic martyrdom, Theomnestus' slanderous name *androphonos* kills him again, this time shamefully at the hands of his own son: so, as the speaker hyperbolically puts it, his brief is not just a prosecution for slander but a defense for murder (31).[35]

[33] Todd 2000a: 103 points out the ambiguity in the word *palaious* between "formally obsolete (i.e. 'former')" and "simply 'ancient'." Cf. Todd 2007: 677 *ad* Lys. 10.15.

[34] It would have been different, the speaker says, if Theomnestus had accused me of killing his father: "if he had accused me of killing his father I would have forgiven him for the charge, for I consider his father vulgar and worthless . . . But as it is, I think it shameful not to punish the man who said these things about my father, who was so valued by you jurors and the city" (2–3). There is debate over whether the *aporrhēta* had to be false in order to be prosecutable. Todd 1993: 260: "as Gernet and Bizos (1955: i.142) point out, the very etymology of *aporrhēta* (lit. 'things which are not to be spoken') logically implies a system in which the words themselves are in issue, irrespective of whether they can reasonably be applied to the plaintiff;" cf. Todd 2007: 634–35. But *contra*, see MacDowell 1978: 128: "a person was guilty of slander only if what he had said was false; if he could show that he had merely spoken the truth, that was sufficient defense." This speaker plays it both ways, suggesting that Theomnestus is guilty both because he (in essence) said the word and because the word is false.

[35] Cf. 26–28: "What greater disaster could I face than to have my father – and a father like he was – slandered so shamefully, a man who served repeatedly as a general and endured many dangers with you . . . Aren't I justified to be angry at the man who said these things and to come to my father's defense? . . . For what could be more painful to him than this: to die at the hands of his enemies and be accused of death by the hand of his children?" The speaker does not identify his father by name, but commentators have proposed that he was Leon, one of the most famous victims of the Thirty. In Plato's *Apology*, Socrates says that he refused to carry out the oligarchs' command to arrest Leon, preferring death to "an unjust and unholy act" (Pl. *Ap.* 32c4–e1): see Hillgruber 1988: 41–42; Todd 2007: 637–38.

The speaker fights at once for the life of his father and the life of the law, saving both from Theomnestus' toxic literalism. He does this not by repudiating the letter of the law but by rediscovering the living spirit within it: the lawmaker's original intent still lives within the stony text, he promises, if only one knows how to read it. The speaker's brief thus becomes a lesson in juridical hermeneutics.

> I think you all know, jurors, that I am speaking accurately and that this man is so stupid that he isn't able to understand what was said. So I want to teach (*didaxai*) him about these laws by the example of other laws, if somehow he might be educated (*paideuthēi*) now on the speaker's stand and in the future not cause you any trouble. (15)

This introduces the extended lesson on the contemporary meaning of Solon's archaic laws. It is not just a pedantic tutorial in translation: "foot-binder" means "stocks"; *stasimos* used to mean "lent at interest" but now means "placed on the balance"; we used to use *draskazein* for "running away" but now we use *apodidraskein*. Instead it is a lesson in reading the spirit of the law from its letter, in recognizing – as Theomnestus is apparently too stupid to do – that although the words change, the *pragmata* behind them stay the same. Those *pragmata* are fully legible, as the speaker's easy translations illustrate. The law's *dianoia* can be read in its *onomata*, if only one knows how to read and what one is reading for.

If the forensic brief is a lesson in hermeneutics, its educational style is Platonic: it does not put new knowledge into its pupils so much as it draws forth (*e-ducere*) a knowledge that is already there inside them.[36] The jurors "all know" (*pantas eidenai*) that his speech is accurate. So, too, they already understand the theory of language that he aims to convey. "I think you all know that those who have killed someone are also man-slayers and those who are man-slayers have also killed someone" (7).[37] This appeal to communal knowledge is a hackneyed trope in forensic oratory, of course, but here it is put in the service of a semiotic theory in which the jury and its collective knowledge span the divide between words and things, the law's spirit and its letter. The lawmaker could not write down every word, but that doesn't matter because the jurors understand that, although the *onomata* may be different, the *dianoia* behind them is the

[36] On the pedagogical metaphor in forensic oratory, see Too 2001, and on the didactic tone in this speech, Todd 2007: 636. Goodrich discusses a similar theory of legal language as the anamnesis of a primary order of being in early English jurisprudential thought: 1992: 58–59, 69–71; cf. 1990a: 53–110.

[37] Cf. 22: "I saw him do what you yourselves know he did [i.e. throw away his shield];" 5: "you all know that I am speaking the truth [about my father's death] but I will provide witnesses nonetheless."

same. So, too, only a moron or an "iron man" like Theomnestus could fail to understand the timeless intent behind Solon's arcane vocabulary. Communal knowledge repairs the rift Theomnestus has opened between words and their meaning, the general and the particular, law and justice. The jurors have heard the voice of the lawmaker speaking in the written text of the law and from his single synoptic word can see the equitable verdict in this case. The speech thus reclaims the eternal and universal spirit of the law from the mortification of the text. Like the speaker in Isaeus 1 (discussed in Chapter 6), who reached back beyond the dead letter of the testament to resuscitate the will behind the will, this speaker frees the spirit of the law from its rigid letter and locates the law's *dianoia* in the *noos* of the jury: all that is needed is the speaker's translation and education.

Theomnestus' posited legal code encodes the law's failure: the failure of its words to say what they mean or to fix that meaning over time, the lawmaker's failure to transcribe his intent in writing or to compose a particular law that elucidates the generality of justice. Even as the speech recoils from the deadening textuality it attributes to Theomnestus, however, it also imagines an alternate legal semiotics and an alternate legal text. In this semiotics, the law speaks a language of truth: Theomnestus may claim that he spoke his charge rashly in a fit of anger, says the speaker, but "the lawmaker doesn't make exceptions for anger but penalizes the speaker unless he shows that what he has said is true" (*alēthē*, 30). Convicting Theomnestus thus means reconnecting law's words with the reality of true *pragmata*, and under the banner of truth it returns to the law its power of efficacious naming: only the law can name a man a murderer because the law, unlike Theomnestus, names truly.

This true language is grounded by the true excellence of the speaker's father. That truth is symbolized by the enemy shields his father had captured and dedicated in the temples of Athens as a memorial (*mnēmeia*) to his *aretē*; likewise, Theomnestus' own baseness and that of his father is signified by their shields, hanging in the temples of the enemy as a memorial to their cowardice (*kakias*, 28). These shields stand as signs, *mnēmeia*, of an ethico-political truth, the *aretē* of the patriotic citizen. Their obvious message indicts both Theomnestus' slander and the reading that rends words from their true meaning. These shields stand for a legal semiotics in which the symbol bears a natural and unequivocal connection to the thing it symbolizes and is in itself a manifest blazon of its intended meaning. The speech ends with a call to the jurors to remember (*memnēmenoi*) the speaker's own patriotism and his father's, and to do justice accordingly (32). In that way, the clear *mnēmeia* of the shields will be translated into the clear message of a verdict. The jurors' correct vote will give voice to the law's true intent.

In so doing, it will serve as a translation of the lawmaker's original word. The passage that lays out Theomnestus' anticipated argument (6–7) hints at the disastrous consequences we have traced: a schism between the law's *onomata* and its *dianoia*, law's spirit crushed beneath its written letter. These negative results are implicit in the passage, but its explicit formulation is positive. The threatened semiotic breakdown is in fact prevented by the lawmaker's single word: "It would have been a tremendous labor for the nomothete to write (*graphein*) every word that holds the same force (*dunamis*), so by speaking about one he elucidated all of them (*peri henos eipōn peri pantōn edēlōsen*) (7). As the speaker presents it, the lawmaker's synoptic speech does comprehend all words; it understands their sense and conveys it clearly. His single word does make manifest (*edēlōsen*) the meaning of everything. In the course of repudiating Theomnestus' vision of legal language, the speaker offers one of his own: a language that is exhaustive and perfectly denotative, that represents the entire world of objects and meanings precisely and accurately with no gaps or ambiguities. This language is also eternal. As the speaker says, the *onomata* may change but the *pragmata* stay the same (20): if the lawmaker speaks a language of pure *pragmata*, his intent can never die, even when encased in stone. Thus the law's spirit is alive in the lawmaker's word, a word spoken in a legal language that is eternal, transparent, and true.[38]

This language of emblematic shields and living words offers an alternative and antidote to the narrow literalism of Theomnestus' legal text, but this speech does not entirely give up on textuality. Instead, it dreams of a perfect text in which the laws' written *onomata* are accurate and permanent transcriptions of both the world's true *pragmata* and the lawmaker's just *dianoia*. This is the text the speaker teaches the jurors to read. In his reading lesson, the law's written text is as perspicuous and true as the paternal shields hung in the temples. His hermeneutics discovers the lawmaker's voice in the silent inscription and grounds the vision of a new – living, speaking – text upon that discovery. And if his hermeneutics posits a speaking text, his pedagogical metaphor suggests that this text speaks through his own clarifying voice. The orator translates not only the lawmaker's archaic language but also his original intent; he changes the *onomata* to reveal the unchanging *pragmata* and *dianoia* behind them. In this way, the orator

[38] Derrida 1976 deconstructs precisely this fantasy by showing that the word was always already a species of writing and haunted by its threat of non-meaning and non-presence. This chapter's debt to his discussion should be obvious. See also Goodrich 1990a: 111–48.

achieves what the lawmaker could not: he unites law's particular words and their larger meaning and closes the divide between law and justice. With his single speech he elucidates everything.

If Demosthenes 24 saves the law through codification, then, Lysias 10 saves it *from* codification. The former speech builds a wall around the legal system and protects its integrity from legal innovation; the latter frees the law from its tomb of text and reanimates its living spirit in its written word. Taken together, the two speeches show juridical discourse's dream of a fixed legal code, whether in the form of Diodorus' bounded system of laws and procedures or this speaker's vision of a lucid and timeless written text. They also express anxiety about the dangers inherent in this code: vulnerability to corruption, on the one hand; petrifying rigidity, on the other. The ambivalence of these speeches toward legal codification (and their own role in it) is resolved neither in the speeches themselves nor in Athenian juridical discourse as a whole. Instead, as we shall see, it is reworked into a positive paradigm that situates the law in a precarious equilibrium between dangerous openness and stultifying closure, an equilibrium that forensic oratory itself must sustain.

THE LAW, THE NOOSE, AND THE ONE-EYED MAN

The scene comes late in Demosthenes 24 (139–41). In Locri, Diodorus tells us, they value their traditional laws so much that if someone wants to establish a new law, he proposes it with his head in a noose (*en brokhōi ton trakhēlon ekhōn nomothetei*). If the law is approved the proposer lives, but if not the noose is drawn. As a result, he says, the Locrians "do not dare to propose new laws but make precise use (*akribōs khrōntai*) of those that were established long ago." In fact, only one new law has been passed there in more than two hundred years. He goes on to describe the circumstances of that solitary innovation. There was a law on the books that if someone knocks out another man's eye, he must allow his own eye to be taken in return. A one-eyed man was harassed by an enemy who threatened to put out his one good eye. "The one-eyed man was upset at this threat and thought that his life would be unlivable if this happened to him. So it is said that he dared to introduce a law that if someone knocks out the eye of a one-eyed man, he must allow both of his eyes to be knocked out in return, so that both men will experience an equivalent misfortune" (*tēi isēi sumphorai amphoteroi khrōntai*, 141).[39]

[39] The story is also told at D.S. 12.17.1–18.1, Plb. 12.16.10–14; cf. Arist. *Rhet.* 1365b16–19.

The episode is offered as a *paradeigma*, a model or example. "I want to explain to you, jurors, how they make laws in Locri. For you will be none the worse for hearing an example (*paradeigma ti*), especially one dealing with a well-governed polis" (139). This offhand introduction belies the significance of the example, which is both typical and exceptional. Thematically, the episode fits neatly with the preoccupations of the speech, epitomizing its desire for a fixed and stable code of law and its anxiety about the potential corruption of legal innovation. On the other hand, this *paradeigma* (literally, "showing on the side") is a side-show to a case dedicated to a side-by-side comparison (*paradeiknumi*) of the laws. It is superfluous to both the specialized arguments about legal procedure and the ideological arguments concerning the civic good that dominate most of the speech and it is poorly integrated in its context, sandwiched between a section on the punishment of past offenders and a harangue against Timocrates and his associates. Rhetorically, too, this episode is more exceptional than typical: its graphic, even gruesome, vividness stands out in striking relief against the backdrop of this oration's generally technical and drab argumentation. Yet that very vividness turns the *paradeigma* into an alternate mode of proof (another meaning of the word), as it stages within its dream-like scenography the ambiguities the speech fails to resolve through logical exposition.[40] In that sense, it is less a side-show than the drama on center stage. A fable about law's violence and authority, its extension into the past and duration into the future, its subjective embodiment and its power over life and death, this episode is paradigmatic of many of the issues raised in this chapter and this book. Thus it seems an exemplary place to conclude and at any rate, as Diodorus says, "you will be none the worse for hearing it."

The Locrian episode presents the dream of an ideal law, a law so ideal that it could exist only in a quasi-mythical and paradigmatically lawful land.[41] It illustrates in full color the desire that motivates Demosthenes 24 as a whole: the desire for the law to be a pure and bounded code. The Locrians are a virtual personification of this desire: their legendary lawmaker Zaleucus

[40] Aristotle lists *paradeigmata* as one of the two modes of rhetorical proof, along with enthymemes (logical syllogisms), but gives them a subordinate and supplementary status: they are most persuasive when used to cap a deductive argument developed through enthymemes (*Rhet.* 1393a23–1394a18). Demosthenes' *paradeigma* would seem to fall into Aristotle's sub-category of "stories" (*logoi*).

[41] Locri, in southern Italy, was for classical Athenians "a fabulous place, legendary for its lawfulness," as Redfield remarks (2003: 260). His interesting study of Locrian culture (2003: 241–307) suggests that this episode is typical of the ancient imagination of the city.

was credited with the first written lawcode.[42] In this exemplary scene, that code is perfect: demanding an eye for an eye, its punishment equals the crime with mathematical precision; it is law as the means and principle of absolute equity.[43] The law that protects the code is likewise perfect: the law of *nomothesia*-in-the-noose ensures that the citizens implement their exact law exactly (*akribōs*) and that the precision of the legal code is mirrored precisely in the precision of legal practice. As in the speech overall, primary laws and secondary laws, statutes and verdicts form an integrated system. And here, as in the speech as a whole, that system is sealed with a human life. The law of an eye for an eye is fixed by the law of the noose and secured by the threat of death. The episode both encapsulates and displaces the rhetorical violence of the oration, which preserves the law by weaving a noose around Timocrates' neck and tightening it.

The Locrians' brutal law is thus simply a less euphemized version of the *graphē nomon mē epitēdeion theinai*. It is a model of that procedure with both its vision of a codified law and the anxieties that vision entails. These imaginary Locrians, like the speaker who imagines them, perceive legal innovation as adulteration or defilement; *nomothesia* introduces the threat of "legislating for the planning and prevarication of crimes" (139). For them, too, the legal system is a fragile being, and the authority of the established laws must be guarded (*peristellein*, 139, literally "enwrapped") by another law. But the same law that enfolds the law risks smothering it. In this episode Demosthenes 24 articulates the possibility explored at length in Lysias 10, the possibility that by fixing the law codification will kill it. In Lysias 10 a law written in stone becomes petrified and obsolete, cut off from human life and from justice. That risk is implicit in the Locrian anecdote, too: the paradigmatically equitable law of the Locrians – an eye for an eye – looks unjust from the unique perspective of the one-eyed man. If it cannot respond to his call for justice, that rigid law will instead become complicit with the blinding that would make his life unlivable. The Locrians fear that innovation will make law an implement of the "planning and prevarication of crimes," just as Diodorus worried that admission of Timocrates' counterfeit law would redefine *nomos* as

[42] Zaleucus is listed along with Solon, Draco, and the Spartan Lycurgus as one of the great lawmakers of Greece (Arist. *Pol.* 1274a22). On the biographical tradition surrounding the legendary lawmakers, see Szegedy-Maszak 1978.

[43] Miller 2006 is an engaging study of justice as evenness. He remarks that the biblical formula of an eye for an eye evokes the possibility of "getting the measure of value right" and the dream of perfect juridical balance (30).

anomia. But this episode, like Lysias 10, also imagines the opposite scenario: that a law impervious to change will become the accomplice of *adikia*.

The one-eyed man's tentative approach to the law raises the possibility that the law will refuse his request and that its universal commandment will be a failure of justice in this particular case. This possibility marks the gap that Aristotle, as we saw, fills with equity, "the rectification of legal justice." But here there is no gap. The law does respond to the particular claim of the one-eyed man, a man defined solely in terms of his particularity. It does so, moreover, without compromising its universality and permanence. The perfectly equitable law of the Locrians requires the supplement of this odd *heterophthalmos* on both sides. On one side, his oddity restores the symmetry of the law's eye for an eye, and his particularity expands the reach of its justice. On the other side, he is the exception that proves the rule this *paradeigma* is designed to illustrate: his anomalous proposal was the sole legal innovation in over two hundred years. This unique individual, nameless and mythic in his abstraction, is the fulcrum upon which balances the perfect law. His demand renders the law open and just, even as his monocular uniqueness secures its closure and fixity. The perfect law may need its noose, but it also needs its one-eyed man. Perhaps it is no coincidence that (according to one report) the Locrian nomothete Zaleucus was himself a *heterophthalmos*.[44]

Of course, this is a fantastic response to the legal problems these speeches raise, and this anonymous, anomalous individual, himself precariously situated between the noose of the unyielding lawcode and the injustice of a justice blind to his blinding, is a precarious foundation for a legal system. This anecdote does not resolve the speech's ambivalence toward codification. Instead it paradigmatizes it. It transmutes a legal problem into a model of legal perfection by reimagining tension as balance and the paired extremes of corrupting openness and petrifying closure as the slim space of justice between the two. Discordant desires – the desire for both a written letter and a living spirit, both a closed system and openness to innovation – are not so much reconciled as simply reconceived as a harmony. With its distant setting, abstract characters, and mythic present tense, the episode places rhetorical closure upon the problem of legal closure and fixes the problem of legal fixity as an idée fixe within juridical discourse. The Locrian

44 The story goes that Zaleucus' law decreed that anyone caught stealing be blinded; when Zaleucus' son was caught, the lawgiver gave up one of his own eyes so that his son wouldn't be left totally blind: Arist. fr. 611 Rose; cf. Aelian *VH* 13.24; Szegedy-Maszak 1978: 206; Redfield 2003: 252.

paradigm, in other words, is a rhetorical non-solution to a problem that is thereby made paradigmatic for the discourse of law.

*

In Demosthenes 24 Diodorus posits that the ideal law must be practical, for if what it commands is not possible, it is not a law but a prayer (68). The Locrian law is a prayer, but it is one that emanates from the very heart of Athenian juridical discourse. We have seen repeatedly throughout the preceding chapters the tension within Athenian legal thought between a drive toward discursive closure and the impossibility of achieving it. Chapter 1 examined how forensic oratory constructs a homogenous and boundless juridical cosmos and secures it rhetorically with "everything but an iron chain" (Dem. 25.28). Forensic oratory tries to ground its legitimacy by erasing its own rhetoricity but this paradoxical self-repudiation, I argued, leaves destabilizing traces within the very cosmos it creates. The Locrian episode might be seen as one such trace. The scene illustrates both the rhetorical construction of a legal cosmos (the Locrian official who expounded Zaleucus' law was called the *kosmopolis*[45]) and its constructedness. The "iron chain" here becomes a noose, closing around the law and closing it off from change or critique. But the morbid hermeticism of that image is countered by the petition of the one-eyed man. Forensic oratory plays the role of both the noose and the one-eyed man: it simultaneously affirms the unchanging authority of the law and exposes its malleability as it shapes and reshapes it to its own rhetorical ends. Through this double role, it constructs a juridical discourse that aims for closure but is never fully closed.

It is also a discourse that aims for justice but is never fully just. The Locrian statute graphically illustrates the violence of the law. We saw in Chapter 2 what it means for law to operate, as Robert Cover says, "in a field of pain and death": the cruel exclusions by which legal discourse secures its boundaries and its quiet complicity with the social violence that it locates beyond them, the disavowed torture by which it produces legal truth, its haunting by those whose pain and death it refuses to acknowledge. All that violence is present in the Locrian scene, which is played out between the pain of blinding and death by the noose. These threats surround and secure the episode's fantasy of an ideal law, a law that is ideal precisely because

[45] Plb. 12.16.9–14. In this passage a young plaintiff argues the meaning of a law with the *kosmopolis*. Each has his head in a noose and the one who loses is to die. The young man remarks that this is unfair as the aged *kosmopolis* has only a few good years left, while he himself has his whole life ahead of him. The magistrates nonetheless find for the *kosmopolis*.

it distributes pain equally: an eye for an eye. They also work to disavow the possibility that the law may have innocent victims, for in this fable only unjust nomothetes are hanged and the law's retributive force operates solely in the interest of equity. But that possibility lurks within the one-eyed man's glimpse of his unlivable life if he is blinded. That momentary vision reveals that the law's relation to justice is always contingent, even as the noose reminds us that the gap between them is bridged only at the risk of one's own life.

That a human life is the ultimate stake in this deadly balancing act indicates the extent to which juridical discourse is invested in its subjects. We saw in Chapters 3 and 4 how the legal cosmos comes to be embodied by its own inhabitants. These fictive legal persons – whether the sketchy and improbable figures of Antiphon's *Tetralogies* or the more fully drawn characters of forensic oratory's *logoi biou* – act as subjective extensions of the logic of the law. Their probable motives and desires mirror the probabilities that govern the legal universe; the rhetorical strategies by which they narrate their life stories tell a story about the rhetorical structure of the law. These chapters showed how legal discourse secures its meaning and metaphysics in the person of its subjects. The Locrian episode reiterates this point with paradigmatic clarity. The ideal law is personified in its one-eyed subject, the unique everyman whose competing fear of death by the noose and desire for a life worth living define the parameters of the legal cosmos he inhabits. As in the speech as a whole, the law's immortality is bought at the price of his mortality, the threat of the noose. At the same time, by saving his life, the law saves its own; it escapes the rigor mortis of codification imagined in Lysias 10 and proves itself both immortal and alive in the present moment. The law is thus biologized: not just an inscribed text or fixed code, it lives in the individual life it has, by its just verdict, made livable.

The Locrian episode also situates the law in relation to time, between the past of "the long established laws" (139) and the open horizon of law's perpetual future. Chapter 5 examined judicial discourse as a mode of memory; it argued that in helping the city forget its traumatic past, forensic oratory also restored the temporality of the law, its chain between past crime, present trial, and future justice. That temporal unity is at stake in the Locrian paradigm, too, as each new law threatens to erase the legal past and undermine the legal future. The Locrians try to repair the bond between past, present, and future, and to tie it off with a hangman's knot. But in the process, the episode evokes the dangerous tricks of memory we saw in the Athenian trials after the civil war: the danger, on the one hand, that the established laws would be forgotten and, on the other, that they would be remembered so well that the future would become nothing more than a mechanical repetition of the past. The paradigmatic status of the episode ensures that what will be remembered is not these dangers but the exemplary law that avoids them both; in this way the anecdote also reminds us of the rhetorical effort required to maintain the temporal unity of the law.

In its recollection of the laws' venerable past and promise for law's eternal future, the Locrian episode dramatizes a crucial moment in the genealogy of the juridical cosmos. Chapter 6 showed how juridical discourse writes its own genealogical history through its domestic narratives: by intervening in the reproduction of the *genos*, I argued, the law reproduces itself. In its family sagas, juridical discourse not only extends its reach into the family's past and future but claims a power over death (through the will) and life (through the woman). In claiming this bio-power for the law, juridical discourse elevates it above the individual: not just vested in the life of its individual subjects, it becomes a force of life itself. One-eyed men may come and go but the laws endure, replicating themselves with every life-and-death decision in perpetuity. Vitality becomes coextensive with legality: life is lived with one's neck always in law's noose, and it is law that makes life livable or consigns it to blindness or death. In this paradigmatic fable, the legal cosmos *is* the cosmos. There is no life or death outside it.

This cosmos is perfect, eternal, just. We might even call it beautiful. Its eye-for-an-eye justice is poetic: perfectly symmetrical, rhythmic, universal. In a land that is itself a model of *eunomia*, metaphorical justice becomes literal law and is secured by another literalized metaphor, the noose. The chiasmus between the two, between the violence of the law and the violence of preserving it, has its own beautiful symmetry. The metaphor of the noose holds the law in a balanced rhetorical homeostasis. Then to a cosmos that hangs suspended between legality and illegality, life and death, the one-eyed man brings forward momentum, a narrative impulse. His oddity disrupts its balance, creating a new moment of suspense both in the anecdote and in the law. Will the law regain its equilibrium? It does. He lives to see (albeit imperfectly) another day, and the law expands to a new and fuller equity: victim and perpetrator will once more share an equivalent misfortune (*tēi isēi sumphorai amphoteroi khrōntai*, 141). The parable itself reflects this legal balance, as it moves from equilibrium through crisis to resolution. This narrative play of odds and evens is rounded out by the moral that makes this scene such a paradigmatic paradigm: "And they say that this was the only law the Locrians passed in more than two hundred years" (141). The entire scene is thus declared a *logos* ("they say") and an allegory. The speaker goes on to compare the wisdom of the Locrians with the legal manipulations of "the orators here in Athens" (142). By this contrast he tries to set off this rhetorical example as exemplarily true, non-rhetorical. But this sleight of hand should not blind us to the rhetorical artfulness of the scene, in which thought and expression, the law and its narrative allegorization, are themselves so well balanced that it is hard to tell which is the model for the other.

The Locrian cosmos is both a legal and an aesthetic order, the order this book has explored in microcosm. If, as Peter Goodrich has argued,[46] the history of Western jurisprudence is a story of the suppression or repudiation of the rhetorical origins of the law, the Locrian episode reminds us that in Athenian jurisprudence the two were neither separate nor separable. In Athens' legal cosmos, judicial order is an effect of the speeches' aesthetic ordering. Literary form and legal matter, legal form and literary matter are inextricable and mutually defining: law and literature, in Athenian forensic oratory, give shape to one another and each enriches the other's thought with its own. The productive dissonances between them – those occasional moments where meaning and its expression strain against one another revealing contradictions within Athens' jurisprudential cosmogony – are resolved into a perfect harmony in the Locrian fantasy. Meaning and expression, law and literature work in unison to create a legal *kosmos* that is at once equitable and exquisite. In the imagined universe of Athens' juridical discourse, lawfulness has a beauty of its own and justice is always poetic.

[46] Goodrich 1990a: 124; 1994b: 95–102 (= 1995: 101–07); 1995: 65–67; 1996: 112–37. Hence the project of genealogical critique he proposes in the passage quoted as an epigram to this chapter (1990a: 110).

Bibliography

Adkins, A. W. H. 1960. *Merit and Responsibility: A Study in Greek Values*. Oxford: Clarendon.

1976. "*Polupragmosunê* and 'Minding One's Own Business': A Study in Greek Social and Political Values." *CP* 71: 301–27.

Allen, D. S. 2000a. *The World of Prometheus: The Politics of Punishing in Democratic Athens*. Princeton University Press.

2000b. "Changing the Authoritative Voice: Lycurgus' *Against Leocrates*." *ClAnt* 19: 5–34.

Althusser, L. 1971. "Ideology and Ideological State Apparatuses (Notes towards an Investigation)." In *Lenin and Philosophy and Other Essays*. Trans. B. Brewster. New York: Monthly Review Press. 127–86.

Andrewes, A. 1970. "Lysias and the Theramenes Papyrus." *ZPE* 6: 35–38.

Arendt, H. 1963. *Eichmann in Jerusalem: A Report on the Banality of Evil*. New York: Penguin.

Arnaoutoglou, I. 1993. "Pollution in the Athenian Homicide Law." *RIDA* 40: 109–37.

Avery, H. C. 1982. "One Antiphon or Two?" *Hermes* 110: 145–58.

Balot, R. 2001. *Greed and Injustice in Classical Athens*. Princeton University Press.

2004. "Free Speech, Courage, and Democratic Deliberation." In Sluiter and Rosen 2004: 233–59.

2008. "Review of Gabriel Herman, *Morality and Behaviour in Democratic Athens: A Social History*." *CP* 103: 320–25.

Barfield, O. 1962. "Poetic Diction and Legal Fiction." In M. Black, ed. *The Importance of Language*. 51–71. Originally published in *Essays Presented to Charles Williams*, Oxford University Press, 1947.

Barron, A. 1993. "The Illusions of the 'I': Citizenship and the Politics of Identity." In A. Norrie, ed. *Closure or Critique: New Directions in Legal Theory*. Edinburgh University Press. 80–100.

Bassi, K. (in press). "Making Prometheus Speak: Dialogue, Torture, and the Power of Secrets in Aeschylus' *Prometheus Bound*." In K. Bassi and J. P. Euben, eds. *When Worlds Elide: Classics, Politics, Culture*. Lanham, MD: Rowman and Littlefield.

Bateman, J. J. 1958. "Lysias and the Law." *TAPA* 89: 276–85.

1962. "Some Aspects of Lysias' Argumentation." *Phoenix* 16: 157–77.

Bauman, R. A. 1990. *Political Trials in Ancient Greece*. London: Routledge.

Bendlin, A. 2007. "Purity and Pollution." In D. Ogden, ed. *A Companion to Greek Religion*. Oxford: Blackwell. 178–89.

Benjamin, W. 1978 [1921]. "Critique of Violence." In *Reflections: Essays, Aphorisms, Autobiographical Writings*. Ed. P. Demetz. Trans. E. Jephcott. New York: Harcourt Brace Jovanovich. 277–300.

Benveniste, E. 1971. *Problems in General Linguistics*. Trans. M. E. Meek. University of Miami Press.

Bers, V. 1985. "Dikastic thorubos." In P. Cartledge and F. D. Harvey, eds. *Crux: Essays Presented to G. E. M. de Ste. Croix*. Exeter: Imprint Academic. 1–15.

1994. "Tragedy and Rhetoric." In I. Worthington, ed. *Persuasion: Greek Rhetoric in Action*. New York: Routledge. 176–95.

Biraud, M. 1991. "La décence ou l'absence du corps: la répresentation sociale du corps dans les plaidoyers des orateurs attiques." *LEC* 59: 335–43.

Biscardi A. 1970. "La 'gnome dikaiotate' et l'interprétation des lois dans la Grèce ancienne." *RIDA* 17: 219–32.

Bizos, M., ed. 1967. *Lysias. Quatre discours*. Paris: Presses universitaires de France.

Blanshard, A. J. L. 2004. "What Counts as the *Demos*? Some Notes on the Relationship Between the Jury and 'the People' in Classical Athens." *Phoenix* 58: 28–48.

Boegehold, A. L. 1991. "Three Court Days." In M. Gagarin, ed. *Symposion 1990: Papers on Greek and Hellenistic Legal History*. Cologne: Böhlau. 165–82.

1994. "Perikles' Citizenship Law of 451/0 B.C." In A. L. Boegehold and A. C. Scafuro, eds. *Athenian Identity and Civic Ideology*. Baltimore, MD: Johns Hopkins University Press. 57–66.

1996. "Resistance to Change in the Law at Athens." In J. Ober and C. Hedrick, eds. *Dêmokratia: A Conversation on Democracies, Ancient and Modern*. Princeton University Press. 203–14.

Bonner, R. J. 1922. "Wit and Humor in Athenian Courts." *CP* 17: 97–103.

Bonner, R. J. and G. Smith. 1930. *The Administration of Justice from Homer to Aristotle*. Volume I. University of Chicago Press.

1938. *The Administration of Justice from Homer to Aristotle*. Volume II. University of Chicago Press.

Bourdieu, P. 1987. "The Force of Law: Toward a Sociology of the Juridical Field." *Hastings Law Journal* 38: 814–53.

1990. *The Logic of Practice*. Trans. R. Nice. Stanford University Press.

Bourriot, F. 1976. *Recherches sur la nature du genos*. Paris: Honoré Champion.

Boyle, J. 1991. "Is Subjectivity Possible? The Postmodern Subject in Legal Theory." *University of Colorado Law Review* 62: 489–524.

Bremer, J. M. 1969. *Hamartia: Tragic Error in the Poetics of Aristotle and in Greek Tragedy*. Amsterdam: Hakkert.

Brooks, P. 2000. *Troubling Confessions: Speaking Guilt in Law and Literature*. University of Chicago Press.

2005. "Law and Literature in Dialogue." *PMLA* 120: 1645–46.

Brooks, P. and P. Gewirtz, eds. 1996. *Law's Stories: Narrative and Rhetoric in the Law*. New Haven, CT: Yale University Press.

Brown, W. 1995a. *States of Injury: Power and Freedom in Late Modernity*. Princeton University Press.

1995b. "Rights and Identity in Late Modernity: Revisiting the 'Jewish Question'." In A. Sarat and T. R. Kearns, eds. *Identities, Politics, and Rights*. Ann Arbor, MI: University of Michigan Press. 85–130.

2001. *Politics Out of History*. Princeton University Press.

Burke, K. 1945. *A Grammar of Motives*. New York: Prentice-Hall.

Bushala, E. W. 1968. "Torture of Non-Citizens in Homicide Investigations." *GRBS* 9: 61–68.

1969. "The *Pallake* of Philoneus." *AJP* 90: 65–72.

Butler, J. 1993. *Bodies that Matter: On the Discursive Limits of "Sex."* New York: Routledge.

1997a. *The Psychic Life of Power: Theories in Subjection*. Stanford University Press.

1997b. *Excitable Speech: A Politics of the Performative*. New York: Routledge.

Butler, J., E. Laclau, and S. Žižek. 2000. *Contingency, Hegemony, Universality: Contemporary Dialogues on the Left*. London: Verso.

Cairns, D. 1996. "*Hybris*, Dishonour, and Thinking Big." *JHS* 116: 1–32.

Calhoun, G. M. 1919. "Oral and Written Pleading in Athenian Courts." *TAPA* 50: 177–93.

Carawan, E. 1983. "Erotesis: Interrogation in the Courts of Fourth Century Athens." *GRBS* 24: 209–26.

1993. "The Tetralogies and Athenian Homicide Trials." *AJP* 114: 235–70.

1998. *Rhetoric and the Law of Draco*. Oxford: Clarendon.

2000. "Deianira's Guilt." *TAPA* 130: 189–237.

2002. "The Athenian Amnesty and the 'Scrutiny of the Laws'." *JHS* 122: 1–23.

2006. "Amnesty and Accountings for the Thirty." *CQ* 56: 57–76.

2007. "Oath and Contract." In A. H. Sommerstein and J. Fletcher, eds. *Horkos: The Oath in Greek Society*. Exeter: Bristol Phoenix Press. 73–80.

Carey, C. 1988. "A Note on Torture in Athenian Homicide Cases." *Historia* 37: 241–45.

ed. 1989. *Lysias: Selected Speeches*. Cambridge University Press.

1990. "Structure and Strategy in Lysias XXIV." *G&R* 37: 44–51.

ed. 1992. *Apollodorus Against Neaira [Demosthenes] 59*. Warminster: Aris and Phillips.

1994a. "Rhetorical Means of Persuasion." In I. Worthington, ed. *Persuasion: Greek Rhetoric in Action*. New York: Routledge. 26–45.

1994b. "'Artless' Proofs in Aristotle and the Orators." *BICS* 39: 95–106.

1995. "Rape and Adultery in Athenian Law." *CQ* 45: 407–17.

1996. "*Nomos* in Attic Rhetoric and Oratory." *JHS* 116: 33–46.

1998. "The Shape of Athenian Laws." *CQ* 48: 93–109.

2004. "Offense and Procedure in Athenian Law." In E. M. Harris and L. Rubinstein, eds. *The Law and the Courts in Ancient Greece*. London: Duckworth. 111–36.

Carey, C. and R. A. Reid, eds. 1985. *Demosthenes: Selected Private Speeches*. Cambridge University Press.

Carter, D. 2007. "Could a Greek Oath Guarantee a Claim Right? Oaths, Contracts and the Structure of Obligation in Classical Athens." In A. H. Sommerstein and J. Fletcher, eds. *Horkos: The Oath in Greek Society*. Exeter: Bristol Phoenix Press. 60–72.

Carter, L. B. 1986. *The Quiet Athenian*. Oxford: Clarendon Press.

Cartledge, P., P. Millett, and S. C. Todd, eds. 1990. *Nomos: Essays in Athenian Law, Politics and Society*. Cambridge University Press.

Caruth, C. 1996. *Unclaimed Experience: Trauma, Narrative, and History*. Baltimore, MD: Johns Hopkins University Press.

Caudill, D. S. 1997. *Lacan and the Subject of Law: Toward a Psychoanalytic Critical Legal Theory*. Atlantic Highlands, NJ: Humanities Press.

Chantraine, P. 1968. *Dictionnaire étymologique de la langue grecque*. 3 vols. Paris: Klincksieck.

Christ, M. R. 1998a. *The Litigious Athenian*. Baltimore, MD: Johns Hopkins University Press.

1998b. "Legal Self-help on Private Property in Classical Athens." *AJP* 119: 521–45.

2006. *The Bad Citizen in Classical Athens*. Cambridge University Press.

2007. Review of G. Herman, *Morality and Behaviour in Democratic Athens*. *BMCR* 2007.07.37.

(in press a). "Helping Behavior in Classical Athens." *Phoenix*.

(in press b). "Helping and Community in the Athenian Lawcourts." In R. M. Rosen and I. Sluiter, eds. *Valuing Others in Classical Antiquity*. Leiden: Brill.

Cloché, P. 1915. *La restauration démocratique à Athènes en 403 avant J.-C.* Paris: Ernest Leroux.

Cohen, D. 1991a. "Demosthenes' *Against Meidias* and Athenian Litigation." In M. Gagarin, ed. *Symposion 1990: Papers on Greek and Hellenistic Legal History*. Cologne: Böhlau. 155–64.

1991b. "Sexuality, Violence and the Athenian Law of 'Hubris'." *G&R* 38: 171–88.

1995a. *Law, Violence and Community in Classical Athens*. Cambridge University Press.

1995b. "The Rule of Law and Democratic Ideology in Classical Athens." In W. Eder, ed. *Die athenische Demokratie im 4. Jahrhundert v. Chr.* Stuttgart: Franz Steiner. 227–44.

2003. "Writing, Law, and Legal Practice in the Athenian Courts." In H. Yunis, ed. *Written Texts and the Rise of Literate Culture in Ancient Greece*. Cambridge University Press. 78–96.

2005. "Crime, Punishment, and the Rule of Law in Classical Athens." In M. Gagarin and D. Cohen, eds. *The Cambridge Companion to Ancient Greek Law*. Cambridge University Press. 211–35.

Cohen, E. 2000. *The Athenian Nation*. Princeton University Press.

2006. "Free and Unfree Sexual Work: An Economic Analysis of Athenian Prostitution." In C. A. Faraone and L. K. McClure, eds. *Prostitutes and Courtesans in the Ancient World.* Madison, WI: University of Wisconsin Press. 95–124.

Cole, S. G. 1984. "Greek Sanctions Against Sexual Assault." *CP* 79: 97–113.

2004. *Landscapes, Gender, and Ritual Space: The Ancient Greek Experience.* Berkeley, CA: University of California Press.

Cole, T. 1991a. *The Origins of Rhetoric in Ancient Greece.* Baltimore, MD: Johns Hopkins University Press.

1991b. "Who Was Corax?" *ICS* 16: 65–84.

Connor, W. R. 1992. *The New Politicians of Fifth-Century Athens.* Indianapolis, IN: Hackett. [Reprint of Princeton University Press, 1971].

Cook, A. 2004. "'Settling Accounts': Law as History in the Trial of the Gang of Four." In A. Lewis and M. Lobban, eds. *Law and History.* Oxford University Press. 413–31.

Copjec, J. 2002. *Imagine There's No Woman: Ethics and Sublimation.* Cambridge, MA: MIT Press.

Cornell, D. 1992a. *The Philosophy of the Limit.* New York: Routledge.

1992b. "From the Lighthouse: The Promise of Redemption and the Possibility of Legal Interpretation." In G. Leyh, ed. *Legal Hermeneutics: History, Theory, and Practice.* Berkeley, CA: University of California Press. 147–72.

1992c. "The Philosophy of the Limit: Systems Theory and Feminist Legal Reform." In Cornell, Rosenfeld, and Carlson 1992: 68–91.

1995a. "Time, Deconstruction, and the Challenge to Legal Positivism: The Call for Judicial Responsibility." In J. D. Leonard, ed. *Legal Studies as Cultural Studies: A Reader in (Post)modern Critical Theory.* Albany, NY: State University of New York Press. 231–66.

1995b. "Bodily Integrity and the Right to Abortion." In A. Sarat and T. R. Kearns, eds. *Identities, Politics, and Rights.* Ann Arbor, MI: University of Michigan Press. 21–83.

1995c. *The Imaginary Domain: Abortion, Pornography and Sexual Harassment.* New York: Routledge.

1996. "The Right to Abortion and the Imaginary Domain." In D. Fuss, ed. *Human, All Too Human.* New York: Routledge. 220–41.

1998. *At the Heart of Freedom: Feminism, Sex, and Equality.* Princeton University Press.

Cornell, D., M. Rosenfeld, and D. G. Carlson, eds. 1992. *Deconstruction and the Possibility of Justice.* London: Routledge.

Cousins, M. 1987. "The Practice of Historical Investigation." In D. Attridge, G. Bennington, and R. Young, eds. *Post-Structuralism and the Question of History.* Cambridge University Press. 126–36.

Cover, R. M. 1986. "Violence and the Word." *Yale Law Journal* 95: 1601–29.

1993. "Nomos and Narrative." In M. Minow, M. Ryan, and A. Sarat, eds. *Narrative, Violence, and the Law: The Essays of Robert Cover.* Ann Arbor, MI: University of Michigan Press. 95–172. [Reprint of "The Supreme Court, 1982

Term – Foreword: Nomos and Narrative," *Harvard Law Review* 97 (1983), 1–68.]

Cox, C. A. 1989. "Incest, Inheritance and the Political Forum in Fifth-Century Athens." *CJ* 85: 34–46.

1996. "Hipponicus' Trapeza: Humour in Andocides 1.130–1." *CQ* 46: 572–75.

1998. *Household Interests: Property, Marriage Strategies, and Family Dynamics in Ancient Athens.* Princeton University Press.

Cronin, J. F. 1936. *The Athenian Juror and His Oath.* University of Chicago Press.

Crook, J. A. 1996. "Legal History and General History." *BICS* 41: 31–36.

Csapo, E. and M. Miller. 1998. "Democracy, Empire, and Art: Toward a Politics of Time and Narrative." In D. Boedeker and K. Raaflaub, eds. *Democracy, Empire, and the Arts in Fifth-Century Athens.* Cambridge, MA: Harvard University Press. 87–125.

Davidson, J. 1997. *Courtesans and Fishcakes: The Consuming Passions of Classical Athens.* New York: St. Martin's Press.

Davies, J. K. 1971. *Athenian Propertied Families, 600–300 B. C.* Oxford: Clarendon.

1977–78. "Athenian Citizenship: The Descent Group and the Alternatives." *CJ* 73: 105–21.

Davis, N. Z. 1987. *Fiction in the Archives: Pardon Tales and Their Tellers in Sixteenth-Century France.* Stanford University Press.

De Brauw, M. 2001–02. "'Listen to the Laws Themselves:' Citations of Laws and Portrayal of Character in Attic Oratory." *CJ* 97: 161–76.

De Certeau, M. 1984. *The Practice of Everyday Life.* Trans. S. Rendall. Berkeley, CA: University of California Press.

Decleva Caizzi, F., ed. 1969. *Antiphontis Tetralogiae.* Milan: Istituto Editoriale Cisalpino.

1989. "Antipho." In F. Adorno *et al.*, eds. *Corpus dei Papiri Filosofici Greci e Latini.* Florence: Olschki. 176–236.

de Man, P. 1979. *Allegories of Reading: Figural Language in Rousseau, Nietzsche, Rilke, and Proust.* New Haven, CT: Yale University Press.

Derrida, J. 1976. *Of Grammatology.* Trans. G. Spivak. Baltimore, MD: Johns Hopkins University Press.

1988. *Limited Inc.* Trans S. Weber and J. Mehlman. Evanston, IL: Northwestern University Press.

1992a. "Force of Law: The 'Mystical Foundation of Authority'." Trans. M. Quaintance. In Cornell, Rosenfeld, and Carlson 1992: 3–67.

1992b. "Before the Law." In D. Attridge, ed. *Acts of Literature.* London: Routledge. 181–220.

2002. *Without Alibi.* Ed. and Trans., P. Kamuf. Stanford University Press.

Dershowitz, A. M. 1996. "Life is Not a Dramatic Narrative." In Brooks and Gewirtz 1996: 99–105.

de Ste. Croix, G. E. M. 1981. *The Class Struggle in the Ancient World.* Ithaca, NY: Cornell University Press.

Detienne, M. 1996. *The Masters of Truth in Archaic Greece.* Trans. J. Lloyd. New York: Zone Books. Originally published as *Les maîtres de vérité dans la grèce archaïque.* Paris, 1967.

Dihle, A. 1982. *The Theory of Will in Classical Antiquity*. Berkeley, CA: University of California Press.

Dillon, M. P. J. 1995. "Payments to the Disabled at Athens: Social Justice or Fear of Aristocratic Patronage?" *AncSoc* 26: 27–57.

Dorjahn, A. P. 1946. *Political Forgiveness in Old Athens: The Amnesty of 403*. Evanston, IL: Northwestern University.

1971. "On Slave-Evidence in the Athenian Courts." *CB* 47: 45–46.

Douglas, L. 2001. *The Memory of Judgment: Making Law and History in the Trials of the Holocaust*. New Haven, CT: Yale University Press.

2004. "The Holocaust, History, and Legal Memory." In A. Lewis and M. Lobban, eds. *Law and History*. Oxford University Press. 405–12.

Douzinas, C. and R. Warrington. 1995. "'A Well-Founded Fear of Justice': Law and Ethics in Postmodernity." In J. D. Leonard, ed. *Legal Studies as Cultural Studies: A Reader in (Post)modern Critical Theory*. Albany, NY: State University of New York Press. 197–229.

Douzinas, C., R. Warrington, and S. McVeigh. 1991. *Postmodern Jurisprudence: The Law of Text in the Texts of Law*. London: Routledge.

Dover, K. J. 1950. "The Chronology of Antiphon's Speeches." *CQ* 44: 44–60.

1968. *Lysias and the* Corpus Lysiacum. Berkeley, CA: University of California Press.

1974. *Greek Popular Morality in the Time of Plato and Aristotle*. Oxford: Blackwell.

1978. *Greek Homosexuality*. Cambridge, MA: Harvard University Press.

Dow, S. 1961. "The Walls Inscribed with Nikomakhos' Law Code." *Hesperia* 30: 58–73.

DuBois, P. 1991. *Torture and Truth*. New York: Routledge.

2003. *Slaves and Other Objects*. University of Chicago Press.

Due, B. 1980. *Antiphon: A Study in Argumentation*. Copenhagen: Museum Tusculanum.

Dunbar, N., ed. 1998. *Aristophanes: Birds*. Oxford: Clarendon.

Duncan, A. 2006. *Performance and Identity in the Classical World*. Cambridge University Press.

Dunn, F. M. 2007. *Present Shock in Late Fifth-Century Greece*. Ann Arbor, MI: University of Michigan Press.

Easterling, P. E. 1999. "Actors and Voices: Reading between the Lines in Aeschines and Demosthenes." In S. Goldhill and R. Osborne, eds. *Performance Culture and Athenian Democracy*. Cambridge University Press. 154–66.

Eden, K. 1986. *Poetic and Legal Fiction in the Aristotelian Tradition*. Princeton University Press.

Edwards, M. J. 1998. "Notes on Pseudo-Plutarch's *Life of Antiphon*." *CQ* 48: 82–92.

ed. 1999. *Lysias: Five Speeches*. Bristol Classical Press.

2000. "Antiphon and the Beginnings of Athenian Literary Oratory." *Rhetorica* 18: 227–42.

Edwards, M. and S. Usher, eds. 1985. *Greek Orators I: Antiphon and Lysias*. Chicago, IL: Bolchazy-Carducci.

Eidinow, E. 2007. "Why the Athenians Began to Curse." In Osborne 2007: 44–71.

Eucken, C. 1996. "Das Tötungsgesetz des Antiphon und der Sinn seiner Tetralogien." *Mus. Helv.* 53: 73–82.

Evjen H. D. 1971. "(Dem.) 47.68–73 and the *dikê phonou.*" *RIDA* 18: 255–65.

Faraone, C. A. 1991. "The Agonistic Context of Early Greek Binding Spells." In C. A. Faraone and D. Obbink, eds. *Magika Hiera: Ancient Greek Magic and Religion*. New York: Oxford University Press. 3–32.

Farenga, V. 2006. *Citizen and Self in Ancient Greece: Individuals Performing Justice and the Law*. Cambridge University Press.

Felman, S. 2002. *The Juridical Unconscious: Trials and Traumas in the Twentieth Century*. Cambridge, MA: Harvard University Press.

Ferguson, R. A. 1996. "Untold Stories in the Law." In Brooks and Gewirtz 1996: 84–98.

Fingarette, A. 1971. "A New Look at the Wall of Nikomakhos." *Hesperia* 40: 330–35.

Fish, S. 1989. *Doing What Comes Naturally: Change, Rhetoric, and the Practice of Theory in Literary and Legal Studies*. Durham, NC: Duke University Press.

1991. "The Law Wishes to Have a Formal Existence." In A. Sarat and T. R. Kearns, eds. *The Fate of Law*. Ann Arbor, MI: University of Michigan Press. 159–208.

Fisher, N. R. E. 1976. "*Hybris* and Dishonour: 1." *G&R* 23: 177–93.

1990. "The Law of *Hubris* in Athens." In Cartledge, Millett, and Todd 1990: 123–38.

1992. *Hybris: A Study in the Values of Honour and Shame in Ancient Greece*. Warminster: Aris and Phillips.

1998. "Violence, Masculinity and the Law in Classical Athens." In L. Foxhall and J. Salmon, eds. *When Men Were Men: Masculinity, Power, and Identity in Classical Antiquity*. London: Routledge. 68–97.

1999. "'Workshops of Villains': Was There Much Organised Crime in Classical Athens?" In K. Hopwood, ed. *Organised Crime in Antiquity*. London: Duckworth. 53–96.

ed. 2001. *Aeschines: Against Timarchus*. Oxford University Press.

Flashar, H. 1966. *Melancholie und Melancholiker in den medizinischen Theorien der Antike*. Berlin: Walter de Gruyter.

Ford, A. 1999. "Reading Homer from the Rostrum: Poems and Laws in Aeschines' *Against Timarchus*." In S. Goldhill and R. Osborne, eds. *Performance Culture and Athenian Democracy*. Cambridge University Press. 231–56.

Foucault, M. 1972. *The Archaeology of Knowledge*. Trans. A. M. Sheridan Smith. New York: Pantheon Books.

1977a. "What is an Author?" In D. F. Bouchard, ed. *Language, Counter-Memory, Practice*. Trans. D. F. Bouchard and S. Simon. Ithaca, NY: Cornell University Press. 113–38.

1977b. "Nietzsche, Genealogy, History." In D. F. Bouchard, ed. *Language, Counter-Memory, Practice*. Trans. D. F. Bouchard and S. Simon. Ithaca, NY: Cornell University Press. 139–64.

1978. *The History of Sexuality. Volume I: An Introduction*. Trans. R. Hurley. New York: Vintage Books.

1980. "Two Lectures." In C. Gordon, ed. *Power/Knowledge: Selected Interviews and Other Writings 1972–1977*. New York: Pantheon. 78–108.

1982. "The Subject and Power." In H. L. Dreyfus and P. Rabinow, eds. *Michel Foucault: Beyond Structuralism and Hermeneutics*. University of Chicago Press. 208–26.

1985. *The History of Sexuality. Volume II: The Use of Pleasure*. Trans. R. Hurley. New York: Vintage Books.

1986. *The History of Sexuality. Volume III: The Care of the Self*. Trans. R. Hurley. New York: Pantheon Books.

1994. "Truth and Juridical Forms." In J. D. Faubion, ed. *Michel Foucault: Power* (Volume III of *Essential Works of Foucault 1954–1984*). Trans. R. Hurley. New York: The New Press. 1–89.

2001. *Fearless Speech*. Ed. J. Pearson. Los Angeles, CA: Semiotext(e).

Foxhall, L. 1989. "Household, Gender and Property in Classical Athens." *CQ* 39: 22–44.

1996. "The Law and the Lady: Women and Legal Proceedings in Classical Athens." In Foxhall and Lewis 1996: 133–52.

Foxhall, L. and A. D. E. Lewis, eds. 1996. *Greek Law in Its Political Setting: Justifications not Justice*. Oxford: Clarendon.

Fredal, J. 2001. "The Language of Delivery and the Presentation of Character: Rhetorical Action in Demosthenes' *Against Meidias*." *Rhetoric Review* 20: 251–67.

2006. *Rhetorical Action in Ancient Athens: Persuasive Artistry from Solon to Demosthenes*. Carbondale, IL: South Illinois University Press.

Freeman, M. and A. D. E. Lewis, eds. 1999. *Law and Literature*. Oxford University Press.

Freud, S. 1953 [1900]. *The Interpretation of Dreams. Standard Edition*, vol. IV. Trans. and ed. J. Strachey. London: Vintage.

1955 [1913]. *Totem and Taboo. Standard Edition*, vol. XIII. Trans. and ed. J. Strachey. London: Vintage. 1–161.

1957 [1917]. "Mourning and Melancholia." *Standard Edition*, vol. XIV. Trans. and ed. J. Strachey. London: Vintage. 243–58.

1960 [1901]. *The Psychopathology of Everyday Life. Standard Edition*, vol. VI. Trans. and ed. J. Strachey. London: Vintage.

1960 [1905]. *Jokes and Their Relation to the Unconscious. Standard Edition*, vol. VIII. Trans. and ed. J. Strachey. London: Vintage.

1961 [1927]. "Fetishism." *Standard Edition*, vol. XXI. Trans. and ed. J. Strachey. London: Vintage. 152–57.

Frug, M. J. 1992. *Postmodern Legal Feminism*. New York: Routledge.

Furley, W. D. 1996. *Andokides and the Herms: A Study of Crisis in Fifth-Century Athenian Religion. BICS* Supplement 65. London: Institute of Classical Studies.

Gagarin, M. 1978a. "Self-defense in Athenian Homicide Law." *GRBS* 19: 111–20.

1978b. "The Prohibition of Just and Unjust Homicide in Antiphon's *Tetralogies*." *GRBS* 19: 291–306.

1979a. "The Athenian Law Against *Hybris*." In G. W. Bowersock, W. Burkert, and M. C. J. Putnam, eds. *Arktouros: Hellenic Studies Presented to Bernard M. W. Knox*. New York: Walter de Gruyter. 229–36.

1979b. "The Prosecution of Homicide in Athens." *GRBS* 20: 301–23.

1981. *Drakon and Early Athenian Homicide Law*. New Haven, CT: Yale University Press.

1989. *The Murder of Herodes: A Study of Antiphon 5. Studien zur Klassischen Philologie* 45. Frankfurt: Peter Lang.

1990a. "The Ancient Tradition on the Identity of Antiphon." *GRBS* 31: 27–44.

1990b. "*Bouleusis* in Athenian Homicide Law." In G. Nenci and G. Thür, eds. *Symposion 1988*. Cologne: Böhlau. 81–99.

1994. "Probability and Persuasion: Plato and Early Greek Rhetoric." In I. Worthington, ed. *Persuasion: Greek Rhetoric in Action*. New York: Routledge. 46–68.

1996. "The Torture of Slaves in Athenian Law." *CP* 91: 1–18.

ed. 1997. *Antiphon: The Speeches*. Cambridge University Press.

1998. "Women in Athenian Courts." *Dike* 1: 39–51.

2000. "Le code de Platon et le droit grec." In E. Lévy, ed. *La Codification des lois dans l'Antiquité*. Paris: Boccard. 215–27.

2001. "Women's Voices in Attic Oratory." In A. Lardinois and L. McClure, eds. *Making Silence Speak: Women's Voices in Greek Literature and Society*. Princeton University Press. 161–76.

2002. *Antiphon the Athenian: Oratory, Law, and Justice in the Age of the Sophists*. Austin, TX: University of Texas Press.

2003a. "Telling Stories in Athenian Law." *TAPA* 133: 197–207.

2003b. "Letters of the Law: Written Texts in Archaic Greek Law." In H. Yunis, ed. *Written Texts and the Rise of Literate Culture in Ancient Greece*. Cambridge University Press. 59–77.

2004. "Writing Athenian Law." In D. L. Cairns and R. A. Knox, eds. *Law, Rhetoric, and Comedy in Classical Athens: Essays in Honour of Douglas M. MacDowell*. Swansea: The Classical Press of Wales. 15–31.

2005. "The Unity of Greek Law." In M. Gagarin and D. Cohen, eds. *The Cambridge Companion to Ancient Greek Law*. Cambridge University Press. 29–40.

2007. "Litigants' Oaths in Athenian Law." In A. H. Sommerstein and J. Fletcher, eds. *Horkos: The Oath in Greek Society*. 39–47.

2008. *Writing Greek Law*. Cambridge University Press.

Garland, R. 1995. *The Eye of the Beholder: Deformity and Disability in the Graeco-Roman World*. London: Duckworth.

Garner, R. 1987. *Law and Society in Classical Athens*. London: Croom Helm.

Gehrke, H.-J. 2000. "Verschriftung und Verschriftlichung sozialer Normen im archaischen und klassischen Griechenland." In E. Lévy, ed. *La Codification des lois dans l'Antiquité*. Paris: Boccard. 141–59.

Gernet, L. 1917. *Recherches sur le développement de la pensée juridique et morale en Grèce*. Paris: Ernest Leroux.

1921. "Sur l'épiclérat." *REG* 34: 337–79.

1955. *Droit et société dans la Grèce ancienne*. Paris: Sirey.

ed. 1957. *Démosthène. Plaidoyers civils*. Vol. II. Paris: Les Belles Lettres.

1981a. "Law and Prelaw in Ancient Greece." In *The Anthropology of Ancient Greece*. Trans. J. Hamilton and B. Nagy. Baltimore, MD: Johns Hopkins University Press. 143–215.

1981b. "The Concept of Time in the Earliest Forms of Law." In *The Anthropology of Ancient Greece*. Trans. J. Hamilton and B. Nagy. Baltimore, MD: Johns Hopkins University Press. 216–39.

Gernet, L. and M. Bizos, eds. 1955. *Lysias. Discours, Vol. I*. Paris: Les Belles Lettres.

Gewirtz, P. 1996. "Victims and Voyeurs: Two Narrative Problems at the Criminal Trial." In Brooks and Gewirtz 1996: 135–61.

Gilhuly, K. 2008. *The Feminine Matrix of Sex and Gender in Classical Athens*. Cambridge University Press.

Gilmore, L. 1994. *Autobiographics: A Feminist Theory of Women's Self-Representation*. Ithaca, NY: Cornell University Press.

Glazebrook, A. 2005. "The Making of a Prostitute: Apollodoros's Portrait of Neaira." *Arethusa* 38: 161–87.

2006. "The Bad Girls of Athens: The Image and Function of *Hetairai* in Judicial Oratory." In C. A. Faraone and L. K. McClure, eds. *Prostitutes and Courtesans in the Ancient World*. Madison, WI: University of Wisconsin Press. 125–38.

Goff, B. 2004. *Citizen Bacchae: Women's Ritual Practice in Ancient Greece*. Berkeley, CA: University of California Press.

Golden, M. 1986. "Names and Naming at Athens: Three Studies." *EMC* 30: 245–69.

2000. "Demosthenes and the Social Historian." In I. Worthington, ed. *Demosthenes: Statesman and Orator*. New York: Routledge. 159–80.

Goldhill, S. 1990. "Character and Action, Representation and Reading: Greek Tragedy and its Critics." In C. Pelling, ed. *Characterization and Individuality in Greek Literature*. Oxford: Clarendon. 100–27.

Goodrich, P. 1984. "Law and Language: An Historical and Critical Introduction." *Journal of Law and Society* 11: 173–206.

1986. *Reading the Law: A Critical Introduction to Legal Method and Techniques*. London: Basil Blackwell.

1987. *Legal Discourse: Studies in Linguistics, Rhetoric and Legal Analysis*. London: MacMillan.

1990a. *Languages of Law: From Logics of Memory to Nomadic Masks*. London: Weidenfeld and Nicolson.

1990b. "Contractions: Rousseau in the Year Two Thousand." In A. Carty, ed. *Post-Modern Law: Enlightenment, Revolution, and the Death of Man*. Edinburgh University Press. 40–70.

1992. "*Ars Bablativa*: Ramism, Rhetoric, and the Genealogy of English Jurisprudence." In G. Leyh, ed. *Legal Hermeneutics: History, Theory, and Practice.* Berkeley, CA: University of California Press. 43–82.

1993. "Fate as Seduction: The Other Scene of Legal Judgment." In A. Norrie, ed. *Closure or Critique: New Directions in Legal Theory*. Edinburgh University Press. 116–41.

1994a. "*Jani anglorum*: Signs, Symptoms, Slips and Interpretation in Law." In C. Douzinas, P. Goodrich, and Y. Hachamovitch, eds. *Politics, Postmodernity and Critical Legal Studies*. London: Routledge. 107–44.

1994b. "Antirrhesis: Polemical Structures of Common Law Thought." In A. Sarat and T. Kearns, eds. *The Rhetoric of Law*. Ann Arbor, MI: University of Michigan Press. 57–102.

1995. *Oedipus Lex: Psychoanalysis, History, Law*. Berkeley, CA: University of California Press.

1996. *Law in the Courts of Love: Literature and Other Minor Jurisprudences*. London: Routledge.

1998. "Law by Other Means." *Cardozo Studies in Law and Literature* 10: 111–16.

2002. "Erotic Melancholia: Law, Literature, and Love." *Law and Literature* 14: 103–29.

Goodrich, P. and Y. Hachamovitch. 1991. "Time Out of Mind: An Introduction to the Semiotics of Common Law." In P. Fitzpatrick, ed. *Dangerous Supplements: Resistance and Renewal in Jurisprudence*. Durham, NC: Duke University Press. 159–81.

Goody, J. 1962. *Death, Property and the Ancestors: A Study of the Mortuary Customs of the LoDagaa of West Africa*. Stanford University Press.

1969. *Comparative Studies in Kinship*. Stanford University Press.

ed. 1976. *Family and Inheritance: Rural Society in Western Europe, 1200–1800*. Cambridge University Press.

Gunderson, E. 2000. *Staging Masculinity: The Rhetoric of Performance in the Roman World.* Ann Arbor, MI: Michigan University Press.

2003. *Declamation, Paternity, and Roman Identity: Authority and the Rhetorical Self.* Cambridge University Press.

Gustafsson, H. 1998. "Immanence of Law." In A. Hirvonen, ed. *Polycentricity: The Multiple Scenes of Law*. London: Pluto Press. 135–75.

Hall, E. 1995. "Lawcourt Dramas: The Power of Performance in Greek Forensic Oratory." *BICS* 40: 39–58.

Halliwell, S. 1986. *Aristotle's Poetics*. London: Duckworth.

1991. "The Uses of Laughter in Greek Culture." *CQ* 41: 279–96.

2004. "Aischrology, Shame, and Comedy." In Sluiter and Rosen 2004: 115–44.

Halperin, D. M. 1990. *One Hundred Years of Homosexuality*. New York: Routledge.

Hamel, D. 2003. *Trying Neaira*. New Haven, CT: Yale University Press.

Hands, A. R. 1968. *Charities and Social Aid in Greece and Rome*. London: Thames and Hudson.

Hansen, M. H. 1971–80. "Athenian Nomothesia in the Fourth Century B. C. and Demosthenes' Speech Against Leptines." *C&M* 32: 87–104.

1974. *The Sovereignty of the People's Court in Athens in the Fourth Century B. C. and the Public Action against Unconstitutional Proposals.* Trans. J. Raphaelsen and S. Holbøll. Odense University Press.

1975. *Eisangelia: The Sovereignty of the People's Court in Athens in the Fourth Century B. C. and the Impeachment of Generals and Politicians.* Odense University Press.

1976. *Apagoge, Endeixis and Ephegesis against Kakourgoi, Atimoi, and Pheugontes.* Odense University Press.

1978. "*Demos, Ecclesia* and *Dicasterion* in Classical Athens." *GRBS* 19: 127–46.

1985. "Athenian Nomothesia." *GRBS* 26: 345–71.

1987. *The Athenian Assembly in the Age of Demosthenes.* Oxford: Blackwell.

1989. "*Demos, Ekklesia*, and *Dikasterion*. A Reply to Martin Ostwald and Josiah Ober." *C&M* 40: 101–06.

1990. "Diokles' Law (Dem. 24.42) and the Revision of the Athenian Corpus of Laws in the Archonship of Eukleides." *C&M* 41: 63–71.

1991. *The Athenian Democracy in the Age of Demosthenes: Structure, Principles and Ideology.* Trans. J. A. Crook. Oxford: Blackwell.

Hardcastle, M. 1980. "Some Non-Legal Arguments in Athenian Inheritance Cases." *Prudentia* 12: 11–22.

Harding, P. 1974. "The Theramenes Myth." *Phoenix* 28: 101–11.

1987. "Rhetoric and Politics in Fourth-Century Athens." *Phoenix* 41: 25–39.

1994. "Comedy and Rhetoric." In I. Worthington, ed. *Persuasion: Greek Rhetoric in Action.* New York: Routledge. 196–221.

Harris, E. M. 1989. "Demosthenes' Speech Against Meidias." *HSCP* 92: 117–36.

1994a. "Law and Oratory." In I. Worthington, ed. *Persuasion: Greek Rhetoric in Action.* New York: Routledge. 130–50.

1994b. "'In the Act' or 'Red-Handed'? *Apagoge* to *the Eleven and Furtum Manifestum.*" In G. Thür, ed. *Symposion 1993.* Cologne: Böhlau. 169–84.

1995. *Aeschines and Athenian Politics.* New York: Oxford University Press.

2000. "Open Texture in Athenian Law." *Dike* 3: 27–79.

2004. "Antigone the Lawyer, or the Ambiguities of Nomos." In E. M. Harris and L. Rubinstein, eds. *The Law and the Courts in Ancient Greece.* London: Duckworth. 19–56. [= Harris 2006: 41–80]

2006. *Democracy and the Rule of Law in Classical Athens: Essays on Law, Society, and Politics.* Cambridge University Press.

Harrison, A. R. W. 1955. "Law-Making at Athens at the End of the Fifth Century B.C." *JHS* 75: 26–35.

1968. *The Law of Athens. Vol. I: The Family and Property.* Oxford: Clarendon Press.

1971. *The Law of Athens. Vol. II: Procedure.* Oxford: Clarendon Press.

Harvey, D. 1990. "The Sykophant and Sykophancy: Vexatious Redefinition?" In Cartledge, Millett, and Todd 1990: 103–21.

Havelock, E. A. 1978. *The Greek Concept of Justice: From Its Shadow in Homer to Its Substance in Plato.* Cambridge, MA: Harvard University Press.

Hedrick, C. W. 1994. "Writing, Reading, and Democracy." In R. Osborne and S. Hornblower, eds. *Ritual, Finance, Politics: Athenian Democratic Accounts Presented to David Lewis.* Oxford: Clarendon. 157–74.

Hegel, G. W. F. 1977 [1807]. *Phenomenology of Spirit.* Trans. A. V. Miller. Oxford University Press.

Heidegger, M. 1996 [1953]. *Being and Time.* Trans. J. Stambaugh. Albany, NY: State University of New York Press.

Henderson, J. 1972. "The Lekythos and *Frogs* 1200–1248." *HSCP* 76: 133–43.

Henrichs, A. 1968. "Zur Interpretation des Michigan-Papyrus über Theramenes." *ZPE* 3: 101–108.

Herman, G. 1993. "Tribal and Civic Codes of Behaviour in Lysias 1." *CQ* 43: 406–19.

1994. "How Violent Was Athenian Society?" In R. Osborne and S. Hornblower, eds. *Ritual, Finance, Politics: Athenian Democratic Accounts Presented to David Lewis.* Oxford: Clarendon Press. 99–117.

1995. "Honour, Revenge and the State in Fourth-Century Athens." In W. Eder, ed. *Die athenische Demokratie im 4. Jahrhundert v. Chr.* Stuttgart: Franz Steiner. 43–60.

1996. "Review of David Cohen, *Law, Violence and Community in Classical Athens.*" *Gnomon* 70: 605–15.

2006. *Morality and Behaviour in Democratic Athens.* Cambridge University Press.

2007. "Herman on Christ on Gabriel Herman, *Morality and Behaviour in Democratic Athens.*" *BMCR* 2007.09.21.

Hesk, J. 1999. "The Rhetoric of Anti-Rhetoric in Athenian Oratory." In S. Goldhill and R. Osborne, eds. *Performance Culture and Athenian Democracy.* Cambridge University Press. 201–30.

2000. *Deception and Democracy in Classical Athens.* Cambridge University Press.

Hillgruber, M. 1988. *Die zehnte Rede des Lysias.* Berlin: Walter de Gruyter.

Hölkeskamp, K.-J. 1992. "Written Law in Archaic Greece." *PCPS* 38: 87–117.

Humphreys, S. C. 1974. "The Nothoi of Kynosarges." *JHS* 94: 88–95.

1983. *The Family, Women and Death.* Ann Arbor, MI: University of Michigan Press.

1985a. "Law as Discourse." *History and Anthropology* 1: 241–64.

1985b. "Social Relations on Stage: Witnesses in Classical Athens." *History and Anthropology* 1: 313–69.

1986. "Kinship Patterns in the Athenian Courts." *GRBS* 27: 57–91.

1988. "The Discourse of Law in Archaic and Classical Greece." *Law and History Review* 6: 465–93.

1989. "Family Quarrels (Dem. 39–40)." *JHS* 109: 182–85.

Hunter, V. J. 1989. "The Athenian Widow and Her Kin." *Journal of Family History* 14: 291–311.

1990. "Gossip and the Politics of Reputation in Classical Athens." *Phoenix* 44: 299–325.

1992. "Constructing the Body of the Citizen: Corporal Punishment in Classical Athens." *EMC* 36: 271–91.

1993. "Agnatic Kinship in Athenian Law and Athenian Family Practice: Its Implications for Women." In B. Halpern and D. W. Hobson, eds. *Law, Politics and Society in the Ancient Mediterranean World.* Sheffield Academic Press. 100–121.

1994. *Policing Athens: Social Control in the Attic Lawsuits, 420–320 B.C.* Princeton University Press.

2000. "Introduction: Status Distinctions in Athenian Law." In V. Hunter and J. Edmondson, eds. *Law and Social Status in Classical Athens.* Oxford University Press. 1–29.

Hyde, A. 1997. *Bodies of Law.* Princeton University Press.

Hyde, W. W. 1917. "The Prosecution of Lifeless Things and Animals in Greek Law." *AJP* 38: 152–75, 285–303.

Hyppolite, J. 1988. "A Spoken Commentary on Freud's *Verneinung.*" In J. Lacan, *The Seminar of Jacques Lacan, Book 1: Freud's Papers on Technique.* Ed. J.-A. Miller. Trans. J. Forrester. New York: W. W. Norton. 289–97.

Isager, S. and M. H. Hansen. 1975. *Aspects of Athenian Society in the Fourth Century B. C.* Trans. J. H. Rosenmeier. Odense University Press.

Jakobson, R. (with M. Halle). 1956. *Fundamentals of Language.* The Hague: Mouton.

Johnstone, S. 1998. "Cracking the Code of Silence: Athenian Legal Oratory and the Histories of Slaves and Women." In S. Joshel and S. Murnaghan, eds. *Women and Slaves in Greco-Roman Culture.* New York: Routledge. 221–35.

1999. *Disputes and Democracy: The Consequences of Litigation in Ancient Athens.* Austin, TX: University of Texas Press.

Jones, J. 1962. *On Aristotle and Greek Tragedy.* Oxford University Press.

Just, R. 1989. *Women in Athenian Law and Life.* New York: Routledge.

Kafka, F. 1992 [1925]. *The Trial.* Trans. W. and E. Muir. New York: Schocken Books.

Kahn, P. W. 1999. *The Cultural Study of Law: Reconstructing Legal Scholarship.* University of Chicago Press.

Kapparis, K. A. 1996. "Humiliating the Adulterer: the Law and the Practice in Classical Athens." *RIDA* 34: 63–77.

ed. 1999. *Apollodorus 'Against Neaira' [D. 59].* Berlin: Walter de Gruyter.

Katz, M. 1992a. "Patriarchy, Ideology and the Epikleros." *SIFC* 10: 692–708.

1992b. "Ox-Slaughter and Goring Oxen: Homicide, Animal Sacrifice, and Judicial Process." *Yale Journal of Law and the Humanities* 4: 249–78.

Kelsen, H. 1967. *Pure Theory of Law.* Trans. M. Knight. Berkeley, CA: University of California Press.

Kennedy, G. 1963. *The Art of Persuasion in Greece.* Princeton University Press.

Kenny, A. 1979. *Aristotle's Theory of the Will.* New Haven, CT: Yale University Press.

Kerferd, G. B. 1981. *The Sophistic Movement.* Cambridge University Press.

Konstan, D. 2000. "Pity and the Law in Greek Theory and Practice." *Dike* 3: 125–45.

2001. *Pity Transformed*. London: Duckworth.

Krentz, P. 1982. *The Thirty at Athens*. Ithaca, NY: Cornell University Press.

1984. "Was Eratosthenes Responsible for the Death of Polemarchos?" *PP* 39: 23–32.

Kurihara, A. 2003. "Personal Enmity as a Motivation in Forensic Speeches." *CQ* 53: 464–77.

Kurke, L. 1997. "Inventing the *Hetaira*: Sex, Politics, and Discursive Conflict in Archaic Greece." *ClAnt* 16: 106–53.

1999. *Coins, Bodies, Games, and Gold: The Politics of Meaning in Archaic Greece*. Princeton University Press.

Lacan, J. 1977a. "The Agency of the Letter in the Unconscious or Reason Since Freud." In *Écrits: A Selection*. Trans. A. Sheridan. New York: W. W. Norton. 146–78.

1977b. "The Subversion of the Subject and the Dialectic of Desire in the Freudian Unconscious." In *Écrits: A Selection*. Trans. A. Sheridan. New York: W. W. Norton. 292–325.

1981. *The Four Fundamental Concepts of Psycho-Analysis*. Ed. J.-A. Miller. Trans. A. Sheridan. New York: W. W. Norton.

1992. *The Ethics of Psychoanalysis: The Seminar of Jacques Lacan, Book VII*. Ed. J.-A. Miller. Trans. D. Porter. New York: W. W. Norton.

1993. *The Psychoses: The Seminar of Jacques Lacan, Book III*. Ed. J.-A. Miller. Trans. R. Grigg. New York: W. W. Norton.

LaCapra, D. 1990. "Violence, Justice, and the Force of Law." *Cardozo Law Review* 11: 1065–78.

1994. *Representing the Holocaust: History, Theory, Trauma*. Ithaca, NY: Cornell University Press.

Lacey, N. 1993. "Closure and Critique in Feminist Jurisprudence: Transcending the Dichotomy or a Foot in Both Camps?" In A. Norrie, ed. *Closure or Critique: New Directions in Legal Theory*. Edinburgh University Press. 194–213.

Lacey, W. K. 1968. *The Family in Classical Greece*. Ithaca, NY: Cornell University Press.

Laclau, E. and C. Mouffe. 1985. *Hegemony and Socialist Strategy: Towards a Radical Democratic Politics*. London: Verso.

Lambert, S. D. 1993. *The Phratries of Attica*. Ann Arbor, MI: University of Michigan Press.

Lane Fox, R. 1985. "Aspects of Inheritance in the Greek World." In. P. Cartledge and F. D. Harvey, eds. *Crux: Essays Presented to G. E. M. de Ste. Croix*. Exeter: Imprint Academic. 208–32.

1994. "Aeschines and Athenian Democracy." In R. Osborne and S. Hornblower, eds. *Ritual, Finance, Politics: Athenian Democratic Accounts Presented to David Lewis*. Oxford: Clarendon. 135–55.

Lanni, A. M. 1997. "Spectator Sport or Serious Politics? οἱ περιεστηκότες and the Athenian Lawcourts." *JHS* 117: 183–89.

2004. "Arguing from 'Precedent': Modern Perspectives on Athenian Practice." In E. M. Harris and L. Rubinstein, eds. *The Law and the Courts in Ancient Greece*. London: Duckworth. 159–71.

2006. *Law and Justice in the Courts of Classical Athens*. Cambridge University Press.

Lape, S. 2002–03. "Solon and the Institution of the 'Democratic' Family Form." *CJ* 98: 117–39.

2004. *Reproducing Athens: Menander's Comedy, Democratic Culture, and the Hellenistic City*. Princeton University Press.

2006. "The Psychology of Prostitution in Aeschines' Speech against Timarchus." In C. A. Faraone and L. K. McClure, eds. *Prostitutes and Courtesans in the Ancient World*. Madison, WI: University of Wisconsin Press. 139–60.

Lateiner, D. 1982. "The Man Who Does Not Meddle in Politics: A 'Topos' in Lysias." *CW* 76: 1–12.

Lavency, M. 2007. "The Written Plea of the Logographer." Trans. G. Kennedy. In E. Carawan, ed. *Oxford Readings in the Attic Orators*. Oxford University Press. 3–26. Translation of "Le Plaidoyer écrit du logographe," in *Aspects de la logographie judiciaire attique*, Université de Louvain, Recueil de Travaux d'Histoire et de Philologie, 4.32 (Louvain, 1964), 124–51.

Legendre, P. 1974. *L'amour du censeur: essai sur l'ordre dogmatique*. Paris: Éditions du Seuil.

1985. *L'inestimable objet de la transmission: étude sur le principe généalogique en Occident*. Paris: Fayard.

Lloyd, G. E. R. 1987. *The Revolutions of Wisdom: Studies in the Claims and Practice of Ancient Greek Science*. Berkeley, CA: University of California Press.

Loening, T. C. 1981. "The Autobiographical Speeches of Lysias and the Biographical Tradition." *Hermes* 109: 280–94.

1987. *The Reconciliation Agreement of 403/402 B.C. in Athens: Its Content and Application. Hermes* Einzelschriften 53. Stuttgart: Franz Steiner.

Loomis, W. T. 1972. "The Nature of Premeditation in Athenian Homicide Law." *JHS* 92: 86–95.

Loraux, N. 1986. *The Invention of Athens: The Funeral Oration in the Classical City*. Trans. A. Sheridan. Cambridge, MA: Harvard University Press.

1993. *The Children of Athena: Athenian Ideas about Citizenship and the Division Between the Sexes*. Trans. C. Levine. Princeton University Press.

2002. *The Divided City: On Memory and Forgetting in Ancient Athens*. Trans. C. Pache and J. Fort. New York: Zone Books.

Luhmann, N. 1988. "The Unity of the Legal System." In Teubner 1988: 12–35.

1990. *Essays on Self-Reference*. New York: Columbia University Press.

1992. "Operational Closure and Structural Coupling: The Differentiation of the Legal System." *Cardozo Law Review* 13: 1419–41.

MacDowell, D. M., ed. 1962. *Andokides: On the Mysteries*. Oxford: Clarendon.

1963. *Athenian Homicide Law in the Age of the Orators*. Manchester University Press.

1975. "Law-Making at Athens in the Fourth Century B.C." *JHS* 95: 62–74.

1976a. "Bastards as Athenian Citizens." *CQ* 26: 88–91.
1976b. "*Hybris* in Athens." *G&R* 23: 14–31.
1978. *The Law in Classical Athens.* Ithaca, NY: Cornell University Press.
1989. "The *Oikos* in Athenian Law." *CQ* 39: 10–21.
ed. 1990. *Demosthenes: Against Meidias.* Oxford: Clarendon.
Macpherson, S. 2003. "Rent to Own; or, What's Entailed in *Pride and Prejudice.*" *Representations* 82: 1–23.
Maffi, A. 1988. "Écriture et pratique juridique dans la Grèce classique." In M. Detienne, ed. *Les savoirs de l'écriture en Grèce ancienne.* Lille: Presses universitaires de Lille. 188–210.
Mannoni, O. 1969. *Clefs pour l'imaginaire ou l'autre scène.* Paris: Seuil.
Markle, M. M. 1985. "Jury Pay and Assembly Pay at Athens." *History of Political Thought* 6: 265–97.
Marr J. L. 1971. "Andocides' Part in the Mysteries and Hermae Affairs 415 B.C." *CQ* 21: 326–38.
Maschke, R. 1968. *Die Willenslehre im griechischen Recht.* Darmstadt: Wissenschaftliche Buchgesellschaft.
McGlew, J. 2002. *Citizens on Stage: Comedy and Political Culture in the Athenian Democracy.* Ann Arbor, MI: University of Michigan Press.
McVeigh, S., P. Rush, and A. Young. 2001. "A Judgment Dwelling in Law: Violence and the Relations of Legal Thought." In A. Sarat, ed. *Law, Violence, and the Possibility of Justice.* Princeton University Press. 101–41.
Merkelbach, R. and H. C. Youtie. 1968. "Ein Michigan-Papyrus über Theramenes." *ZPE* 2: 161–69.
Meyer-Laurin, H. 1965. *Gesetz und Billigkeit im attischen Prozess.* Weimar: Hermann Böhlaus Nachfolger.
Miller, W. I. 2006. *Eye for an Eye.* Cambridge University Press.
Minda, G. 1997. "Law and Literature at Century's End." *Cardozo Studies in Law and Literature* 9: 245–58.
Miner, J. 2003. "Courtesan, Concubine, Whore: Apollodorus' Deliberate Use of Terms for Prostitutes." *AJP* 124: 19–37.
Mirhady, D. C. 1996. "Torture and Rhetoric in Athens." *JHS* 116: 119–31.
2000a. "Demosthenes as Advocate: The Private Speeches." In I. Worthington, ed. *Demosthenes: Statesman and Orator.* London: Routledge. 181–204.
2000b. "The Athenian Rationale for Torture." In V. Hunter and J. Edmondson, eds. *Law and Social Status in Classical Athens.* Oxford University Press. 53–74.
2004. "Contracts in Athens." In D. L. Cairns and R. A. Knox, eds. *Law, Rhetoric, and Comedy in Classical Athens: Essays in Honour of Douglas M. MacDowell.* Swansea: The Classical Press of Wales. 51–63.
2007. "The Dikasts' Oath and the Question of Fact." In A. H. Sommerstein and J. Fletcher, eds. *Horkos: The Oath in Greek Society.* Exeter: Bristol Phoenix Press. 48–59.
Missiou, A. 1992. *The Subversive Oratory of Andokides: Politics, Ideology and Decision-making in Democratic Athens.* Cambridge University Press.

Monoson, S. 1994. "Frank Speech, Democracy, and Philosophy: Plato's Debt to a Democratic Strategy of Civic Discourse." In J. P. Euben, J. R. Wallach, and J. Ober, eds. *Athenian Political Thought and the Reconstruction of American Democracy*. Ithaca, NY: Cornell University Press. 172–97.

Montiglio, S. 2000. *Silence in the Land of Logos*. Princeton University Press.

Morford, M. P. O. 1966. "Ethopoiia and Character-Assassination in the Conon of Demosthenes." *Mnemosyne* 19: 241–48.

Morrison, J. S. 1961. "Antiphon." *PCPS* 187: 49–58.

Mossé, C. 1987. "Égalité démocratique et inégalités sociales: le débat à Athènes au IVème siècle." *Métis* 2: 165–76, 195–206.

1991. "La place de la *pallakê* dans la famille athénienne." In M. Gagarin, ed. *Symposion 1990: Papers on Greek and Hellenistic Legal History*. Cologne: Böhlau. 273–79.

Moulinier, L. 1952. *Le pur et l'impur dans la pensée des Grecs d'Homère à Aristote*. Paris: Klincksieck.

Munn, M. 2000. *The School of History: Athens in the Age of Socrates*. Berkeley, CA: University of California Press.

Murnaghan, S. 1988. "How a Woman Can Be More Like a Man: the Dialogue between Ischomachus and His Wife in Xenophon's *Oeconomicus*." *Helios* 15: 9–22.

Murphy, T. 1994. "As if: camera juridica." In C. Douzinas, P. Goodrich, and Y. Hachamovitch, eds. *Politics, Postmodernity and Critical Legal Studies*. London: Routledge. 69–106.

Murphy, T. M. 1989. "The Vilification of Eratosthenes and Theramenes in Lysias 12." *AJP* 110: 40–49.

Murray, O. 1990a. "The Solonian Law of *Hubris*." In Cartledge, Millett, and Todd 1990: 139–45.

1990b. "The Affair of the Mysteries: Democracy and the Drinking Group." In *Sympotica: A Symposium on the Symposion*. Oxford: Clarendon Press. 149–61.

Nedelsky, J. 1990. "Law, Boundaries, and the Bounded Self." *Representations* 30: 162–89.

Nietzsche, F. 1967 [1887]. *On the Genealogy of Morals*. Trans. W. Kaufmann and R. J. Hollingdale. New York: Random House.

Nightingale, A. W. 1999. "Plato's Lawcode in Context: Rule by Written Law in Athens and Magnesia." *CQ* 49: 100–22.

Nora, P. 1989. "Between Memory and History: *Les Lieux de Mémoire*." Trans. M. Roudebush. *Representations* 26: 7–24.

Norris, C. 1988. "Law, Deconstruction, and the Resistance to Theory." *Journal of Law and Society* 15: 166–87.

Nouhaud, M. 1982. *L'utilisation de l'histoire par les orateurs attiques*. Paris: Les Belles Lettres.

Ober, J. 1989a. *Mass and Elite in Democratic Athens: Rhetoric, Ideology, and the Power of the People*. Princeton University Press.

1989b. "Review Article: The Nature of Athenian Democracy." *CP* 84: 322–34.

1994. "Power and Oratory in Democratic Athens: Demosthenes 21, Against Meidias." In I. Worthington, ed. *Persuasion: Greek Rhetoric in Action*. New York: Routledge. 85–108.

2005. "Law and Political Theory." In M. Gagarin and D. Cohen, eds. *The Cambridge Companion to Ancient Greek Law*. Cambridge University Press. 394–411.

Ober, J. and B. Strauss. 1990. "Drama, Political Rhetoric, and the Discourse of Athenian Democracy." In J. J. Winkler and F. I. Zeitlin, eds. *Nothing To Do With Dionysus? Athenian Drama in its Social Context*. Princeton University Press. 237–70.

Ogden, D. 1996. *Greek Bastardy in the Classical and Hellenistic Periods*. Oxford: Clarendon.

Oliver, J. H. 1950. *The Athenian Expounders of the Sacred and Ancestral Law*. Baltimore, MD: Johns Hopkins University Press.

Omitowoju, R. 2002. *Rape and the Politics of Consent in Classical Athens*. Cambridge University Press.

Osborne, R. 1985. "Law in Action in Classical Athens." *JHS* 105: 40–58.

1990. "Vexatious Litigation in Classical Athens: Sykophancy and the Sykophant." In Cartledge, Millett, and Todd 1990: 83–102.

1997. "Law, the Democratic Citizen and the Representation of Women in Classical Athens." *P&P* 155: 3–33.

2000. "Religion, Imperial Politics, and the Offering of Freedom to Slaves." In V. Hunter and J. Edmondson, eds. *Law and Social Status in Classical Athens*. Oxford University Press. 75–92.

ed. 2007. *Debating the Athenian Cultural Revolution: Art, Literature, Philosophy, and Politics 430–380 BC*. Cambridge University Press.

Ostwald, M. 1969. *Nomos and the Beginnings of the Athenian Democracy*. Oxford: Clarendon Press.

1973. "Was There a Concept ἄγραφος νόμος in Classical Greece?" In E. N. Lee, A. P. D. Mourelatos, and R. M. Rorty, eds. *Exegesis and Argument: Studies in Greek Philosophy Presented to Gregory Vlastos*. New York: Humanities Press. 70–104.

1986. *From Popular Sovereignty to the Sovereignty of Law: Law, Society, and Politics in Fifth-Century Athens*. Berkeley, CA: University of California Press.

O'Sullivan, N. 1995. "Aristotle on Dramatic Probability." *CJ* 91: 47–63.

Padel, R. 1995. *Whom Gods Destroy: Elements of Greek and Tragic Madness*. Princeton University Press.

Papillon, T. L. 1998. *Rhetorical Studies in the Aristocratea of Demosthenes*. New York: Peter Lang.

Parke, H. W. 1977. *Festivals of the Athenians*. Ithaca, NY: Cornell University Press.

Parker, R. 1983. *Miasma: Pollution and Purification in Early Greek Religion*. Oxford: Clarendon Press.

Parsons, T. 1861. *Memoir of Theophilus Parsons*. Boston, MA: Ticknor and Fields.

Patterson, C. 1990. "Those Athenian Bastards." *ClAnt* 9: 40–73.

1991. "Response to Claude Mossé." In M. Gagarin, ed. *Symposion 1990: Papers on Greek and Hellenistic Legal History*. Cologne: Böhlau. 281–87.

1994. "The Case against Neaira and the Public Ideology of the Athenian Family." In A. L. Boegehold and A. C. Scafuro, eds. *Athenian Identity and Civic Ideology*. Baltimore, MD: Johns Hopkins University Press. 199–216.

1998. *The Family in Greek History*. Cambridge, MA: Harvard University Press.

2000. "The Hospitality of Athenian Justice: the Metic in Court." In V. Hunter and J. Edmondson, eds. *Law and Social Status in Classical Athens*. Oxford University Press. 93–112.

2005. "Athenian Citizenship Law." In M. Gagarin and D. Cohen, eds. *The Cambridge Companion to Ancient Greek Law*. Cambridge University Press. 267–89.

Pearson, L. 1976. *The Art of Demosthenes*. (*Beiträge zur Klassischen Philologie* 68.) Meisenheim: Verlag Anton Hain.

Pendrick, G. J. 1987. "Once Again Antiphon the Sophist and Antiphon of Rhamnus." *Hermes* 115: 47–60.

1993. "The Ancient Tradition on Antiphon Reconsidered." *GRBS* 34: 215–28.

ed. 2002. *Antiphon the Sophist: the Fragments*. Cambridge University Press.

Perlman, S. 1963. "The Politicians in the Athenian Democracy of the Fourth Century B.C." *Athenaeum* 41: 327–55.

1964. "Quotations from Poetry in Attic Orators of the Fourth Century B. C." *AJP* 85: 155–72.

Peseley, G. 1989. "The Origin and Value of the Theramenes Papyrus." *AHB* 3: 29–35.

Peters, J. S. 2005. "Law, Literature, and the Vanishing Real: On the Future of an Interdisciplinary Illusion." *PMLA* 120: 442–53.

Pigeaud, J. 1981. *La maladie de l'âme*. Paris: Les Belles Lettres.

1988. *Aristote, l'homme de génie et la mélancolie*. Marseille: Rivages.

Porter, J. R. 1997. "Adultery By The Book: Lysias 1 (*On the Murder of Eratosthenes*) and Comic *Diegesis*." *EMC* 16: 421–53.

Pringsheim, F. 1950. *The Greek Law of Sale*. Weimar: Hermann Böhlaus.

Quillin, J. M. 2002. "Achieving Amnesty: The Role of Events, Institutions, and Ideas." *TAPA* 132: 71–107.

Redfield, J. M. 2003. *The Locrian Maidens: Love and Death in Greek Italy*. Princeton University Press.

Rhodes, P. J. 1978. "Bastards as Athenian Citizens." *CQ* 28: 89–92.

1981. *A Commentary on the Aristotelian* Athenaion Politeia. Oxford: Clarendon.

1985. "Nomothesia in Fourth-century Athens." *CQ* 35: 55–60.

1991. "The Athenian Code of Laws, 410–399 B. C." *JHS* 111: 87–100.

1998. "Enmity in Fourth-Century Athens." In P. Cartledge, P. Millett, and S. von Reden, eds. *Kosmos: Essays in Order, Conflict and Community in Classical Athens*. Cambridge University Press. 144–61.

Rickert, G. 1989. *EKΩN and AKΩN in Early Greek Thought*. Atlanta, GA: Scholars Press.

Riley, D. 1988. *Am I That Name? Feminism and the Category of 'Women' in History.* Minneapolis, MN: University of Minnesota Press.

Robb, K. 1994. *Literacy and Paideia in Ancient Greece.* New York: Oxford University Press.

Robertson, N. 1990. "The Laws of Athens, 410–399 BC: The Evidence for Review and Publication." *JHS* 110: 43–75.

Roisman, J. 2004. "Speaker-Audience Interaction in Athens: A Power Struggle." In Sluiter and Rosen 2004: 261–78.

2005. *The Rhetoric of Manhood: Masculinity in the Attic Orators.* Berkeley, CA: University of California Press.

2006. *The Rhetoric of Conspiracy in Ancient Athens.* Berkeley, CA: University of California Press.

de Romilly, J. 1971. *La loi dans la pensée grecque des origines à Aristote.* Paris: Les Belles Lettres.

Rosenbloom, D. 2003. "Aristogeiton Son of Cydimachus and the Scoundrel's Drama." In J. Davidson and A. Pomeroy, eds. *Theatres of Action: Papers for Chris Dearden.* Auckland: Polygraphia. 88–117.

2004. "*Ponêroi* vs. *Chrêstoi*: The Ostracism of Hyperbolos and the Struggle for Hegemony in Athens after the Death of Perikles." *TAPA* 134: 55–105, 323–58.

Rosivach, V. J. 1991. "Some Athenian Presuppositions about 'the Poor'." *G&R* 38: 189–98.

Roussel, L. 1966. *Lysias. L'invalide.* Paris: Presses universitaires de France.

Roy, J. 1999. "*Polis* and *Oikos* in Classical Athens." *G&R* 46: 1–18.

Rubinstein, L. 1993. *Adoption in IV. Century Athens.* Copenhagen: Museum Tusculanum.

1998. "The Athenian Political Perception of the *Idiotes.*" In P. Cartledge, P. Millett, and S. von Reden, eds. *Kosmos: Essays in Order, Conflict and Community in Classical Athens.* Cambridge University Press. 125–43.

2000. *Litigation and Cooperation: Supporting Speakers in the Courts of Classical Athens. Historia* Einzelschriften 147. Stuttgart: Franz Steiner.

2005. "Differentiated Rhetorical Strategies in the Athenian Courts." In M. Gagarin and D. Cohen, eds. *The Cambridge Companion to Ancient Greek Law.* Cambridge University Press. 129–45.

2007. "Arguments from Precedent in Attic Oratory." In E. Carawan, ed. *Oxford Readings in the Attic Orators.* Oxford University Press. 359–71. Translation of "Praecedensargumenter i de attiske retstaler," in C. G. Tortzen and T. H. Nielsen, eds. *Gammel Dansk. studiere et alia til œre for Mogens Herman Hansen på hans 55-års fødeselsdag 20. august 1995* (Copenhagen, 1995), 80–84.

Rudhardt, J. 1962. "La reconnaissance de la paternité, sa nature et sa portée dans la société athénienne." *MH* 19: 39–64.

Ruschenbusch, E. 1957. "ΔΙΚΑΣΤΗΡΙΟΝ ΠΑΝΤΩΝ ΚΥΡΙΟΝ." *Historia* 6: 257–74.

Russell, D. A. 1990. "*Ēthos* in Oratory and Rhetoric." In C. Pelling, ed. *Characterization and Individuality in Greek Literature.* Oxford: Clarendon Press. 197–212.

Ryan, M. 1989. *Politics and Culture: Working Hypotheses for a Post-Revolutionary Society*. Baltimore, MD: Johns Hopkins University Press.

Sarat, A. 2001. "Situating Law Between the Realities of Violence and the Claims of Justice: An Introduction." In A. Sarat, ed. *Law, Violence, and the Possibility of Justice*. Princeton University Press. 3–16.

Sarat, A. and T. R. Kearns. 1991. "A Journey Through Forgetting: Toward a Jurisprudence of Violence." In A. Sarat and T. R. Kearns, eds. *The Fate of Law*. Ann Arbor, MI: University of Michigan Press. 209–73.

1992. "Making Peace with Violence: Robert Cover on Law and Legal Theory." In A. Sarat and T. R. Kearns, eds. *Law's Violence*. Ann Arbor, MI: University of Michigan Press. 211–50.

1994. "Editorial Introduction." In A. Sarat and T. R. Kearns, eds. *The Rhetoric of Law*. Ann Arbor, MI: University of Michigan Press. 1–27.

Sattler, W. M. 1947. "Conceptions of *Ethos* in Ancient Rhetoric." *Speech Monographs* 14: 55–65.

Saxonhouse, A. W. 2006. *Free Speech and Democracy in Ancient Athens*. Cambridge University Press.

Sayre, F. B. 1931–32. "Mens Rea." *Harvard Law Review* 45: 974–1026.

Scafuro, A. C. 1994. "Witnessing and False Witnessing: Proving Citizenship and Kin Identity in Fourth-Century Athens." In A. L. Boegehold and A. C. Scafuro, eds. *Athenian Identity and Civic Ideology*. Baltimore, MD: Johns Hopkins University Press. 156–98.

1997. *The Forensic Stage: Settling Disputes in Graeco-Roman New Comedy*. Cambridge University Press.

Scarry, E. 1985. *The Body in Pain: The Making and Unmaking of the World*. New York: Oxford University Press.

Schaps, D. M. 1975. "Women in Greek Inheritance Law." *CQ* 25: 53–57.

1977. "The Woman Least Mentioned: Etiquette and Women's Names." *CQ* 27: 323–30.

1979. *Economic Rights of Women in Ancient Greece*. Edinburgh University Press.

Schlag, P. 1991. "The Problem of the Subject." *Texas Law Review* 69: 1627–1743.

Schloemann, J. 2002. "Entertainment and Democratic Distrust: The Audience's Attitudes Towards Oral and Written Oratory in Classical Athens." In I. Worthington and J. M. Foley, eds. *Epea and Grammata: Oral and Written Communication in Ancient Greece*. Leiden: Brill. 133–46.

Schmitz, T. A. 2000. "Plausibility in the Greek Orators." *AJP* 121: 47–77.

Seager, R. 1978. "Andocides' Confession: A Dubious Note." *Historia* 27: 221–23.

Sealey, R. 1967. "Pseudo-Demosthenes xiii and xxv." *REG* 80: 250–55.

1975. "Pap. Mich. inv. 5982: Theramenes." *ZPE* 16: 279–88.

1982. "On the Athenian Concept of Law." *CJ* 77: 289–302.

1984a. "On Lawful Concubinage in Athens." *ClAnt* 3: 111–33.

1984b. "The Tetralogies Ascribed to Antiphon." *TAPA* 114: 71–85.

1987. *The Athenian Republic: Democracy or the Rule of Law*. University Park, PA: Pennsylvania State University Press.

1990. *Women and Law in Classical Greece*. Chapel Hill, NC: University of North Carolina Press.
1993. *Demosthenes and His Time: A Study in Defeat*. Oxford University Press.
1994. *The Justice of the Greeks*. Ann Arbor, MI: University of Michigan Press.
Shear, J. 2007. "Cultural Change, Space, and the Politics of Commemoration in Athens." In Osborne 2007: 91–115.
Shrimpton, G. S. 1997. *History and Memory in Ancient Greece*. Montreal: McGill-Queen's University Press.
Sickinger, J. P. 1999. *Public Records and Archives in Classical Athens*. Chapel Hill, NC: University of North Carolina Press.
2002. "Literacy, Orality, and Legislative Procedure in Classical Athens." In I. Worthington and J. M. Foley, eds. *Epea and Grammata: Oral and Written Communication in Ancient Greece*. Leiden: Brill. 147–69.
2004. "The Laws of Athens: Publication, Preservation, Consultation." In E. M. Harris and L. Rubinstein, eds. *The Law and the Courts in Ancient Greece*. London: Duckworth. 93–110.
Silverman, K. 1983. *The Subject of Semiotics*. New York: Oxford University Press.
Simon, E. 1983. *Festivals of Attica: An Archaeological Commentary*. Madison, WI: University of Wisconsin Press.
Sinclair, R. K. 1988. *Democracy and Participation in Athens*. Cambridge University Press.
Sissa, G. 1999. "Sexual Bodybuilding: Aeschines Against Timarchus." In J. Porter, ed. *Constructions of the Classical Body*. Ann Arbor, MI: University of Michigan Press. 147–68.
Sluiter, I. and R. M. Rosen, eds. 2004. *Free Speech in Classical Antiquity*. Leiden: Brill.
Sommerstein, A. H. 1984. "The Murder of Polemarchos." *PP* 39: 370–72.
Sorabji, R. 1980. *Necessity, Cause, and Blame: Perspectives on Aristotle's Theory*. Ithaca, NY: Cornell University Press.
Sosin, J. 1997. "A Word for Woman?" *GRBS* 38: 75–83.
Steiner, D. T. 1994. *The Tyrant's Writ: Myths and Images of Writing in Ancient Greece*. Princeton University Press.
Sternberg, R. H. 2006. *Tragedy Offstage: Suffering and Sympathy in Ancient Athens*. Austin, TX: University of Texas Press.
Stewart, I. 1987. "Closure and the Legal Norm: An Essay in Critique of Law." *The Modern Law Review* 50: 908–33.
Stinton, T. C. W. 1975. "*Hamartia* in Aristotle and Greek Tragedy." *CQ* 25: 221–54.
Strauss, B. S. 1986. *Athens after the Peloponnesian War: Class, Faction and Policy 403–386* BC. London: Croom Helm.
1993. "Andocides' *On the Mysteries* and the Theme of the Father in Late Fifth-Century Athens." In R. M. Rosen and J. Farrell, eds. *Nomodeiktes: Greek Studies in Honor of Martin Ostwald*. Ann Arbor, MI: University of Michigan Press. 255–68.
Stroud, R. S. 1968. *Drakon's Law on Homicide*. Berkeley, CA: University of California Press.

Sundahl, M. J. 2003. "The Rule of Law and the Nature of the Fourth-Century Athenian Democracy." *C&M* 54: 127–56.

2005. "When Literature Becomes Law: An Example from Ancient Greece." *Texas Wesleyan Law Review* 12: 331–43.

Svenbro, J. 1993. *Phrasikleia: An Anthropology of Reading in Ancient Greece*. Trans. J. Lloyd. Ithaca, NY: Cornell University Press.

Szegedy-Maszak, A. 1978. "Legends of the Greek Lawgivers." *GRBS* 19: 199–209.

Teubner, G., ed. 1988. *Autopoietic Law: A New Approach to Law and Society*. Berlin: Walter de Gruyter.

Thomas, B. 1991. "Reflections on the Law and Literature Revival." *Critical Inquiry* 17: 510–39.

Thomas C. G. 1977. "Literacy and the Codification of Law." *Studia et Documenta Historiae et Iuris* 43: 455–58.

Thomas, R. 1989. *Oral Tradition and Written Record in Classical Athens*. Cambridge University Press.

1992. *Literacy and Orality in Ancient Greece*. Cambridge University Press.

1994. "Law and the Lawgiver in the Athenian Democracy." In R. Osborne and S. Hornblower, eds. *Ritual, Finance, Politics: Athenian Democratic Accounts Presented to David Lewis*. Oxford: Clarendon Press. 119–33.

1996. "Written in Stone? Liberty, Equality, Orality and the Codification of Law." In Foxhall and Lewis 1996: 9–31.

2005. "Writing, Law, and Written Law." In M. Gagarin and D. Cohen, eds. *The Cambridge Companion to Ancient Greek Law*. Cambridge University Press. 41–60.

Thompson W. E. 1970. "Some Attic Kinship Terms." *Glotta* 48: 75–81.

1976. *De Hagniae Hereditate: An Athenian Inheritance Case*. Leiden: Brill.

1981. "Athenian Attitudes Toward Wills." *Prudentia* 13: 13–23.

Thür, G. 1977. *Beweisführung vor den Schwurgerichtshöfen Athens: die Proklesis zur Basanos*. Vienna: Austrian Academy of Science.

1996. "Reply to D. C. Mirhady: Torture and Rhetoric in Athens." *JHS* 116: 132–34.

2005. "The Role of the Witness in Athenian Law." In M. Gagarin and D. Cohen, eds. *The Cambridge Companion to Ancient Greek Law*. Cambridge University Press. 146–69.

Todd, S. C. 1990a. "The Use and Abuse of the Attic Orators." *G&R* 37: 159–78.

1990b. "The Purpose of Evidence in Athenian Courts." In Cartledge, Millett, and Todd 1990: 19–39.

1990c. "*Lady Chatterley's Lover* and the Attic Orators: The Social Composition of the Athenian Jury." *JHS* 110: 146–73.

1993. *The Shape of Athenian Law*. Oxford: Clarendon.

1996. "Lysias Against Nikomachos: The Fate of the Expert in Athenian Law." In Foxhall and Lewis 1996: 101–31.

trans. 2000a. *Lysias*. Austin, TX: University of Texas Press.

2000b. "How to Execute People in Fourth-Century Athens." In V. Hunter and J. Edmondson, eds. *Law and Social Status in Classical Athens*. Oxford University Press. 31–51.

2007. *A Commentary on Lysias, Speeches 1–11*. Oxford University Press.

Todd, S. C. and P. Millett. 1990. "Law, Society and Athens." In Cartledge, Millett, and Todd 1990: 1–18.

Too, Y. L. 2001. "Legal Instructions in Classical Athens." In Y. L. Too, ed. *Education in Greek and Roman Antiquity*. Leiden: Brill. 111–32.

Toohey, P. 2004. *Melancholy, Love, and Time: Boundaries of the Self in Ancient Literature*. Ann Arbor, MI: University of Michigan Press.

Trevett, J. 1992. *Apollodoros the Son of Pasion*. Oxford: Clarendon.

1996. "Aristotle's Knowledge of Athenian Oratory." *CQ* 46: 371–79.

Tulin, A. 1996. *Dike Phonou: The Right of Prosecution and Attic Homicide Procedure*. Stuttgart: Teubner.

Usher, S. 1965. "Individual Characterisation in Lysias." *Eranos* 63: 99–119.

1968. "Xenophon, Critias and Theramenes." *JHS* 88: 128–35.

1976. "Lysias and his Clients." *GRBS* 17: 31–40.

Vernant, J.-P. 1988. "Intimations of the Will in Greek Tragedy." In J.-P. Vernant and P. Vidal-Naquet, *Myth and Tragedy in Ancient Greece*. Trans. J. Lloyd. New York: Zone. 49–84.

1990. *Myth and Society in Ancient Greece*. Trans. J. Lloyd. New York: Zone.

Versnel, H. S. 1991. "Beyond Cursing: The Appeal to Justice in Judicial Prayers." In C. A. Faraone and D. Obbink, eds. *Magika Hiera: Ancient Greek Magic and Religion*. New York: Oxford University Press. 60–106.

Volonaki, E. 2001. "The Re-Publication of the Athenian Laws in the Last Decade of the Fifth Century B.C." *Dike* 4: 137–67.

Von Fritz, K. 1940. "Atthidographers and Exegetae." *TAPA* 71: 91–126.

Wallace, R. W. 1994. "The Athenian Laws against Slander." In G. Thür, ed. *Symposion 1993*. Cologne: Böhlau. 109–24.

1996. "Law, Freedom, and the Concept of Citizens' Rights in Democratic Athens." In J. Ober and C. Hedrick, eds. *Dēmokratia: A Conversation on Democracies, Ancient and Modern*. Princeton University Press. 105–19.

2004. "The Power to Speak – and Not to Listen – in Ancient Athens." In Sluiter and Rosen 2004: 221–32.

Ward, I. 1995. *Law and Literature: Possibilities and Perspectives*. Cambridge University Press.

Weisberg, R. 1992. "Private Violence as Moral Action: The Law as Inspiration and Example." In A. Sarat and T. Kearns, eds. *Law's Violence*. Ann Arbor, MI: University of Michigan Press. 175–210.

West, R. 1993. *Narrative, Authority, and Law*. Ann Arbor, MI: University of Michigan Press.

Westbrook, R. 2000. "Codification and Canonization." In E. Lévy, ed. *La Codification des lois dans l'Antiquité*. Paris: Boccard. 33–47.

Westlake, H. D. 1958. 'Ὡς εἰκός in Thucydides." *Hermes* 86: 447–52.

White, H. 1973. *Metahistory: The Historical Imagination in Nineteenth-Century Europe*. Baltimore, MD: Johns Hopkins University Press.

1978. *Tropics of Discourse: Essays in Cultural Criticism*. Baltimore, MD: Johns Hopkins University Press.

White, J. B. 1985. *Heracles' Bow: Essays on the Rhetoric and Poetics of the Law*. Madison, WI: University of Wisconsin Press.

1990. *Justice as Translation: An Essay in Cultural and Legal Criticism*. University of Chicago Press.

1999. "Writing and Reading in Philosophy, Law, and Poetry." In Freeman and Lewis 1999: 1–20.

Whitehead, D. 1977. *The Ideology of the Athenian Metic*. Cambridge Philological Society.

Wicke, J. 1991. "Postmodern Identity and the Legal Subject." *University of Colorado Law Review* 62: 455–73.

Williams, B. 1993. *Shame and Necessity*. Berkeley, CA: University of California Press.

Williams, P. 1991. *The Alchemy of Race and Rights*. Cambridge, MA: Harvard University Press.

Wilson, L. 2000. *Theaters of Intention: Drama and the Law in Early Modern England*. Stanford University Press.

Wilson, P. 1991. "Demosthenes 21 (*Against Meidias*): Democratic Abuse." *PCPS* 37: 164–95.

1996. "Tragic Rhetoric: The Use of Tragedy and the Tragic in the Fourth Century." In M. S. Silk, ed. *Tragedy and the Tragic: Greek Theatre and Beyond*. Oxford: Clarendon. 310–31.

2000. *The Athenian Institution of the Khoregia: The Chorus, the City and the Stage*. Cambridge University Press.

Winkler, J. J. 1990a. "Phallos Politikos: Representing the Body Politic in Athens." *Differences* 2: 29–45.

1990b. *The Constraints of Desire: The Anthropology of Sex and Gender in Ancient Greece*. New York: Routledge.

Wohl, V. 1997. "Scenes from a Marriage: Love and Logos in Plutarch's *Coniugalia Praecepta*." *Helios* 24: 170–92.

2002. *Love Among the Ruins: The Erotics of Democracy in Classical Athens*. Princeton University Press.

2009. "Sexual Difference and the Aporia of Justice in Sophocles' *Antigone*." In D. McCoskey and E. Zakin, eds., *Bound by the City: Greek Tragedy, Sexual Difference, and the Formation of the Polis*. Albany, NY: SUNY Press. 119–48.

(in press). "A Tragic Case of Poisoning: Intention between Tragedy and the Law." *TAPA*.

Wolff, H. J. 1944. "Marriage Law and Family Organization in Ancient Athens." *Traditio* 2: 43–95.

1957. "Die Grundlagen des griechischen Vertragsrechts." *ZRG* 74: 26–72.

1970. *'Normenkontrolle' und Gesetzesbegriff in der attischen Demokratie*. Heidelberg: C. Winter.

Wolpert, A. 2001. "Lysias 1 and the Politics of the Oikos." *CJ* 96: 415–24.

2002a. *Remembering Defeat: Civil War and Civic Memory in Ancient Athens.* Baltimore, MD: Johns Hopkins University Press.

2002b. "Lysias 18 and Athenian Memory of Civil War." *TAPA* 132: 109–26.

Worman, N. 2002. *The Cast of Character: Style in Greek Literature.* Austin, TX: University of Texas Press.

2004. "Insult and Oral Excess in the Disputes Between Aeschines and Demosthenes." *AJP* 125: 1–25.

2008. *Abusive Mouths in Classical Athens.* Cambridge University Press.

Worthington, I. 1991. "Greek Oratory, Revision of Speeches and the Problem of Historical Reliability." *C&M* 42: 55–74.

1994. "History and Oratorical Exploitation." In I. Worthington, ed. *Persuasion: Greek Rhetoric in Action.* New York: Routledge. 109–29.

1996. "Greek Oratory and the Oral/Literate Division." In I. Worthington, ed. *Voice into Text: Orality and Literacy in Ancient Greece.* Leiden: Brill. 165–77.

Wyse, W., ed. 1904. *The Speeches of Isaeus.* Cambridge University Press.

Yunis, H. 1988. "Law, Politics, and the *Graphe Paranomon* in Fourth-Century Athens." *GRBS* 29: 361–82.

1996. *Taming Democracy: Models of Political Rhetoric in Classical Athens.* Ithaca, NY: Cornell University Press.

2000–01. "Politics as Literature: Demosthenes and the Burden of the Athenian Past." *Arion* 8: 97–118.

2005. "The Rhetoric of Law in Fourth-Century Athens." In M. Gagarin and D. Cohen, eds. *The Cambridge Companion to Ancient Greek Law.* Cambridge University Press. 191–208.

Zeitlin, F. 1984. "The Dynamics of Misogyny: Myth and Mythmaking in the *Oresteia.*" In J. Peradotto and J. P. Sullivan, eds. *Women in the Ancient World.* Albany, NY: SUNY Press. 159–94.

Žižek, S. 1991. *For They Know Not What They Do: Enjoyment as a Political Factor.* London: Verso.

Zuntz, G. 1939. "Earliest Attic Prose-Style." *C&M* 2: 121–44.

Index locorum

General index